MW00388341

222306001

Mathematics

6

MYP 1

third edition

Michael Haese

Mark Humphries

Ngoc Vo

for use with
IB Middle Years
Programme

MATHEMATICS 6 MYP 1 third edition

Michael Haese   B.Sc.(Hons.), Ph.D.
Mark Humphries   B.Sc.(Hons.)
Ngoc Vo   B.Ma.Sc.

Published by Haese Mathematics
152 Richmond Road, Marleston, SA 5033, AUSTRALIA
Telephone: +61 8 8210 4666
Email: info@haesemathematics.com
Web: www.haesemathematics.com

National Library of Australia Card Number & ISBN 978-1-922416-28-5

© Haese & Harris Publications 2021

First Edition	2008
Reprinted	2009, 2011, 2012
Second Edition	2014
Reprinted	2015, 2016, 2017 (twice), 2018, 2019
Third Edition	2021

Cartoon artwork by Yi-Tung Huang, John Martin, and Ngoc Vo.

Artwork by Hannah Coleman, Brian Houston, and Bronson Mathews.

Computer software by Patrick French, Ben Hensley, Huda Kharrufa, Rachel Lee, Bronson Mathews, Linden May, and Han Zong Ng.

Production work by Hannah Coleman and Michael Mampusti.

Typeset in Australia by Charlotte Frost and Deanne Gallasch. Typeset in Times Roman $10\frac{1}{2}$.

Printed in China by Prolong Press Limited.

Acknowledgements: Maps that have been provided by OpenStreetMap are available freely at www.openstreetmap.org. Licensing terms can be viewed at www.openstreetmap.org/copyright. While every attempt has been made to trace and acknowledge copyright, the authors and publishers apologise for any accidental infringement where copyright has proved untraceable. They would be pleased to come to a suitable agreement with the rightful owner.

Disclaimer: All the internet addresses (URLs) given in this book were valid at the time of printing. While the authors and publisher regret any inconvenience that changes of address may cause readers, no responsibility for any such changes can be accepted by either the authors or the publisher.

FOREWORD

Mathematics 6 MYP 1 third edition has been designed and written for the International Baccalaureate Middle Years Programme (IB MYP) Mathematics framework, providing complete coverage of the content and expectations outlined.

Discussions, Activities, Investigations, and Research exercises are used throughout the chapters to develop conceptual understanding. Material is presented in a clear, easy-to-follow style to aid comprehension and retention, especially for English Language Learners. Each chapter ends with extensive review sets and an online multiple choice quiz.

The associated digital Snowflake subscription supports the textbook content with interactive and engaging resources for students and educators.

The Global Context projects highlight the use of mathematics in understanding history, culture, science, society, and the environment. We have aimed to provide a diverse range of topics and styles to create interest for all students and illustrate the real-world application of mathematics.

We have developed this book in consultation with experienced teachers of IB Mathematics internationally but independent of the International Baccalaureate Organisation (IBO). It is not endorsed by the IBO.

We have endeavoured to publish a stimulating and thorough textbook and digital resource to develop and encourage student understanding and nurture an appreciation of mathematics.

Many thanks to Rob Colaiacovo and our other contributors for their recommendations and advice.

We welcome your feedback.　　　Email:　info@haesemathematics.com

　　　　　　　　　　　　　　　　Web:　　www.haesemathematics.com

ONLINE FEATURES

Each textbook comes with a 12 month subscription to the online edition and its range of interactive features. This can be accessed through the **SNOWFLAKE** online learning platform via a web browser or our offline viewer.

To activate your electronic textbook, please contact Haese Mathematics by emailing info@haesemathematics.com with your proof of purchase such as a copy of your receipt.

For general queries regarding **SNOWFLAKE** and online subscriptions:
- Visit our help page: snowflake.haesemathematics.com.au/help
- Contact Haese Mathematics: info@haesemathematics.com

SELF TUTOR

Self Tutor is an engaging feature that supports students learning independently and in classrooms.

Click on any example box to access a step-by-step animation with teacher voice support providing explanation and understanding.

Example 5 ◄)) **Self Tutor**

Consider the matchstick pattern: $\sqcup$, $\sqcup\sqcup$, $\sqcup\sqcup\sqcup$, ...

a Draw the next two diagrams in the pattern.

b Copy and complete this table:

Diagram number	1	2	3	4	5
Number of matches	3	5			

c Write a rule describing the number of matches in each diagram.

a The next two diagrams are: $\sqcup\sqcup\sqcup\sqcup$, $\sqcup\sqcup\sqcup\sqcup\sqcup$

b

Diagram number	1	2	3	4	5
Number of matches	3	5	7	9	11

+2 +2 +2 +2

c The number of matches starts at 3, and increases by 2 each time.

See **Chapter 14, Sequences,** p. 263

INTERACTIVE LINKS

The **SNOWFLAKE** icons direct you to interactive tools to enhance learning and teaching.

These features include:
- demonstrations to illustrate and animate concepts
- multiple choice quizzes to test understanding
- games to practise and build skills
- tools for graphing and statistics
- printable pages for use in class.

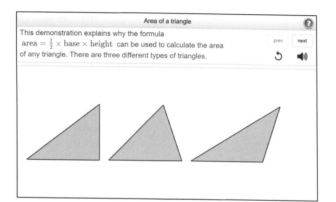

DEMO

Here are some examples from **SNOWFLAKE**.

GAME

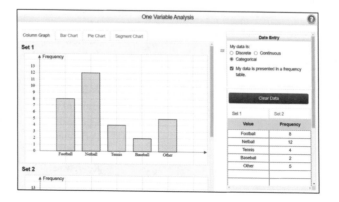

TOOL

TABLE OF CONTENTS

GLOBAL CONTEXTS

The International Baccalaureate Middle Years Programme focuses teaching and learning through six Global Contexts:

- Identities and relationships
- Orientation in space and time
- Personal and cultural expression
- Scientific and technical innovation
- Globalisation and sustainability
- Fairness and development

The Global Contexts help students to develop connections between different subject areas in the curriculum.

GLOBAL CONTEXT	CICADAS
Global context: Orientation in space and time	
Statement of inquiry: Mathematics can be used to explain occurrences in nature.	**GLOBAL CONTEXT**
Criterion: Investigating patterns	Click on the icon to access the online link.

Each project contains a series of questions, divided into:

- Factual questions (in green)
- Conceptual questions (in blue)
- Debatable questions (in red).

The projects are also accompanied by the general descriptor and a task-specific descriptor for one of the four assessment criteria.

Chapter

1

Whole numbers

OPENING PROBLEM

Last Saturday, 24 068 runners took part in the city marathon.

Things to think about:

a What is the value of the 4 in 24 068?

b The 0 in 24 068 has no value. Why is it still important?

c Can you write 24 068 in words?

d How would you *approximate* the number of runners in the marathon?

In ancient times, people used items to represent numbers:

scratches on a cave wall showed the number of new moons since the buffalo herd came through	knots on a rope showed the number of corn rows planted	pebbles on the sand showed the number of traps set for fish	notches cut on a branch showed the number of new lambs born

In time, humans learned to write numbers more efficiently. They did this by developing **number systems**.

The number system we use today was developed in India about 2000 years ago. It was introduced to European nations by Arab traders about 1000 years later. The system is therefore called the **Hindu-Arabic** number system.

We represent numbers using **numerals**. They are formed using the symbols 1, 2, 3, 4, 5, 6, 7, 8, 9, and 0, which are known as **digits**.

number	one	two	three	four	five	six	seven	eight	nine
Hindu-Arabic numeral	𝗜	૮	३	૪	૫	૬	7	8	9
modern numeral	1	2	3	4	5	6	7	8	9

The digits 3 and 8 can be used to form the numeral 38 for the number "thirty eight", and the numeral 83 for the number "eighty three". The order of symbols is therefore important.

In this Chapter, we will study **whole numbers**. These include:

- the **counting numbers**   1, 2, 3, 4, 5, 6, 7, 8, 9, 10, 11, ...
- the **natural numbers**   0, 1, 2, 3, 4, 5, 6, 7, 8, 9, 10, 11, ...

The dots "...." tell us that these sets go on forever. We say they are **infinite**.

The Hindu-Arabic system is more efficient than the number systems used by other ancient people such as the Egyptians, Romans, and Mayans.

- It uses only 10 digits.
- It has a **place value system** where the value of each digit depends on the column it is written in.

A		**PLACE VALUE**

The **place** of a digit in a number determines its value.

units	1
tens	10
hundreds	100
thousands	1000
ten thousands	10 000
hundred thousands	100 000

Using the place value system, we can write a number in:

- numeral form $\qquad$ 6794

- expanded form $\qquad$ $6000 + 700 + 90 + 4$

- words $\qquad$ six thousand, seven hundred, and ninety four

- a place value chart

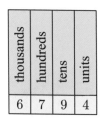

thousands	hundreds	tens	units
6	7	9	4

The digit **zero** or 0 is used to show an empty place value.

> Although zero has no value, it is needed to make sure other digits are in the correct place.

EXERCISE 1A

1 Write down the value of the digit 4 in:

    a 349   **b** 124   **c** 408   **d** 5461

    e 7843   **f** 4902   **g** 11 634   **h** 64 286

2 Write down the value of the digit 8 in:

    a 458   **b** 847   **c** 1981   **d** 8247

    e 2861   **f** 84 019   **g** 78 794   **h** 860 137

3 For the number 382 014, write down the value of the:

    a 2   **b** 1   **c** 3   **d** 4   **e** 8   **f** 0

4 Write in numeral form:

    a $80 + 6$ **b** $600 + 70 + 4$

    c $9000 + 600 + 30 + 8$ **d** $50\,000 + 200 + 40$

    e $20\,000 + 7000 + 3$ **f** $500\,000 + 300 + 70 + 5$

    g $70\,000 + 3000 + 200 + 90 + 8$ **h** $800\,000 + 9000 + 300 + 2$

5 Write in expanded form:

    a 975   **b** 680   **c** 3874   **d** 9083

    e 56 742   **f** 75 007   **g** 600 829   **h** 354 718

6 Write in words:

    a 49   **b** 352   **c** 7186   **d** 3029

    e 401   **f** 6850   **g** 18 714   **h** 263 083

7 Write in numeral form:

    a twenty seven   **b** eighty

    c six hundred and eight   **d** one thousand and sixteen

    e eight thousand, two hundred

    f nineteen thousand, five hundred, and thirty eight

    g seventy five thousand, four hundred, and three

    h six hundred and two thousand, eight hundred, and eighteen.

PUZZLE

one, two, three, four, five, ...

When the counting numbers are written in words, there is only one number whose letters are in alphabetical order.

Which number is it?

B   NUMBER LINES

A **number line** has equally spaced points marked with numbers in the correct position relative to one another. Arrowheads are used to show that the line continues indefinitely.

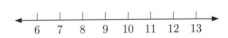

As we move from left to right on a number line, the numbers increase in value. We can therefore use a number line to *order* numbers.

For example, 7 is to the right of 4 on the number line. We can say that:

- 7 is *greater than* 4
- 4 is *less than* 7.

We can use the symbols $>$ and $<$ when comparing numbers.

> $>$ means "**is greater than**".
> $<$ means "**is less than**".

So, we can write $7 > 4$ and $4 < 7$.

Example 1

◀)) **Self Tutor**

Show the numbers 9, 15, 3, and 6 with dots on a number line.

Hence write the numbers in ascending order.

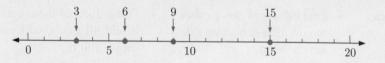

In ascending order, the numbers are 3, 6, 9, 15.

> **Ascending** means increasing.
> **Descending** means decreasing.

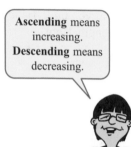

EXERCISE 1B

1 Find the missing value(s) in each number line:

a

b

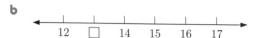

c

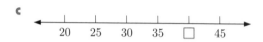

d

e

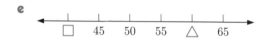

f

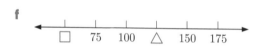

g

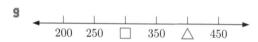

h

2 Using a number line to help you, insert $<$ or $>$ to make each statement correct:

   a 5 □ 9   **b** 8 □ 2   **c** 7 □ 13

   d 4 □ 16   **e** 14 □ 11   **f** 19 □ 15

3 Show each set of numbers on a number line, and hence write them in *ascending* order.

   a 9, 4, 8, 2, 7   **b** 14, 19, 16, 18, 13   **c** 28, 31, 23, 30, 34

   d 70, 30, 60, 90, 40   **e** 250, 75, 200, 25, 125 **f** 4000, 3000, 500, 2500, 1500

4 Show each set of numbers on a number line, and hence write them in *descending* order.

   a 11, 8, 15, 6, 13   **b** 24, 19, 32, 28, 21   **c** 350, 425, 300, 275, 375

C   BIG NUMBERS

We can extend the place value system beyond hundred thousands to write even bigger numbers.

> A **million** is 1000 thousand or 1 000 000.
>
> A **billion** is 1000 million or 1 000 000 000.
>
> A **trillion** is 1000 billion or 1 000 000 000 000.

To help you understand how big these numbers are, consider a cube with side length 1 cm.

1 cm

- One million of these cubes would fill a cube with side length 1 m.

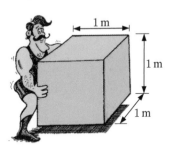

- One billion of these cubes would fill a cube with side length 10 m.

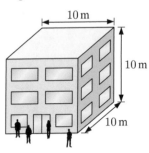

- One trillion of these cubes would fill a cube with side length 100 m.

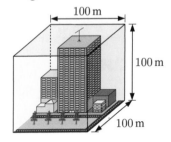

When we write big numbers in a place value chart, we separate the digits into units, thousands, millions, billions, and trillions.

trillions			billions			millions			thousands			units		
H	T	U	H	T	U	H	T	U	H	T	U	H	T	U
	6	3	5	8	0	0	0	0	0	0	0	0	0	0

The number in this place value chart is sixty three trillion, five hundred and eighty billion.

EXERCISE 1C

1 Write in a place value chart:
   a 27 406 593
   b 18 275 623 115
   c 32 403 976 813 214

2 Write down the value of the digit 7 in:
   a 2 713 506
   b 7 142 066
   c 715 094 126
   d 4 672 514 016
   e 7 628 085 543
   f 273 514 039

3 Write each number in the place value chart in words:

	trillions			billions			millions			thousands			units		
	H	T	U	H	T	U	H	T	U	H	T	U	H	T	U
a							2	3	6	0	0	0	0	0	0
b				7	6	1	4	0	0	0	0	0	0	0	0
c		1	8	9	4	8	0	0	0	0	0	0	0	0	0

4 Write in words:
   a 5 784 000
   b 43 200 000
   c 198 030 000
   d 2 015 000 000
   e 302 000 000 000
   f 7 382 000 000 000

5 Write the big number in each sentence as a numeral:

   a A heart beating at a rate of 70 beats per minute would beat about thirty seven million times in a year.

   b A hamburger chain bought two hundred million bread buns in one year.

   c The Jurassic era was about one hundred and fifty million years ago.

   d Saturn is approximately one billion, four hundred and twenty seven million kilometres from the Sun.

   e There are about three billion, nine hundred and forty million email users in the world.

   f One tebibyte of data is one trillion, ninety nine billion, five hundred and eleven million, six hundred and twenty seven thousand, seven hundred and seventy six bytes.

PUZZLE   NUMBER SEARCH PROBLEMS

Click on the icon to obtain these printable puzzles.

NUMBER SEARCH

ACTIVITY   ROMAN NUMERALS

The ancient Romans did not use the digits 0, 1, 2, 3, ..., 9 to write numbers.

Instead, they used the letters:

- I   to represent one (1)
- V   to represent five (5)
- X   to represent ten (10)
- L   to represent fifty (50)
- C   to represent one hundred (100)
- D   to represent five hundred (500)
- M   to represent one thousand (1000).

Many clocks and watches still have Roman numerals on their faces.

Notice that we do not write any symbol more than three times in a row.

Instead:

- "4" is written **IV** which is "one before five"
- "6" is written **VI** which is "one after five".

Larger numbers are written in Roman numerals by describing each place value in turn.

$$\underbrace{L}\ \underbrace{X\ X}\ \underbrace{I\ X}$$

"fifty ten ten"   "one before 10"

70 + 9 = 79

What to do:

1 Use the clock face to determine what number is represented by:

    a II   **b** X   **c** VIII   **d** XII

2 Use the clock face to write the Roman numerals for:

    a 3   **b** 7   **c** 9   **d** 11

3 Write down the number meant by the Roman numerals:

    a XV   **b** XXIV   **c** XLVII   **d** LXXXI

    e XCVI   **f** CCLXIX   **g** DCXII   **h** MMXX

4 Write using Roman numerals:

    a 16   **b** 19   **c** 32   **d** 36

    e 49   **f** 74   **g** 108   **h** 496

5 **a** Each week Octavius sharpens CCCLIV swords for his general. Write this as an ordinary number.

> The **denarius** (plural: **denarii**) was the unit of currency used by the Romans.

    b Octavius charges his general 8 denarii for each sword sharpened. Write this number using Roman numerals.

    c In Roman numerals, how many denarii does the general need to pay in total?

6 Write in ascending order: XII, XIX, XXX, XXI, III

7 Write in descending order: LXI, XCI, XLV, CLX, XVI

8 Which number less than one hundred is represented by the greatest number of Roman numerals?

9 A stroke above a symbol makes the number 1000 times larger.

    For example: • $\overline{V}$ is used to represent 5000

                     • $\overline{C}$ is used to represent 100 000.

    a Write down the number meant by the Roman numerals:

        i $\overline{X}$ **ii** $\overline{LX}$ **iii** $\overline{DL}DCV$ **iv** $\overline{MMCCC}$

    b Write using Roman numerals:

        i 50 000   **ii** 260 000   **iii** 1 024 000   **iv** 555 501

10 Discuss why the Romans did not need a symbol for zero to write numbers.

    Research whether they used a *word* for zero, and how it would have been used.

D ROUNDING NUMBERS

When a quantity is described, we often do not need to know the *exact* number.

For example, if there were 306 competitors at an athletics carnival, we might say "There were about 300 competitors."

> To approximate a number of objects, we can **round** the number to a particular place value.

For example, to round a number to the nearest 10, we choose the multiple of 10 which is nearest to our number.

> Multiples of 10 end in 0.

Consider this number line from 40 to 50.

40 and 50 are both multiples of 10.

- 41, 42, 43, and 44 are all nearer to 40 than to 50, so they are **rounded down** to 40.
- 46, 47, 48, and 49 are all nearer to 50 than to 40, so they are **rounded up** to 50.
- 45 is midway between 40 and 50. We choose 45 to be **rounded up** to 50.

So, to round to the nearest *ten*, we need to look at the digit in the *units* place.

> To **round** to a particular place value, look at the digit in the place value to the right of it.
> - If this digit is 0, 1, 2, 3, or 4, we round down.
> - If this digit is 5, 6, 7, 8, or 9, we round up.

Example 2   ◀》 Self Tutor

Round to the nearest 10:

a 63   **b** 475   **c** 3029

a 63 is nearer to 60 than 70, so we round 63 *down* to 60.

b 475 is midway between 470 and 480, so we round 475 *up* to 480.

c 3029 is nearer to 3030 than 3020, so we round 3029 *up* to 3030.

> When we round to the nearest *ten*, we look at the digit in the *units* place.

EXERCISE 1D

1 Look at the number in **bold**. Write down which multiple of 10 it is nearer to, or write "midway" if it is midway between them.

a 30, **38**, 40   **b** 70, **71**, 80   **c** 90, **95**, 100

d 130, **132**, 140   **e** 450, **457**, 460   **f** 730, **735**, 740

g 810, **818**, 820   **h** 1220, **1225**, 1230   **i** 6740, **6743**, 6750

2 Write down the nearest multiple of 10 on *either* side of:

a 21   **b** 46   **c** 65   **d** 93   **e** 199

f 461   **g** 785   **h** 1733   **i** 2801   **j** 3947

3 Round to the nearest 10:

a 17   **b** 53   **c** 35   **d** 71   **e** 97

f 206   **g** 311   **h** 502   **i** 888   **j** 659

k 444   **l** 705   **m** 696   **n** 4075   **o** 3122

p 4777   **q** 6564   **r** 7099   **s** 8183   **t** 4996

Example 3	◀)) **Self Tutor**

Round to the nearest 100:

a 183   **b** 241   **c** 1650

---

a 183 is nearer to 200 than 100, so we round 183 *up* to 200.

b 241 is nearer to 200 than 300, so we round 241 *down* to 200.

c 1650 is midway between 1600 and 1700, so we round 1650 *up* to 1700.

Multiples of 100 end in 00. When we round to the nearest *hundred*, we look at the digit in the *tens* place.

---

4 Look at the number in **bold**. Write down which multiple of 100 it is nearer to, or write "midway" if it is midway between them.

a 500, **547**, 600   **b** 600, **679**, 700   **c** 900, **950**, 1000

d 7600, **7631**, 7700   **e** 2900, **2985**, 3000   **f** 11 300, **11 360**, 11 400

5 Write down the nearest multiple of 100 on *either* side of:

a 470   **b** 634   **c** 1841   **d** 2015   **e** 4950

6 Round to the nearest 100:

a 175   **b** 211   **c** 572   **d** 793   **e** 1050

f 2684   **g** 6998   **h** 3950   **i** 9015   **j** 13 208

k 27 660   **l** 18 611   **m** 38 457   **n** 55 443   **o** 85 074

7 Write down the nearest multiple of 1000 on *either* side of:

   a 6219   **b** 14 386   **c** 86 250

8 Round to the nearest 1000:

   a 834   **b** 2495   **c** 1089

   d 5485   **e** 7800   **f** 6500

   g 9990   **h** 9399   **i** 13 095

   j 7543   **k** 246 088   **l** 499 859

> Multiples of 1000 end in 000. When we round to the nearest *thousand*, we look at the digit in the *hundreds* place.

9 Round to the nearest 10 000:

   a 18 124   **b** 47 600   **c** 54 500

   d 75 850   **e** 89 888   **f** 52 749

   g 90 555   **h** 99 776   **i** 104 968

10 Round to the nearest 100 000:

   a 181 000   **b** 342 000   **c** 654 000   **d** 709 850

   e 139 888   **f** 450 749   **g** 290 555   **h** 989 512

11 Round 38 485 to the nearest: **a** 10   **b** 100   **c** 1000   **d** 10 000

12 Round to the accuracy given:

   a There are 37 musicians in an orchestra.   (to the nearest 10)

   b There are 55 singers in a youth choir.   (to the nearest 10)

   c I received a payment of $582.   (to the nearest $10)

   d My tax bill is €4095.   (to the nearest €10)

   e Each load of bricks weighs 687 kg.   (to the nearest 100 kg)

   f My new car cost $24 995.   (to the nearest $100)

   g The journey was 35 621 km.   (to the nearest 100 km)

   h I am paid $1378 per fortnight.   (to the nearest $100)

   i The circumference of the Earth is 40 008 km.   (to the nearest 10 000 km)

   j The cost of a house is £463 590.   (to the nearest £10 000)

   k The population of Moscow is 11 924 706.   (to the nearest 100 000)

PUZZLE   **ROUNDING WHOLE NUMBERS**

Click on the icon to obtain a printable puzzle for rounding numbers.   **PRINTABLE PUZZLE**

MULTIPLE CHOICE QUIZ   **QUICK QUIZ**

REVIEW SET 1A

1 Write in expanded form:

    a 742   **b** 5063   **c** 29 188

2 Write seventeen thousand, three hundred and four, in numeral form.

3 Find the missing value(s) in each number line:

  a    **b**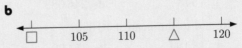

4 Show each set of numbers on a number line, and hence write them in ascending order.

    a 5, 2, 7, 9   **b** 20, 80, 40, 30, 10

5 Write in words:

    a 24 350 000   **b** 410 700 000 000   **c** 8 500 200 000 000

6 The average person will travel five million, eight hundred and ninety thousand metres during their lifetime. Write this number using numerals.

7 Round:

    a 35 to the nearest 10   **b** 4384 to the nearest 1000

    c 463 994 to the nearest 10 000   **d** 853 941 to the nearest 100 000.

REVIEW SET 1B

1 Write down the value of the digit 4 in:

    a 3409   **b** 41 076   **c** 4 613 598

2 For the number 583 214, write down the value of the:

    a 2   **b** 1   **c** 5

3 Write $2000 + 400 + 90 + 7$ in numeral form.

4 Write in words:

    a 426   **b** 7086   **c** 930 541

5 Show the set of numbers 72, 79, 64, 67 on a number line, and hence write the numbers in descending order.

6 Write 246 503 041 in a place value chart.

7 Round to the accuracy given:

    a There are 16 610 spectators at the stadium.   (to the nearest 1000)

    b My internet bill is €82.   (to the nearest €10)

    c The dog ran 2309 m along the beach.   (to the nearest 100 m)

    d The festival cost $951 820 to organise.   (to the nearest $100 000)

Chapter 2

Operations

Contents:

OPENING PROBLEM

A concert hall has 20 sections of seating, each holding the same number of people. In total, there is seating for 3000 people.

A band called *The Angles* performed 5 concerts at the hall. There was a full audience each night, and each ticket cost $30.

Things to think about:

a What *operations* do we use in mathematics?

b Can you use a mathematical operation to find:

   i the number of seats in each section

   ii the total number of people who attended the concerts

   iii the total value of the tickets they bought?

In this Chapter we will study the mathematical operations of addition, subtraction, multiplication, and division.

When solving real world problems, there are often words or phrases which tell us which operation we need to perform.

DISCUSSION

Discuss how each of these words or phrases might indicate which mathematical operation we need:

- total
- decrease
- times
- product
- increase
- share
- less
- difference
- lots of.
- more
- sum

A   ADDITION

> To find the **sum** of two or more numbers, we **add** them together.

When we add three or more numbers together, the order we add them in is not important.

For example:

$$8 + 2 + 5$$
$$= \ \ 10 \ \ + 5$$
$$= 15$$

$$8 + 5 + 2$$
$$= \ \ 13 \ \ + 2$$
$$= 15$$

$$2 + 5 + 8$$
$$= \ \ 7 \ \ + 8$$
$$= 15$$

The sum of 2, 5, and 8 is 15 no matter which order we add them in.

INVESTIGATION 1   ORDER OF ADDITION

Since we can perform additions in whichever order we like, is there a strategy we can use to make some additions easier?

What to do:

1   Find each pair of sums using the given order of addition:

   a $3 + 5 + 7$ and $3 + 7 + 5$ **b** $6 + 9 + 4$ and $6 + 4 + 9$

   c $13 + 6 + 7$ and $13 + 7 + 6$ **d** $8 + 9 + 12$ and $8 + 12 + 9$

2   In each pair of sums, what made it easier to calculate the second sum?

When we add three or more numbers together, we can look for numbers whose sum ends in 0 or 00. We add these first to make the calculation easier.

Example 1	◀) **Self Tutor**
Find:	
a $74 + 23 + 7$	**b** $16 + 67 + 14$

a $74 + \underbrace{23 + 7}$
   $= 74 + \quad 30$
   $= 104$

b $16 + 67 + 14$
   $= \underbrace{16 + 14} + 67$
   $= \quad 30 \quad + 67$
   $= 97$

COLUMN ADDITION

When we add larger numbers, we write them in columns so the place values line up. We then add each column, working from right to left.

Example 2	◀) **Self Tutor**
Find $32 + 427 + 3274$.	$\begin{array}{r} 3\ 2 \\ 4\ 2\ 7 \\ +\ 3\ {}_1 2\ {}_1 7\ 4 \\ \hline 3\ 7\ 3\ 3 \end{array}$

EXERCISE 2A

1   Find each sum mentally:

   a $6 + 9$ **b** $8 + 11$ **c** $13 + 9$ **d** $14 + 12$

   e $16 + 19$ **f** $24 + 13$ **g** $18 + 15$ **h** $56 + 14$

2 Find each sum by adding in the most convenient order:

    a $3+6+7$
    b $19+8+2$
    c $3+6+7+4$

    d $18+41+32$
    e $21+98+19$
    f $45+14+26$

    g $98+57+102$
    h $107+14+23$
    i $28+13+12+37$

3 Copy and complete:

    a
$$\begin{array}{r} 5\ 2 \\ +\ 3\ 5 \\ \hline \end{array}$$

    b
$$\begin{array}{r} 7\ 4 \\ +\ 3\ 7 \\ \hline \end{array}$$

    c
$$\begin{array}{r} 6\ 2\ 8 \\ +\ \ \ 4\ 7 \\ \hline \end{array}$$

    d
$$\begin{array}{r} 4\ 9\ 2 \\ +\ \ \ 6\ 9 \\ \hline \end{array}$$

    e
$$\begin{array}{r} 7\ 5\ 3 \\ +\ 1\ 8\ 4 \\ \hline \end{array}$$

    f
$$\begin{array}{r} 1\ 9\ 1\ 7 \\ +\ 2\ 0\ 7\ 8 \\ \hline \end{array}$$

    g
$$\begin{array}{r} 9\ 1\ 3 \\ 2\ 4 \\ +\ 7\ 0\ 7 \\ \hline \end{array}$$

    h
$$\begin{array}{r} 2\ 1\ 7 \\ 1\ 0\ 6 \\ +\ 1\ 2\ 7\ 4 \\ \hline \end{array}$$

    i
$$\begin{array}{r} 9\ 0\ 0\ 4 \\ 2\ 1\ 6 \\ 2\ 7 \\ +\ 3\ 8\ 1\ 6 \\ \hline \end{array}$$

4 Find:

    a $42+37$
    b $72+35$
    c $421+327$

    d $624+77$
    e $921+1234$
    f $6214+324+27$

    g $90+784+2173$
    h $32+627+4296$
    i $912+6+427+3274$

5 Check each of these sums. If a sum is incorrect, rewrite it correctly.

    a
$$\begin{array}{r} 2\ 3\ 9 \\ +\ 4\ 7\ 8 \\ \hline 7\ 0\ 7 \end{array}$$

    b
$$\begin{array}{r} 7\ 0\ 2 \\ 8\ 7 \\ +\ 1\ 0\ 1 \\ \hline 8\ 9\ 0 \end{array}$$

    c
$$\begin{array}{r} 3\ 1\ 1 \\ 1\ 9\ 7 \\ +\ 6\ 4\ 8 \\ \hline 1\ 1\ 5\ 5 \end{array}$$

    d
$$\begin{array}{r} 5\ 5\ 5\ 5 \\ +\ 6\ 7\ 6\ 7 \\ \hline 1\ 2\ 3\ 2\ 2 \end{array}$$

6 Clive bought 450 g of potatoes, 175 g of carrots, and 340 g of onions. Find the total weight of Clive's vegetables.

> When solving worded problems, write your final answer in a sentence.

7 Hetty had $87 in her bank account. She made two deposits of $246 and $113 into the account. How much is in the account now?

8 An ice cream store sold 78 ice creams on Friday, 154 ice creams on Saturday, and 129 ice creams on Sunday. How many ice creams did the store sell in total?

9 Xuen bought a game console for $255. She also purchased an extra controller for $50, a game for $95, and a bag to store these in for $32. How much did Xuen pay altogether?

10 Rima went on an overseas trip that required three plane flights. The first flight was 2142 km, the second was 732 km, and the third was 1049 km. Find the total distance that Rima flew.

B # SUBTRACTION

When we **subtract** a number, we take it away from what was there previously.

To find the **difference** between two numbers, we **subtract** the smaller number from the larger one.

INVESTIGATION 2   STRATEGY FOR SUBTRACTION

In this Investigation we look for a strategy that will allow us to do more subtractions mentally.

What to do:

1 Perform each pair of subtractions:

     a $14 - 9$ and $15 - 10$ **b** $22 - 9$ and $23 - 10$

     c $23 - 19$ and $24 - 20$ **d** $17 - 8$ and $19 - 10$

2 You should have found that the subtractions in each pair gave the same result.

     a Did you find the second subtractions easier?

     b How can we convert the first subtraction in each pair into the second?

When we subtract two numbers, we can first increase them both by the same amount so we are subtracting a number ending in 0 or 00.

Example 3	◀) **Self Tutor**
Find:	
a the difference between 12 and 27	**b** $42 - 29$

a The difference between 12 and 27
   $= 27 - 12$ {larger $-$ smaller}
   $= 15$
	b $42 - 29$
	   $= 43 - 30$ {adding 1 to both}
	   $= 13$

COLUMN SUBTRACTION

When we subtract larger numbers, we write them in columns so the place values line up. We then subtract each column, working from right to left.

Example 4	◀) **Self Tutor**
Find $519 - 345$.	$\begin{array}{r} ^4\not{5}\,^{11}\not{1}\ \ 9 \\ -\ 3\ \ 4\ \ 5 \\ \hline 1\ \ 7\ \ 4 \end{array}$

EXERCISE 2B

1 Find the difference between:

    a 7 and 3   **b** 3 and 7   **c** 27 and 14   **d** 8 and 15.

2 Find without using column subtraction:

    a $24 - 12$ **b** $24 - 17$ **c** $32 - 19$ **d** $36 - 16$

    e $32 - 18$ **f** $38 - 29$ **g** $66 - 43$ **h** $164 - 99$

3 Copy and complete:

a   9 7
   − 1 5
	b 6 3
	   − 1 9
		c 4 5 2
		   − 1 3 8

d   5 1 7
   − 2 7 3
	e 6 2 8
	   − 3 3 3
		f 2 4 7
		   − 1 3 8

g   6 0 2
   − 1 4 9
	h 4 0 1 5
	   − 1 7 3 2
		i 6 0 0 5
		   − 2 3 4 9

4 Find:

    a $93 - 27$ **b** $765 - 143$ **c** $214 - 132$

    d $861 - 437$ **e** $2002 - 1236$ **f** $3000 - 583$

5 Find the difference between:

    a 33 and 87   **b** 147 and 223   **c** 503 and 1127.

6 Check each of the subtractions. If a subtraction is incorrect, rewrite it correctly.

a   5 6 3
   − 2 8 1
 ‾‾‾‾‾
    3 8 2
	b 5 9 0 0
	   − 3 8 1 4
	 ‾‾‾‾‾
	    2 1 8 6
		c 6 9 1 3
		   − 5 8 7
		 ‾‾‾‾‾
		    6 3 2 6
			d 3 2 1 5
			   − 3 1 8 6
			 ‾‾‾‾‾
			       3 9

7 Justyn bought a jumper for \$42. Sylvia bought a shirt for \$26. How much more did Justyn spend than Sylvia?

8 At a tennis tournament, the first prize was \$175 000 and second prize was \$115 000. Find the difference between the prizes.

9 Erika has 120 minutes of international calls included with her phone plan. If she spends 38 minutes talking to her grandparents who live overseas, how many minutes of international call time remain?

10 During a 365 day year, it rained in New York on 192 days. On how many days did it *not* rain?

11 Darryl likes fishing. He caught 48 fish during June, 97 fish during July, and 74 fish during August.

    a How many more fish did Darryl catch in July than in June?

    b How many fewer fish did Darryl catch in August than in July?

GAME   SNAKES AND ADDERS

Click on the icon to play a game of Snakes and Adders. You must add and subtract your way to the finish before being bitten by a snake!

SNAKES AND ADDERS

PUZZLE   NUMBER PUZZLES

In these number puzzles each letter stands for a different digit from 0 to 9. There are several solutions to each puzzle. Can you find one of them? Can you find all of them?

a
```
    D O G
  + C A T
  ‾‾‾‾‾‾‾
  H A T E
```

b
```
    S U R F
  - S A N D
  ‾‾‾‾‾‾‾‾‾
      S E A
```

C   MULTIPLICATION

To find the **product** of two or more numbers, we **multiply** them.

For example, the product of 6 and 7 is 6×7 or 42.

MULTIPLYING BY 10, 100, AND 1000

When we multiply a number by 10, each digit moves one place value to the *left*.

We write a zero to fill in the empty units place value.

Since $100 = 10 \times 10$ and $1000 = 10 \times 10 \times 10$, we conclude that:

> To multiply a whole number by 10, we place one zero on the end of it.
>
> To multiply a whole number by 100, we place two zeros on the end of it.
>
> To multiply a whole number by 1000, we place three zeros on the end of it.

Example 5			◀) Self Tutor
Find:	**a** 23×10	**b** 200×6	**c** 30×400

a
$$23 \times 10$$
$$= 230$$

b
$$200 \times 6$$
$$= 2 \times 100 \times 6$$
$$= 12 \times 100$$
$$= 1200$$

c
$$30 \times 400$$
$$= 3 \times 10 \times 4 \times 100$$
$$= 12 \times 1000$$
$$= 12\,000$$

ORDER OF MULTIPLICATION

When we multiply three or more numbers together, we can perform the multiplication in whichever order we like.

For example:

$$3 \times 5 \times 4$$
$$= \ 15 \ \times 4$$
$$= 60$$

$$4 \times 5 \times 3$$
$$= \ 20 \ \times 3$$
$$= 60$$

INVESTIGATION 3	ORDER OF MULTIPLICATION

Since we can perform multiplications in whichever order we like, is there a strategy we can use to make some multiplications easier?

What to do:

1 Find each pair of products using the given order of multiplication:

  a $5 \times 9 \times 2$ and $5 \times 2 \times 9$ **b** $2 \times 7 \times 5$ and $2 \times 5 \times 7$

  c $4 \times 6 \times 5$ and $4 \times 5 \times 6$ **d** $8 \times 3 \times 5$ and $8 \times 5 \times 3$

2 In each pair of products, what made it easier to calculate the second product?

When we multiply three or more numbers together, we can look for numbers whose product ends in 0 or 00. We multiply these first to make the calculation easier.

Example 6	◀) Self Tutor

Find: **a** $5 \times 19 \times 2$ **b** $16 \times 25 \times 8$

a $5 \times 19 \times 2$
$= 5 \times 2 \times 19$
$= \ 10 \ \times 19$
$= 190$

b $16 \times 25 \times 8$
$= 16 \times \ \ 200$
$= 3200$

EXERCISE 2C

1 Find each product mentally:

  a 6×9 **b** 8×12 **c** 11×5 **d** 7×3

  e $2 \times 3 \times 2$ **f** $4 \times 2 \times 3$

2 Find:

  a 50×10 **b** 50×100 **c** 50×1000 **d** 69×100

  e 69×1000 **f** $69 \times 10\,000$ **g** 123×100 **h** 246×1000

  i 960×100 **j** $49 \times 10\,000$ **k** 490×100 **l** 4900×100

3 Find:

    a 3×2 **b** 30×2 **c** 30×20 **d** 300×20

    e 5×7 **f** 5×70 **g** 50×70 **h** 50×700

    i 3×11 **j** 30×11 **k** 300×11 **l** 300×1100

4 Find each product by multiplying in the most convenient order:

    a $5 \times 13 \times 2$ **b** $25 \times 19 \times 4$ **c** $50 \times 21 \times 2$ **d** $125 \times 19 \times 8$

    e $4 \times 21 \times 25$ **f** $200 \times 97 \times 5$ **g** $500 \times 27 \times 2$ **h** $12 \times 125 \times 8$

5 60 rows of pine trees were planted, each containing 80 trees. How many pine trees were planted altogether?

D   COLUMN MULTIPLICATION

When we multiply larger numbers, we write them in columns so the place values line up.

We multiply the first number by the digits of the second number one at a time, then if necessary add the results.

Example 7   ◀) **Self Tutor**

Find:

   a 567×4 **b** 253×16

a
$$
\begin{array}{r}
5\;\;6\;\;7 \\
\times\;\; {}_2{}_2\,4 \\
\hline
2\;\;2\;\;6\;\;8
\end{array}
$$

b
$$
\begin{array}{r}
2\;\;5\;\;3 \\
\times\;\;\;\;1\;\;6 \\
\hline
1\;\;{}^3 5\;\;{}^1 1\;\;8 \quad \leftarrow 253 \times 6 = 1518 \\
+\;\;{}_1 2\;\;5\;\;3\;\;0 \quad \leftarrow 253 \times 10 = 2530 \\
\hline
4\;\;0\;\;4\;\;8 \quad \leftarrow 253 \times 16 = 4048
\end{array}
$$

EXERCISE 2D

1 Copy and complete:

    a
$$
\begin{array}{r}
7\;\;2 \\
\times\;\;\;\;3 \\
\hline
\end{array}
$$
    b
$$
\begin{array}{r}
5\;\;9 \\
\times\;\;\;\;4 \\
\hline
\end{array}
$$
    c
$$
\begin{array}{r}
1\;\;2\;\;5 \\
\times\;\;\;\;\;\;7 \\
\hline
\end{array}
$$
    d
$$
\begin{array}{r}
3\;\;1\;\;8 \\
\times\;\;\;\;\;\;9 \\
\hline
\end{array}
$$

2 Find:

    a 37×4 **b** 62×8 **c** 174×7 **d** 541×6

3 Copy and complete:

    a
$$
\begin{array}{r}
2\;\;8 \\
\times\;\;1\;\;2 \\
\hline
\end{array}
$$
    b
$$
\begin{array}{r}
3\;\;1 \\
\times\;\;2\;\;6 \\
\hline
\end{array}
$$
    c
$$
\begin{array}{r}
7\;\;5 \\
\times\;\;4\;\;1 \\
\hline
\end{array}
$$
    d
$$
\begin{array}{r}
1\;\;5\;\;2 \\
\times\;\;\;\;2\;\;3 \\
\hline
\end{array}
$$

4   Find:

    a 27×15 **b** 56×49 **c** 85×43

    d 415×34 **e** 324×45 **f** 642×36

5   Carlos lifted five 18 kg bags of potatoes onto a truck. How many kilograms of potatoes did he lift altogether?

6   A flute teacher charges \$80 per lesson. She gives 17 lessons in one week. How much money does she earn?

7   A greengrocer agrees to buy 217 baskets of fresh cherries at \$38 for each basket.
    How much does the greengrocer pay?

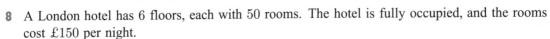

8   A London hotel has 6 floors, each with 50 rooms. The hotel is fully occupied, and the rooms cost £150 per night.

    a How many rooms does the hotel have?

    b How much income does the hotel receive for the night?

E   DIVISION

To find the **quotient** of two numbers, we **divide** the first number by the second number.

The number being divided is the **dividend**, and the number we are dividing by is called the **divisor**.

For example, the quotient of 63 and 9 is $63 \div 9$, which is 7.

$$63 \quad \div \quad 9 \quad = \quad 7$$
$$\uparrow \qquad\quad \uparrow \qquad\qquad \uparrow$$
$$\text{dividend} \quad \text{divisor} \qquad \text{quotient}$$

DIVIDING BY 10, 100, AND 1000

When we divide a number by 10, each digit moves one place to the *right*.

We conclude that:

If a whole number ends in 0, we divide it by 10 by removing the zero from the end.

If a whole number ends in 00, we divide it by 100 by removing the two zeros from the end.

If a whole number ends in 000, we divide it by 1000 by removing the three zeros from the end.

Example 8		◄)) *Self Tutor*
Find:		
a $34\,000 \div 10$	**b** $34\,000 \div 100$	**c** $34\,000 \div 1000$
a $34\,000 \div 10$ $= 3400$	**b** $34\,000 \div 100$ $= 340$	**c** $34\,000 \div 1000$ $= 34$

DIVIDING LARGER NUMBERS

When dividing larger numbers, we divide each place value in turn, starting with the highest.

If a digit is too small to be divided on its own, we exchange it in the next column.

If the resulting quotient is not a whole number, we are left with a **remainder**.

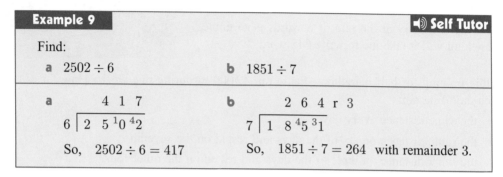

Example 9	◀) **Self Tutor**

Find:

a $2502 \div 6$ b $1851 \div 7$

a $\begin{array}{r} 4\ 1\ 7 \\ 6\,\overline{)2\ 5\ ^{1}0\ ^{4}2} \end{array}$ b $\begin{array}{r} 2\ 6\ 4\ r\ 3 \\ 7\,\overline{)1\ 8\ ^{4}5\ ^{3}1} \end{array}$

So, $2502 \div 6 = 417$ So, $1851 \div 7 = 264$ with remainder 3.

EXERCISE 2E

1 Find the quotient of:

  a   12 and 3   b   28 and 7   c   99 and 9   d   144 and 12.

2 Find:

a $2000 \div 10$	b $2000 \div 100$	c $2000 \div 1000$
d $57\,000 \div 10$	e $57\,000 \div 100$	f $57\,000 \div 1000$
g $243\,000 \div 10$	h $243\,000 \div 100$	i $243\,000 \div 1000$
j $45\,000 \div 10$	k $45\,000 \div 100$	l $45\,000 \div 1000$
m $720\,000 \div 10$	n $720\,000 \div 100$	o $720\,000 \div 1000$
p $6\,000\,000 \div 10$	q $6\,000\,000 \div 100$	r $6\,000\,000 \div 1000$

3 Find these quotients:

a $6 \div 2$	b $60 \div 2$	c $600 \div 2$	d $6000 \div 2$
e $35 \div 7$	f $350 \div 7$	g $3500 \div 7$	h $35\,000 \div 7$
i $12 \div 3$	j $120 \div 3$	k $1200 \div 3$	l $12\,000 \div 3$

4 Copy and complete:

a $3\,\overline{)4\ 2}$ b $4\,\overline{)2\ 1\ 6}$ c $8\,\overline{)1\ 6\ 8}$ d $6\,\overline{)5\ 0\ 4}$

e $5\,\overline{)3\ 7\ 5}$ f $4\,\overline{)1\ 1\ 6\ 4}$ g $5\,\overline{)6\ 8\ 0\ 9}$ h $7\,\overline{)6\ 3\ 1\ 7}$

5 Find:

a $48 \div 4$	b $125 \div 5$	c $312 \div 6$	d $240 \div 5$
e $203 \div 7$	f $624 \div 3$	g $328 \div 8$	h $7353 \div 9$

6 Find:

  a $86 \div 3$ b $193 \div 5$ c $974 \div 6$ d $3948 \div 9$

7 My three brothers and I received a gift of $320. If we share the money equally between us, how much will each person get?

8 A relay team of nine people took 738 minutes to complete a charity relay. If each team member ran for the same amount of time, how long did each person spend running?

9 I can write a story at the rate of 8 words per minute. How long will it take me to write 648 words?

10 While training for half marathons, Paulo ran 42 000 m during one week. How far did he run each day if he ran:

    a the same distance every day

    b the same distance on six of the days and rested on the seventh

    c the same distance on three of the days and rested on the other four?

F PROBLEMS WITH MULTIPLE OPERATIONS

Sometimes we need to perform more than one operation to solve a problem. In these situations we need to carefully choose which operations we need, and what order we need to perform them in.

Example 10 ◀)) **Self Tutor**

Each week Clancy is paid $350, plus $65 for each vacuum cleaner he sells. How much does Clancy earn if he sells 13 vacuum cleaners in a week?

$$\text{Money from sales} = \$65 \times 13$$
$$= \$845$$

In total, Clancy earns $\$845 + \$350$
$$= \$1195$$

```
      6 5
  ×   1 3
  1 ¹9 5
+ ₁6 5 0
  8 4 5
```

```
    8 4 5
  + 3 5 0
  1 1 9 5
```

EXERCISE 2F

1 Deloris bought a shirt costing $69, a pair of jeans costing $75, and a pair of shoes costing $109.

    a How much did Deloris spend in total?

    b How much change did she get from $300?

2 Yesterday, June bought 7 coffees for her coworkers, costing $42 in total. Today it is Colin's turn, and he needs to buy 9 coffees.

    a How much did each coffee cost June?

    b How much will Colin need to pay?

3 Anne and Alan have a herd of 183 goats. Anne puts 75 goats into their largest paddock, then Alan divides the rest equally between two smaller paddocks. How many goats did Alan put in each smaller paddock?

4 The cost of placing a notice in a newspaper is $38, plus $13 for each line of type. If my notice takes 10 lines, how much will I pay in total?

5 Marcia saved $620 during the year, and her sister saved twice that amount.

    a How much money did Marcia's sister save?

    b How much money did the sisters save in total?

6 Yuan worked 45 hours at one job for $24 per hour, then 35 hours at another job for $26 per hour.

    a In total, how much did Yuan earn over this period?

    b Yuan had hoped to earn $2000. Did he succeed or fail, and by how much?

7 Alicia ran 6 km each day during March, and 8 km each day during April. How far did she run in total over the two months?

8 A plastic crate contains 100 boxes of pens. Each box of pens weighs 86 grams. The total mass of the crate and pens is 9200 grams. Find the mass of the crate.

9 It takes 24 minutes for Rodney to chainsaw a log into 3 pieces. In total, how long would it take Rodney to chainsaw the log into 4 pieces?

G   EXPONENT NOTATION

We sometimes need to multiply the same number together many times.

To avoid writing long lists of identical numbers multiplied together, we can instead use **exponent notation**.

For example, we can write $2 \times 2 \times 2 \times 2 \times 2$ as 2^5.

The 2 is called the **base**.

The 5 is called the **exponent**, **index**, or **power**. It is the number of times the base appears in the product.

$$2^5$$
    ← exponent, index, or power

    ← base number

The following table demonstrates correct language when talking about exponent notation.

Natural number	Expanded form	Exponent notation	Spoken form
2	2	2^1	2 *or* 2 to the power 1
4	2×2	2^2	2 squared *or* 2 to the power 2
8	$2 \times 2 \times 2$	2^3	2 cubed *or* 2 to the power 3
16	$2 \times 2 \times 2 \times 2$	2^4	2 to the fourth *or* 2 to the power 4
32	$2 \times 2 \times 2 \times 2 \times 2$	2^5	2 to the fifth *or* 2 to the power 5

Example 11
◀) **Self Tutor**

Write using exponent notation:

   a $5 \times 5 \times 5$ **b** $2 \times 2 \times 3 \times 3 \times 3 \times 5$

  a $5 \times 5 \times 5$ **b** $\underbrace{2 \times 2}_{2^2} \times \underbrace{3 \times 3 \times 3}_{3^3} \times \underbrace{5}_{5^1 \text{ or } 5}$

      $= 5^3$

                             $= 2^2 \times 3^3 \times 5$

EXERCISE 2G

1 Write using exponent notation:

  a $2 \times 2 \times 2$ **b** 7×7 **c** $9 \times 9 \times 9 \times 9$

  d 13×13 **e** $3 \times 3 \times 3 \times 3 \times 3$ **f** $4 \times 4 \times 4 \times 4 \times 4 \times 4 \times 4$

2 Write using exponent notation:

  a $5 \times 7 \times 7$ **b** $2 \times 2 \times 2 \times 3$ **c** $3 \times 3 \times 5 \times 5$

  d $2 \times 2 \times 2 \times 3 \times 3$ **e** $4 \times 4 \times 7 \times 7 \times 7 \times 7$ **f** $2 \times 2 \times 5 \times 7$

  g $2 \times 3 \times 3 \times 5$ **h** $3 \times 5 \times 5 \times 7 \times 7$ **i** $3 \times 3 \times 3 \times 5 \times 7 \times 7$

3 Copy and complete this table showing powers of 10:

Numeral	Words	Exponent notation
100		
1000	one thousand	
10 000		10^4
100 000		
	one million	
	ten million	10^7
1 000 000 000		
1 000 000 000 000	one trillion	

> To find a power of 10, we can count the number of zeros after the 1.

Example 12
◀) **Self Tutor**

Find: **a** 3^4 **b** $2^3 \times 4^2$

  a 3^4 **b** $2^3 \times 4^2$

     $= 3 \times 3 \times 3 \times 3$ $= 2 \times 2 \times 2 \times 4 \times 4$

     $= 81$ $= 8 \times 16$

                                  $= 128$

4 Find the value of:

  a 3^2 **b** 2^3 **c** 4^2 **d** 3^3

  e 4^3 **f** 2^4 **g** 5^3 **h** 9^2

  i $6^2 \times 2^3$ **j** $3^3 \times 2^2$ **k** $5^2 \times 3^3$ **l** $8^2 \times 10^3$

5 Which is larger?

   a 2^3 or 3^2 **b** 2^4 or 4^2 **c** 5^2 or 2^5

H — ORDER OF OPERATIONS

DISCUSSION

What do you think is the value of $20 + 8 \div 4$?

Share your answer with your classmates. Did everybody in the class get the same answer?

From your discussion, you will probably have decided that the value of $20 + 8 \div 4$ depends on the order in which the operations are performed.

If we do the addition first and then the division, we get $20 + 8 \div 4 = 28 \div 4$
$$= 7$$

If we do the division first and then the addition, we get $20 + 8 \div 4 = 20 + 2$
$$= 22$$

To avoid confusion, there is a set of rules for the order of operations:

- Perform the operations within **Brackets** first.
- Calculate any part involving **Exponents**.
- Starting from the left, perform all **Divisions** and **Multiplications** as you come to them.
- Restart from the left, performing all **Additions** and **Subtractions** as you come to them.

> The word **BEDMAS** may help you remember this order.

The rule of BEDMAS does *not* mean that division should be performed before multiplication, or that addition should be performed before subtraction.

- If an expression contains only $\times$ and $\div$ operations, we work from left to right.
- If an expression contains only $+$ and $-$ operations, we work from left to right.

Using the rule of BEDMAS, $20 + 8 \div 4$ $\{\div$ before $+\}$
$$= 20 + 2$$
$$= 22$$

Example 13	◀) Self Tutor
Find:	
a $11 - 6 + 8$	**b** $8 \times 3 \div 2$

  a $11 - 6 + 8$ $\{-$ and $+$ from left$\}$ **b** $8 \times 3 \div 2$ $\{\times$ and $\div$ from left$\}$

       $= 5 + 8$ $= 24 \div 2$

       $= 13$ $= 12$

EXERCISE 2H

1 Find the value of:

a $12 - 6 + 2$	**b** $12 + 6 - 8$	**c** $24 \div 3 \div 4$	**d** $6 \times 2 \div 3$
e $12 \div 3 \times 2$	**f** $15 - 6 - 4$	**g** $6 \times 6 \div 2$	**h** $12 + 6 + 13$
i $17 - 8 - 6$	**j** $30 - 10 + 2$	**k** $32 \div 4 \times 2$	**l** $36 \div 6 \div 2$

Example 14   ◀)) **Self Tutor**

Find: **a** $12 \div 6 + 8$ **b** $30 - 6 \times 2$

a $12 \div 6 + 8$ $\{\div$ before $+\}$ **b** $30 - 6 \times 2$ $\{\times$ before $-\}$
  $= 2 + 8$ $= 30 - 12$
  $= 10$ $= 18$

---

2 Find the value of:

a $5 \times 7 - 6$	**b** $12 \div 3 + 2$	**c** $17 - 7 \times 2$	**d** $30 - 10 \div 2$
e $12 + 6 \div 3$	**f** $3 \times 8 - 6$	**g** $15 \div 3 - 2$	**h** $4 + 4 \div 4$
i $100 - 10 \div 2$	**j** $3 + 9 \times 7$	**k** $16 \div 8 + 2$	**l** $3 \times 12 + 4$

3 To find $15 - 7 + 3$, Derrick performed these steps:

$$15 - 7 + 3 \qquad \{\text{perform addition first}\}$$
$$= 15 - 10 \qquad \{\text{then perform subtraction}\}$$
$$= 5$$

a Explain the error in Derrick's working.

b Find the correct value of $15 - 7 + 3$.

Example 15   ◀)) **Self Tutor**

Find: **a** $7 + 3 \times 2 - 4$ **b** $9 \div 3 + 7 \times 2$

a $7 + 3 \times 2 - 4$ $\{\times$ before $+$ and $-\}$
  $= 7 + 6 - 4$ $\{+$ and $-$ from left$\}$
  $= 13 - 4$
  $= 9$

b $9 \div 3 + 7 \times 2$ $\{\div$ and $\times$ before $+\}$
  $= 3 + 14$
  $= 17$

---

4 Find the value of:

a $7 + 6 - 5 \times 2$	**b** $9 + 2 \times 5 - 4$	**c** $18 \div 3 + 10 \times 3$
d $8 \times 3 - 4 \times 5$	**e** $30 - 3 \times 5 + 1$	**f** $5 + 7 - 3 \times 4$
g $22 \div 2 + 5 \times 4$	**h** $60 - 24 \div 3 + 12$	**i** $20 \div 2 + 8 \div 4$

Example 16   ◀) **Self Tutor**

Find the value of:

   a $18 \div 2 \times 3 - 1$ **b** $16 - 12 \times 2 \div 3$

   a $18 \div 2 \times 3 - 1$ $\{\div$ and $\times$ from left before $-\}$
         $= 9 \times 3 - 1$ $\{\times$ before $-\}$
         $= 27 - 1$
         $= 26$

   b $16 - 12 \times 2 \div 3$ $\{\div$ and $\times$ from left before $-\}$
         $= 16 - 24 \div 3$ $\{\div$ before $-\}$
         $= 16 - 8$
         $= 8$

5   Find the value of:

   a $18 \div 3 \times 5 + 7$ **b** $60 - 24 \div 8 \times 3$ **c** $8 \times 5 \div 2 - 13$

   d $4 \times 9 \div 12 + 5$ **e** $13 + 21 \div 7 \div 3$ **f** $3 \times 4 \times 5 + 8$

   g $30 - 2 \times 9 \div 2$ **h** $50 - 32 \div 8 \times 2$ **i** $70 \div 7 \div 5 - 1$

Example 17   ◀) **Self Tutor**

Find the value of: $23 - (17 - 2)$

        $23 - (17 - 2)$ {brackets first}
    $= 23 - 15$
    $= 8$

6   Find the value of:

   a $(8 - 4) \div 2$ **b** $11 - (2 + 3)$ **c** $5 \times (6 + 1)$

   d $14 \div (10 - 3)$ **e** $(11 + 19) \div 5$ **f** $60 \div (3 \times 4)$

   g $(5 + 3) \times 4 - 1$ **h** $5 + (3 \times 4) - 1$ **i** $5 + 3 \times (4 - 1)$

   j $(6 + 19 - 3) \div 2$ **k** $11 - 6 \div (3 - 1)$ **l** $(7 + 17) \div (40 \div 5)$

Example 18   ◀) **Self Tutor**

Find the value of:

   a $45 \div 3^2$ **b** $2 + (4 - 1)^2$

   a $45 \div 3^2$ {exponent first}   **b** $2 + (4 - 1)^2$ {brackets first}
       $= 45 \div 9$ $= 2 + 3^2$ {exponent next}
       $= 5$ $= 2 + 9$
                                        $= 11$

7 Find the value of:

a $10 - 3^2$

b $28 \div 2^2$

c $8^2 \div 4$

d $21 - 2^4 + 6$

e $2 + 5^2$

f $(2 + 5)^2$

g 2×3^2

h $(2 \times 3)^2$

i $(4 - 2)^3 \div 8$

j $(30 \div 6)^3$

k $5 + (4 + 5)^2$

l $3^4 - (3 \times 2)^2$

8 Insert $+$, $-$, $\times$, or $\div$ to make each statement true:

a $4 + 18 \,\square\, 3 = 10$

b $6 \,\square\, 7 - 12 = 30$

c $(17 \,\square\, 3) \div 5 = 4$

d $(18 - 2) \,\square\, 8 = 2$

e $3^3 \,\square\, 2^2 = 23$

f $4 + (21 \,\square\, 7) = 7$

PUZZLE

Click on the icon to obtain a printable version of this puzzle.

1		2		3	4
		5	6		
7	8		9		
	10	11		12	13
14			15		
16			17		

PUZZLE

Across

1   $40 \times 5 - 17$

3   $100 - (7 - 1)$

5   $(1 + 5 \times 50) \times 25$

7   $3 \times (3 + 20)$

9   $8 \times 11 - 7$

10   $100 - 9 \times 2$

12   $5 \times (6 + 7)$

14   $153 \div 3 + 3 \times 1000$

16   $90 - 4 \times 4$

17   $9 \times 100 + 8 \times 5$

Down

1   $100 + 24 \div 4$

2   $10 \times 4 - 20 \div 5$

3   $10\,000 - 3 \times 100 + 2 \times 8$

4   $7 \times 7 - 2 \times 2$

6   $(7 - 3) \times (6 + 1)$

8   $100 \times 100 - 14 \times 14$

11   $625 \div (20 + 5)$

13   $10 \times (9 \times 6)$

14   $70 - 3 \times 11$

15   $2 \times 5 + 3 \times 3$

MULTIPLE CHOICE QUIZ

QUICK QUIZ

REVIEW SET 2A

1 Find:

a the sum of 19 and 27

b the difference between 28 and 51.

2 Copy and complete:

a
```
    2 1 7
  + 5 4 1
  _____
```

b
```
    6 2 9
  - 1 6 6
  _____
```

c
```
    1 7 8
    2 3 0 7
  +   7 6 5
  _____
```

3 Find:

    a $18 + 17 + 32$ **b** $2 \times 27 \times 5$ **c** $108 - 29$ **d** $23 \times 40 \times 5$

4 David scored 570 points in a diving competition. Victor scored 486 points. Find the difference between their scores.

5 Copy and complete:

    a
$$\begin{array}{r} 5\ 6 \\ \times\ \ \ 6 \\ \hline \end{array}$$

    b $4\,\overline{)1\ 3\ 6}$

    c
$$\begin{array}{r} 4\ 7 \\ \times\ 1\ 3 \\ \hline \end{array}$$

    d $7\,\overline{)3\ 9\ 2}$

6 Find:

    a 56×9 **b** $344 \div 8$ **c** 491×6

7 Find the total cost of 24 opera tickets at €112 each.

8 Kathryn was paid $608 wages for the week. She also earned $24 per hour for 5 hours overtime. How much did Kathryn earn in total?

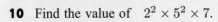

9 Write using exponent notation:

    a $6 \times 6 \times 6 \times 6$

    b $2 \times 2 \times 2 \times 7 \times 7 \times 7 \times 7 \times 7$

10 Find the value of $2^2 \times 5^2 \times 7$.

11 Find the value of:

    a $19 - 8 + 2$ **b** $10 + 6 \div 2$ **c** $24 \div (6 - 4)$

    d $48 \div 4 \times 2$ **e** $72 \div 3^2$ **f** $36 \div (12 \div 6)^2$

12 Insert $+$, $-$, $\times$, or $\div$ to make $2 \times 8 \ \square \ 4 + 2 = 6$ a correct statement.

REVIEW SET 2B

1 Copy and complete:

    a
$$\begin{array}{r} 8\ 5 \\ -\ 3\ 2 \\ \hline \end{array}$$

    b
$$\begin{array}{r} 3\ 5\ 7\ 6 \\ +\ 4\ 3\ 8\ 5 \\ \hline \end{array}$$

    c
$$\begin{array}{r} 2\ 3\ 0\ 6 \\ -\ \ \ 5\ 1\ 2 \\ \hline \end{array}$$

2 Find:

    a $108 + 16 + 84$ **b** $25 \times 17 \times 4$ **c** $206 + 47 + 195$ **d** $3040 - 197$

3 Damien bought some shorts for $39, and a polo shirt for $32. How much did he spend in total?

4 Find:

    a 34×100 **b** $59\,000 \div 1000$ **c** 70×400

5 Copy and complete:

    a
$$\begin{array}{r} 1\ 2\ 7 \\ \times\ \ \ \ \ \ 4 \\ \hline \end{array}$$

    b $5\,\overline{)3\ 8\ 5}$

    c
$$\begin{array}{r} 4\ 3 \\ \times\ 2\ 8 \\ \hline \end{array}$$

    d $9\,\overline{)5\ 5\ 3}$

6 Find:

    a $408 \div 8$ **b** 23×39 **c** $3632 \div 7$

7 5000 tickets were sold in a raffle. The cost of each ticket was \$20. How much money was raised?

8 Derek takes 6 minutes to construct one section of fence. How many sections can he construct in 90 minutes?

9 At a sports store, Mildred bought 4 footballs for a total cost of \$68.

    a How much does each football cost?

    b Julie bought 3 footballs and 2 cricket balls. Each cricket ball costs \$15.

        i How much did Julie pay in total?

        ii How much change did Julie receive from \$100?

10 Write using exponent notation:

    a $2 \times 2 + 7 \times 7 \times 7$ **b** $11 \times 11 \times 11 - 3 \times 3 \times 3 \times 3$

11 Find:

    a $18 - 12 \div (1 + 5)$ **b** $9 \times 3 - 4 \times 6$ **c** $7 + (20 \div 4)^2$

12 Answer the **Opening Problem** on page **22**.

13 **a** Find the value of $30 - 12 \div 2 \times 3$.

    b Add a set of brackets to make each statement correct:

        i $30 - 12 \div 2 \times 3 = 28$ **ii** $30 - 12 \div 2 \times 3 = 27$

        iii $30 - 12 \div 2 \times 3 = 72$

Chapter 3

Lines and angles

Contents:

OPENING PROBLEM

Henry was studying two straight roads on a map. He observed that at their point of intersection, there were four angles made. They are marked red, blue, black, and green.

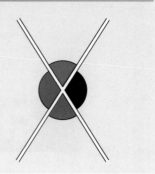

Things to think about:

a Is the blue angle larger or smaller than the red angle?

b How could you *measure* the sizes of the angles?

c Which angles are equal in size?

DISCUSSION   POINTS

In small groups, discuss:

- What is meant by a *point*?
- What are some specific *points* in your classroom?
- How can we *represent* a point?

A **point** is used to mark a position or location.

A point does not have any size. However, we use small dots to represent points so that we can see them.

To help identify a point, we can label it with a capital letter.

We can then make statements like:

- "The distance from A to B is ...."
- "The angle at B measures ...."

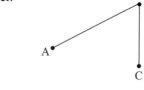

In the figure alongside, the corner points are A, B, C, and D.

Each corner point is called a **vertex**.

The plural of vertex is **vertices**.

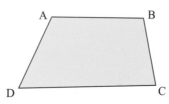

A   LINES

A **straight line**, usually just called a **line**, is a continuous infinite collection of points in a particular direction. A line has no beginning and no end.

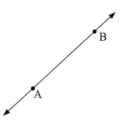

The line alongside passes through points A and B. We use arrowheads to show that the line continues endlessly in both directions. We can call this line "line AB" or "line BA".

We use the following bracket notation to describe lines and parts of lines:

 (AB) is the **line** which passes through A and B and continues endlessly in both directions.

 [AB] is the **line segment** which joins the two points A and B. It is only a part of the line (AB).

 [AB) is the **ray** which starts at A, passes through point B, and continues on endlessly.

PARALLEL AND INTERSECTING LINES

Parallel lines are lines which are always a fixed distance apart and never meet.

In mathematics, a **plane** is a flat surface like a table top or a sheet of paper.

Two straight lines on a plane are either **parallel** or **intersecting**.

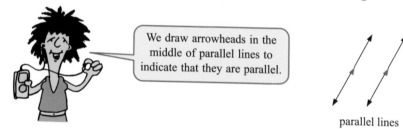

We draw arrowheads in the middle of parallel lines to indicate that they are parallel.

parallel lines

point of intersection

intersecting lines

DISCUSSION

1 The edges of a long straight road are parallel lines. To the people in the yellow car, the parallel lines appear to meet in the distance.
Do the parallel lines really meet?

2 Find examples in your classroom of:
   a parallel line segments
   b intersecting line segments.

3 Why do we call it a *ray* of sunshine?

EXERCISE 3A

1 Describe, including a sketch, the meaning of:
   a a line
   b a line segment
   c a ray
   d a vertex
   e a point of intersection
   f parallel lines.

2 Give *all* ways of naming:

a    **b**

3 Use bracket notation to describe:

a 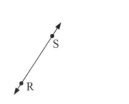   **b**   **c**

d 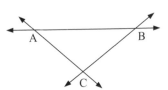   **e**   **f**

4   State the intersection of:

a (AB) and (BC)

b (CB) and (CA).

5 **a** At which point does [AB) intersect (CD)?

   b Which points do *not* lie on (AD)?

   c Which two lines are parallel?

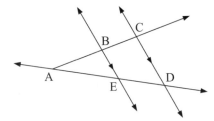

6 Find the intersection of:

   a [AB] and [BC]

   b [AB) and [BC]

   c [AB] and [AC].

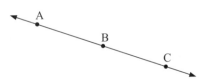

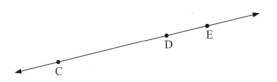

DISCUSSION   **LINES**

- How many different straight lines could be drawn through the single point A?
- Suppose A and B are two distinct points. How many straight lines can be drawn which pass through *both* A and B?
- Suppose P, Q, and R are three distinct points. How many straight lines could be drawn which pass through P, Q, and R?

ACTIVITY 1   **STRAIGHT LINE SURPRISES**

In this online Activity, you will see how straight lines can be used to produce some surprising patterns.

STRAIGHT LINE
SURPRISES

B   # ANGLES

An **angle** is formed where two straight lines meet.

The point where the lines meet is called the **vertex** of the angle, and the lines are called the **arms**.

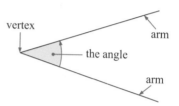

Here are some examples of angles we see around us:

- the angle between scissor blades

- the angle between a wall and a door

- the angle between the hands on a watch

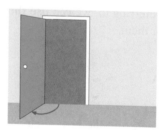

CLASSIFYING ANGLES

The **size** or **measure** of an angle is the amount of *turn* between its arms.

We measure the turn in **degrees**, and use the symbol °.

Ancient Babylonian astronomers decided that there would be 360 degrees in a **complete turn** or **revolution**.

We write this as 360°.

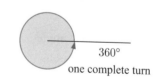

360°
one complete turn

360 was probably chosen because it can be divided by 2, 3, 4, 5, 6, 8, 9, 10, 12, and 15, to give whole number answers.

We can measure other angles by comparing their size with a complete turn.

Revolution	Straight angle	Right angle
One complete turn. 360°	$\frac{1}{2}$ turn. 180°	$\frac{1}{4}$ turn. 90°

We use a small square to indicate a right angle.

Acute angle	Obtuse angle	Reflex angle
Less than $\frac{1}{4}$ turn. Between 0° and 90°.	Between $\frac{1}{4}$ turn and $\frac{1}{2}$ turn. Between 90° and 180°.	Between $\frac{1}{2}$ turn and a complete turn. Between 180° and 360°.

THREE POINT NOTATION

To make it clear what angle we are referring to, we can use **three point notation**. This uses a point on each arm, and the vertex between them.

For example:

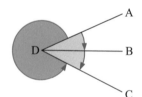

- the green angle is $A\widehat{D}B$ or $B\widehat{D}A$
- the blue angle is $B\widehat{D}C$ or $C\widehat{D}B$
- $A\widehat{D}C$ is made up of the green angle and the blue angle
- the red angle is *reflex* $A\widehat{D}C$, since its size is greater than 180°.

EXERCISE 3B

1 Draw a diagram to illustrate:

   a a $\frac{1}{2}$ turn   **b** a $\frac{1}{4}$ turn   **c** a revolution

   d an obtuse angle   **e** a straight angle   **f** a right angle

   g an acute angle   **h** a reflex angle.

2 Name the shaded angle using three point notation, and classify the angle:

   a   **b**   **c**

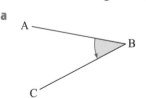
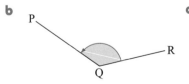
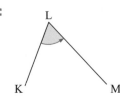

d

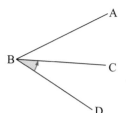

e

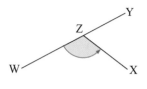

f

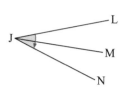

g

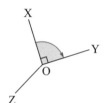

h

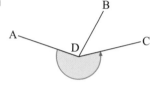

i

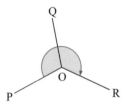

3 State whether each angle is acute, right, obtuse, straight, or reflex:

a 73°   b 194°   c 90°   d 114°

e 13°   f 180°   g 277°   h 93°

4 Copy this figure into your book.

a Label vertices B, C, and D such that:

- $\hat{ADC}$ is a right angle
- there is a straight angle at B.

b Name *two* other right angles in the figure.

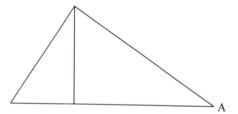

C MEASURING ANGLES

Angles are measured using a **protractor**.

Every mark around the edge of the protractor represents 1°.

There are two scales on the protractor, one for measuring in each direction.

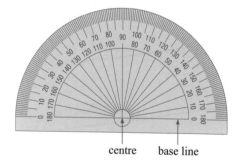

centre   base line

To measure an angle:

- the centre of the protractor must be over the vertex of the angle
- the base line of the protractor must be directly over one arm of the angle.

We start at 0° and measure to the other arm of the angle.

Example 1

◀)) **Self Tutor**

Measure these angles:

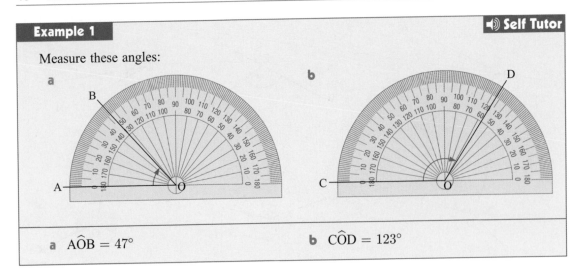

a $\widehat{AOB} = 47°$

b $\widehat{COD} = 123°$

EXERCISE 3C

1   Measure these angles:

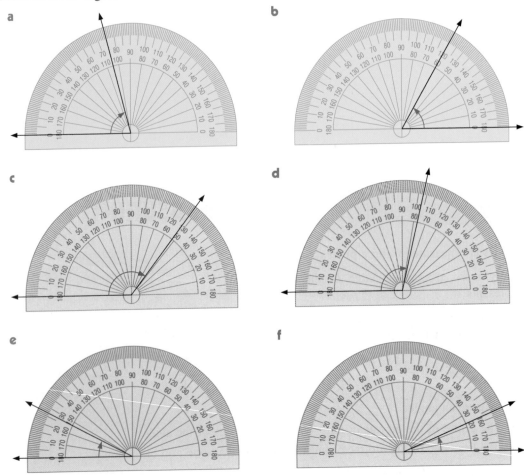

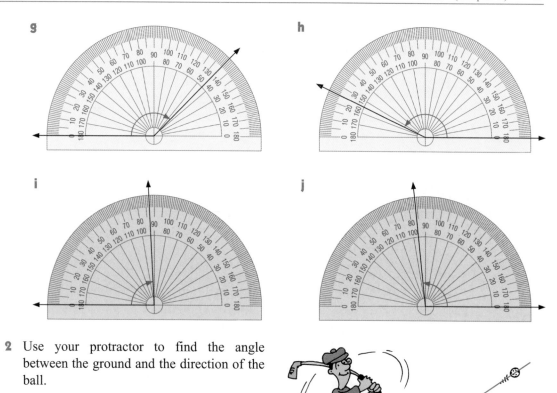

2 Use your protractor to find the angle between the ground and the direction of the ball.

3 Measure *all* angles of the following figures. Use three point notation to record your answers.

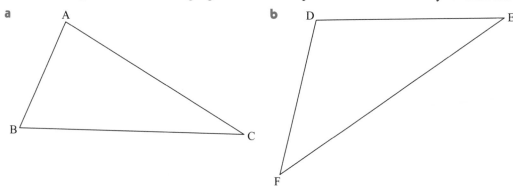

4 Use your ruler and protractor to draw each angle:

    a $\widehat{ABC} = 60°$ **b** $\widehat{PQR} = 115°$ **c** $\widehat{LMN} = 48°$

    d $\widehat{DEF} = 151°$ **e** $\widehat{JKL} = 137°$ **f** $\widehat{XYZ} = 17°$

Ask a classmate to check your answers.

5 For each pair of angles:

    i Measure $\widehat{ABC}$ and $\widehat{XYZ}$.   **ii** Determine whether $\widehat{ABC}$ or $\widehat{XYZ}$ is larger.

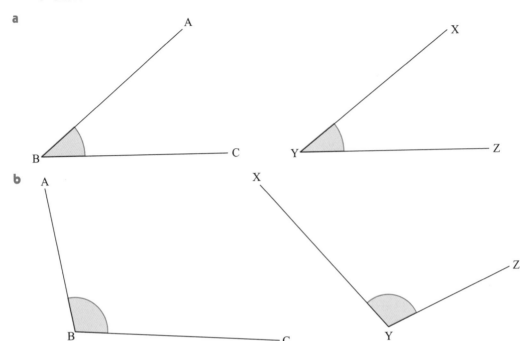

a

b

D

CALCULATING ANGLES

We are often able to calculate the size of an angle using other angles we already know.

When working with angles, we can either refer to them using three point notation, or else label the unknown angle with a letter such as x.

Example 2   ◀)) **Self Tutor**

In each diagram:

    i Find the size of $\widehat{ABC}$ *without* using a protractor.   **ii** Classify $\widehat{ABC}$.

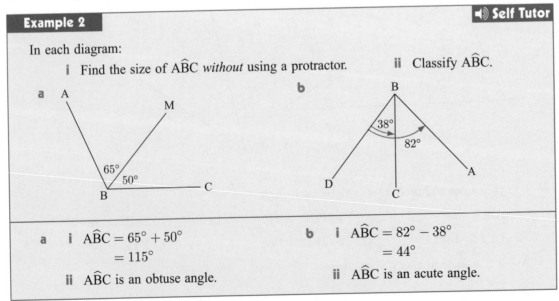

a **i** $\widehat{ABC} = 65° + 50°$

          $= 115°$

  ii $\widehat{ABC}$ is an obtuse angle.

b **i** $\widehat{ABC} = 82° - 38°$

          $= 44°$

  ii $\widehat{ABC}$ is an acute angle.

It is useful to remember that:

- **angles in a right angle** add to 90°

- **angles on a line** add to 180°

- **angles at a point** add to 360°.

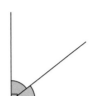

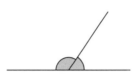

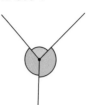

| **Example 3** | ◀)) **Self Tutor** |

Find the value of x without using a protractor:

a

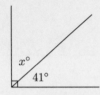

b

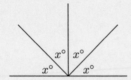

c

a The angles add to 90°

so $x = 90 - 41$

$= 49$

b The angles add to 180°

so $x = 180 \div 4$

$= 45$

c The angles add to 360° so

$x = 360 - 135 - 90 - 110$

$= 25$

EXERCISE 3D

1 In each diagram:

   i Find the size of $\widehat{ABC}$ without using a protractor.

   ii Classify $\widehat{ABC}$.

a

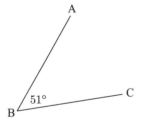

b

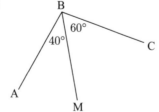

c

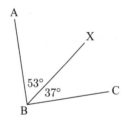

d

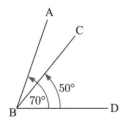

e

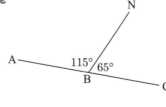

f

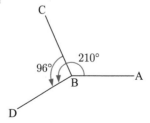

2 Find the unknown value without using a protractor:

a

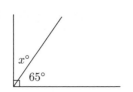

b

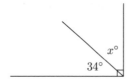

c

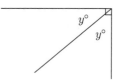

d

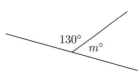

e

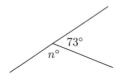

f

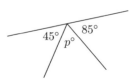

g

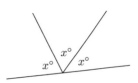

h

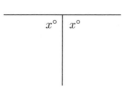

i

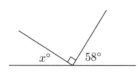

3 Find the unknown value without using a protractor:

a

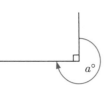

b

c

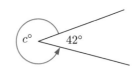

d

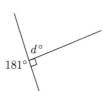

e

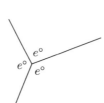

f

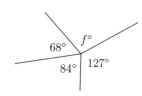

g

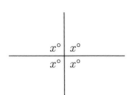

h

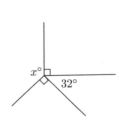

i

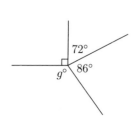

4 Without using a protractor, find the values of x, y, and z.

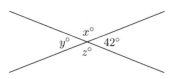

E | VERTICALLY OPPOSITE ANGLES

Vertically opposite angles are formed when two straight lines intersect.

They are directly opposite each other through the vertex.

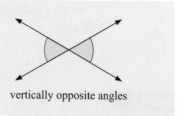

vertically opposite angles

INVESTIGATION | VERTICALLY OPPOSITE ANGLES

In this Investigation we will discover the relationship between the sizes of vertically opposite angles.

What to do:

1   For each set of intersecting line segments, use a protractor to measure each of the vertically opposite angles shaded.

a

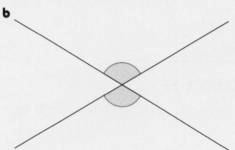

b

c

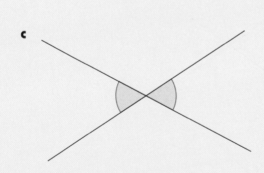

d

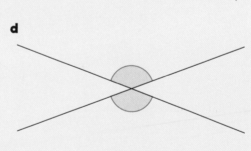

2   What do you suspect from **1**?

3   In the diagram alongside, $A\hat{O}D = x°$.
     $A\hat{O}C$ and $B\hat{O}D$ are vertically opposite angles.

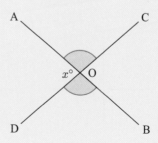

   a   Explain why $A\hat{O}C = (180 - x)°$.
   b   Explain why $B\hat{O}D = (180 - x)°$.
   c   What can you conclude?

From the **Investigation** you should have discovered that:

Vertically opposite angles are **equal in size**.

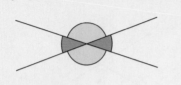

The red angles are equal in size
and
the blue angles are equal in size.

Example 4

◀)) **Self Tutor**

Find the unknown value:

a

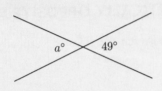

b

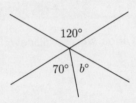

a $a = 49$ {vertically opposite angles}

b $b + 70 = 120$ {vertically opposite angles}
But $50 + 70 = 120$
So, $b = 50$

EXERCISE 3E

1   Name the angle which is vertically opposite $\widehat{ABC}$:

a

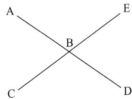

b

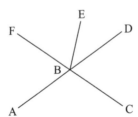

c

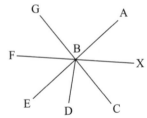

2   Find the unknown value:

a

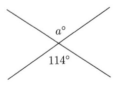

b

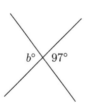

c

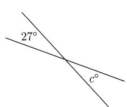

d

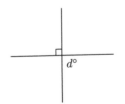

e

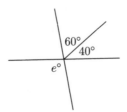

f

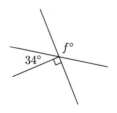

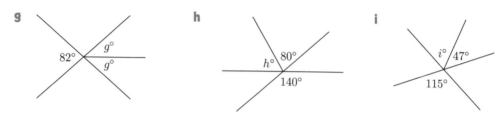

ACTIVITY 2   BISECTING ANGLES

When we **bisect** an angle with a straight line, we divide it into two angles of equal size.

In this Activity we see how to bisect an angle using a compass and ruler only. We call this a **geometric construction**.

Before you begin, you need to know:

- The **radius** of a compass means the distance from the sharp point to the tip of your pencil.

- An **arc** is a curve which is *part* of a circle.

Be careful with your compass. It is sharp!

What to do:

1 Draw AB̂C similar to this. It does not have to be exact.

DEMO

Follow these steps to bisect AB̂C:

Step 1: With centre B, draw an arc which cuts [BA] and [BC] at P and Q respectively.

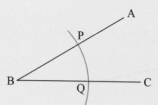

Step 2: With centre Q and radius [PQ], draw an arc within AB̂C.

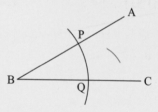

Step 3:   With centre P and the same radius [PQ], draw another arc to intersect the previous one at M.

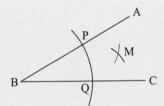

Step 4:   Draw [BM].
[BM] bisects $\widehat{ABC}$ with $\widehat{ABM} = \widehat{CBM}$.

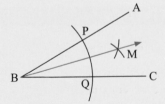

2 a Use your protractor to draw $\widehat{ABC}$ of size $80°$. Bisect $\widehat{ABC}$ using a compass and ruler only.

b Use your protractor to find the size of each of the two angles you constructed.

3 Draw an obtuse $\widehat{ABC}$ of your own choice. Bisect the angle using a compass and ruler only. Check your construction using your protractor.

4 a Draw a large triangle ABC and carefully bisect its three angles.

b What do you notice about the angle bisectors?

c Check that your classmates made the same observation.

d Copy and complete: "The three angle bisectors of a triangle ....".

5 Use your protractor to draw an angle of size $140°$. Hence, using a compass and ruler, construct an angle of size $35°$.

QUICK QUIZ

MULTIPLE CHOICE QUIZ

REVIEW SET 3A

1 Use bracket notation to describe:

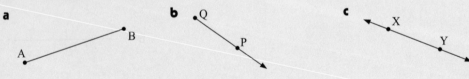

a   **b**   **c**

2 Draw a diagram to illustrate a $\frac{3}{4}$ turn.

3 Name the shaded angle using three point notation, and classify the angle:

a

b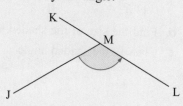

4 State whether each angle is acute, right, obtuse, straight, or reflex:

    a $139°$ **b** $90°$ **c** $187°$ **d** $24°$

5 Use a protractor to find the angle between the ground and the direction of the plane.

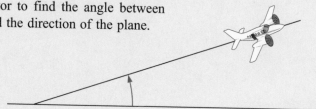

6 Use a protractor to measure the angle. Hence classify the angle.

    a   **b**

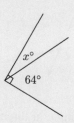
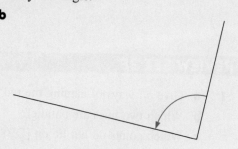

7 Find the unknown value without using a protractor:

    a   **b**   **c**

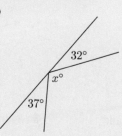
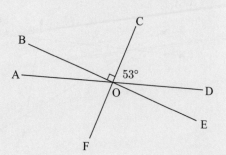

8   **a** Name the angle which is vertically opposite $A\widehat{O}B$.

      b Find the size of $A\widehat{O}E$.

9 **a** Find the value of:

   i a **ii** b

   b Find the size of the shaded angle.

   c Classify the shaded angle.

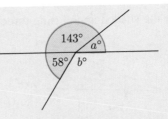

10

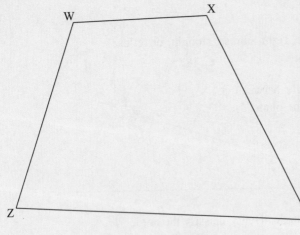

a Use a protractor to measure each angle of this shape.

b Which angle is the largest?

c Classify each angle.

d Find the sum of the angles.

REVIEW SET 3B

1 **a** Give *all* ways of naming the red line.

   b Which two lines are parallel?

   c Which points do not lie on [DB)?

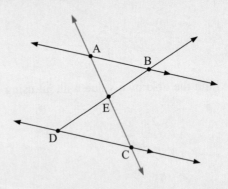

2 State the intersection of (AB) and (AC).

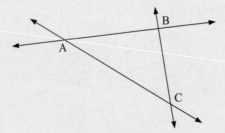

3 Name the shaded angle in three point notation, and classify the angle.

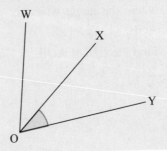

4 Measure AB̂C and DÊF. Hence determine which angle is larger.

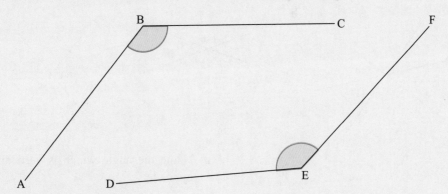

5 Find the size of AB̂C without using a protractor:

a

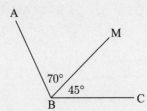

b

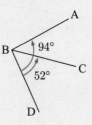

c

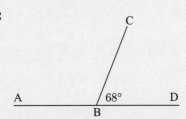

d

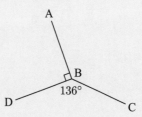

6 **a** Use a protractor to measure each angle in this triangle.

   b Find the sum of the angles.

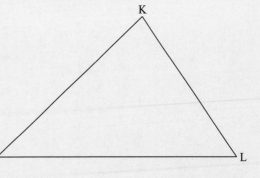

7 Find the value of a without using a protractor:

a

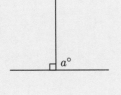

b

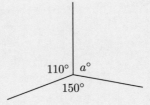

c

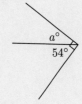

8 Find the unknown value without using a protractor:

a

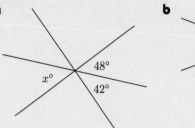

b

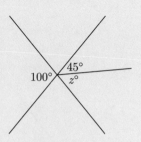

c

9

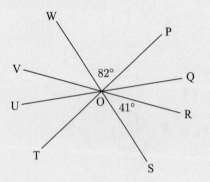

a Name the angle which is vertically opposite:

    i $P\hat{O}Q$ **ii** $W\hat{O}V$

b Find the size of:

    i $S\hat{O}T$ **ii** $P\hat{O}V$

Chapter 4

Number properties

Contents:

OPENING PROBLEM

There are 24 students in a class. The teacher wants to divide the students into smaller groups of equal size to work on a project.

Things to think about:

a Can the students be divided into 6 equal groups? How many students would be in each group?

b Can the students be divided into 5 equal groups?

c What other size groups can the students be divided into equally?

d Suppose one student has gone home sick, so there are only 23 students left in the class. Is it still possible to divide the class into smaller groups of equal size?

The questions in the **Opening Problem** are about *divisibility*, or whether a number can be divided by smaller whole numbers with no remainder.

In this Chapter we will study some *properties* of numbers, including divisibility.

 # ZERO AND ONE

Zero (0) and one (1) are very special numbers which have important properties.

ZERO

- Zero is the **identity** for addition. This means that:
  ▶ When 0 is added to a number, the number remains the same.
  ▶ When 0 is subtracted from a number, the number remains the same.
- When a number is multiplied by 0, the result is 0.
- It is meaningless to divide by 0. We say the result is **undefined**.
- When 0 is divided by a non-zero number, the result is 0.

For example:

$12 + 0 = 12$, $12 - 0 = 12$, $12 \times 0 = 0$, $12 \div 0$ is undefined, $0 \div 12 = 0$.

ONE

One is the **identity** for multiplication. This means that if we multiply or divide a number by 1, the number remains the same.

For example:

$12 \times 1 = 12$, $12 \div 1 = 12$.

DISCUSSION

You should have observed previously that with both addition and multiplication, we can swap the order of the numbers without changing the result.

For example: $3 + 5 = 5 + 3$

$3 \times 5 = 5 \times 3$

1 What does this property tell us about:

    a $0 + 12$ **b** 0×12 **c** 1×12?

2 Do subtraction and division have this property?

3 Research the special name given to this property.

EXERCISE 4A

1 Find, if possible:

    a $7 + 0$ **b** $7 - 0$ **c** 7×0 **d** $7 \div 0$ **e** $0 \div 7$

    f $0 + 7$ **g** 0×7 **h** 7×1 **i** $7 \div 1$ **j** 1×7

2 Find, if possible:

    a 11×0 **b** 11×1 **c** $0 + 11$ **d** $11 \div 1$ **e** $11 - 0$

    f $0 \div 11$ **g** $11 + 0$ **h** 1×11 **i** $11 \div 0$ **j** 0×11

3 Find, if possible:

    a $0 + 0$ **b** 0×1 **c** 0×0 **d** 1×0

    e $1 + 0$ **f** $0 \div 1$ **g** $0 + 1$ **h** $0 \div 0$

4 Find, if possible:

    a 235×1 **b** 30×0 **c** $0 \div 480$ **d** $0 + 26$

    e $48 \div 0$ **f** 0×19 **g** 1×125 **h** $684 \div 1$

5 Find, if possible:

    a $15 + 0 - 8$ **b** $15 + 0 \times 8$ **c** $(15 + 0) \times 8$

    d $14 + 2 \times 1$ **e** $(14 + 2) \times 1$ **f** $14 \times 2 \times 0$

    g $18 - 6 \times 0$ **h** $13 \div 1 + 7$ **i** $1 \times 8 \div 0$

    j $0 + 9 \div 1$ **k** $(0 + 9) \div 1$ **l** $1 + 0 \div 9$

HISTORICAL NOTE

Neither the Ancient Greeks nor the Romans had a symbol to represent nothing, but other ancient peoples such as the Babylonians did.

The symbol 0 was originally called *sifr* in Arabic. It was later called *zephirum* in Latin, from which the word "zero" originates.

B   SQUARE NUMBERS

> The product of two identical whole numbers is a **square number**.

We call it a square number because it can be represented by a square array of dots.

For example:

"one squared"	"two squared"	"three squared"	"four squared"
$1^2 = 1 \times 1 = 1$	$2^2 = 2 \times 2 = 4$	$3^2 = 3 \times 3 = 9$	$4^2 = 4 \times 4 = 16$

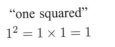
1, 4, 9, and 16 are all square numbers.

EXERCISE 4B

1   By counting the number of dots in these arrangements, find the fifth and sixth square numbers.

a $5 \times 5 = ...$
$5^2 = ...$

b $6 \times 6 = ...$
$6^2 = ...$

2   List the first ten square numbers.

3   Find the:
   a   12th square number
   b   15th square number
   c   22nd square number.

4   Find two square numbers whose sum is another square number.

5   **a**   Find 0^2.
   b   Which numbers are equal to their own squares?

6   Find the smallest square number greater than 300.

7   Find the largest square number smaller than 200.

8   Explain why the product of two square numbers is itself a square number.

ACTIVITY 1   TRIANGULAR NUMBERS

Triangular numbers are numbers which can be represented by a triangular arrangement of dots.

The first three triangular numbers are 1, 3, and 6.

$$1 \qquad 1 + 2 = 3 \qquad 1 + 2 + 3 = 6$$

What to do:

1 **a** Redraw this set of bowling pins as a triangular arrangement of dots.

   b Write a sum for the number of dots, and hence find the fourth triangular number.

2 **a** Redraw this set of billiard balls as a triangular arrangement of dots.

   b Write a sum for the number of dots, and hence find the fifth triangular number.

3 **a** Draw a diagram to represent the 6th triangular number.

   b Write a sum for the number of dots, and hence find the sixth triangular number.

4 Look at the sums for the first six triangular numbers. Describe what happens when you move from one triangular number to the next.

5 Write down the 7th, 8th, 9th, and 10th triangular numbers.

6 **a** Find:

   i $1 + 3$ **ii** $3 + 6$ **iii** $6 + 10$ **iv** $10 + 15$

   b Copy and complete:

   "When two consecutive triangular numbers are added together, the result is a ......"

   c Use a diagram to explain this result.

7 **a** Find:

   i $(1 \times 2) \div 2$ **ii** $(2 \times 3) \div 2$ **iii** $(3 \times 4) \div 2$ **iv** $(4 \times 5) \div 2$

   b Can you describe a calculation which you can use to quickly find a particular triangular number?

   c Use your method to find the 20th triangular number.

   d Use a diagram to explain *why* this method works.

CUBIC NUMBERS

> The product of three identical whole numbers is a **cubic number**.

We call it a cubic number because it can be represented by a cubic array of blocks.

For example:

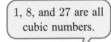
1, 8, and 27 are all cubic numbers.

"one cubed"	"two cubed"	"three cubed"
$1^3 = 1 \times 1 \times 1 = 1$	$2^3 = 2 \times 2 \times 2 = 8$	$3^3 = 3 \times 3 \times 3 = 27$

EXERCISE 4C

1   **a**   Draw an arrangement of blocks to represent the fourth cubic number.

     b   Find the fourth cubic number.

2   List the first ten cubic numbers.

3   Find the difference between the sixth cubic number and the sixth square number.

4   Find two cubic numbers whose sum is a square number.

5   Find two square numbers whose sum is a cubic number.

6   **a**   Find 0^3.

     b   Which natural numbers are equal to their own cubes?

DIVISIBILITY

> One number is **divisible** by another if, when we divide, the quotient is a whole number.

For example: 12 is divisible by 4 because $12 \div 4 = 3$.

               12 is not divisible by 5 because $12 \div 5 = 2$ remainder 2.

EVEN AND ODD NUMBERS

> A natural number is **even** if it is divisible by 2.
> A natural number is **odd** if it is not divisible by 2.

For example: 14 is even because $14 \div 2 = 7$.

               19 is odd because $19 \div 2 = 9$ with remainder 1.

EXERCISE 4D

1 Determine whether:

    a 15 is divisible by 2   **b** 18 is divisible by 3   **c** 20 is divisible by 7

    d 40 is divisible by 10   **e** 67 is divisible by 10   **f** 27 is divisible by 4

    g 35 is divisible by 5   **h** 31 is divisible by 9   **i** 88 is divisible by 11.

2 Determine whether each number is even or odd:

    a 12   **b** 27   **c** 39   **d** 34   **e** 60   **f** 53   **g** 79   **h** 104

3 Find the number between 50 and 60 which is divisible by 7.

4 Is zero odd or even? Explain your answer.

5 What is the smallest non-zero number which is divisible by 6 *and* by 8?

6   **a** Beginning with 8, write three consecutive even numbers.

    b Beginning with 17, write five consecutive odd numbers.

7   **a** Write down all of the pairs of non-consecutive even numbers which add to 10.

    b Write down all of the pairs of non-consecutive odd numbers which add to 20.

    c Write down all of the sets of three *different* even numbers which add to 20.

8 Use the words "even" and "odd" to complete these sentences:

    a The sum of two even numbers is always ......

    b The sum of two odd numbers is always ......

    c The sum of an odd number and an even number is always ......

    d When an even number is subtracted from an odd number, the result is ......

    e When an odd number is subtracted from an odd number, the result is ......

    f The product of two odd numbers is always ......

    g The product of an even number and an odd number is always ......

E   DIVISIBILITY TESTS

INVESTIGATION 1   DIVISIBILITY BY 3

In this Investigation we will discover a test to determine whether a number is divisible by 3.

What to do:

1 Copy the table below. Complete it by determining whether each number is divisible by 3, and by finding the sum of its digits.

Number	15	22	27	34	39	47	55	69	126	152
Divisible by 3?	yes	no								
Sum of digits	$1 + 5 = 6$	$2 + 2 = 4$								

2 Look at the sum of the digits for numbers which are divisible by 3. What do you notice?

3 Can you describe a test to determine whether a number is divisible by 3?

Here are some tests we can use to determine whether one number is divisible by another, without actually doing the division:

Number	Divisibility Test
2	If the last digit is even, then the number is divisible by 2.
3	If the sum of the digits is divisible by 3, then the number is divisible by 3.
4	If the number formed by the last *two* digits is divisible by 4, then the original number is divisible by 4.
5	If the last digit is 0 or 5, then the number is divisible by 5.
6	If the number is divisible by both 2 and 3, then it is divisible by 6.
10	If the last digit is 0, then the number is divisible by 10.

Example 1   ◀)) **Self Tutor**

Determine whether 768 is divisible by:

a 2   b 3   c 6.

a 768 ends in 8, which is even.
   So, 768 is divisible by 2.
b The sum of the digits $= 7 + 6 + 8 = 21$.
   Now 21 is divisible by 3.   {as $21 \div 3 = 7$}
   So, 768 is divisible by 3.
c Since 768 is divisible by both 2 and 3, 768 is divisible by 6.

EXERCISE 4E

1 Determine whether each number is divisible by 2:
   a 216   b 3184   c 827   d 4770   e 123 456

2 Determine whether each number is divisible by 10:
   a 341   b 520   c 4313   d 87 600   e 211 003

3 Determine whether each number is divisible by 3:
   a 84   b 123   c 437   d 111 114   e 707 052

4 Determine whether each number is divisible by 5:
   a 400   b 628   c 735   d 21 063   e 384 005

5 Determine whether each number is divisible by 4:
   a 482   b 2556   c 8762   d 12 368   e 213 186

6 Determine whether each number is divisible by 6:
   a 162   b 381   c 1602   d 2156   e 5364

7 Consider the numbers of the form 37□. Which digits could replace □ so that the number is:
   a even   b divisible by 3   c divisible by 4   d divisible by 5?

8 What digits could replace □ so that these numbers are divisible by 3?

    a 3□2   **b** 8□5   **c** 3□14   **d** □229

F   FACTORS

The **factors** of a natural number are the natural numbers which divide it exactly.

For example:

- $24 \div 6 = 4$, so 6 is a factor of 24.
- $24 \div 4 = 6$, so 4 is a factor of 24.
- $24 \div 7 = 3$ remainder 3, so 7 is *not* a factor of 24.

We can write 24 as 6×4 where 6 and 4 are both factors of 24. We say that 6 and 4 are a **factor pair**.

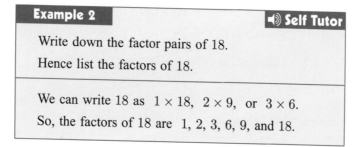

Example 2	◀) **Self Tutor**

Write down the factor pairs of 18.

Hence list the factors of 18.

We can write 18 as 1×18, 2×9, or 3×6.

So, the factors of 18 are 1, 2, 3, 6, 9, and 18.

EXERCISE 4F

1   **a** Is 5 a factor of 30?   **b** Is 4 a factor of 18?

    c Is 8 a factor of 26?   **d** Is 7 a factor of 35?

2 List the factors of:

    a 5   **b** 6   **c** 7   **d** 8

    e 9   **f** 10   **g** 11   **h** 12

3 Determine whether each number is a factor of 40:

    a 1   **b** 3   **c** 4   **d** 6

    e 8   **f** 12   **g** 15   **h** 40

4 Copy and complete each factor pair:

    a $22 = 2 \times$ ......   **b** $45 = 9 \times$ ......   **c** $30 = 3 \times$ ......

    d $49 = 7 \times$ ......   **e** $72 = 12 \times$ ......   **f** $85 = 5 \times$ ......

5 List the factors of:

    a 14   **b** 15   **c** 18   **d** 23

    e 24   **f** 36   **g** 43   **h** 45

    i 60   **j** 64   **k** 72   **l** 100

6 How many factors do these numbers have?

    a 19   **b** 28   **c** 54   **d** 66

7 Explain why every natural number greater than 1 has at least two factors.

8 Explain why every square number has an odd number of factors.

G   PRIME AND COMPOSITE NUMBERS

A **prime** number is a natural number which has exactly two different factors, 1 and itself.

A **composite** number is a natural number which has more than two factors.

For example:

- 5 is a prime number because its only factors are 1 and 5.
- 6 is a composite number because it has four factors: 1, 2, 3, and 6.

Every natural number greater than 1 is either prime or composite.

The number 1 is special since its only factor is itself.

The number **1** is neither prime nor composite.

EXERCISE 4G

1 Copy and complete the table below, describing each number as "prime" or "composite":

1	neither	11		21		31	
2	prime	12		22		32	
3	prime	13		23		33	
4	composite	14		24		34	
5		15		25		35	
6		16		26		36	
7		17		27		37	
8		18		28		38	
9		19		29		39	
10		20		30		40	

2 How many even prime numbers are there?

3 List the prime numbers between 40 and 70.

4 Explain why 57 932 560 195 is a composite number.

5 Find the smallest two consecutive odd numbers which are both composite.

6
    a Find two composite numbers whose *sum* is a prime number.

    b Is it possible to find two composite numbers whose *product* is a prime number? Explain your answer.

Example 3

  a List the factors of 24.   **b** List the *prime* factors of 24.

  c Write 24 as a product of prime factors.

---

  a The factors of 24 are 1, 2, 3, 4, 6, 8, 12, and 24.

  b The prime factors of 24 are 2 and 3.

$$\begin{aligned} \textbf{c} \quad 24 &= 2 \times 12 \\ &= 2 \times 4 \times 3 \\ &= 2 \times 2 \times 2 \times 3 \end{aligned}$$

---

7 **a** List the factors of 20.   **b** List the *prime* factors of 20.

    c Write 20 as a product of prime factors.

8 **a** List the factors of 27.   **b** List the *prime* factors of 27.

    c Write 27 as a product of prime factors.

9 Write as a product of prime factors:

    a 8   **b** 12   **c** 14   **d** 15

    e 18   **f** 28   **g** 30   **h** 32

PUZZLE

1 Fill the 3×3 square with the numbers 1 to 9, so that the sum of each row and column is a prime number.

2 Fill the 4×4 square with the numbers 1 to 16, so that the sum of each row and column is a prime number.

ACTIVITY 2

What to do:

1 Write out the numbers from 1 to 100 in a square.

2 Draw a circle around each prime number.

3 Cross out each square number.

4 Notice that $4 = 2 + 2$ and $9 = 7 + 2$. Can all of the perfect squares other than 1 be written as the sum of two prime numbers?

PRINTABLE NUMBERS

H   HIGHEST COMMON FACTOR

The **highest common factor** or **HCF** of two natural numbers is the largest factor which is common to both of them.

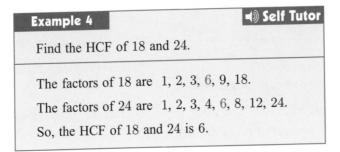

Example 4   ◀)) **Self Tutor**

Find the HCF of 18 and 24.

The factors of 18 are 1, 2, 3, 6, 9, 18.

The factors of 24 are 1, 2, 3, 4, 6, 8, 12, 24.

So, the HCF of 18 and 24 is 6.

EXERCISE 4H

1 Find the HCF of:

  a 3 and 6

  b 4 and 6

  c 4 and 10

  d 6 and 8

  e 6 and 9

  f 9 and 15

  g 8 and 14

  h 10 and 15

  i 12 and 16

  j 14 and 21

  k 16 and 20

  l 28 and 42

2 At my school there are 42 students in Year 6 and 54 students in Year 7.
   On Sports Day the students are divided into teams.
   Each team has the same number of Year 6 students in it, and the same number of Year 7 students in it.

  a Find the largest number of teams there could be.

  b How many students from each year level would be in each team?

I   MULTIPLES

The **multiples** of any natural number have that number as a factor. They are obtained by multiplying it by 1, then 2, then 3, then 4, and so on.

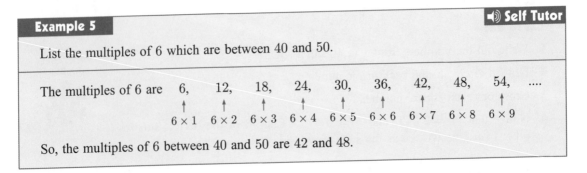

Example 5   ◀)) **Self Tutor**

List the multiples of 6 which are between 40 and 50.

The multiples of 6 are   6,   12,   18,   24,   30,   36,   42,   48,   54, ...
                          ↑   ↑   ↑   ↑   ↑   ↑   ↑   ↑   ↑
                        6 × 1 6 × 2 6 × 3 6 × 4 6 × 5 6 × 6 6 × 7 6 × 8 6 × 9

So, the multiples of 6 between 40 and 50 are 42 and 48.

EXERCISE 4I

1 List the first ten multiples of:

   a 4   **b** 9   **c** 11

2 List the multiples of 3 which are between 10 and 20.

3 List the multiples of 12 which are between 40 and 70.

4   **a** List the first twelve multiples of 7.

    b Use your list to determine which of these numbers are multiples of 7:

      i 12   **ii** 21   **iii** 30   **iv** 47   **v** 63

5   **a** List the first twelve multiples of 8.

    b List the first ten multiples of 10.

    c Write down the numbers less than 100 which are multiples of both 8 and 10.

    d What is the *lowest* common multiple of 8 and 10?

6   **a** Write down the numbers less than 100 which are multiples of both 8 and 12.

    b What is the *lowest* common multiple of 8 and 12?

7 Find the largest multiple of 11 which is less than 200.

8 Find the smallest multiple of 12 which is greater than 300.

PUZZLE   WHICH NUMBER AM I?

I am one of the numbers shown alongside.

The number to the left of me is a multiple of 6.

The number to the right of me is a multiple of 4.

The number above me is a multiple of 3.

The number below me is a multiple of 7.

Which number am I?

1	2	3	4	5	6	7	8	9	10
11	12	13	14	15	16	17	18	19	20
21	22	23	24	25	26	27	28	29	30
31	32	33	34	35	36	37	38	39	40
41	42	43	44	45	46	47	48	49	50
51	52	53	54	55	56	57	58	59	60
61	62	63	64	65	66	67	68	69	70
71	72	73	74	75	76	77	78	79	80
81	82	83	84	85	86	87	88	89	90
91	92	93	94	95	96	97	98	99	100

GLOBAL CONTEXT   CICADAS

Global context: Orientation in space and time

Statement of inquiry: Mathematics can be used to explain occurrences in nature.

Criterion: Investigating patterns

GLOBAL CONTEXT

INVESTIGATION 2   DIFFERENCES BETWEEN SQUARE NUMBERS

In this Investigation we will discover some patterns formed by the differences between the square numbers.

What to do:

1 List the perfect squares from 0^2 to 12^2.

2 Copy and complete:

   a $1^2 - 0^2 = \dots$ b The differences between consecutive square numbers
       $2^2 - 1^2 = \dots$ are the ...... numbers.
       $3^2 - 2^2 = \dots$
       $4^2 - 3^2 = \dots$
       $\vdots$
       $12^2 - 11^2 = \dots$

3 Copy and complete:

   a $2^2 - 0^2 = \dots$ b The differences between every second square number
       $3^2 - 1^2 = \dots$ form the ......
       $4^2 - 2^2 = \dots$
       $\vdots$
       $12^2 - 10^2 = \dots$

4   a Copy and complete: $3^2 - 0^2 = \dots$
                              $4^2 - 1^2 = \dots$
                              $5^2 - 2^2 = \dots$
                              $\vdots$
                              $12^2 - 9^2 = \dots$

    b What do you notice about the differences between every third square number?

MULTIPLE CHOICE QUIZ

QUICK QUIZ

REVIEW SET 4A

1 Find, if possible:

   a $13 - 0$ b 23×0 c $0 \div 18$ d $21 \div 0$

2   a Find the sum of the 1st and the 8th square numbers.

    b Find two other square numbers whose sum is the same as that in **a**.

3 How many cubic numbers are between 100 and 500?

4 Write down all the sets of three *different* odd numbers that add to 25.

5 Determine whether:

   a 43 is divisible by 9   **b** 132 is divisible by 12.

6 What digits could $\square$ be if $2\square8$ is divisible by:

   a 3   **b** 4?

7 **a** Find the sum of the first 5 prime numbers.

   b Is this number prime or composite?   **c** List the factors of the number.

8 List the factors of:

   a 16   **b** 35   **c** 75

9 Determine whether the following numbers are prime or composite:

   a 44   **b** 51   **c** 83   **d** 87

10 Find the HCF of:

   a 12 and 20   **b** 18 and 42

11 List the multiples of 6 which are between 50 and 70.

REVIEW SET 4B

1 Find, if possible:

   a 243×1 **b** $243 \div 1$ **c** $243 \div 0$ **d** $(243 - 1) \times 0$

2 Find the sum of the first three cubic numbers.

3 Find the first square number greater than 200.

4 Determine whether 37 952 is divisible by:

   a 5   **b** 4   **c** 3

5 Copy and complete each factor pair:

   a $42 = 7 \times \ldots\ldots$ **b** $72 = 9 \times \ldots\ldots$ **c** $110 = 10 \times \ldots\ldots$

6 List the factors of:

   a 63   **b** 65   **c** 80

7 How many natural numbers smaller than 30 are composite?

8 Find:

   a the smallest multiple of 9 which is larger than 100

   b the largest multiple of 7 which is smaller than 100.

9 **a** List the factors of 30.   **b** List the *prime* factors of 30.

   c Write 30 as the product of prime factors.

10 A box of chocolates contains 40 milk chocolates and 24 white chocolates. The chocolates are shared equally between the children at a party. Each child received the same number of milk chocolates, and received the same number of white chocolates.

Find the largest number of children there could be.

11 **a** Find:

  i $7 + 9$ **ii** $21 + 23$ **iii** $29 + 31$ **iv** $37 + 39$

  b Copy and complete:

  "When two consecutive odd numbers are added together, the result is always divisible by ......"

12 **a** List the first thirteen multiples of 6.

  b List the first ten multiples of 8.

  c Write down the numbers less than 80 which are multiples of both 6 and 8.

  d What is the *lowest* common multiple of 6 and 8?

Chapter 5

Geometric shapes

Contents:

OPENING PROBLEM

The three-dimensional shape alongside is called a *tetrahedron*.

All of the edges of the tetrahedron have the same length.

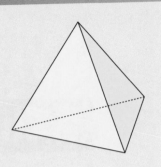

Things to think about:

a What do we mean by *three-dimensional*? Is the drawing on the page three-dimensional?

b How can we indicate on the diagram that the lengths of the edges are equal?

c What shape is each *face* of the tetrahedron?

d How can the tetrahedron be constructed by folding a piece of paper?

A **plane** is a flat surface.

Any figure drawn on a page is **two-dimensional**. Its dimensions are height and width.

By contrast, an object in space is **three-dimensional**. Its dimensions are height, width, and depth.

In this Chapter we will explore two-dimensional **polygons** and **circles**, and three-dimensional **solids**.

A   POLYGONS

A **polygon** is a closed two-dimensional figure which has only straight line sides and which does not cross itself.

A **closed** figure has no gaps.

These figures are polygons:

Here are some examples of polygons that we often see around us:

These figures are **not** polygons:

This figure has a curved side.   This figure crosses itself.   This figure is not closed.

NAMING POLYGONS

We name polygons according to how many sides and vertices they have:

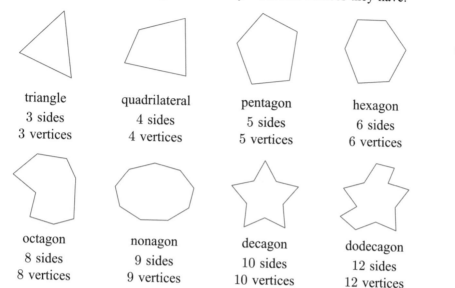

triangle	quadrilateral	pentagon	hexagon	heptagon
3 sides	4 sides	5 sides	6 sides	7 sides
3 vertices	4 vertices	5 vertices	6 vertices	7 vertices

octagon	nonagon	decagon	dodecagon
8 sides	9 sides	10 sides	12 sides
8 vertices	9 vertices	10 vertices	12 vertices

REGULAR POLYGONS

A **regular polygon** is a polygon with all sides the same length and all angles the same size.

The polygons below are marked to show that they are regular.
• Equal sides are shown by small markings.
• Equal angles are shown by using the same symbols.

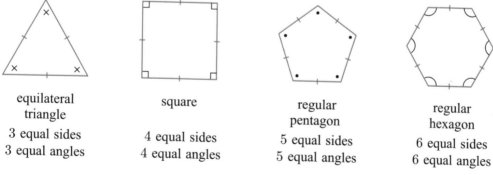

equilateral triangle	square	regular pentagon	regular hexagon
3 equal sides	4 equal sides	5 equal sides	6 equal sides
3 equal angles	4 equal angles	5 equal angles	6 equal angles

EXERCISE 5A

1   Name each polygon:

a 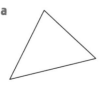   b 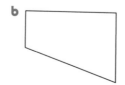   c 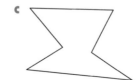   d

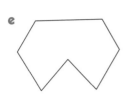 e
 f
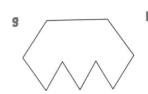 g
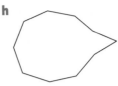 h

2 Explain why these shapes are *not* polygons:

a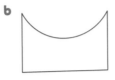
b
c
d

3 Explain whether each shape is regular or irregular:

a
b
c

> *Irregular* means "not regular".

d
e
f

4 Draw:
- **a** a quadrilateral with 3 equal sides
- **b** a regular pentagon
- **c** an octagon with equal sides but unequal angles
- **d** a hexagon with 3 right angles.

5 **a** Draw a quadrilateral with three right angles.
- **b** Measure the fourth angle.
- **c** What can you say about the opposite sides?

6 Use a ruler and protractor to determine whether each polygon is regular:

a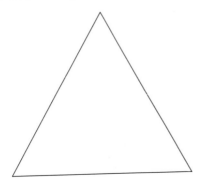
b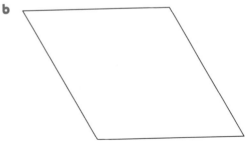

c

d

B   TRIANGLES

A **triangle** is a polygon with three sides.

DISCUSSION

We often see triangles in buildings and bridges because they provide strength and stability.

Why do triangles provide strength and stability?

We can classify triangles according to the number of sides which are equal in length.

A triangle is:

- **scalene**   if its three sides all have different lengths

- **isosceles**   if at least two sides have the same length

- **equilateral**   if its three sides all have the same length.

EXERCISE 5B

1 Classify each triangle as scalene, isosceles, or equilateral:

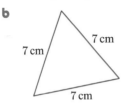

a 9 cm, 6 cm, 8 cm

b 7 cm, 7 cm, 7 cm

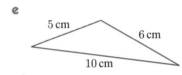

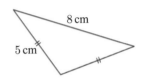

c 6 cm, 8 cm, 8 cm

d 4 cm

e 5 cm, 6 cm, 10 cm

f 8 cm, 5 cm

2 Use a ruler to measure each side of these triangles. Hence classify each triangle.

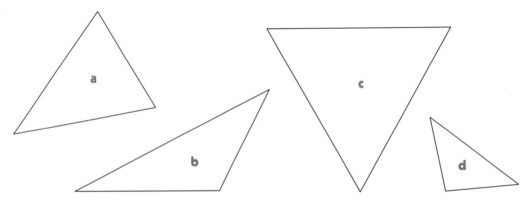

3 Show how you can arrange 12 matchsticks of equal length to form:

   a an equilateral triangle

   b an isosceles triangle

   c a scalene triangle.

PUZZLE

How many triangles can you find in each figure?

a

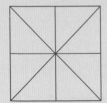

b

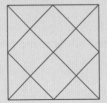

c

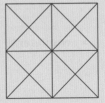

ACTIVITY 1   CONSTRUCTING TRIANGLES

In this Activity we construct triangles using:

VIDEO CLIP

- a compass and a ruler
- a protractor and a ruler.

What to do:

1 Follow these steps to construct a triangle ABC with sides 4 cm, 3 cm, and 2 cm long:

Step 1: Draw a line segment [AB] of length 4 cm.

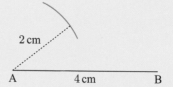

Step 2: Open your compass to a radius of 2 cm.
Using this radius, draw an arc from A.

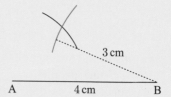

Step 3: Open your compass to a radius of 3 cm.
Draw an arc from B to intersect the first arc.

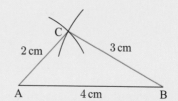

Step 4: The point of intersection of the two arcs is the third vertex C of the triangle ABC.
Draw line segments [AC] and [BC] to complete the triangle.

2 Accurately construct a triangle with side lengths:

a 4 cm, 5 cm, and 6 cm   **b** 3 cm, 6 cm, and 7 cm.

3 Is it possible to construct a triangle with sides 3 cm, 4 cm, and 9 cm long? Explain your answer.

4 Use a protractor and ruler to accurately construct these triangles:

a

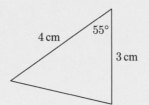

b

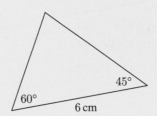

5 **a** Construct a triangle ABC whose side lengths are all 6 cm.

   b What type of triangle is ABC?

   c Measure the angles of the triangle using a protractor.

   d Copy and complete: "All angles of an equilateral triangle measure ......°".

 # QUADRILATERALS

A **quadrilateral** is a polygon with four sides.

The shapes alongside are all quadrilaterals.

To classify quadrilaterals, we need to consider side lengths and angles, and also whether opposite sides are parallel.

There are six special quadrilaterals:

- A **parallelogram** has both pairs of opposite sides parallel.
  The opposite sides of a parallelogram are equal in length.

- A **rectangle** is a parallelogram with right angled corners.
  The opposite sides of a rectangle are equal in length.

- A **rhombus** is a quadrilateral with all four sides equal in length.
  The opposite sides of a rhombus are parallel.

- A **square** is a rectangle with all sides equal in length.

- A **trapezium** has one pair of opposite sides which are parallel.

- A **kite** has two pairs of adjacent sides which are equal in length.

EXERCISE 5C

1 In the diagram alongside, identify a:
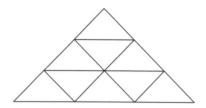
  a square
  b rectangle
  c parallelogram
  d trapezium.

2 Draw an example of a:
  a rhombus   **b** rectangle   **c** trapezium   **d** kite.

3 Classify each quadrilateral:

  a    **b**    **c**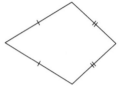

  d    **e**    **f**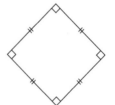

4 True or false?
  a A square has four right angled corners.
  b The adjacent sides of a rectangle are parallel.
  c The opposite sides of a kite are equal in length.
  d The opposite sides of a rhombus are parallel.

5 True or false?
  a A square is a special type of rhombus.
  b A rectangle is a special type of square.
  c A square is a special type of parallelogram.
  d A rectangle is a special type of parallelogram.

6 **a** Use a ruler and protractor to draw a square with side
    length 6 cm.
  b Draw the diagonals of the square.
  c Measure the lengths of the diagonals. What do you
    notice?

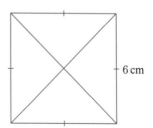

6 cm

ACTIVITY 2

What to do:

1 Print the shapes and cut them out.

PRINTABLE
SHAPES

Trapezia is the plural of trapezium!

2 Show how to use:

   a the two squares to form a rectangle

   b the two rectangles to form a square

   c the two trapezia to form a parallelogram

   d the two equilateral triangles to form a rhombus

   e the two isosceles triangles to form a kite.

ACTIVITY 3   MAKING PARALLELOGRAMS

To make parallelograms with different angles you could use ice-block sticks.

What to do:

1 Join the ice-block sticks with four small bolts and nuts. You do not need to tighten the bolts.

2 Use a pencil to draw the parallelogram inside the frame.

3 Change the parallelogram by moving the wooden frame.
   Hence draw *five* different parallelograms.

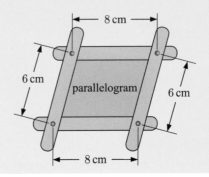

D   CIRCLES

A **circle** is the set of points which are the same distance from a fixed point called its **centre**.

The distance from the centre to the circle is called the **radius** of the circle.

The plural of radius is **radii**.

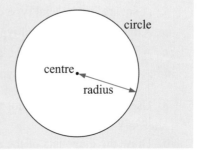

You can use a **compass** to draw a circle with a particular radius.

VIDEO DEMO

The point of the compass is placed at the centre of the circle. The arms are set so the distance from the needle to the tip of your pencil is the radius that you have chosen.

EXERCISE 5D

1 Explain why a circle is not a polygon.

2 This circle has radius 2 cm.

What can we say about the distance between the centre of the circle and:

a point A

b point B

c point C?

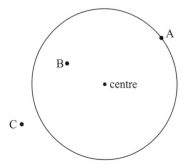

3 Using the same centre, draw circles with radii 1 cm, 2 cm, and 3 cm.

ACTIVITY 4

What to do:

Use your compass to draw these patterns:

1

2

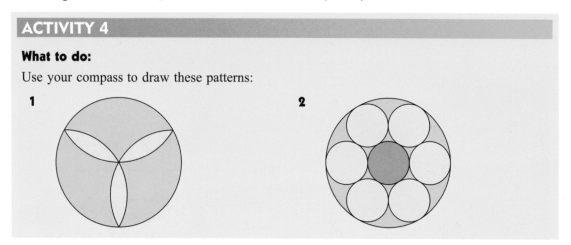

E   SOLIDS

A **solid** is a three-dimensional object which occupies space.

Each solid has the three dimensions width, height, and depth.

The boundaries of a solid are called **surfaces**.

Solids may have flat surfaces, curved surfaces, or a combination of both.

Each flat surface of a solid is called a **face**.

The diagram alongside shows a solid. Notice that:

- an **edge** is where two surfaces meet
- a **vertex** is a "corner" of the solid
- we can use dashed lines to show "hidden" edges which are at the back of the solid, so we understand the solid is three-dimensional.

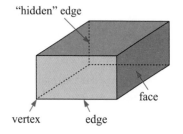

CROSS-SECTIONS OF SOLIDS

A **cross-section** of a solid is the shape of a slice through it.

For some solids, when we make a series of parallel slices along its length, the cross-section is always the same. These solids are called **solids of uniform cross-section**.

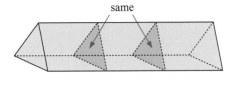

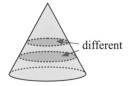

uniform cross-section   not uniform cross-section

CLASSIFYING SOLIDS

We classify solids according to their surfaces and their cross-section.

	Uniform cross-section	Tapered solids	Other solids
All flat surfaces	prisms	pyramids	
At least one curved surface	cylinders	cones	spheres

PRISMS

A **prism** is a solid with a uniform cross-section that is a polygon.

Each end has the shape of the cross-section. The remaining faces are all rectangles.
Prisms are named according to the shape of the cross-section.

Name	Figure	Cross-section
Triangular prism		
Hexagonal prism		

A rectangular prism whose edges are all the same length is called a **cube**.

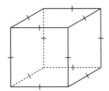

CYLINDERS

A **cylinder** is a solid with a uniform cross-section that is a circle.

A cylinder has two flat circular faces and one curved surface.

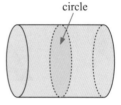

circle

PYRAMIDS

A **pyramid** is a solid with a polygon base, and triangular faces which come from its base to meet at a point called the **apex**.

Pyramids are named according to the shape of their base.

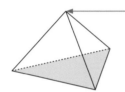

apex

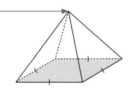

triangular-based pyramid
or tetrahedron

square-based pyramid

CONES

A **cone** is a solid with a circular base and a curved surface from the base to the apex.

apex

cone

SPHERES

A **sphere** is a ball-shaped solid.

A sphere has no edges, but we often draw an "equator" around it to distinguish our drawing from a circle.

sphere

EXERCISE 5E

1 Name each solid:

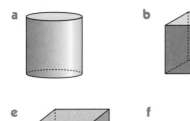

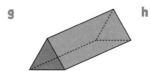

2 Draw the uniform cross-section of:

3 State whether the following solids have:

      A only flat surfaces   **B** only curved surfaces   **C** both flat and curved surfaces.

   a triangular prism   **b** sphere   **c** square-based pyramid   **d** cylinder

4 Copy and complete this table:

Solid	Number of faces	Shapes of faces	Sketch
	6	rectangles	
pentagonal prism			
square-based pyramid			
	4	triangles	

5 Explain why a cylinder is *not* a prism.

DISCUSSION

- Why are pyramids and cones called *tapered* solids?
- Are these solids pyramids?

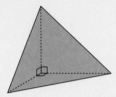 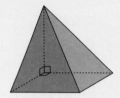

F   DRAWING SOLIDS

Edges which cannot be seen because they are at the back of a solid are called **hidden edges**.

Adding dotted or dashed lines helps us to understand where the hidden edges are.

To draw your own solids, follow these steps.

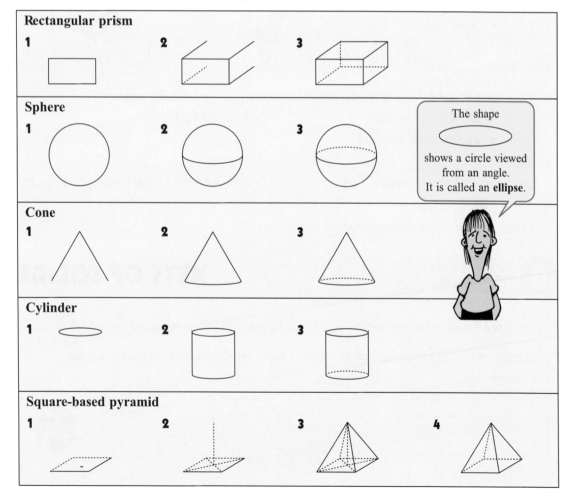

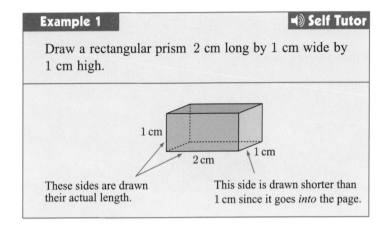

| Example 1 | ◄)) **Self Tutor** |

Draw a rectangular prism 2 cm long by 1 cm wide by 1 cm high.

We call this a 2 cm × 1 cm × 1 cm rectangular prism.

1 cm

2 cm   1 cm

These sides are drawn their actual length.

This side is drawn shorter than 1 cm since it goes *into* the page.

EXERCISE 5F

1 Draw a rectangular prism that is:

a 1 cm × 1 cm × 2 cm   **b** 3 cm × 2 cm × 1 cm   **c** 4 cm × 2 cm × 3 cm

2 Copy these solids and draw in the hidden edges. Name each solid you have drawn.

a 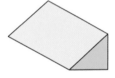   **b**   **c**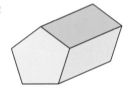

3 Draw each of the following solids, using dotted lines to show hidden edges:

a a square-based pyramid   **b** a hexagonal prism

c a hexagonal-based pyramid

4 Draw:

a a cube with edge lengths 2 cm   **b** a cylinder 3 cm high with base 2 cm wide

c a cone 4 cm high with base 3 cm wide.

5 Sketch a sphere. Use shading to show how it curves.

G   NETS OF SOLIDS

A **net** is a two-dimensional pattern which can be folded to form a three-dimensional solid.

For example, when this net is cut out and folded along the dashed lines, we form a **cube**.

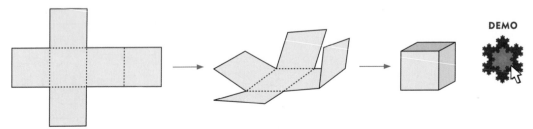

DEMO

ACTIVITY 5   NETS

Click on the icon to obtain these printable nets.

Print them onto light card, and use them to construct a:

PRINTABLE NETS

- rectangular prism
- tetrahedron
- cube
- square-based pyramid
- triangular prism
- cylinder
- cone

EXERCISE 5G

1 Match the net given in the first column with the correct solid and the correct name.

Net	Solid	Name
a	A	1 pentagonal-based pyramid
b	B	2 cylinder
c	C	3 triangular prism
d	D	4 square-based pyramid

2 Decide whether each net could be used to make a cube:

a 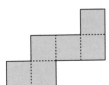   **b** 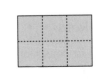   **c**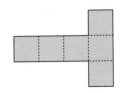

d 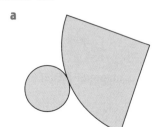   **e** 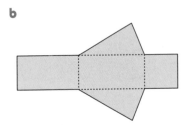   **f**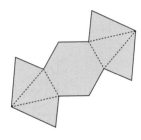

3 Draw and name the solid which can be formed from the net:

a   **b**   **c**

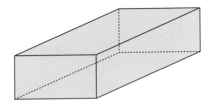

4 **a** Draw a net which could be used to construct a box like this one.

   b How would you change your net so that the box is open at the top?

   c How would you change the sketch of the box to show it is open at the top?

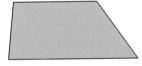

5 Draw a net for a prism with cross-section:

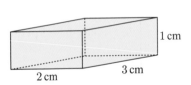

6 Draw a net for a tetrahedron with all edges of equal length.

7 Draw *to scale* a net which could be used to construct:

a   **b**

8 Three students were asked to draw a net for a square-based pyramid. The nets they drew are shown below:

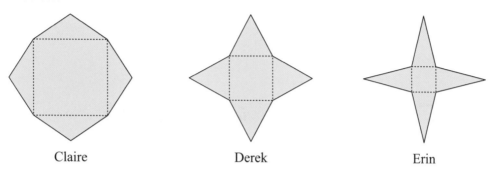

Claire   Derek   Erin

a Explain why it is not possible to construct a pyramid from Claire's net.

b Which of the remaining nets will produce a higher pyramid? Explain your answer.

DISCUSSION

Discuss whether this statement is true:

"A sphere can have no net because it has no edges."

ACTIVITY 6   MODELS OF SOLIDS

You will need: plastic straws, modelling clay

What to do:

1 Using straws as the edges and modelling clay to hold the edges together, create:

    a a cube

    b a rectangular prism

    c a triangular prism

    d a square-based pyramid

    e a triangular-based pyramid

We call this a **wireframe** model because it only includes the edges.

2 Experiment using straws of different lengths. For each solid, determine which edges must be the same length, and which edges can be different lengths.

GLOBAL CONTEXT   PLATONIC SOLIDS

Global context:	Scientific and technical innovation
Statement of inquiry:	Solids can be classified according to their properties.
Criterion:	Communicating

GLOBAL CONTEXT

MULTIPLE CHOICE QUIZ

REVIEW SET 5A

1 Name each polygon:

a

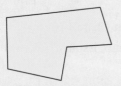

b

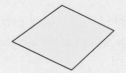

c

2 Draw:

  a an isosceles triangle **b** a regular hexagon **c** a rhombus.

3 Classify each triangle:

a

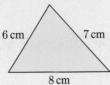

b

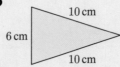

c

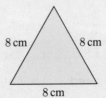

4 Draw two points P and Q which are 1 cm apart. Construct circles of radius 1 cm centred at P and Q.

5 Name each quadrilateral:

a

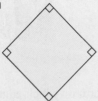

b

c

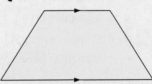

6 True or false?

  a The opposite sides of a kite are always parallel.

  b A rectangle has four right angled corners.

  c A tetrahedron is a type of pyramid.

7 Explain whether:

  a an equilateral triangle is also isosceles

  b a square is a special type of kite.

8 Name each solid:

a

b

c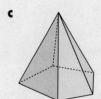

9 Draw a cylinder which is 5 cm high and has a base 3 cm wide.

10 Draw and name the solid which can be formed from the net:

a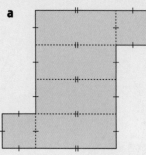

b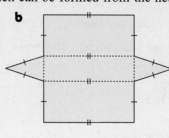

c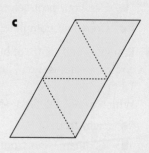

REVIEW SET 5B

1 Using a ruler and protractor, determine whether these polygons are regular:

a

b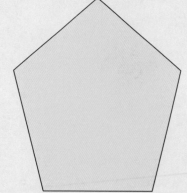

2 Classify this triangle by measuring its sides:

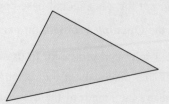

3 Draw a quadrilateral which has 3 obtuse angles.

4 Is a rhombus a special type of parallelogram?

5   **a** What type of quadrilateral is shown below?

    b Use your protractor to measure each angle of the quadrilateral.

    c Copy and complete: "The opposite angles of a ...... are ......".

6   Point C is the centre of both of these circles. The larger circle has radius 2 cm, and the smaller circle has radius 1 cm.

Which of the labelled points is:

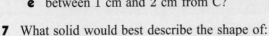

    a 2 cm from C

    b less than 1 cm from C

    c 1 cm from C

    d more than 2 cm from C

    e between 1 cm and 2 cm from C?

7   What solid would best describe the shape of:

    a a marble   **b** a washing machine?

8   Use your ruler to draw:

    a a cube   **b** a 2 cm × 1 cm × 3 cm rectangular prism.

9   Draw the net for a hexagonal-based pyramid.

10 Answer the **Opening Problem** on page **78**.

11 **a** Use a ruler and protractor to draw a rectangle which is 4 cm long and 3 cm wide.

    b Draw the diagonals of the rectangle.

    c Measure the length of the diagonals. What do you notice?

    d Sketch the net for a 4 cm × 3 cm × 2 cm rectangular prism. Label each length.

Chapter

6

Fractions

Contents:

OPENING PROBLEM

The students in Amelia's class have all been given a week to do a project. So far, Amelia has done $\frac{3}{8}$, Charlie has done $\frac{5}{8}$, and Matilda has done $\frac{1}{2}$.

Things to think about:

a Who has completed more of their project:
  i Amelia or Charlie
  ii Amelia or Matilda?

b Which of the problems in **a** was easier to solve? What made the other one harder?

c The next night, Amelia completed another $\frac{1}{2}$ of her project.

  i What total fraction has she completed now?
  ii How much of her project does Amelia still have to do?

A **fraction** helps us to divide a whole into parts.

Every day we see quantities which can be expressed as fractions. It is therefore important that we can understand, compare, add, and subtract fractions.

$\frac{1}{2}$ apple

$\frac{1}{4}$ remaining

$\frac{1}{3}$ OFF SALE

$\frac{1}{3}$ full

size $8\frac{1}{2}$

$16\frac{1}{2}$ hands

A   FRACTIONS

A chocolate bar is broken into 5 equal pieces.

George takes 2 of the pieces.

We say that George has taken *two fifths* of the chocolate bar.

This is a **fraction** which can be written as $\frac{2}{5}$.

> A written fraction includes a **numerator**, a **bar**, and a **denominator**.
>
> The **denominator** is the number of **equal** parts in a whole.
>
> The **numerator** is the number of parts we are looking at.

$$\frac{2}{5}$$ ← numerator
← bar
← denominator

The name given to each part is determined by the denominator of the fraction.

For most denominators, we name each part by adding "th" to the number.

The table alongside lists some exceptions!

Number of equal parts	Name of each part
2	half (plural halves)
3	third
4	quarter
5	fifth
8	eighth
9	ninth
12	twelfth
20	twentieth

EXERCISE 6A

1 State the numerator of each fraction:

   a $\frac{2}{3}$ **b** $\frac{4}{5}$ **c** $\frac{3}{7}$ **d** $\frac{1}{8}$

2 State the denominator of each fraction:

   a $\frac{2}{3}$ **b** $\frac{4}{5}$ **c** $\frac{3}{7}$ **d** $\frac{1}{8}$

3 Write down the number of equal parts there are if a whole has been divided into:

   a halves   **b** quarters   **c** sixths   **d** thirds

   e tenths   **f** elevenths   **g** twelfths   **h** hundredths.

4 Write as a fraction:

   a three quarters   **b** one third   **c** four fifths

   d three eighths   **e** five eighths   **f** two sevenths

   g three tenths   **h** seven hundredths   **i** six thousandths

5 Write in words:

  a $\dfrac{2}{3}$ **b** $\dfrac{2}{4}$ **c** $\dfrac{3}{5}$ **d** $\dfrac{5}{7}$ **e** $\dfrac{9}{10}$

  f $\dfrac{7}{8}$ **g** $\dfrac{5}{12}$ **h** $\dfrac{3}{100}$ **i** $\dfrac{84}{100}$ **j** $\dfrac{5}{1000}$

6 What fraction of the diagram is shaded?

  a   **b**   **c**

  d   **e**   **f**

  g   **h**   **i**

7 Is $\dfrac{3}{8}$ of this triangle shaded? Explain your answer.

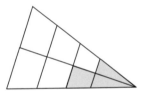

8 Copy each figure and shade the given fraction:

  a $\dfrac{2}{6}$ **b** $\dfrac{7}{8}$ **c** $\dfrac{11}{12}$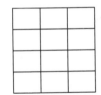

9 Draw a diagram to represent:

  a $\dfrac{5}{8}$ **b** $\dfrac{1}{6}$ **c** $\dfrac{8}{9}$ **d** $\dfrac{4}{12}$ **e** $\dfrac{11}{15}$

Example 1   ◀)) **Self Tutor**

Describe using a sentence, the fraction represented by the diagram.

The beaker is three fifths full of liquid.

10 Describe using a sentence, the fraction represented by the diagram:

a

b

c

Example 2 ◀) **Self Tutor**

What fraction of the cats are black?

There are 8 cats in total, and 5 of them are black.

So, $\frac{5}{8}$ of the cats are black.

---

11 What fraction of the dots are red?

a

b

c

12

What fraction of the children are:
- **a** wearing a hat
- **b** not wearing a hat
- **c** wearing glasses
- **d** wearing a yellow shirt?

13

a What fraction of the flowers are:
   i in the vase   **ii** lying on the table?

b What fraction of the flowers are:
   i tulips   **ii** daisies?

c What fraction of the tulips are in the vase?

d What fraction of the daisies are lying on the table?

ACTIVITY 1   DIVIDING SHAPES

In this online Activity we consider the properties of different shapes which allow us to divide them into different numbers of equal parts.

DIVIDING
SHAPES

B   FRACTIONS AS DIVISION

INVESTIGATION 1

In this Investigation we see how fractions are related to division.

What to do:

1   2 circular pies are shared equally between 3 people.

   a Use the diagram to find what fraction of a pie each person receives.

   b Copy and complete:
       "...... pies ÷ ...... people = ... of a pie each".

2   3 baguettes are shared equally between 4 people.

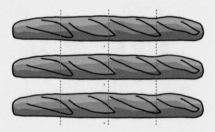

   a Use the diagram to find what fraction of a baguette each person receives.

   b Copy and complete:
       "...... baguettes ÷ ...... people = ... of a baguette each".

3   Copy and complete:
   $$\frac{\text{numerator}}{\text{denominator}} = ... \div ......$$

HISTORICAL NOTE

The symbol for division ÷ is called an *obelus*. It was first used by the Swiss mathematician **Johann Heinrich Rahn** in his book *Teutsche Algebra*.

Notice how the division symbol looks like a fraction.

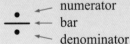

— numerator
— bar
— denominator

When we write a fraction, the bar indicates division. For example, $\frac{3}{4} = 3 \div 4$.

Example 3 ◀ᴺ Self Tutor

Write $\frac{42}{6}$ as a division, and hence as a whole number.

$$\frac{42}{6} = 42 \div 6$$
$$= 7$$

EXERCISE 6B

1 Write as a fraction:

a $4 \div 5$ b $1 \div 7$ c $3 \div 10$

d $8 \div 9$ e $2 \div 11$ f $12 \div 13$

2 Write as a division:

a $\frac{1}{3}$ b $\frac{2}{5}$ c $\frac{7}{8}$ d $\frac{3}{4}$ e $\frac{8}{13}$ f $\frac{11}{20}$

3 Write as a division, and hence as a whole number:

a $\frac{20}{5}$ b $\frac{27}{3}$ c $\frac{55}{11}$ d $\frac{7}{7}$

e $\frac{24}{12}$ f $\frac{19}{19}$ g $\frac{0}{8}$ h $\frac{108}{9}$

C   PROPER AND IMPROPER FRACTIONS

A fraction which has numerator **less** than its denominator is called a **proper fraction**.

A fraction which has numerator **greater** than its denominator is called an **improper fraction**.

For example: $\frac{2}{3}$ is a proper fraction.

$\frac{5}{3}$ is an improper fraction. $\frac{5}{3} = \frac{3}{3} + \frac{2}{3} = 1 + \frac{2}{3}$

When an improper fraction is written as a whole number and a proper fraction, it is called a **mixed number**.

For example, we can write $\frac{5}{3}$ as the mixed number $1\frac{2}{3}$.

EXERCISE 6C

1 Decide whether each number is a proper fraction, an improper fraction, or a mixed number:

   a $\dfrac{3}{5}$ **b** $\dfrac{7}{6}$ **c** $\dfrac{1}{9}$ **d** $3\dfrac{1}{3}$

   e $\dfrac{11}{8}$ **f** $\dfrac{8}{11}$ **g** $4\dfrac{2}{5}$ **h** $\dfrac{40}{7}$

2

This diagram shows $3\dfrac{1}{2}$ pizzas.

   a How many halves are there in $3\dfrac{1}{2}$ pizzas?

   b Copy and complete: $3\dfrac{1}{2} = \dfrac{....}{2}$

3   **a** What mixed number is represented by this diagram?

    b How many fifths are shaded?

    c Copy and complete: ...... $= \dfrac{....}{5}$

4 Describe the shaded region using a mixed number:

  a

  b

  c

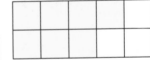

  d

5 Write down the mixed number shown in the diagram:

  a   **b**   **c**

d

Example 4

Write $2\frac{1}{3}$ as an improper fraction.

There are 6 thirds in the 2 wholes.

$$2\frac{1}{3} = 2 + \frac{1}{3}$$
$$= \frac{6}{3} + \frac{1}{3}$$
$$= \frac{7}{3}$$

$2 = \frac{6}{3}$

---

6 Write as an improper fraction:

a $1\frac{1}{4}$ **b** $2\frac{1}{2}$ **c** $3\frac{2}{3}$ **d** $2\frac{5}{6}$ **e** $1\frac{3}{5}$

f $5\frac{1}{3}$ **g** $6\frac{1}{2}$ **h** $2\frac{3}{8}$ **i** $4\frac{1}{6}$ **j** $2\frac{9}{10}$

Example 5

Write $\frac{13}{4}$ as a mixed number.

$$\frac{13}{4} = \frac{12}{4} + \frac{1}{4}$$
$$= 3 + \frac{1}{4}$$
$$= 3\frac{1}{4}$$

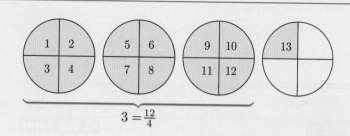

$3 = \frac{12}{4}$

---

7 After the school picnic there were 17 quarter sandwiches left over.

  a How many whole sandwiches can be formed from the quarters?

  b Once the whole sandwiches have been formed, how many quarters are left over?

  c Copy and complete: $\frac{17}{4} = \ ......$

8 Write as a mixed number:

   a $\dfrac{4}{3}$ **b** $\dfrac{9}{4}$ **c** $\dfrac{11}{6}$ **d** $\dfrac{16}{5}$ **e** $\dfrac{19}{4}$

   f $\dfrac{15}{2}$ **g** $\dfrac{14}{3}$ **h** $\dfrac{17}{7}$ **i** $\dfrac{33}{10}$ **j** $\dfrac{35}{8}$

9 19 carrots are shared equally between 5 horses. How many carrots does each horse receive? Give your answer as a mixed number.

10 Yiu Min cut 8 chillies into fifths.

   a How many fifths did she have?

   b Yiu Min added 11 pieces of chilli into one saucepan, 22 pieces of chilli into a wok, and the rest into a bowl to use later.

      Copy and complete this table for the amount of chilli in each container.

	Improper fraction	Mixed number
saucepan		
wok		
bowl		

D   FRACTIONS ON A NUMBER LINE

We can place whole numbers on a number line.

We can also place fractions and mixed numbers on a number line by dividing the space between the whole numbers into *equal parts*.

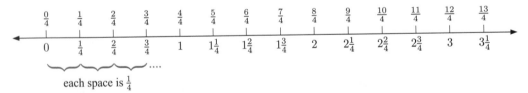

each space is $\frac{1}{4}$

Example 6   ◀ৠ **Self Tutor**

   a Place $\dfrac{5}{7}$, $\dfrac{11}{7}$, and $1\dfrac{3}{7}$ on a number line.

   b Hence write the numbers in ascending order.

   a

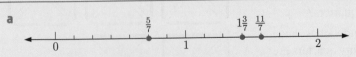

   b In ascending order, the numbers are $\dfrac{5}{7}$, $1\dfrac{3}{7}$, $\dfrac{11}{7}$.

We divide each whole into 7 equal parts.

EXERCISE 6D

1 Place each set of fractions on a number line:

    a $\frac{2}{5}$ and $\frac{3}{5}$ **b** $\frac{3}{6}$ and $\frac{5}{6}$ **c** $\frac{1}{4}$ and $1\frac{3}{4}$

    d $\frac{2}{3}$ and $2\frac{1}{3}$ **e** $\frac{3}{5}$ and $\frac{8}{5}$ **f** $\frac{9}{8}$ and $2\frac{3}{8}$

    g $\frac{2}{10}$, $\frac{5}{10}$, and $\frac{9}{10}$ **h** $\frac{1}{6}$, $\frac{11}{6}$, and $1\frac{1}{6}$ **i** $\frac{6}{7}$, $\frac{12}{7}$, and $2\frac{2}{7}$

2 State the value indicated by each red dot:

    a    **b**

    c    **d**

    e    **f**

    g 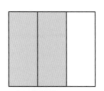   **h**

3   **a** Place $1\frac{2}{5}$, $\frac{4}{5}$, and $\frac{6}{5}$ on a number line.

    b Hence write the numbers in ascending order.

4   **a** Place $2\frac{1}{6}$, $\frac{15}{6}$, $\frac{10}{6}$, and $1\frac{5}{6}$ on a number line.

    b Hence write the numbers in descending order.

E   EQUAL FRACTIONS

> Two fractions are **equal** if they describe the same amount.
> Equal fractions lie at the same place on the number line.

For example, we can represent the fractions $\frac{2}{3}$ and $\frac{4}{6}$ by shading diagrams.

We see the same amount is shaded in each case, so $\frac{2}{3} = \frac{4}{6}$.

$\frac{2}{3}$ is shaded $\frac{4}{6}$ is shaded

We can also observe this on a number line, since $\frac{2}{3}$ and $\frac{4}{6}$ lie at the same place.

INVESTIGATION 2   EQUAL FRACTIONS

Equal fractions lie at the *same place* along a fraction wall.

1											
$\frac{1}{2}$						$\frac{1}{2}$					
$\frac{1}{3}$				$\frac{1}{3}$				$\frac{1}{3}$			
$\frac{1}{4}$			$\frac{1}{4}$			$\frac{1}{4}$			$\frac{1}{4}$		
$\frac{1}{6}$		$\frac{1}{6}$		$\frac{1}{6}$		$\frac{1}{6}$		$\frac{1}{6}$		$\frac{1}{6}$	
$\frac{1}{8}$	$\frac{1}{8}$	$\frac{1}{8}$	$\frac{1}{8}$		$\frac{1}{8}$	$\frac{1}{8}$	$\frac{1}{8}$	$\frac{1}{8}$			
$\frac{1}{9}$	$\frac{1}{9}$	$\frac{1}{9}$	$\frac{1}{9}$	$\frac{1}{9}$	$\frac{1}{9}$	$\frac{1}{9}$	$\frac{1}{9}$	$\frac{1}{9}$			
$\frac{1}{12}$	$\frac{1}{12}$	$\frac{1}{12}$	$\frac{1}{12}$	$\frac{1}{12}$	$\frac{1}{12}$	$\frac{1}{12}$	$\frac{1}{12}$	$\frac{1}{12}$	$\frac{1}{12}$	$\frac{1}{12}$	$\frac{1}{12}$

For example, $\frac{1}{6}$ and $\frac{2}{12}$ lie at the same place on the fraction wall, so $\frac{1}{6} = \frac{2}{12}$.

What to do:

1 Use the fraction wall to complete these equal fraction statements:

    a $\frac{1}{2} = \frac{....}{4}$ **b** $\frac{8}{12} = \frac{....}{3}$ **c** $\frac{3}{4} = \frac{....}{8}$ **d** $\frac{9}{12} = \frac{....}{4}$

2 Write down ten more pairs of equal fractions.

In the **Investigation**, you should have found that $\frac{1}{2} = \frac{2}{4}$ and $\frac{8}{12} = \frac{2}{3}$.

Notice how these numbers are related:

$$\overset{\times 2}{\frac{1}{2}} = \underset{\times 2}{\frac{2}{4}} \qquad\qquad \overset{\div 4}{\frac{8}{12}} = \underset{\div 4}{\frac{2}{3}}$$

This suggests that:

> Multiplying or dividing both the numerator and the denominator by the same non-zero number produces an equal fraction.

This rule allows us to write a given fraction with a different numerator or with a different denominator, without changing the fraction's value.

Example 7 ◀)) **Self Tutor**

Express with denominator 18:

a $\dfrac{7}{9}$ b $\dfrac{5}{6}$ c $\dfrac{22}{36}$

a $\dfrac{7}{9}$ b $\dfrac{5}{6}$ c $\dfrac{22}{36}$

$= \dfrac{7 \times 2}{9 \times 2}$ $\{9 \times 2 = 18\}$ $= \dfrac{5 \times 3}{6 \times 3}$ $\{6 \times 3 = 18\}$ $= \dfrac{22 \div 2}{36 \div 2}$ $\{36 \div 2 = 18\}$

$= \dfrac{14}{18}$ $= \dfrac{15}{18}$ $= \dfrac{11}{18}$

EXERCISE 6E

1 Write a fraction equal to $\dfrac{6}{10}$ by:

  a multiplying both the numerator and denominator by 3

  b dividing both the numerator and denominator by 2.

2 Write a fraction equal to $\dfrac{4}{12}$ by:

  a multiplying both the numerator and denominator by 5

  b dividing both the numerator and denominator by 4.

3 Write $\dfrac{3}{4}$ with denominator:

  a 8 **b** 12 **c** 16 **d** 20

4 Write $\dfrac{4}{10}$ with denominator:

  a 20 **b** 30 **c** 50 **d** 5

5 Write $\dfrac{2}{12}$ with numerator:

  a 4 **b** 10 **c** 16 **d** 1

6 Write with denominator 8:

  a $\dfrac{1}{4}$ **b** $\dfrac{1}{2}$ **c** $\dfrac{3}{4}$ **d** 1 **e** $\dfrac{10}{16}$

7 Write with denominator 30:

  a $\dfrac{1}{2}$ **b** $\dfrac{4}{5}$ **c** $\dfrac{5}{6}$ **d** $\dfrac{3}{10}$ **e** $\dfrac{1}{5}$

  f $\dfrac{2}{3}$ **g** 1 **h** $\dfrac{3}{5}$ **i** $\dfrac{14}{60}$ **j** $\dfrac{13}{10}$

8 Write with denominator 60:

    a $\dfrac{1}{3}$ **b** $\dfrac{2}{5}$ **c** $\dfrac{1}{4}$ **d** $\dfrac{5}{12}$ **e** $\dfrac{17}{20}$

9 Write with denominator 100:

    a $\dfrac{1}{2}$ **b** $\dfrac{1}{4}$ **c** $\dfrac{4}{5}$ **d** $\dfrac{9}{10}$ **e** $\dfrac{7}{25}$

    f $\dfrac{13}{50}$ **g** 1 **h** $\dfrac{17}{20}$ **i** $\dfrac{34}{200}$ **j** $\dfrac{61}{50}$

GAME   EQUAL FRACTIONS

Click on the icon to play a game where you must find equal fractions.

GAME

F   LOWEST TERMS

A fraction is written in **lowest terms** or **simplest form** if it is written with the smallest possible whole number numerator and denominator.

For example:

- $\dfrac{5}{6}$ is in lowest terms.

- $\dfrac{9}{15}$ is *not* in lowest terms, since we can write it as $\dfrac{3}{5}$.

$$\dfrac{9}{15} \overset{\div 3}{\underset{\div 3}{=}} \dfrac{3}{5}$$

DISCUSSION

- How do we know whether a fraction is in lowest terms?

- $\dfrac{16}{24}$ is not in lowest terms, since we can write it as $\dfrac{8}{12}$.

$$\dfrac{16}{24} \overset{\div 2}{\underset{\div 2}{=}} \dfrac{8}{12}$$

    ▸ Is $\dfrac{8}{12}$ written in lowest terms?

    ▸ If not, what do we need to divide both the numerator and denominator of $\dfrac{16}{24}$ by, in order to write it in lowest terms?

    ▸ How do we *know* that we are dividing by the correct number?

To write a fraction in **lowest terms**, we must divide both the numerator and denominator by their **highest common factor** (HCF).

Example 8 🔊 **Self Tutor**

Write in lowest terms:

a $\dfrac{5}{20}$ 　　　　　　　　　　　b $\dfrac{8}{12}$

A fraction is in lowest terms when its numerator and denominator do not have any factors in common, except 1 .

a $\dfrac{5}{20}$

$= \dfrac{5 \div 5}{20 \div 5}$ $\{$HCF of 5 and 20 is 5$\}$

$= \dfrac{1}{4}$

b $\dfrac{8}{12}$

$= \dfrac{8 \div 4}{12 \div 4}$ $\{$HCF of 8 and 12 is 4$\}$

$= \dfrac{2}{3}$

EXERCISE 6F

1 Write in lowest terms:

a $\dfrac{4}{8}$ 　　b $\dfrac{3}{9}$ 　　c $\dfrac{2}{10}$ 　　d $\dfrac{5}{15}$ 　　e $\dfrac{4}{24}$

f $\dfrac{6}{10}$ 　　g $\dfrac{20}{30}$ 　　h $\dfrac{18}{21}$ 　　i $\dfrac{24}{32}$ 　　j $\dfrac{30}{100}$

k $\dfrac{45}{100}$ 　　l $\dfrac{12}{10}$ 　　m $\dfrac{24}{14}$ 　　n $\dfrac{40}{28}$ 　　o $\dfrac{54}{12}$

2 Which of these fractions is written in lowest terms?

A $\dfrac{6}{8}$ 　　**B** $\dfrac{3}{12}$ 　　**C** $\dfrac{10}{21}$ 　　**D** $\dfrac{14}{20}$ 　　**E** $\dfrac{7}{28}$

3 Write, in lowest terms, the fraction of solids which are:

a cones

b spheres

c pyramids

d cylinders

e prisms.

G 　 COMPARING FRACTIONS

DISCUSSION

If you were offered $\dfrac{3}{5}$ or $\dfrac{7}{10}$ of a block of chocolate, which would you choose?

How can we *compare* the size of two fractions?

If two fractions are written with the same denominator, we can compare their numerators.

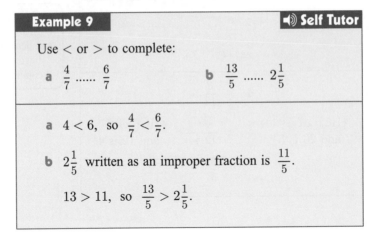

If two fractions have *different* denominators, we first write them with the *same* denominator.

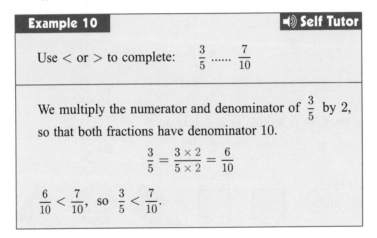

EXERCISE 6G

1 Use < or > to complete:

    a $\dfrac{5}{12}$ ...... $\dfrac{7}{12}$ **b** $\dfrac{4}{5}$ ...... $\dfrac{3}{5}$ **c** $\dfrac{8}{9}$ ...... $\dfrac{13}{9}$

    d $\dfrac{11}{7}$ ...... $1\dfrac{3}{7}$ **e** $\dfrac{19}{4}$ ...... $5\dfrac{1}{4}$ **f** $\dfrac{28}{6}$ ...... $4\dfrac{5}{6}$

2 Keith and Caroline ate sushi for dinner. Keith ate $3\dfrac{1}{3}$ pieces of sushi. Caroline cut her sushi pieces into thirds, and ate 8 of the thirds. Who had more sushi for dinner?

3 Use < or > to complete:

    a $\dfrac{1}{2}$ ...... $\dfrac{3}{4}$ **b** $\dfrac{1}{3}$ ...... $\dfrac{3}{6}$ **c** $\dfrac{3}{4}$ ...... $\dfrac{7}{8}$

    d $\dfrac{5}{8}$ ...... $\dfrac{1}{2}$ **e** $\dfrac{2}{3}$ ...... $\dfrac{5}{9}$ **f** $\dfrac{4}{3}$ ...... $\dfrac{5}{6}$

    g $\dfrac{13}{15}$ ...... $\dfrac{6}{5}$ **h** $\dfrac{15}{4}$ ...... $3\dfrac{1}{2}$ **i** $4\dfrac{1}{4}$ ...... $\dfrac{33}{8}$

4 Arnold spends $\frac{1}{3}$ of his income on rent, and $\frac{2}{9}$ of his income on groceries. Does he spend more on rent or on groceries?

5 Trent and Meredith each own a cage of birds.

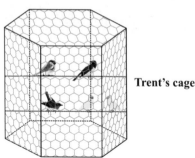
Trent's cage

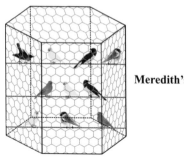
Meredith's cage

   a What fraction of Trent's birds are yellow?

   b What fraction of Meredith's birds are yellow?

   c In which cage is there a greater fraction of yellow birds?

6 Place each group of fractions on a number line. Use the number line to rewrite the fractions in ascending order.

   a $\frac{5}{8}, \frac{7}{8}, \frac{3}{4}$ **b** $\frac{5}{2}, \frac{12}{5}, 2\frac{1}{10}$

7 Rewrite each group of fractions in ascending order:

   a $\frac{2}{6}, \frac{3}{12}, \frac{5}{12}$ **b** $\frac{8}{12}, \frac{11}{12}, \frac{5}{6}$ **c** $\frac{3}{5}, \frac{11}{20}, \frac{7}{20}$ **d** $\frac{11}{8}, 1\frac{1}{4}, \frac{3}{2}$

8 Rewrite each group of fractions in descending order:

   a $\frac{3}{10}, \frac{4}{5}, \frac{7}{10}$ **b** $\frac{5}{8}, \frac{3}{4}, \frac{9}{16}$ **c** $\frac{2}{3}, \frac{7}{15}, \frac{3}{5}$ **d** $2\frac{2}{3}, \frac{7}{3}, \frac{22}{9}$

9 Imogen kept a record of how much her cat Freckles ate in one week.

She recorded the fraction of a can of food that Freckles ate each day.

   a On which day did Freckles eat the most food?

   b On which days did Freckles eat the same amounts of food?

Day	Fraction of a can
Monday	$\frac{2}{3}$
Tuesday	$\frac{3}{4}$
Wednesday	$\frac{5}{6}$
Thursday	$\frac{2}{12}$
Friday	$\frac{4}{6}$
Saturday	$\frac{6}{12}$
Sunday	$\frac{1}{6}$

10 Are improper fractions always larger in size than proper fractions? Explain your answer.

H   ADDING AND SUBTRACTING FRACTIONS

A loaf of garlic bread is divided into 8 equal pieces.

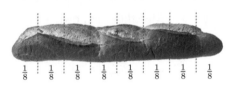

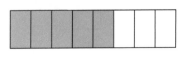

Sam takes 3 pieces and Pam takes 2 pieces. Together, they have taken 5 pieces.

Sam has taken $\frac{3}{8}$.   Pam has taken $\frac{2}{8}$.   Together, they have taken $\frac{5}{8}$.

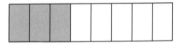

$$\frac{3}{8} \qquad + \qquad \frac{2}{8} \qquad = \qquad \frac{5}{8}$$

Having taken 3 pieces of garlic bread, Sam eats one of his pieces. He has two pieces remaining.

Sam took $\frac{3}{8}$.   He ate $\frac{1}{8}$.   He has $\frac{2}{8}$ remaining.

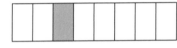

$$\frac{3}{8} \qquad - \qquad \frac{1}{8} \qquad = \qquad \frac{2}{8}$$

To **add** or **subtract** fractions *with the same denominator*, we add or subtract the numerators. The denominator stays the same.

Example 11   ◄》 **Self Tutor**

Find, giving your answer in lowest terms:

a $\frac{4}{9} + \frac{7}{9}$ **b** $\frac{2}{5} - \frac{1}{5}$ **c** $\frac{3}{8} - \frac{2}{8} + \frac{5}{8}$

a $\quad \frac{4}{9} + \frac{7}{9}$ **b** $\quad \frac{2}{5} - \frac{1}{5}$ **c** $\quad \frac{3}{8} - \frac{2}{8} + \frac{5}{8}$

$\quad = \frac{4+7}{9}$ $\quad = \frac{2-1}{5}$ $\quad = \frac{3-2+5}{8}$

$\quad = \frac{11}{9}$ $\quad = \frac{1}{5}$ $\quad = \frac{6}{8}$

$\qquad\qquad\qquad\qquad\qquad\qquad\qquad\quad = \frac{6 \div 2}{8 \div 2}$ {HCF of 6 and 8 is 2}

$\qquad\qquad\qquad\qquad\qquad\qquad\qquad\quad = \frac{3}{4}$

EXERCISE 6H.1

1 Find:

a $\dfrac{1}{7} + \dfrac{2}{7}$

b $\dfrac{2}{3} - \dfrac{1}{3}$

c $\dfrac{4}{5} + \dfrac{2}{5}$

d $\dfrac{5}{4} - \dfrac{2}{4}$

e $\dfrac{3}{8} + \dfrac{4}{8}$

f $\dfrac{6}{5} + \dfrac{3}{5}$

g $\dfrac{11}{7} - \dfrac{3}{7}$

h $\dfrac{9}{20} + \dfrac{8}{20}$

i $\dfrac{21}{25} - \dfrac{13}{25} + \dfrac{1}{25}$

j $\dfrac{10}{13} + \dfrac{8}{13} + \dfrac{11}{13}$

k $\dfrac{11}{14} + \dfrac{13}{14} - \dfrac{1}{14}$

l $\dfrac{10}{7} - \dfrac{8}{7} + \dfrac{6}{7}$

2 Find, giving your answer in lowest terms:

a $\dfrac{3}{4} - \dfrac{1}{4}$

b $\dfrac{2}{9} + \dfrac{1}{9}$

c $\dfrac{7}{6} - \dfrac{3}{6}$

d $\dfrac{5}{8} + \dfrac{2}{8} + \dfrac{3}{8}$

e $\dfrac{8}{4} - \dfrac{3}{4} - \dfrac{3}{4}$

f $\dfrac{3}{10} + \dfrac{7}{10} - \dfrac{2}{10}$

Example 12	🔊 Self Tutor
Find: $2 + \dfrac{4}{7} + \dfrac{6}{7}$	$2 + \dfrac{4}{7} + \dfrac{6}{7}$ $= 2 + \dfrac{4+6}{7}$ $= 2 + \dfrac{10}{7}$ $= 2 + 1\dfrac{3}{7}$ $= 3\dfrac{3}{7}$

3 Find:

a $3 + \dfrac{1}{9} + \dfrac{4}{9}$

b $2 + \dfrac{3}{10} + \dfrac{4}{10}$

c $5 + \dfrac{6}{7} - \dfrac{4}{7}$

d $1 + \dfrac{5}{6} + \dfrac{2}{6}$

e $4 + \dfrac{13}{15} - \dfrac{4}{15}$

f $7 + \dfrac{12}{17} + \dfrac{10}{17}$

4 Rob is planting flowers in his garden. He planted $\dfrac{2}{8}$ of the flowers on the first day, and $\dfrac{3}{8}$ of the flowers on the second day. What fraction of the flowers has he planted so far?

5 Spiros had $\dfrac{9}{10}$ of a bag of fertiliser. He used $\dfrac{6}{10}$ of a bag for his tomatoes. What fraction of the bag of fertiliser is left?

6 Beth takes $\dfrac{5}{6}$ of a bag of rice from her cupboard. She uses $\dfrac{3}{6}$ of a bag in her recipe. She then finds another $\dfrac{4}{6}$ of a bag in her cupboard. How much rice does she have left?

Example 13   🔊 **Self Tutor**

Find:

a $1\frac{3}{5} + 3\frac{4}{5}$

b $4 - 1\frac{2}{3}$

a $\quad 1\frac{3}{5} + 3\frac{4}{5}$

$= \frac{8}{5} + \frac{19}{5}$

$= \frac{8 + 19}{5}$

$= \frac{27}{5}$

$= 5\frac{2}{5}$

b $\quad 4 - 1\frac{2}{3}$

$= \frac{12}{3} - \frac{5}{3} \quad \{4 = 12 \div 3\}$

$= \frac{12 - 5}{3}$

$= \frac{7}{3}$

$= 2\frac{1}{3}$

To add or subtract mixed numbers, we can convert them to improper fractions. We write our answer as a mixed number again at the end.

7 Find:

a $2\frac{2}{3} + 1\frac{2}{3}$

b $3\frac{3}{5} - 2\frac{1}{5}$

c $1\frac{2}{7} + 2\frac{3}{7}$

d $4\frac{2}{8} - 1\frac{5}{8}$

e $1\frac{5}{9} + 3\frac{2}{9} + 2\frac{7}{9}$

f $8\frac{1}{10} - 5\frac{7}{10} + 6\frac{3}{10}$

8 Find:

a $1 - \frac{4}{9}$

b $3 - 1\frac{5}{8}$

c $7 - 4\frac{2}{7}$

d $9 - 6\frac{5}{12}$

9 Leah wrote $1\frac{1}{4}$ pages of a story before dinner, and another $2\frac{1}{4}$ pages after dinner. How many pages has she completed?

10 Sarah and Jane went apple picking. Sarah picked $1\frac{3}{5}$ bags and Jane picked $2\frac{4}{5}$ bags.

a How many bags of apples did they pick altogether?

b How many more bags did Jane pick than Sarah?

DISCUSSION

Michael uses the method alongside to find $4\frac{2}{5} + 2\frac{4}{5}$.

- Does Michael's method give the correct answer?
- What advantages and disadvantages does Michael's method have?
- Can you use a similar method to find $4\frac{2}{5} - 2\frac{4}{5}$?

$4\frac{2}{5} + 2\frac{4}{5}$

$= 4 + 2 + \frac{2}{5} + \frac{4}{5}$

$= 6 + \frac{6}{5}$

$= 6 + 1\frac{1}{5}$

$= 7\frac{1}{5}$

ADDING AND SUBTRACTING FRACTIONS WITH UNEQUAL DENOMINATORS

To **add** or **subtract** fractions with *different* denominators, we first write them with the *same* denominator.
We then add or subtract the numerators.

Example 14

Find:

a $\dfrac{3}{5} + \dfrac{1}{10}$

b $\dfrac{5}{9} - \dfrac{1}{3}$

a $\quad \dfrac{3}{5} + \dfrac{1}{10}$

$= \dfrac{3 \times 2}{5 \times 2} + \dfrac{1}{10}$ {writing $\dfrac{3}{5}$ with denominator 10}

$= \dfrac{6}{10} + \dfrac{1}{10}$

$= \dfrac{7}{10}$

b $\quad \dfrac{5}{9} - \dfrac{1}{3}$

$= \dfrac{5}{9} - \dfrac{1 \times 3}{3 \times 3}$ {writing $\dfrac{1}{3}$ with denominator 9}

$= \dfrac{5}{9} - \dfrac{3}{9}$

$= \dfrac{2}{9}$

EXERCISE 6H.2

1 Find:

a $\dfrac{1}{2} + \dfrac{1}{4}$

b $\dfrac{1}{6} + \dfrac{2}{3}$

c $\dfrac{5}{8} - \dfrac{1}{4}$

d $\dfrac{1}{3} - \dfrac{1}{9}$

e $\dfrac{1}{3} + \dfrac{1}{12}$

f $\dfrac{4}{5} + \dfrac{3}{10}$

g $\dfrac{19}{30} - \dfrac{2}{5}$

h $\dfrac{13}{12} + \dfrac{5}{6}$

i $\dfrac{7}{9} + \dfrac{21}{45}$

j $\dfrac{30}{49} - \dfrac{2}{7}$

k $\dfrac{9}{25} + \dfrac{51}{100}$

l $\dfrac{53}{40} - \dfrac{3}{10}$

2 Find:

a $2 + \dfrac{1}{2} + \dfrac{1}{4}$

b $4 + \dfrac{2}{3} + \dfrac{1}{9}$

c $3 + \dfrac{7}{10} + \dfrac{2}{5}$

3 Find, giving your answer in lowest terms:

a $\dfrac{1}{2} + \dfrac{1}{6}$

b $\dfrac{7}{10} - \dfrac{1}{5}$

c $\dfrac{2}{3} + \dfrac{7}{12}$

d $\dfrac{5}{3} - \dfrac{4}{15}$

e $3 + \dfrac{1}{2} + \dfrac{1}{10}$

f $1 + \dfrac{3}{4} + \dfrac{5}{12}$

4 Lisa ate $\dfrac{2}{9}$ of a cake, and Rebecca ate $\dfrac{1}{3}$ of the cake. What fraction of the cake did the girls eat between them?

5 Every day, Angus feeds his chickens $\dfrac{1}{5}$ of a large tub of feed. If Angus' tub is $\dfrac{9}{10}$ full at the start of the day, how much is left after he has fed his chickens?

Example 15   ◀) **Self Tutor**

Find $1\frac{1}{4} + 2\frac{1}{2}$.

$1\frac{1}{4} + 2\frac{1}{2}$

$= \frac{5}{4} + \frac{5}{2}$ {writing as improper fractions}

$= \frac{5}{4} + \frac{5 \times 2}{2 \times 2}$ {writing $\frac{5}{2}$ with denominator 10}

$= \frac{5}{4} + \frac{10}{4}$

$= \frac{15}{4}$

$= 3\frac{3}{4}$

6 Find:

a $1\frac{1}{2} + 2\frac{3}{8}$

b $3\frac{1}{3} - 2\frac{1}{6}$

c $1\frac{2}{5} + 1\frac{9}{10}$

d $7\frac{1}{2} - 5\frac{3}{4}$

e $2\frac{2}{7} + 1\frac{10}{21}$

f $6\frac{2}{3} - 3\frac{2}{15}$

7 Samantha is an artist. She spends $3\frac{1}{2}$ hours on Saturday painting a portrait, and a further $2\frac{1}{4}$ hours finishing it on Sunday.

In total, how long did it take her to paint the portrait?

8 Paul spends $2\frac{2}{3}$ hours replacing door locks and $4\frac{1}{6}$ hours replacing lights.

In total, how much time does Paul spend doing this work?

9 $12\frac{1}{3}$ tonnes of earth must be removed to level a housing block. A truck moves $6\frac{1}{2}$ tonnes in the first load.

How much earth still needs to be moved?

10 Anita and Melissa each have a can of soft drink. Anita drinks $\frac{2}{3}$ of her can. Melissa drinks $\frac{3}{4}$ of her can.

a In total, how much soft drink have the girls drunk?

b In total, how much soft drink remains?

I MULTIPLYING A FRACTION BY A WHOLE NUMBER

The multiplication $\frac{2}{5} \times 4$ means "4 lots of $\frac{2}{5}$".

In total, we have shaded $\frac{8}{5}$.

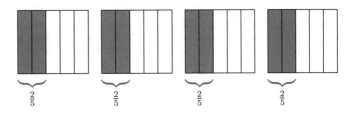

Notice that   2 fifths $\times 4 = 2 \times 4$ fifths $= 8$ fifths

$$\frac{2}{5} \times 4 = \frac{2 \times 4}{5} \qquad = \frac{8}{5}$$

> To multiply a fraction by a whole number, the numerator is multiplied by the whole number. The denominator stays the same.

Example 16 ◀)) Self Tutor

Find:

a $\frac{3}{7} \times 2$ **b** $\frac{1}{4} \times 20$ **c** $\frac{5}{8} \times 6$

a $\quad \frac{3}{7} \times 2$

$= \frac{3 \times 2}{7}$

$= \frac{6}{7}$

b $\quad \frac{1}{4} \times 20$

$= \frac{1 \times 20}{4}$

$= \frac{20}{4}$

$= 5$

c $\quad \frac{5}{8} \times 6$

$= \frac{5 \times 6}{8}$

$= \frac{30 \div 2}{8 \div 2}$

$= \frac{15}{4}$

EXERCISE 6I

1 Find:

a $\frac{1}{3} \times 2$ **b** $\frac{2}{9} \times 4$ **c** $\frac{3}{25} \times 6$ **d** $2 \times \frac{3}{11}$

2 Find:

a $\frac{1}{5} \times 5$ **b** $\frac{1}{3} \times 12$ **c** $\frac{2}{5} \times 15$ **d** $\frac{5}{6} \times 12$

3 Find:

a $\frac{2}{3} \times 5$ **b** $\frac{7}{9} \times 4$ **c** $7 \times \frac{3}{4}$ **d** $5 \times \frac{4}{7}$

4 Find, giving your answer in lowest terms:

a $\frac{1}{10} \times 2$ b $4 \times \frac{3}{16}$ c $3 \times \frac{2}{9}$ d $\frac{5}{6} \times 9$

e $\frac{7}{12} \times 10$ f $6 \times \frac{5}{12}$ g $\frac{2}{15} \times 10$ h $6 \times \frac{4}{15}$

J | A FRACTION OF A QUANTITY

Erica has 4 pumpkins. Her mother tells her they will need $\frac{2}{5}$ of the pumpkins to make soup.

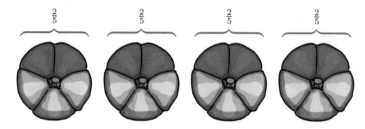

To understand how much is needed, Erica imagines taking $\frac{2}{5}$ out of each of the 4 whole pumpkins.

Erica realises that $\frac{2}{5}$ of 4 pumpkins $= \frac{2}{5} \times 4$ pumpkins $= \frac{8}{5}$ pumpkins.

Example 17	🔊 **Self Tutor**

Find:

a $\frac{1}{5}$ of 30   b $\frac{3}{8}$ of 32

a $\frac{1}{5}$ of 30

$= \frac{1}{5} \times 30$

$= \frac{30}{5}$

$= 6$

b $\frac{3}{8}$ of 32

$= \frac{3}{8} \times 32$

$= \frac{96}{8}$

$= 12$

"of" means that we multiply.

EXERCISE 6J

1 Find:

a $\frac{1}{2}$ of 10   b $\frac{1}{3}$ of 12   c $\frac{1}{4}$ of 20   d $\frac{1}{6}$ of 30

e $\frac{1}{8}$ of 48   f $\frac{1}{10}$ of 70   g $\frac{1}{12}$ of 108   h $\frac{1}{5}$ of 120

2 Find:

a $\frac{2}{3}$ of 9   b $\frac{3}{4}$ of 24   c $\frac{2}{5}$ of 45   d $\frac{3}{5}$ of 35

e $\frac{4}{7}$ of 21   f $\frac{5}{6}$ of 54   g $\frac{7}{10}$ of 120   h $\frac{8}{9}$ of 72

3 Find:

a $\frac{1}{3}$ of 30 people   **b** $\frac{2}{5}$ of 35 drinks   **c** $\frac{7}{10}$ of 40 g

d $\frac{1}{2}$ of 38 lollies   **e** $\frac{3}{4}$ of 60 minutes   **f** $\frac{5}{8}$ of $40

4 Viktor played 15 games of tennis for his school team. He won one third of them. How many games did Viktor win?

5 Ling had $900 in her bank account. She spent one fifth of her money on a new badminton racket. How much did the racket cost?

6 Evan had 96 tomato plants in his greenhouse. While he was on holidays, one eighth of the plants died.

  a How many plants died?

  b What fraction of the plants were still alive?

  c How many plants were still alive?

7 55 passengers were on the bus one morning. Two fifths of the passengers were school children. How many school children were on the bus?

8 Richard spent three quarters of his working day installing computers, and the remainder of the time travelling between jobs. If his working day was 9 hours, how much time did Richard spend installing computers?

9 A business hired a truck to transport boxes of equipment. The total weight of the equipment was 3000 kg, but the truck could only carry $\frac{5}{8}$ of the weight in one load.

What weight did the truck carry in the:

  a first load   **b** second load?

MULTIPLE CHOICE QUIZ

QUICK QUIZ

REVIEW SET 6A

1 What fraction of the diagram is shaded?

a   **b**   **c**

2 What fraction of the cars in this car park are blue?

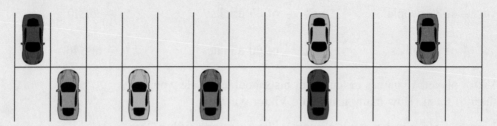

3 Write as a fraction:

    a $6 \div 11$ **b** $15 \div 19$

4 Write as a mixed number:

    a $\frac{9}{5}$ **b** $\frac{13}{3}$ **c** $\frac{35}{6}$

5 Write with denominator 12:

    a $\frac{5}{6}$ **b** $\frac{2}{3}$ **c** $\frac{10}{24}$

6 Place each pair of fractions on a number line:

    a $\frac{1}{6}$ and $\frac{4}{6}$ **b** $\frac{4}{8}$ and $\frac{11}{8}$ **c** $\frac{6}{7}$ and $1\frac{4}{7}$

7 Use $<$ or $>$ to complete:

    a $\frac{6}{10}$ ...... $\frac{3}{10}$ **b** $\frac{19}{7}$ ...... $2\frac{3}{7}$ **c** $\frac{4}{5}$ ...... $\frac{22}{25}$ **d** $5\frac{2}{3}$ ...... $\frac{31}{6}$

8 Find:

    a $\frac{12}{7} - \frac{8}{7}$ **b** $\frac{8}{11} + \frac{9}{11}$ **c** $\frac{3}{8} + \frac{1}{4}$ **d** $5\frac{1}{3} - 1\frac{1}{9}$

9 Find:

    a $\frac{4}{9} \times 2$ **b** $\frac{3}{8} \times 24$ **c** $\frac{5}{6} \times 3$

10 Find:

    a $\frac{1}{4}$ of \$200   **b** $\frac{2}{5}$ of 100 g   **c** $\frac{3}{8}$ of 56 cm

11 An athlete runs $\frac{2}{5}$ of a 20 km race in the first hour and $\frac{3}{10}$ in the second hour.

    a What fraction of the race has he completed?

    b How far has he run?

    c What fraction of the race does he still have remaining?

    d How far away is the finish line?

12 Answer the **Opening Problem** on page **100**.

REVIEW SET 6B

1 Copy this circle and shade $\frac{5}{8}$ of it.

2 **a** What mixed number is represented by this diagram?

   b Write the mixed number as an improper fraction.

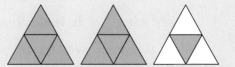

3 Write as a division, and hence as a whole number:

   a $\frac{40}{8}$ **b** $\frac{72}{9}$ **c** $\frac{99}{11}$

4 Sarah went on a holiday for 20 days. It rained on one quarter of the days. On how many days did it rain?

5 Write as an improper fraction:

   a $3\frac{5}{6}$ **b** $4\frac{3}{7}$ **c** $5\frac{2}{5}$

6 Write in lowest terms:

   a $\frac{2}{16}$ **b** $\frac{25}{45}$ **c** $\frac{60}{32}$

7 Rewrite each set of fractions in ascending order:

   a $\frac{4}{5}, \frac{7}{10}, \frac{2}{5}$ **b** $1\frac{5}{6}, \frac{19}{12}, \frac{5}{3}$

8 Find:

   a $3 + \frac{3}{5} + \frac{4}{5}$ **b** $4\frac{1}{10} - 2\frac{3}{10}$ **c** $\frac{11}{6} + \frac{14}{18}$

9 At a barbecue, Adam ate $5\frac{1}{3}$ sausages, and Jill ate $3\frac{2}{3}$ sausages.

   a Write each of these numbers as an improper fraction.

   b How many sausages did Adam and Jill eat in total?

   c How many more sausages did Adam eat than Jill?

10 Kanlin works at a fast food restaurant. He worked for $5\frac{3}{4}$ hours on Monday, and $3\frac{1}{2}$ hours on Tuesday.

   a How much longer did he work on Monday than on Tuesday?

   b How long did he work in total for the two days?

11 Find:

    a $\dfrac{3}{5} \times 4$ **b** $\dfrac{2}{7} \times 21$ **c** $8 \times \dfrac{7}{10}$

12 Judy has to write 60 Christmas cards to send to her friends and family. She writes $\dfrac{1}{3}$ of them on Monday.

    a How many cards did Judy write on Monday?

    b How many cards does she still need to write?

    c Judy writes $\dfrac{2}{5}$ of the *remaining* cards on Tuesday.

        i How many cards did she write on Tuesday?

        ii How many cards does she still need to write?

Chapter 7

Decimals

OPENING PROBLEM

When Taniya takes 8 steps, she moves a distance of 6.8 m.

Things to think about:

a Between which two whole numbers is the value 6.8?

b How can you write 6.8 as a fraction?

c Taniya would like to know what distance she moves with each step.

    i What calculation does Taniya need to perform?

    ii What distance does Taniya move with each step?

d What distance would Taniya move if she took 45 steps?

We have seen how fractions can be used to describe values between the whole numbers. These values can also be described using **decimal numbers** by extending our place value system.

In this Chapter we will explore the relationship between fractions and decimal numbers, and learn how to perform operations with decimals.

A   DECIMAL NUMBERS

In our number system, we write whole numbers using digits in different **place value columns**.

To the right of the units place, we write a **decimal point**. This separates the *wholes* on its left from the *fractions* on its right.

thousands	hundreds	tens	units
3	1	8	4

Every place value is $\frac{1}{10}$ of the value of the place value to its left. So, the place values to the right of the decimal point are **tenths**, **hundredths**, and **thousandths**.

Whole number part				decimal point	Fraction part			
...	thousands	hundreds	tens	units	.	tenths	hundredths	thousandths	...
			8	4	.	7	3		

The number 84.73 has 8 tens, 4 units, 7 tenths, and 3 hundredths.

It is read as "eighty four point seven three".

Example 1	◀)) **Self Tutor**

Write in words: **a** 0.37   **b** 11.407

a 0.37 is "zero point three seven".

b 11.407 is "eleven point four zero seven".

If the whole number part is zero, we write 0 in front of the decimal point.

DISCUSSION

- Why do you think we write 0.37 instead of .37?
- Are the numbers 1.5 and 1.05 the same?
- Are the numbers 1.5 and 1.50 the same?
- In what situations would we write 1.50 instead of 1.5?

EXERCISE 7A

1 Write as a decimal number:

  a eight point three seven   b zero point four nine

  c twenty one point zero five   d seventy point six one

  e nine point zero zero four   f thirty eight point two zero six

2 Write in words:

  a 0.6   b 0.45   c 0.908   d 8.3

  e 11.7   f 6.08   g 20.15   h 96.02

  i 5.864   j 34.003   k 7.581   l 60.264

3 Between which two whole numbers does each decimal number lie?

  a 5.7   b 13.4   c 9.8

  d 6.27   e 19.76   f 32.09

  g 0.46   h 111.05   i 8.506

4 State the number of decimal places in these decimal numbers:

  a 9.1   b 3.26   c 17.2

  d 47.94   e 2.507   f 57.813

  g 34.0   h 13.80   i 23.006

The "number of decimal places" is the number of digits after the decimal point.

Example 2   ◀) Self Tutor

Write in a place value table and as a decimal number:

  a 8 units and 7 hundredths   b $23 + \frac{4}{10} + \frac{9}{1000}$

Number	tens	units	decimal point	tenths	hundredths	thousandths	Decimal number
a 8 units and 7 hundredths		8	.	0	7		8.07
b $23 + \frac{4}{10} + \frac{9}{1000}$	2	3	.	4	0	9	23.409

5 Write in a place value table and as a decimal number:

    a 8 tenths   **b** 4 hundredths

    c 3 thousandths   **d** 7 tens and 8 tenths

    e 5 units and 6 hundredths   **f** 9 thousands and 2 thousandths

    g 2 hundreds, 9 units, and 4 hundredths   **h** 8 thousands, 4 tenths, and 2 thousandths

    i 6 tens, 8 tenths, and 9 hundredths

6 Write in a place value table and as a decimal number:

    a $\dfrac{8}{10} + \dfrac{3}{100}$ **b** $4 + \dfrac{1}{10} + \dfrac{2}{100} + \dfrac{8}{1000}$ **c** $9 + \dfrac{4}{1000}$

    d $28 + \dfrac{6}{10} + \dfrac{9}{100} + \dfrac{9}{1000}$ **e** $\dfrac{5}{100} + \dfrac{6}{1000}$ **f** $139 + \dfrac{7}{100} + \dfrac{7}{1000}$

7 State the value of the digit 3 in:

    a 325.9   **b** 6.37   **c** 32.098   **d** 0.953

    e 43.444   **f** 82.738   **g** 3874.9   **h** 4.843

8 State the value of the digit 5 in:

    a 18.945   **b** 596.08   **c** 4.597   **d** 94.857

    e 5948.26   **f** 275.183   **g** 0.0504   **h** 0.005

Example 3   🔊 **Self Tutor**

Write 5.706 in expanded form.

$$5.706 = 5 + \dfrac{7}{10} + \dfrac{0}{100} + \dfrac{6}{1000}$$

$$= 5 + \dfrac{7}{10} + \dfrac{6}{1000}$$

---

9 Write in expanded form:

    a 5.4   **b** 14.9   **c** 2.03   **d** 32.86

    e 1.308   **f** 3.002   **g** 0.952   **h** 4.024

    i 20.816   **j** 9.008   **k** 808.808   **l** 0.064

10 Write as a decimal number:

    a $\dfrac{6}{10}$ **b** $\dfrac{4}{10} + \dfrac{3}{100}$ **c** $\dfrac{8}{10} + \dfrac{9}{1000}$

    d $\dfrac{9}{100}$ **e** $\dfrac{7}{1000}$ **f** $2 + \dfrac{5}{10} + \dfrac{3}{1000}$

    g $4 + \dfrac{3}{100} + \dfrac{7}{1000}$ **h** $6 + \dfrac{5}{10} + \dfrac{2}{100}$ **i** $\dfrac{5}{10} + \dfrac{6}{100} + \dfrac{8}{1000}$

    j $\dfrac{2}{1000} + \dfrac{3}{10\,000}$ **k** $\dfrac{3}{100} + \dfrac{8}{10\,000}$ **l** $\dfrac{6}{1000} + \dfrac{2}{100\,000}$

Example 4 ◀)) Self Tutor

Write $\dfrac{39}{1000}$ as a decimal number.

$$\dfrac{39}{1000} = \dfrac{3\cancel{0}}{100\cancel{0}} + \dfrac{9}{1000}$$
$$= \dfrac{3}{100} + \dfrac{9}{1000}$$
$$= 0.039$$

The cancellations Ø show that we have divided both the numerator and denominator by 10.

11 Write as a decimal number:

a $\dfrac{3}{10}$ b $\dfrac{15}{100}$ c $\dfrac{23}{100}$ d $\dfrac{65}{100}$

e $\dfrac{79}{100}$ f $\dfrac{117}{1000}$ g $\dfrac{83}{1000}$ h $\dfrac{307}{1000}$

12 Write as a decimal number:

a $13\dfrac{5}{10}$ b $1\dfrac{91}{100}$ c $2\dfrac{137}{1000}$ d $8\dfrac{34}{1000}$

e $\dfrac{27}{10}$ f $\dfrac{384}{100}$ g $\dfrac{4068}{1000}$ h $\dfrac{5172}{100}$

13 Write as a fraction with denominator 100:

a 0.07   b 0.10   c 0.28   d 0.45   e 0.61

14 Write as a fraction with denominator 1000:

a 0.009   b 0.010   c 0.038   d 0.217   e 0.806

ACTIVITY 1   TALKING MONEY

In **decimal currencies**, each major unit is divided into 100 minor units. For example, one dollar is divided into 100 cents.

Suppose you have 12 dollars and 85 cents. This amount is $12\dfrac{85}{100}$ dollars, which we write as $12.85.

We would not *say* this value as the decimal "twelve point eight five dollars", but instead say "twelve dollars eighty five".

What to do:

1 Write in dollars using a decimal point:

   a one dollar thirty cents   b ten dollars ninety five cents

   c forty five cents   d thirty seven dollars eight cents

2 Write down how you would *say*:

   a $6.50   b $11.05   c $18.95   d $32.14

3 Discuss other variations you might hear people say.

4 Do you think these ways of writing and saying values are most efficient?

B DECIMAL NUMBERS ON A NUMBER LINE

We can place decimal numbers on a number line in the same way as we do whole numbers and fractions. We divide each interval according to the place value of the last decimal place.

Example 5   🔊 Self Tutor

What decimal numbers are at A, B, C, and D?

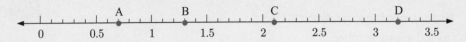

Each division on the number line represents 0.1.

$A = 0.7$, $B = 1.3$, $C = 2.1$,   and $D = 3.2$.

EXERCISE 7B

1 What decimal numbers are at M and N?

a    b

c    d

e    f

2 Copy each number line and mark on it the given numbers:

a $A = 1.6$, $B = 2.5$, $C = 2.9$, $D = 4.1$

PRINTABLE
NUMBER LINES

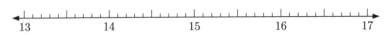

b $E = 13.7$, $F = 16.5$, $G = 15.0$, $H = 14.2$

Example 6   🔊 Self Tutor

What decimal numbers are at A, B, C, and D?

Each division on the number line represents 0.01.

$A = 2.43$, $B = 2.51$, $C = 2.57$,   and $D = 2.62$.

3 What decimal numbers are at P, Q, and R?

a

b

c
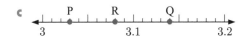

d

e

f

4 Copy each number line, and mark on it the given numbers:

a A = 4.61, B = 4.78, C = 4.83, D = 4.97

b E = 10.62, F = 10.79, G = 10.35, H = 10.46

5 Copy each number line. At each mark, write the equivalent decimal number above the line.

a

b
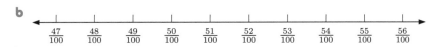

C ORDERING DECIMAL NUMBERS

We can use a number line to help order decimal numbers.

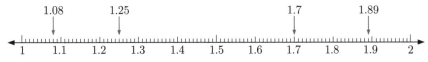

As we look from left to right, the numbers are increasing.

So, $1.08 < 1.25 < 1.7 < 1.89$

$<$ means "is less than".
$>$ means "is greater than".

To compare decimal numbers without having to construct a number line, we compare digits starting with the highest place values.

Example 7   ◀)) **Self Tutor**

Insert >, <, or = to make each statement true:

   a 0.305 ☐ 0.35   b 0.883 ☐ 0.88

---

  a Each number has 0 units and 3 tenths.
     0.305 has less hundredths than 0.35.
     So, 0.305 < 0.35
  b Each number has 0 units, 8 tenths, and 8 hundredths.
     0.883 has more thousandths than 0.88.
     So, 0.883 > 0.88

EXERCISE 7C

1 **a** Place the numbers 2.34, 2.4, 2.26, and 2.3 on this number line.

  b Hence write the numbers in ascending order.

2 **a** Place the numbers 4.02, 4.12, 4.1, 4.01, and 4.2 on this number line.

  b Hence write the numbers in descending order.

3 Insert >, <, or = to make each statement true:

a 0.7 ☐ 0.8	**b** 0.06 ☐ 0.05	**c** 0.2 ☐ 0.19
d 5.01 ☐ 5.1	**e** 0.81 ☐ 0.803	**f** 2.5 ☐ 2.50
g 0.304 ☐ 0.34	**h** 0.03 ☐ 0.2	**i** 6.05 ☐ 60.50
j 0.29 ☐ 0.290	**k** 5.01 ☐ 5.016	**l** 1.15 ☐ 1.035
m 21.021 ☐ 21.210	**n** 8.09 ☐ 8.090	**o** 0.904 ☐ 0.94

4 Write in ascending order:

  a 0.8, 0.4, 0.6   **b** 0.4, 0.1, 0.9

  c 0.14, 0.09, 0.06   **d** 0.46, 0.5, 0.51

  e 1.06, 1.59, 1.61   **f** 2.6, 2.06, 0.206

  g 0.095, 0.905, 0.0905   **h** 15.5, 15.05, 15.55

5 Write in descending order:

  a 0.9, 0.4, 0.3, 0.8   **b** 0.51, 0.49, 0.5, 0.47

  c 0.6, 0.596, 0.61, 0.609   **d** 0.02, 0.04, 0.42, 0.24

  e 6.27, 6.271, 6.027, 6.277   **f** 0.31, 0.031, 0.301, 0.311

  g 8.088, 8.008, 8.080, 8.880 **h** 7.61, 7.061, 7.01, 7.06

6 Shana threw a shot put 5 times. The distances thrown were:

4.11 m,   4.08 m,   4.4 m,   4.1 m,   4.01 m

Write these distances in order from shortest to longest.

7 This table shows the lap times of a motorcycle racer. Write the lap times in order from slowest to fastest.

Lap	Time (seconds)
1	47.045
2	46.980
3	47.009
4	47.103
5	46.982

D   ROUNDING DECIMAL NUMBERS

We are often given measurements as decimal numbers. For example, my digital bathroom scales tell me I weigh 59.4 kg. In reality I do not weigh *exactly* 59.4 kg, but this is an *approximation* of my actual weight. My weight has been *rounded* to one decimal place.

We round off decimal numbers in the same way we do whole numbers. We look at values on the number line either side of our number, which have the required number of decimal places. We round our number to the value which is nearer.

For example, suppose we want to round the numbers below to one decimal place.

≈ means "is approximately equal to".

- 1.23 is nearer to 1.2 than 1.3, so we round *down*.
  We write $1.23 \approx 1.2$.
- 1.28 is nearer to 1.3 than 1.2, so we round *up*.
  We write $1.28 \approx 1.3$.
- 1.25 is midway between 1.2 and 1.3. In this case we choose to round *up*. So, $1.25 \approx 1.3$.

Example 8	◀) Self Tutor

Round to 1 decimal place:

a 3.26 **b** 5.73

a 3.26 lies between 3.2 and 3.3.
It is nearer to 3.3, so we round up.
So, $3.26 \approx 3.3$

b 5.73 lies between 5.7 and 5.8.
It is nearer to 5.7, so we round down.
So, $5.73 \approx 5.7$

"Rounding to 1 decimal place" means rounding to the nearest *tenth*.

DISCUSSION

When rounding whole numbers, we used this rule:

> To round to a particular place value, look at the digit in the place value to the right of it.
> - If this digit is 0, 1, 2, 3, or 4, we round down.
> - If this digit is 5, 6, 7, 8, or 9, we round up.

Can this rule also be used to round decimal numbers?

EXERCISE 7D

1 Look at the number in **bold**. Write down which of the outer two numbers it is nearer to, or write "midway" if it is midway between them.

  a 2.6, **2.63**, 2.7   b 4.1, **4.16**, 4.2   c 0.3, **0.35**, 0.4

  d 5.9, **5.928**, 6.0   e 18.2, **18.253**, 18.3   f 11, **11.05**, 11.1

2 Round to 1 decimal place:

  a 2.43   b 3.57   c 4.92   d 7.75   e 0.639   f 4.274

3 Round to the nearest tenth:

  a 1.52   b 7.16   c 0.08   d 6.473   e 8.95   f 13.205

Example 9	◀) **Self Tutor**

Round to 2 decimal places:

  a 2.584   b 17.945

a 2.584 lies between 2.58 and 2.59.
   It is nearer to 2.58, so we round down.
   So, $2.584 \approx 2.58$

b 17.945 lies between 17.94 and 17.95.
   It is midway between them, so we choose to round up.
   So, $17.945 \approx 17.95$

"Rounding to 2 decimal places" means rounding to the nearest *hundredth*.

---

4 Look at the number in **bold**. Write down which of the outer two numbers it is nearer to, or write "midway" if it is midway between them.

  a 4.62, **4.626**, 4.63   b 9.11, **9.113**, 9.12   c 12.37, **12.375**, 12.38

5 Round to 2 decimal places:

  a 4.236   b 2.731   c 5.625   d 10.006

  e 4.377   f 6.5237   g 1.0871   h 26.3047

6 a Between which two whole numbers does the number 4.6 lie?

   b Round 4.6 to the nearest whole number.

7 Round to the nearest whole number:

  a 3.7   b 6.1   c 7.48   d 12.63   e 21.082   f 45.512

8 Round 0.486 to:

  a 1 decimal place   **b** 2 decimal places.

9 Round 3.789 to the nearest:

  a whole number   **b** tenth   **c** hundredth.

10 Round 5.1837 to:

  a the nearest whole number   **b** 1 decimal place

  c 2 decimal places   **d** 3 decimal places.

11 Round:

  a 3.87 to the nearest tenth   **b** 4.3 to the nearest whole number

  c 6.09 to 1 decimal place   **d** 0.461 72 to 3 decimal places

  e 2.9467 to 2 decimal places   **f** 0.175 61 to 3 decimal places.

12 Round each value to the accuracy given:

  a Frank's cat weighs 4.327 kg.   {1 decimal place}

  b The maximum temperature today was 32.694°C. {1 decimal place}

  c The tree in Tina's backyard is 2.9381 m high. {2 decimal places}

  d Nick swam 100 m in 86.825 seconds. {whole number}

E CONVERTING DECIMALS TO FRACTIONS

We have seen that decimals and fractions can both be used to describe values between whole numbers.

Since the decimal places correspond to tenths, hundredths, thousandths, and so on, we can easily convert decimals into fractions whose denominators are powers of 10.

We can then look to write the fraction in lowest terms.

Example 10   ◀) **Self Tutor**

Write as a fraction or mixed number in lowest terms:

  a 0.7   **b** 0.72   **c** 2.175

a 0.7

$= \dfrac{7}{10}$

b 0.72

$= \dfrac{72}{100}$

$= \dfrac{72 \div 4}{100 \div 4}$

$= \dfrac{18}{25}$

c 2.175

$= 2 + \dfrac{175}{1000}$

$= 2 + \dfrac{175 \div 25}{1000 \div 25}$

$= 2 + \dfrac{7}{40}$

$= 2\dfrac{7}{40}$

EXERCISE 7E

1 Write as a fraction or mixed number:

   a 0.1
   b 0.9
   c 0.19
   d 0.67

   e 0.07
   f 0.191
   g 0.523
   h 0.049

   i 4.3
   j 6.13
   k 0.011
   l 5.271

2 Write as a fraction or mixed number in lowest terms:

   a 0.8
   b 0.5
   c 0.26
   d 0.35

   e 0.25
   f 0.106
   g 0.015
   h 0.075

   i 0.125
   j 7.6
   k 4.56
   l 3.95

F   CONVERTING FRACTIONS TO DECIMALS

We have already seen how to convert fractions with denominators 10, 100, and 1000 into decimal numbers.

For example:

- $\dfrac{4}{10} = 0.4$
- $\dfrac{57}{100} = 0.57$
- $\dfrac{129}{1000} = 0.129$

If the denominator is not a power of 10, we can sometimes write the fraction so that the denominator is a power of 10.

Example 11   ◀) Self Tutor

Write as a decimal:

  a $\dfrac{3}{4}$
  b $\dfrac{7}{20}$
  c $\dfrac{23}{125}$

> When we multiply the numerator and denominator by the same number, we do not change the value of the fraction.

a $\dfrac{3}{4}$

$= \dfrac{3 \times 25}{4 \times 25}$

$= \dfrac{75}{100}$

$= 0.75$

b $\dfrac{7}{20}$

$= \dfrac{7 \times 5}{20 \times 5}$

$= \dfrac{35}{100}$

$= 0.35$

c $\dfrac{23}{125}$

$= \dfrac{23 \times 8}{125 \times 8}$

$= \dfrac{184}{1000}$

$= 0.184$

EXERCISE 7F

1 Write as a decimal:

  a $\dfrac{8}{10}$
  b $\dfrac{21}{100}$
  c $1\dfrac{4}{10}$
  d $\dfrac{319}{1000}$
  e $2\dfrac{83}{100}$

2 By what whole number would you multiply the following, to obtain a power of 10?

  a 2
  b 5
  c 4
  d 20
  e 25

  f 50
  g 125
  h 8
  i 40
  j 250

3   Write as a decimal:

a $\dfrac{1}{2}$ b $\dfrac{2}{5}$ c $\dfrac{1}{4}$ d $\dfrac{3}{20}$ e $\dfrac{17}{20}$ f $\dfrac{9}{25}$

g $\dfrac{21}{25}$ h $\dfrac{13}{50}$ i $\dfrac{138}{500}$ j $\dfrac{6}{250}$ k $\dfrac{91}{250}$ l $\dfrac{11}{500}$

m $\dfrac{9}{125}$ n $\dfrac{9}{40}$ o $\dfrac{3}{8}$ p $5\dfrac{3}{4}$ q $7\dfrac{11}{20}$ r $3\dfrac{21}{125}$

4   Copy and complete these conversions to decimals:

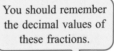

You should remember the decimal values of these fractions.

a $\dfrac{1}{2} = \ldots\ldots$

b $\dfrac{1}{5} = \ldots\ldots,\quad \dfrac{2}{5} = \ldots\ldots,\quad \dfrac{3}{5} = \ldots\ldots,\quad \dfrac{4}{5} = \ldots\ldots$

c $\dfrac{1}{4} = \ldots\ldots,\quad \dfrac{2}{4} = \ldots\ldots,\quad \dfrac{3}{4} = \ldots\ldots$

d $\dfrac{1}{8} = \ldots\ldots,\quad \dfrac{2}{8} = \ldots\ldots,\quad \dfrac{3}{8} = \ldots\ldots,\quad \dfrac{4}{8} = \ldots\ldots,$

$\dfrac{5}{8} = \ldots\ldots,\quad \dfrac{6}{8} = \ldots\ldots,\quad \dfrac{7}{8} = \ldots\ldots$

5   a Write the fractions $\dfrac{7}{10}$, $\dfrac{13}{20}$, and $\dfrac{18}{25}$ as decimals.

b Hence write $\dfrac{7}{10}$, 0.63, $\dfrac{13}{20}$, 0.74, and $\dfrac{18}{25}$ in ascending order.

6   Write as a decimal:

a $\dfrac{4}{5}$ kg   b $2\dfrac{1}{2}$ g   c $4\dfrac{3}{4}$ hours

d $\dfrac{7}{20}$ m   e $2\dfrac{9}{20}$ tonnes   f $7\dfrac{7}{8}$ L

G ADDING AND SUBTRACTING DECIMAL NUMBERS

To **add** or **subtract** decimal numbers, we write the numbers under one another so the decimal points and the place values line up. We then add or subtract each column, working from right to left, in the same way as for whole numbers.

Example 12	◀ᴥ **Self Tutor**

Find $3.84 + 0.372$

```
      3 . 8  4  0
  + ₁0 .₁3  7  2
      4 . 2  1  2
```

We write 0 on the end of 3.84 so that both numbers have the same number of decimal places.

EXERCISE 7G

1 Find:

a $0.4 + 0.5$

b $0.6 + 2.7$

c $0.9 + 0.23$

d $0.64 + 0.09$

e $0.57 + 0.96$

f $3.04 + 4.78$

g $15.79 + 2.64$

h $0.4 + 0.3 + 4$

i $0.009 + 0.435$

j $0.261 + 2.948$

k $0.03 + 0.697$

l $0.3 + 0.9 + 0.65$

m $0.41 + 0.12 + 0.6$

n $7.1 + 2.4 + 3.81$

o $0.95 + 1.638 + 8.78$

Example 13   ◀) **Self Tutor**

Find: a $26.9 - 9.5$ b $5 - 2.32$

a
$$
\begin{array}{r}
^1 2 ^{16}\!\!\not{6} \,.\, 9 \\
- \quad 9 \,.\, 5 \\
\hline
1\;7\,.\,4
\end{array}
$$

b
$$
\begin{array}{r}
^4\!\not{5} \,.\, ^9\!\not{0} \,^{10}\!\not{0} \\
- \quad 2 \,.\, 3 \;2 \\
\hline
2\,.\,6\;8
\end{array}
$$

---

2 Find:

a $5.8 - 2.4$

b $8.7 - 3.5$

c $9.65 - 4.2$

d $0.86 - 0.34$

e $1.75 - 0.41$

f $16.42 - 3.3$

g $1.7 - 0.9$

h $2.3 - 0.8$

i $4.2 - 3.8$

j $2 - 0.6$

k $4 - 1.7$

l $3 - 0.74$

m $4.5 - 1.83$

n $2 - 0.57$

o $10 - 3.06$

3 Find the sum of:

a 31.1, 8.4, and 4.7

b 3.56, 1.12, and 9.7

c 1.01, 0.101, and 10.1

d 4, 4.004, 0.044, and 0.404

4 Subtract:

a 29.5 from 35.6

b 1.3 from 23.48

c 6.08 from 7.1

d 3.7 from 171.2

e 9.67 from 68.3

f 8.096 from 10.11

5 John gets \$5.40 pocket money, Pat gets \$3.85, and Jill gets \$7.85. How much pocket money do they get altogether?

6 Helena is 1.75 m tall and Fred is 1.38 m tall. How much taller is Helena than Fred?

7 At a golf tournament, Janet's first two shots travel 132.6 m and 104.8 m. How far has the ball travelled in total?

8 Jeff went trout fishing and caught five fish. Their weights were 10.6 kg, 3.45 kg, 6.23 kg, 1.83 kg, and 5.84 kg. Find the total weight of the five fish.

9 Three pieces of timber measure 2.755 m, 3.084 m, and 7.24 m. Find the total length of the timber pieces.

10 Elizabeth bought items costing $10.85, $37.65, $19.05, and $24.35.

   a How much did she spend in total?

   b How much change will she receive from $100?

H   MULTIPLYING BY POWERS OF 10

When we multiply a whole number by 10, each digit moves one place to the left.

Since 10 tenths make 1 unit, 10 hundredths make 1 tenth, and 10 thousandths make 1 hundredth, the same is true for decimal numbers.

hundreds	tens	units	tenths	hundredths	thousandths
	5	9 .	1	2	3
5	9	1 .	2	3	

$59.123 \times 10 = 591.23$

This has the effect of moving the decimal point one place to the *right*.

> When multiplying by 10, we move the decimal point one place to the right.

Since $100 = 10 \times 10$, and $1000 = 10 \times 10 \times 10$, we conclude that:

- When multiplying by 100, we move the decimal point two places to the right.
- When multiplying by 1000, we move the decimal point three places to the right.

If necessary, we use a zero to fill an empty place value.

Example 14   ◄)) **Self Tutor**

Multiply 2.14 by:

  a 10   **b** 100   **c** 1000

  a 2.14×10 **b** 2.14×100 **c** 2.140×1000
    $= 21.4$ $= 214$ $= 2140$

EXERCISE 7H

1 Multiply by 10:

  a 2.5   **b** 6.3   **c** 0.2   **d** 0.01   **e** 0.238   **f** 60.6

2 Multiply by 100:

  a 6.7   **b** 9.2   **c** 0.7   **d** 0.54   **e** 70.4   **f** 0.05798

3 Multiply by 1000:

  a 7.4   **b** 16.2   **c** 0.8   **d** 0.38   **e** 6.75   **f** 0.0824

4 Copy and complete this table of multiplications.

	Number	× 10	× 100	× 1000
a	0.009			
b	0.12			
c	0.5			
d	4.6			
e	19.07			

5 Complete these products:

  a $9 \times \ldots\ldots = 900$ **b** $33 \times \ldots\ldots = 330$ **c** $3.4 \times \ldots\ldots = 34$

  d $0.02 \times \ldots\ldots = 2$ **e** $0.003 \times \ldots\ldots = 0.03$ **f** $5.64 \times \ldots\ldots = 5640$

6 An ice cream costs \$2.80. Find the cost of:

  a 10 ice creams   **b** 100 ice creams   **c** 1000 ice creams.

7 A baseball weighs 0.147 kg. Find the weight of:

  a 10 baseballs   **b** 100 baseballs   **c** 1000 baseballs.

I   DIVIDING BY POWERS OF 10

When we divide a whole number by 10, each digit moves one place to the right.

The same is true for decimal numbers.

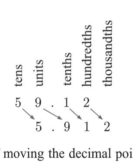

$$59.12 \div 10 = 5.912$$

This has the effect of moving the decimal point one place to the *left*.

- When dividing by 10, we move the decimal point one place to the left.
- When dividing by 100, we move the decimal point two places to the left.
- When dividing by 1000, we move the decimal point three places to the left.

Example 15	◀)) Self Tutor

Divide 60.9 by:

  a 10   **b** 100   **c** 1000

  a $60.9 \div 10$ **b** $60.9 \div 100$ **c** $60.9 \div 1000$

  $= 6.09$ $= 0.609$ $= 060.9 \div 1000$

  $= 0.0609$

EXERCISE 71

1 Divide by 10:

    a 2   **b** 6.3   **c** 0.82   **d** 0.01   **e** 54.02   **f** 606

2 Divide by 100:

    a 6   **b** 9.2   **c** 0.7   **d** 53   **e** 166   **f** 300.7

3 Divide by 1000:

    a 7   **b** 6.2   **c** 56.1   **d** 499   **e** 70.15   **f** 6854.9

4 Copy and complete this table of divisions.

	Number	÷ 10	÷ 100	÷ 1000
a	8			
b	4.6			
c	50			
d	19.07			
e	231.4			

5 Complete these divisions:

    a $6 \div \ldots\ldots = 0.6$ **b** $33 \div \ldots\ldots = 0.33$ **c** $3.4 \div \ldots\ldots = 0.34$

    d $0.2 \div \ldots\ldots = 0.002$ **e** $49 \div \ldots\ldots = 0.49$ **f** $634.1 \div \ldots\ldots = 0.6341$

6 A family of 10 elephants eats 914 kg of food in a day. Find the average amount eaten by each elephant.

7 A prize of $27 565 is divided equally between 100 people. How much money does each person receive?

8 A farmer grows 1000 pumpkins for Halloween. Their total mass is 6284 kg. Find the average mass of each pumpkin.

J   MULTIPLYING DECIMALS BY A WHOLE NUMBER

We know that 3×4 means "4 lots of 3" which is $3 + 3 + 3 + 3 = 12$.

In the same way, 3.6×4 means "4 lots of 3.6" which is $3.6 + 3.6 + 3.6 + 3.6$.

$$
\begin{array}{r}
3 \,.\, 6 \\
3 \,.\, 6 \\
3 \,.\, 6 \\
+ \quad {}_2 3 \,.\, 6 \\
\hline
1 \; 4 \,.\, 4 \\
\end{array}
$$

So, $3.6 \times 4 = 14.4$

INVESTIGATION

In this Investigation we look for a relationship between the multiplication of a decimal number and a whole number, and the corresponding multiplication of two whole numbers.

What to do:

1   **a** Use repeated addition to find 1.9×3.

   b Use column multiplication to find 19×3.

   What do you notice?

2 Use repeated addition and column multiplication to find these products:

   a 1.7×2 and 17×2 **b** 2.4×3 and 24×3

   c 0.26×4 and 26×4 **d** 0.37×5 and 37×5

3 Can you explain the relationship between each pair of products in **1** and **2**?

When a decimal number is multiplied by a whole number, the result has the same digits in the same order as the corresponding multiplication of two whole numbers.

To explain this, consider 3.6×4 and 36×4.

Using column multiplication, $36 \times 4 = 144$

$$
\begin{array}{ccc}
 & 3 & 6 \\
\times & {}_2 4 \\
\hline
1 & 4 & 4
\end{array}
$$

Now $3.6 = \frac{36}{10}$, so $3.6 \times 4 = \frac{36}{10} \times 4$

$$= \frac{36 \times 4}{10}$$

$$= \frac{144}{10} \qquad \{\text{using the column multiplication}\}$$

$$= 14.4$$

So, to multiply a decimal number by a whole number, we first convert the decimal number to a fraction with a denominator that is a power of 10.

Example 16   ◀) Self Tutor

Find: **a** 7×2.8 **b** 8.62×3

a 7×2.8

$= 7 \times \frac{28}{10}$

$= \frac{7 \times 28}{10}$

$= \frac{196}{10}$

$= 19.6$

$$
\begin{array}{ccc}
 & 2 & 8 \\
\times & {}_5 7 \\
\hline
1 & 9 & 6
\end{array}
$$

b 8.62×3

$= \frac{862}{100} \times 3$

$= \frac{862 \times 3}{100}$

$= \frac{2586}{100}$

$= 25.86$

$$
\begin{array}{cccc}
 & 8 & 6 & 2 \\
\times & {}_1 & & 3 \\
\hline
2 & 5 & 8 & 6
\end{array}
$$

EXERCISE 7J

1 Find:

  a 0.7×3 **b** 0.8×4 **c** 0.5×5 **d** 8×0.9

  e 0.03×2 **f** 7×0.07 **g** 4×0.05 **h** 6×0.008

2 Find:

  a 2.1×6 **b** 5×1.2 **c** 4.8×4 **d** 7.2×9

  e 17.3×5 **f** 32.5×6 **g** 9×30.7 **h** 134.8×2

3 Find:

  a 0.23×3 **b** 0.87×4 **c** 0.29×8 **d** 1.42×3

  e 4.05×9 **f** 2.77×8 **g** 3.64×7 **h** 14.25×4

4 Find:

  a 13×0.2 **b** 17×0.3 **c** 22×0.5 **d** 0.4×36

  e 42×0.9 **f** 15×0.03 **g** 37×0.06 **h** 24×0.05

Example 17	◄)) Self Tutor

Find: 3.7×23

$$3.7 \times 23$$
$$= \frac{37}{10} \times 23$$
$$= \frac{37 \times 23}{10}$$
$$= \frac{851}{10}$$
$$= 85.1$$

$$\begin{array}{rrr} & 3 & 7 \\ \times & 2 & 3 \\ \hline 1 \,^2 1 & 1 \\ + \,^1 7 & 4 & 0 \\ \hline 8 & 5 & 1 \end{array}$$

5 Find:

  a 1.6×12 **b** 3.9×15 **c** 8.4×21

  d 10.7×18 **e** 35.1×26 **f** 0.83×14

  g 5.08×19 **h** 9.35×42 **i** 17.14×35

6 A building has 7 storeys. Each storey is 2.8 m high. Find the height of the building.

7 Dawn can sew a skirt hem in 10.4 minutes. How long will it take her to sew nine skirt hems if she works at the same rate?

8 23 students went on an excursion. Their bus tickets cost \$4.35 each. Find the total amount paid.

9 Find the total weight of 75 boxes of muesli bars if each box weighs 0.18 kg.

ACTIVITY 2   ESTIMATION

When we multiply a decimal number by a whole number, it is important to think about what answer to expect. An **estimate** can warn us of an error we may have made.

We can estimate the product by rounding the decimal to the nearest whole number.

For example, $12 \times 3.9 \approx 12 \times 4$, so we expect the value of 12×3.9 to be close to 48.

What to do:

1 Estimate the following products, then use your estimate to choose the correct answer.

   a $4.387 \times 6 = \ldots.$

      A 263.22   **B** 26.322   **C** 2.6322   **D** 2632.2

   b $150 \times 2.8 = \ldots.$

      A 4.2   **B** 42   **C** 420   **D** 4200

   c $7.234 \times 11 = \ldots.$

      A 795.74   **B** 79.574   **C** 7.9574   **D** 0.795 74

2 **a** Estimate the product 17×3.1

   b Will your estimate be more or less than the actual value? Explain your answer.

K   DIVIDING DECIMALS BY A WHOLE NUMBER

We divide a decimal by a whole number using the same method we previously used for whole numbers:

- We divide each place value in turn, starting with the highest.
- If a digit is too small to be divided on its own, we exchange it in the next column.
- We place the decimal point in the answer directly above the decimal point in the question.

Example 18   ◀) Self Tutor

Find: **a** $4.64 \div 4$ **b** $5.28 \div 8$

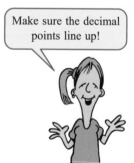
Make sure the decimal points line up!

a
$$\begin{array}{r} 1.1\ 6 \\ 4\ \overline{|\ 4.6\,^24} \end{array}$$
$$4.64 \div 4 = 1.16$$

b
$$\begin{array}{r} 0.6\ 6 \\ 8\ \overline{|\ 5.\,^52\,^48} \end{array}$$
$$5.28 \div 8 = 0.66$$

EXERCISE 7K

1 Find:

   a $9.6 \div 3$ **b** $7.5 \div 5$ **c** $0.72 \div 9$ **d** $1.26 \div 3$

   e $3.57 \div 7$ **f** $43.4 \div 7$ **g** $81.6 \div 4$ **h** $0.315 \div 7$

   i $24.16 \div 8$ **j** $67.14 \div 3$ **k** $7.224 \div 8$ **l** $8.046 \div 6$

Example 19   ◀)) **Self Tutor**

Find:

  a $6.3 \div 5$ **b** $3.5 \div 4$

a		**b**	
	$\begin{array}{r} 1 \,.\, 2 \;\; 6 \\ \hline 5 \,\big|\, 6 \,.\, {}^1 3 \,{}^3 0 \end{array}$		$\begin{array}{r} 0 \,.\, 8 \;\; 7 \;\; 5 \\ \hline 4 \,\big|\, 3 \,.\, 5 \,{}^3 0 \,{}^2 0 \end{array}$
	$6.3 \div 5 = 1.26$		$3.5 \div 4 = 0.875$

> Sometimes we need to write extra zeros at the end of the decimal number we are dividing into.

2 Find:

  a $5.3 \div 2$ **b** $6.1 \div 5$ **c** $23.4 \div 4$ **d** $12.41 \div 2$

  e $3.4 \div 8$ **f** $5.9 \div 4$ **g** $9.17 \div 4$ **h** $26.1 \div 8$

3 A 10.75 kg tub of ice cream is divided equally among 5 people. How much ice cream does each person receive?

4 Simone bought 4 kg of bananas for \$9.16. How much did each kilogram of bananas cost?

5 Ingrid completed 8 laps of a bicycle circuit, which was a total distance of 26.8 km. Find the length of each lap.

6 Use division to attempt to write the following fractions as decimal numbers:

  a $\dfrac{1}{6}$ **b** $\dfrac{2}{3}$ **c** $\dfrac{4}{9}$ **d** $\dfrac{1}{7}$

Discuss your results.

PUZZLE

Across

  1 23.2×4
  3 $17.25 \div 5$
  5 $291.6 \div 6$
  7 $528.4 + 302.1$
  8 0.036×1000
  9 $11.59 - 7.25$
10 $38.1 \div 10$
11 $18.36 + 9.04$

13 6.3×7
15 0.6×100
16 $906 \div 1000$
17 0.32×8
18 $80.39 - 21.59$
19 0.93×9

PRINTABLE CROSSWORD

Down

  1 $12.74 - 2.89$
  2 28.16×3
  3 $56.1 - 19.7$
  4 108.36×4
  6 $595.7 \div 7$
10 $64.076 \div 2$
11 $205 \div 100$

12 17.92×4
13 0.428×10
14 $15.9 + 20.8$

MULTIPLE CHOICE QUIZ

QUICK QUIZ

REVIEW SET 7A

1 Write as a decimal number:

  a $\dfrac{7}{10} + \dfrac{3}{100}$ **b** $\dfrac{1}{10} + \dfrac{7}{1000}$ **c** $5 + \dfrac{6}{100} + \dfrac{9}{1000}$

2 What decimal numbers are at A and B?

  a    **b**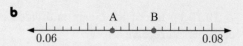

3 Write the decimal numbers 0.69, 0.609, 0.069, 0.096, and 0.6 in ascending order.

4 Round 3.8551 to:

  a one decimal place   **b** two decimal places.

5 Convert to a fraction in lowest terms:

  a 0.23 **b** 0.2 **c** 0.059 **d** 0.68

6 Convert to a decimal:

  a $\dfrac{71}{100}$ **b** $\dfrac{4}{5}$ **c** $\dfrac{19}{20}$ **d** $\dfrac{81}{500}$

7 Find:

  a $0.41 + 0.27$ **b** $7.39 - 5.16$

  c $16.5 + 3.74$ **d** $8 - 2.49$

8 In three seasons, a vineyard produced 638.17 tonnes, 582.35 tonnes, and 717.36 tonnes of grapes. Find the total harvest of grapes for the three years.

9 Find:

  a 6.2×10 **b** 2.158×100 **c** $5.6 \div 10$ **d** $4.2 \div 1000$

10 Find:

  a 3.4×6 **b** 6.09×7 **c** 0.7×15 **d** 2.18×24

11 Find:

  a $8.4 \div 6$ **b** $0.721 \div 7$ **c** $3.92 \div 5$ **d** $0.15 \div 4$

12 **a** Place the decimal numbers 2.39 and 2.46 on this number line.

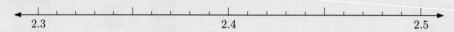

  b Find the sum of 2.39 and 2.46.

  c Round the sum to 1 decimal place.

13 Find the total cost of 14 showbags valued at $7.85 each.

14 Kim sent some birthday presents to his cousins overseas using three parcels.

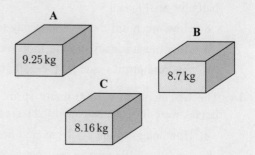

   a Find the total weight of the parcels.

   b How much heavier is parcel **A** than parcel **C**?

   c The parcels cost $9 per kilogram to send. Find the cost of sending parcel **B**.

REVIEW SET 7B

1 Write "sixteen point five seven four" as a decimal.

2 Write $\dfrac{31}{1000}$ as a decimal number.

3 State the value of the digit 3 in 10.003.

4 Write 2.049 in expanded form.

5 Mark A = 2.7 and B = 3.4 on this number line.

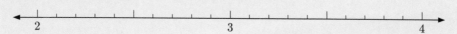

6 Round 5.4906 to:

   a the nearest whole number   **b** 3 decimal places   **c** the nearest tenth.

7 Insert >, <, or = to make each statement true:

   a 0.709 □ 0.79   **b** 3.04 □ 3.046   **c** 8.13 □ 8.130

8 Write the following amounts as decimals:

   a $\dfrac{17}{20}$ km   **b** $\dfrac{3}{25}$ L   **c** $4\dfrac{21}{50}$ kg

9 Complete the following statements:

   a 203 ÷ ...... = 2.03   **b** 2.03 × ...... = 2030   **c** 0.203 ÷ ...... = 0.002 03

10 Find:

   a 1.7 + 12.42   **b** 5.07 − 1.46   **c** 4.3 × 7   **d** 8.46 ÷ 9

   e 7.9 ÷ 5   **f** 0.231 + 0.69   **g** 6.81 − 4.25   **h** 23 × 1.6

11 Damien deposited amounts of $153.95 and $68.25 in a new bank account.

   a How much has Damien deposited in total?

   b How much more will he need to save, to reach his target of $300?

12 A set of 8 batteries has total weight 94.2 g. Find the weight of each battery.

13 A golf shop bought 1000 golf balls from a manufacturer at $3.15 each. It sells the golf balls for $6.40 each.

  a How much did the golf shop pay to buy the golf balls?

  b How much money did the shop receive from selling the balls?

  c Find the profit made by the golf shop from buying and selling the balls.

14 The first horse in a 1000 metre sprint finished in 56.98 seconds. The second and third horses were 0.07 seconds and 0.23 seconds behind the winner.

  a How long did the   **i** second horse   **ii** third horse   take to finish the sprint?

  b Find the difference in time between the second horse and the third horse.

  c Find the average number of seconds the winner took to gallop each metre.

15 Anna decided to go to a movie. She spent $2.85 on a bus ticket, $15.50 on the movie ticket, $4.55 on a drink, and $6.85 on an ice cream.

  a How much did Anna spend in total?

  b How much change would she have from $50?

  c Four of Anna's friends went to the movies with her, and they each spent the same amount as Anna. In total, how much was spent by the five children?

Measurement:
Introduction

Contents:
A Units
B Reading scales
C Mass

OPENING PROBLEM

Jackson took his hamster and his cat to the vet for a check-up. The information in this table was collected.

Quantity	Hamster	Cat
Age	2 years	7 years
Height	7 cm	25 cm
Mass	200 g	3.4 kg
Length	15 cm	45 cm
Body temperature	38.9°C	37.6°C
Vet visits in last year	3	1

Thing to think about:

a Which of the quantities have been *measured*?

b Which two quantities are the same *type* of measurement?

c Why are different *units* used for the masses of the pets?

d How many times heavier is the cat than the hamster?

In our everyday life we **measure** many things. Measurement tells us the **size** of a quantity.

There are several *types* of quantities we commonly measure:

Type of quantity	Example
Distance or length	How far we have travelled.
Mass	How heavy we are.
Time	How long a tennis match will last.
Temperature	How hot it is.
Area	The size of a farm.
Volume	How big the parcel I am receiving is.
Capacity	How much hot chocolate my mug can hold.
Speed	How fast the car is travelling.

The different types of quantities are measured in different **units**, and require different **devices** to measure them.

ACTIVITY 1   MEASURING DEVICES

What to do:

1 Make a list of the measuring devices that you use:

   a in your house   b at school   c outside.

2 Describe what each device is used to measure.

3 Draw *three* of the devices you have thought of.

RESEARCH — WHAT DOES THAT MEASURE?

Some measuring devices have interesting names. They are not used within the home and a person needs to be trained to use them correctly.

What to do:

Find out what these devices measure, and who would use them:

- sextant
- clinometer
- sphygmomanometer.

Find pictures or make drawings to support your answers.

ACTIVITY 2 — MEASUREMENT IN JOBS

What to do:

1 Joanne is a tailor. Her duties include:
- selling lengths of fabric by the metre
- sewing clothes requested by customers
- making alterations to clothes that customers bring in.

a What things will Joanne need to measure to do her job?

b Describe *how* Joanne might measure these things.

c Why is it important that Joanne's measurements are accurate?

2 Joey is a nurse.
a List at least 3 things Joey will need to measure to do his job.

b Describe how Joey might measure these things.

c Why is it important that Joey's measurements are accurate?

3 Ask a parent or older relative:
- what their job is
- what they need to measure to do their job
- how they measure it
- how important accuracy is in their measurements.

Compare your findings with your classmates.

A — UNITS

When we write whole numbers, we use a **units** place value column. It is the smallest whole part that we consider.

H	T	U
7	2	4

When we *count* items, the **unit** we use describes what we are counting. It tells us what one whole *means*.

For example:

- When counting kangaroos, the units are "kangaroos".

- When counting people, the units are "people".

4 kangaroos

3 people

When we *measure* a quantity, we also need to use units to describe what it is we are measuring. Again, the unit tells us what one whole *means*.

ACTIVITY 3   UNITS

What to do:

1 Write down all the units you know, that are used when measuring:

    a length   **b** mass   **c** time   **d** temperature

    e area   **f** volume   **g** capacity   **h** speed.

2 Discuss how the units for each *type* of quantity are related. Which are the biggest units? Which are the smallest?

For each *type* of quantity, there is a set of related units that can be used to describe the quantity. This table shows some commonly used units.

Type of quantity	*Units*	
Distance or length	• millimetre (mm)	• centimetre (cm)
	• metre (m)	• kilometre (km)
Mass	• milligram (mg)	• gram (g)
	• kilogram (kg)	• tonne (t)
Time	• second (s)	• minute (min)
	• hour (h)	• day
Temperature	• degrees Celsius (°C)	• degrees Fahrenheit (°F)
Area	• square millimetre (mm^2)	• square centimetre (cm^2)
	• square metre (m^2)	• square kilometre (km^2)
Volume	• cubic millimetre (mm^3)	• cubic centimetre (cm^3)
	• cubic metre (m^3)	
Capacity	• millilitres (mL)	• litres (L)
	• kilolitres (kL)	
Speed	• kilometres per hour (km/h)	• metres per second (m/s)

When describing a quantity, you should choose an appropriate unit so that you are dealing with sensibly sized numbers.

For example, we would describe the distance from Johannesburg to Cape Town as 1398 km, rather than 1 398 000 m.

EXERCISE 8A

1   Write down the unit which describes each counting situation:

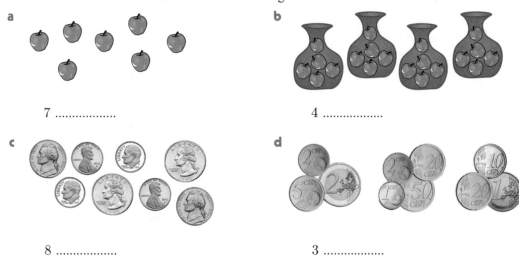

a 7 ....

b 4 ....

c 8 ....

d 3 ....

2   Match each statement with the correct measurement:

    a The mass of a rock.

    b The length of a spoon.

    c The maximum temperature in Manila today.

    d The time Hazel spent running.

    e The area of a classroom.

    A 80 m^2

    B 25 minutes

    C 300 g

    D 15 cm

    E 32°C

3   Look at the conversation alongside.
State *two types* of quantity that the person on the right could be talking about.
For each type, state the *unit* the person would use.

4   This nail weighs 1.2 grams.
Explain why it would not be sensible to describe the weight of a bulldozer in grams.

DISCUSSION

Does it make sense to use fractions or decimals when:
- *counting* items such as cars or people
- *measuring* quantities such as distances or mass?

ACTIVITY 4

Look at this recipe for scones.

What to do:

1 In a table like the one below:
- List all of the measurements given in the recipe.
- Describe what *type* of quantity is being measured in each case.

Measurement	Type of quantity

2 Discuss how each measurement would be done.

3 Which measurements do you think are most important to be done accurately?

Ingredients
80 g salted butter
3 cups of self-raising flour
$1\frac{1}{4}$ cups milk
5 tablespoons jam

Method
Preheat the oven to 200°C. Rub the butter into the flour. Add the milk then knead until smooth.
Pat the dough into a 2 cm thick layer. Use a 5 cm cutter to cut out 12 rounds. Place the rounds onto a tray, 1 cm apart. Bake for 20 minutes, then serve with the jam.

B   READING SCALES

Measuring devices usually have a **scale** marked on them.

We are all familiar with a **ruler** for measuring lengths. Rulers usually have a scale marked in both millimetres and centimetres.

Example 1   ◄)) Self Tutor

Read each length measurement:

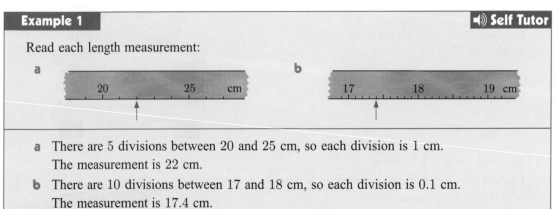

a There are 5 divisions between 20 and 25 cm, so each division is 1 cm.
The measurement is 22 cm.

b There are 10 divisions between 17 and 18 cm, so each division is 0.1 cm.
The measurement is 17.4 cm.

EXERCISE 8B

1 Read each length measurement in cm:

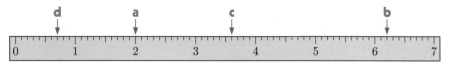

2 Read each length measurement:

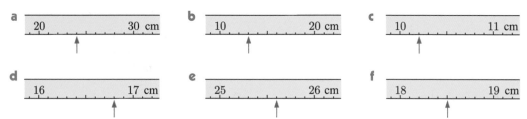

3 Read the temperature on each thermometer:

4 Read, as accurately as possible, the speed on each speedometer:

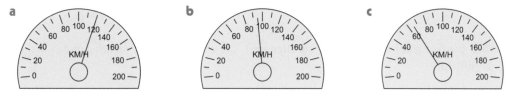

5 Read the mass, in kilograms, on each bathroom scale:

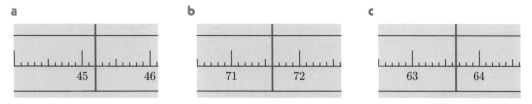

6 Read the amount of water in each jug:

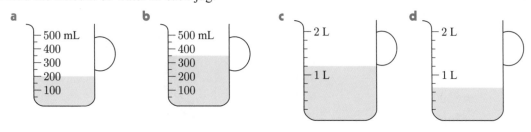

MASS

> The **mass** of an object is a measure of how heavy the object is.

The units of mass we use are:

- **milligrams** (mg)

  A house fly has mass about 10 mg.

- **grams** (g)

  A potato has mass about 150 g.

- **kilograms** (kg)

  A horse has mass about 550 kg.

- **tonnes** (t)

  A truck has mass about 3 t.

MASS CONVERSIONS

The units of mass are related as shown in the table:

$$1 \text{ t} = 1000 \text{ kg}$$
$$1 \text{ kg} = 1000 \text{ g}$$
$$1 \text{ g} = 1000 \text{ mg}$$

When we convert from one unit to a **smaller** unit, there will be more smaller units. We therefore need to **multiply**.

When we convert from one unit to a **larger** unit, there will be less larger units. We therefore need to **divide**.

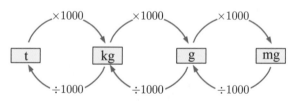

Example 2	◀)) **Self Tutor**

Write in kilograms:

a 8.5 t   **b** 350 g

a   8.5 t
$= 8.5 \times 1000$ kg
$= 8500$ kg

b   350 g
$= 350 \div 1000$ kg
$= 0.35$ kg

> To multiply by 1000, we move the decimal point 3 places to the right.
>
> To divide by 1000, we move the decimal point 3 places to the left.

EXERCISE 8C

1 State the units you would use to measure the mass of:

    a a sheep   **b** a ship   **c** a book

    d a banana   **e** a lounge suite   **f** a raindrop

    g your school lunch   **h** a baseball bat   **i** a refrigerator

    j a dinner plate   **k** a school ruler   **l** a bulldozer.

2 Match each object with the correct mass:

    a   **b**   **c**

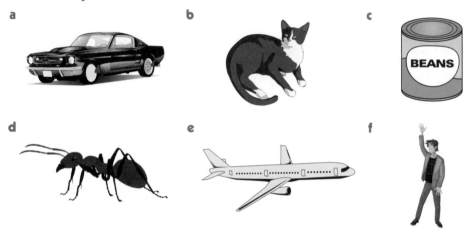

    d   **e**   **f**

    A 500 g   **B** 400 t   **C** 4 kg   **D** 1.6 t   **E** 5 mg   **F** 70 kg

3 Write in grams:

    a 8 kg   **b** 3.2 kg   **c** 380 mg   **d** 4250 mg

4 Write in kilograms:

    a 3.4 t   **b** 0.15 t   **c** 13 870 g   **d** 786 g

5 Convert:

    a 7 g into mg   **b** 3400 mg into g   **c** 860 g into kg

    d 12.4 kg into g   **e** 2.516 t into kg   **f** 4150 kg into t.

6 Ervin bought a 1.5 kg box of cereal and a 700 g box of cereal. Find the total mass of the cereal.

7 A block of chocolate has mass 120 g. Find the mass of 200 chocolate blocks, giving your answer in kilograms.

8 350 sandbags are used to stop floodwaters from reaching a school. Each sandbag has mass 20 kg. Find the total mass of the sandbags, giving your answer in tonnes.

9 There are 30 students in Jacqui's science class. Her teacher has placed a dish containing 4 g of purple powder on the front bench. Each student requires 110 mg of the powder for an experiment. Will there be enough powder?

10 A bale of lucerne hay has mass 14 kg.

   a A truck is loaded with 66 bales of hay. Find the mass of hay on the truck.

   b Is the truck carrying more or less than a tonne of hay?

11 A tree trunk with mass 3.2 tonnes is cut into 80 planks of equal size. Find, in kilograms, the mass of each plank.

12 An aeroplane takes off carrying 108 tonnes of fuel. During the flight, it burns 150 kg of fuel per minute.
How much fuel is the plane still carrying after 40 minutes?

ACTIVITY 5   NETT MASS

You may have noticed that many food packages use the word "nett" when describing the mass of their contents.

Nett mass is the mass of the contents, *not* including the mass of the container.

Gross mass is the total mass of the contents *and* the container.

The jam has mass 550 g.

The gross mass of the jam and the jar is 800 g.

So, the mass of the jar is   800 g − 550 g = 250 g.

What to do:

1 Collect some food items which are packed in cardboard, plastic, or glass. Record the nett mass stated on each container in a table like this:

Item	Nett mass	Gross mass	Mass of container

2 Measure the gross mass of each container with its contents.

3 Hence find the mass of each container.

4 Discuss why food packages state the nett mass rather than the gross mass.

GLOBAL CONTEXT   CALCULATING YOUR CARBON FOOTPRINT

Global context: Globalisation and sustainability

Statement of inquiry: Examining the resources we use helps us to measure our impact on the environment.

Criterion: Applying mathematics in real-life contexts

QUICK QUIZ

MULTIPLE CHOICE QUIZ

REVIEW SET 8A

1 Match each statement with the correct measurement:

  a The amount of juice in a bottle.   **A** 50 km/h

  b The time Billy slept last night.   **B** 4 m^3

  c The speed of a car.   **C** 7 hours

  d The volume of sand in a sand pit.   **D** 55°C

  e The temperature of a cup of coffee.   **E** 350 mL

2 Read these scales:

  a   **b**   **c**

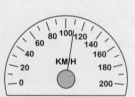

3 State the units you would use to measure the mass of:

  a a phone   **b** a bus   **c** a cupboard.

4 Write in kilograms:

  a 2.7 t   **b** 0.89 t   **c** 6230 g

5 My suitcase has mass 21.2 kg. Write this mass in:

  a grams   **b** tonnes.

6 A truck can carry 800 kg of soil. How many tonnes of soil can be carried in 25 truckloads?

7 A crane has mass 2.5 tonnes.

  a Write the mass of the crane in:

    i kilograms   **ii** grams   **iii** milligrams.

  b Explain why it is not sensible to use milligrams to describe the mass of a crane.

8 Answer the **Opening Problem** on page **152**.

REVIEW SET 8B

1 A swimming pool holds approximately 50 kL of water.
Explain why it would not be sensible to use kilolitres to describe the amount of water in a cup.

2 Read each measurement:

a

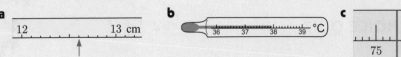

b   c

3 Match each object with the correct mass:

a   b   c

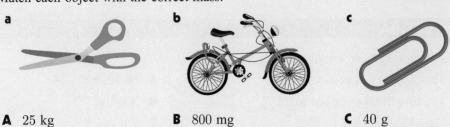

A 25 kg   **B** 800 mg   **C** 40 g

4 Convert:

    a 3200 g to kg   **b** 4.6 g to mg   **c** 0.7 t to kg.

5 Finn wants to send a book with mass 1.2 kg and a scarf with mass 500 g to his sister who lives interstate. Find the total mass of the items Finn will send.

6 How many 600 g cans of tomatoes can be made from 48 kg of tomatoes?

7 The mass of a cricket ball is shown on the scales alongside.

    a Find the mass of the cricket ball.

    b Find the mass, in kilograms, of a box containing 40 cricket balls.

    c A shipping van has a maximum load limit of 1.2 tonnes. How many boxes of cricket balls can be loaded into the van?

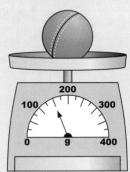

Chapter **9**

Measurement: Length

Contents:

OPENING PROBLEM

Byron is about to play a game of football on the pitch illustrated alongside. You may have a pitch like this at your school.

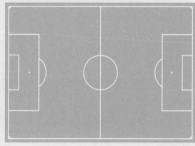

Scale: 1 represents 2000

Things to think about:

a What units would you use to measure the length of the field:

   i on the diagram   **ii** in real life?

b What does the statement "1 represents 2000" mean?

c How can you use this diagram to determine the actual dimensions of the pitch?

d How could you calculate the total distance around the boundary of the pitch?

A **length** is a measure of distance.

Lengths are used to express how far one object is from another.

For example:

   "I live 5 kilometres from school."

   "His ball is 150 metres from the hole."

   "Rule a margin 2 centimetres from the edge of the page."

A   UNITS OF LENGTH

DISCUSSION

The earliest units of length were related to parts of the body.

- We still talk about the **span** of your hand.
- A **cubit** was the length from your elbow to the tip of your fingers.
- A **yard** was the distance from your nose to your fingertip.

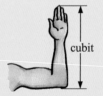

What disadvantages are there to using parts of the body to measure length?

The modern units of length we now use are:

- **millimetre** (mm)

  A coin is about 1 mm thick.

- **centimetre** (cm)

  A fingernail is about 1 cm wide.

- **metre** (m)

  A large dog is about 1 m tall.

- **kilometre** (km)

  $2\frac{1}{2}$ laps of an athletics track is 1 km.

  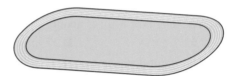

LENGTH CONVERSIONS

The units of length are related as shown in the table:

1 cm = 10 mm
1 m = 100 cm
1 km = 1000 m

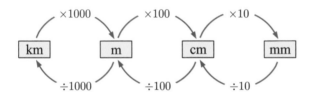

To convert larger units to smaller units we multiply. To convert smaller units to larger units we divide.

Example 1	◀) Self Tutor
Convert:	
a 2.1 cm into mm	**b** 5830 m into km.
a 2.1 cm = 2.1 × 10 mm	**b** 5830 m = 5830 ÷ 1000 km
= 21 mm	= 5.83 km

EXERCISE 9A

1   Write down the missing unit of length:

a

10 ......

b

54 ....

c
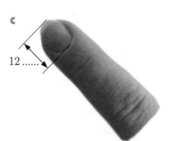
12 ......

d

84 ......

e

156 ......

f

5 ......

2 Choose the correct answer.

   a The length of a fly is about:

      A 7 cm   **B** 7 mm   **C** 7 m   **D** 7 km

   b The flight distance from Rome to Moscow is about:

      A 23 800 m   **B** 238 cm   **C** 23.8 mm   **D** 2380 km

   c The width of a public swimming pool is:

      A 200 m   **B** 200 cm   **C** 20 m   **D** 20 km

3 Use a ruler to find the length of each line. Give your answer in millimetres.

   a   **b**

   c

4 Convert:

   a 6 cm into mm   **b** 9.7 cm into mm   **c** 8 m into cm

   d 11.4 m into cm   **e** 2.08 m into cm   **f** 4 km into m

   g 0.7 km into m   **h** 5.26 km into m   **i** 13.145 km into m.

5 Convert:

   a 50 mm into cm   **b** 143 mm into cm   **c** 300 cm into m

   d 930 cm into m   **e** 76 cm into m   **f** 10 000 m into km

   g 21 900 m into km   **h** 4740 m into km   **i** 607 m into km.

6 **a** How many millimetres are there in a metre?

   b Convert:

      i 2 m into mm   **ii** 1.24 m into mm

      iii 1740 mm into m   **iv** 835 mm into m.

7 Jodie measured the length of a big black ant as 2.35 cm. Write this length in millimetres.

8 Peter's long jump distance was measured as 4.265 metres. Write this length in centimetres.

9 **a** Write each of these lengths in centimetres: 0.13 m, 7.8 cm, 95 mm, 0.08 m.

   b Hence write the lengths in order from shortest to longest.

ACTIVITY 1   STEP ESTIMATION

In Roman times, a **pace** was the length of two steps. There were 1000 paces in a Roman mile.

However, we know that the length of a step varies from one person to the next.

By knowing your own step length, you can estimate long distances with reasonable accuracy.

Consider this experiment:

> Seani set up two flags which she measured to be 100 metres apart. Using her usual walking step, she took $128\frac{1}{2}$ steps to walk between the flags.
>
> Seani calculated that $100 \text{ m} \div 128.5 \approx 0.78 \text{ m}$, so she concluded that her usual step length is about 0.78 m.
>
> When Seani walked to school, she took 2186 steps.
>
> Since $2186 \times 0.78 \approx 1705$, she estimated the distance from her house to her school is about 1705 metres.

What to do:

1 Use a long tape measure or trundle wheel to help place two flags exactly 100 metres apart.

2 Walk with your usual step from one flag to the other. Count the steps you take.

3 Using Seani's method and your calculator, calculate your usual step length. Round your answer to 2 decimal places.

4 Choose *three* suitable distances around the school to estimate. Use Seani's method to estimate them.

5 Compare your estimates with other students who estimated the same lengths.

B   OPERATIONS WITH LENGTHS

Before we can add or subtract two lengths, we need to write them with the *same units*.

DISCUSSION

Why is it important that the lengths are written with the same units?

EXERCISE 9B

1 Find the sum of these lengths:

   a 19 cm, 38 cm   **b** 6.4 m, 3.7 m

   c 450 mm, 210 mm, 600 mm   **d** 38.2 cm, 56.5 cm, 71.9 cm

2 By first writing each length in metres, find the sum of:

   a 3 km, 580 m   **b** 1 km, 38 m

   c 5 km, 674 m, 22 cm   **d** 48 m, 91 cm, 6 mm

Make sure you use the correct units.

3 To get to school, Katrina walks 600 m to the train station, travels 7 km by train, then travels by bus for 4.1 km.

Find the total distance travelled by Katrina in:

   a metres   **b** kilometres.

4 Zhen must climb 800 steps to reach the top of a lookout. Each step is 20 cm high. Find the height of the lookout in metres.

5 How many laps of a 50 m swimming pool must be completed in a 1.5 km race?

6 Joe is building this wooden cot frame for his baby's nursery. Each slat is 50 cm long.

   a Find the total length of timber required for the slats, in metres.

   b Find the total length of timber required for the posts and horizontal beams.

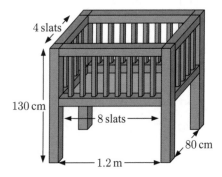

4 slats

130 cm

8 slats

80 cm

1.2 m

C   PERIMETER

The **perimeter** of a closed figure is the distance around its boundary.

For example, suppose you stood at one corner of this playground area, then walked around the boundary until you returned to your starting point.

The distance you have walked is the **perimeter** of the playground.

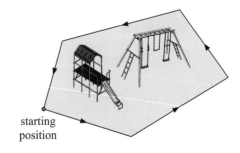

starting position

The perimeter of a polygon is found by adding the lengths of its sides.

Before you add the side lengths, make sure they are written with the *same units*.

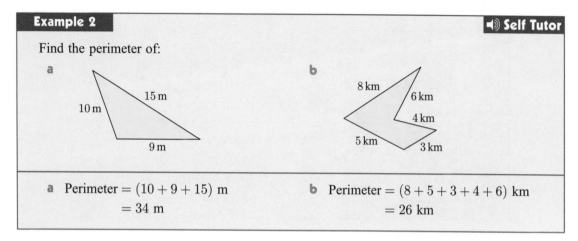

| **Example 2** | ◀》 **Self Tutor** |

Find the perimeter of:

a Perimeter $= (10 + 9 + 15)$ m
   $= 34$ m

b Perimeter $= (8 + 5 + 3 + 4 + 6)$ km
   $= 26$ km

EXERCISE 9C

1 Find the perimeter of:

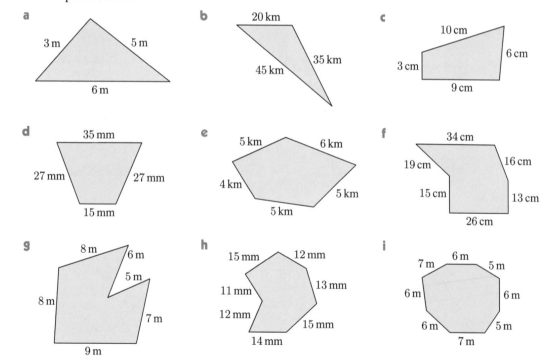

2 By first writing the side lengths in the same units, find the perimeter of each figure:

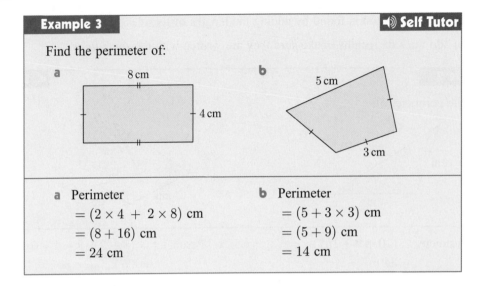

Example 3

◀)) **Self Tutor**

Find the perimeter of:

a

8 cm

4 cm

b

5 cm

3 cm

a Perimeter
$$= (2 \times 4 + 2 \times 8) \text{ cm}$$
$$= (8 + 16) \text{ cm}$$
$$= 24 \text{ cm}$$

b Perimeter
$$= (5 + 3 \times 3) \text{ cm}$$
$$= (5 + 9) \text{ cm}$$
$$= 14 \text{ cm}$$

3 Find the perimeter of each rectangle:

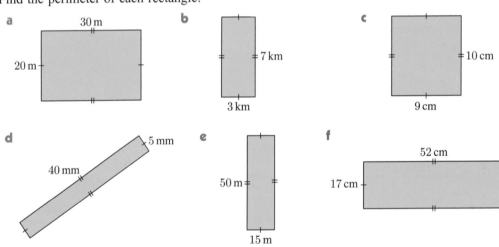

a 30 m, 20 m

b 7 km, 3 km

c 10 cm, 9 cm

d 5 mm, 40 mm

e 50 m, 15 m

f 52 cm, 17 cm

4 Find the perimeter of each figure:

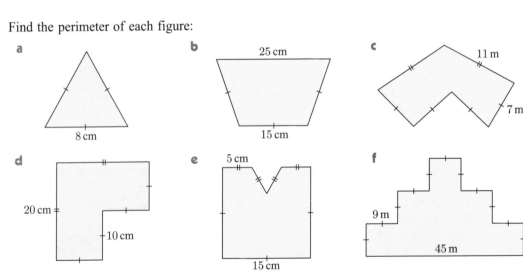

a 8 cm

b 25 cm, 15 cm

c 11 m, 7 m

d 20 cm, 10 cm

e 5 cm, 15 cm

f 9 m, 45 m

5 By first writing the side lengths in the same units, find the perimeter of each figure:

a

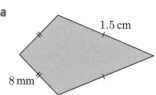
1.5 cm
8 mm

b

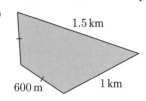
1.5 km
600 m   1 km

c

1.23 cm
8.4 mm

6 **a** Use a ruler to find the perimeter of each figure:

A

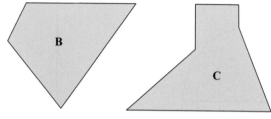

B   C

b Which figure has the longest perimeter?

7 Find the length of the fence around:

a a 120 m by 260 m rectangular paddock

b an 18 m by 9.5 m house block.

8 Martine has a rectangular tablecloth with the dimensions shown. She wants to sew lace trim along its border.

a Find the length of the lace required.

b The lace costs $4.65 per metre. Find the total cost of the lace Martine needs.

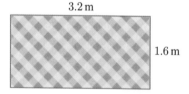
3.2 m
1.6 m

9 A city block has the given dimensions.

a If I run one lap of the block, how far do I run?

b Find the total distance that I would run in 5 laps.

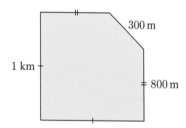
300 m
1 km
800 m

10 Find the length of each side of:

a an equilateral triangle with perimeter 27 cm

b a square with perimeter 49.2 cm.

11 When two identical regular octagons are joined exactly on one side, the perimeter of the resulting figure is 98 cm.

What was the perimeter of each original octagon?

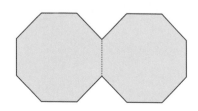

ACTIVITY 2

What to do:

Use a piece of string to estimate, as accurately as possible, the perimeter of:

PRINTABLE DIAGRAMS   **VIDEO DEMO**

a   b   c

D   SCALE DIAGRAMS

A **scale diagram** is a drawing which is smaller than the original, in which all lengths of the original are divided by the same **scale factor**.

We say that the sides are *in proportion* with the original.

The scale factor is recorded with the diagram in a **scale**.

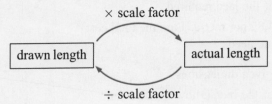

This house plan is a scale diagram.

The scale "1 represents 200" tells us the scale factor is 200.

Lengths on the scale diagram are 200 times longer in reality.

For example, since the house plan is 5 cm wide, the actual width of the house is   5 cm × 200 = 1000 cm

= 10 m.

Scale: 1 represents 200

Example 4 ◀) **Self Tutor**

On a scale diagram, the scale is "1 represents 20". Find:
a the actual length if the drawn length is 3.4 cm
b the drawn length if the actual length is 2.4 m.

To find the actual length, we **multiply** the drawn length by the scale factor.

To find the drawn length, we **divide** the actual length by the scale factor.

a actual length = drawn length × scale factor
$$= 3.4 \text{ cm} \times 20$$
$$= 68 \text{ cm}$$

b drawn length = actual length ÷ scale factor
$$= 2.4 \text{ m} \div 20$$
$$= 240 \text{ cm} \div 20$$
$$= 24 \text{ cm} \div 2$$
$$= 12 \text{ cm}$$

EXERCISE 9D

1 The scale on a diagram is "1 represents 200".
  a Find the actual length if the drawn length is:
    i 3 cm   **ii** 7 cm   **iii** 8.2 cm   **iv** 0.8 cm
  b Find the drawn length if the actual length is:
    i 200 m   **ii** 18 m   **iii** 70 m   **iv** 124 m

2 The scale on a diagram is "1 represents 5000".
  a Find the actual length if the drawn length is:
    i 4 cm   **ii** 6 cm   **iii** 1.2 cm   **iv** 0.7 cm
  b Find the drawn length if the actual length is:
    i 500 m   **ii** 300 m   **iii** 450 m   **iv** 950 m

3 The drawing of the truck has the scale "1 represents 100". Find:
  a the actual length of the truck
  b the maximum height of the truck.

4

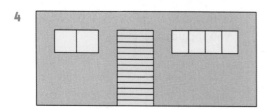

This plan of a factory wall has been drawn with the scale "1 represents 200". Find the actual:
  a length of the wall
  b height of the wall
  c measurements of the door
  d measurements of the windows.

5 Match each diagram with the correct scale:

a

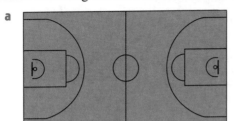

b

c

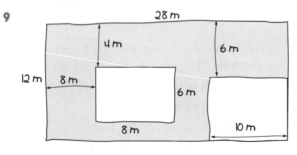

d

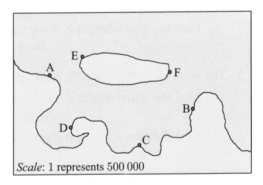

A "1 represents 30"   **B** "1 represents 400"

C "1 represents 125 000"   **D** "1 represents 30 000 000"

6 **a** Find the actual distance represented by 1 cm on this map.

  b Find the actual distance from:
    i A to B   **ii** D to E
   iii C to F.

Scale: 1 represents 500 000

7 A scale diagram of a building is drawn using the scale "1 represents 50". If the building is 10 m high, how high will the building appear on the diagram?

8 The rectangular park outside Kerri's house is 80 m long and 60 m wide. Use the scale "1 represents 2000" to draw a scale diagram of the park. Make sure you include the scale.

9

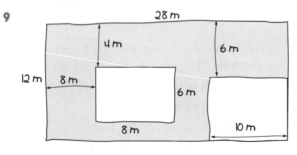

Use the measurements on this rough sketch to draw an accurate scale diagram with scale "1 represents 400". Make sure you include the scale.

10 Use the measurements on this sketch to draw an accurate scale diagram with scale "1 represents 60". Make sure you include the scale.

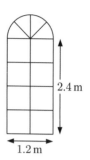

2.4 m

1.2 m

11 Find the scale if:

   a an aeroplane has wingspan 50 m and on its scale diagram it is 5 cm

   b a truck is 15 m long and on its scale diagram it has length 12 cm.

12 Look at this scale diagram of a garden. The actual distance between the tap and the bird bath is 6 m.

   a Find the scale for the map.

   b Which two trees are 4 m apart?

   c Find the distance between the dog kennel and the apple tree.

   d Find the dimensions of the garden shed.

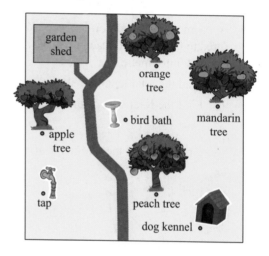

MULTIPLE CHOICE QUIZ

QUICK QUIZ

REVIEW SET 9A

1 Write down the missing unit of length:

   a

80 ....

   b

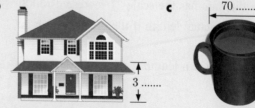

3 ....

   c

70 ....

2 Convert:

   a 356 cm into m

   b 450 m into km

   c 7.63 m into mm.

3 A house brick is 23 cm long. Find the total length of 8 bricks laid end to end. Give your answer in metres.

4 By first writing each length in metres, find the sum of:

  a 6 km and 207 m

  b 9 m, 38 cm, and 4 mm

5 Find the perimeter of:

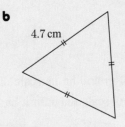

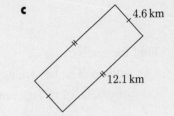

6 A room with this floorplan needs skirting board fitted to the bottom of each wall. The skirting board costs $20 per metre.

  a Find the total length of skirting board required.

  b Find the total cost of the skirting board.

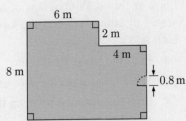

7 Use a ruler to find the perimeter of each figure:

  a

  b

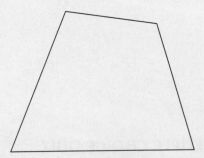

8 A farmer fences a 250 m by 400 m rectangular paddock with a 3 strand wire fence.

  a Find the perimeter of the paddock.

  b Find the total length of wire needed.

  c The wire costs $2.40 per metre. Find the total cost of the wire.

9 A scale diagram has the scale "1 represents 5000".

  a Find the actual length if the drawn length is:

    i 3 cm   **ii** 6.4 cm

  b Find the drawn length if the actual length is:

    i 500 m   **ii** 200 m

10 A boat is 30 m long, and on its scale diagram it has length 15 cm. Find the scale for the scale diagram.

11 Answer the **Opening Problem** on page **164**.

REVIEW SET 9B

1 Use a ruler to find the length of each line, giving your answer in centimetres.

    a _____   **b** _____

2 Convert:

    a 8.1 km into m   **b** 595 mm into cm   **c** 4060 mm into m.

3 Write these lengths in order from smallest to largest:

    423 mm,   21 cm,   0.35 m,   47.1 mm.

4 A rabbit travels 30 cm with each jump. How many jumps are needed for the rabbit to travel 15 m?

5 Find the perimeter of each figure:

    a 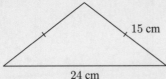   **b**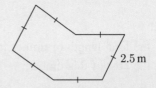

6 A regular pentagon has perimeter 60 cm. Find the length of each side of the pentagon.

7 The roof of Paul's house is shown alongside. Gutters need to be installed around the edge of the roof. Find the length of gutters required.

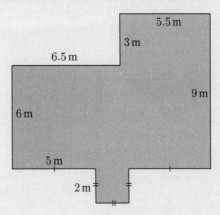

8 Use a ruler to find the perimeter of each figure:

    a 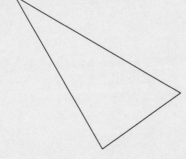   **b**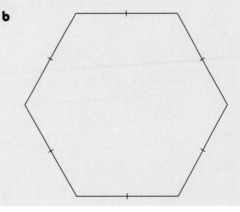

9 This scale diagram of a tennis court has the scale "1 represents 400". Find the actual length of:

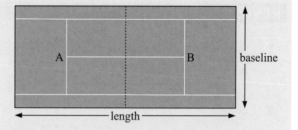

a the court

b the centre service line [AB]

c the baseline.

10 A 2.3 cm line on a scale diagram represents an actual length of 460 m. What is the scale?

11 Jeff's bedroom is 3.5 m long and 3 m wide. Use the scale "1 represents 100" to draw a scale diagram of the bedroom.

12 A builder needs to construct a pergola with the dimensions shown. The support posts cost $15 per metre, and the timber for the top costs $4.50 per metre.

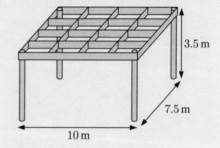

a Find:

  i the total length of timber for the top

  ii the cost of this timber.

b Find the cost of the posts.

c The cost of nails and other extra materials is $27. Find the total cost of building the pergola.

Chapter **10**

Measurement: Area, volume, and capacity

Contents:

OPENING PROBLEM

Peter is building a raised garden bed for his son's primary school. The garden bed will be 4 m long, 2 m wide, and 0.3 m high.

Things to think about:

a What *area* of weed mat is needed to cover the base of the garden bed?

b What *volume* of soil is needed to fill the garden bed?

c Peter buys soil in bags with *capacity* 20 litres. How many bags of soil will Peter need to fill the garden bed?

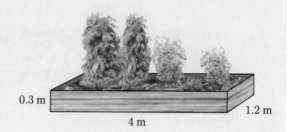

A   AREA

When we talk about how large a shape is, we are usually interested in how much *surface* it covers.

Area is a measurement of the size of a surface.

DISCUSSION

- Why might you want to measure the area of:
  ▸ a classroom floor   ▸ the walls of a room?
- What areas do these people need to measure?
  ▸ a tiler   ▸ a dressmaker   ▸ a glazier

ACTIVITY 1   SQUARE UNITS

One way to measure an area is to cover it with identical shapes and then count them.

Since it is easy to place identical squares together with no gaps between them, a **square unit** can be used to measure area. We write a square unit as 1 unit^2. ← 1 unit^2

What to do:

1 Find the area of each shape in square units:

a   **b**   **c**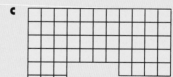

d    **e** 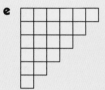   **f**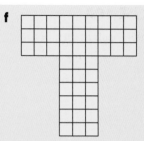

2 Which of the shapes in **1** has the:
  a largest area   **b** smallest area?

3 Use 20 square units to construct:
  a a rectangle   **b** a hexagon   **c** a decagon
  d a polygon with as many sides as possible.

4 **a** What other *regular* shapes can be placed together with no gaps between them?
   b Why do you think the square was chosen to be the unit for measuring area?

In **Chapter 9** we used **millimetres**, **centimetres**, **metres**, and **kilometres** to measure length.

We use these units of length as a basis for commonly used square units of area.

1 square millimetre (mm²) is the area enclosed by a square of side length 1 mm.

□ ◀——— 1 mm²

1 square centimetre (cm²) is the area enclosed by a square of side length 1 cm.

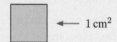

◀— 1 cm²

1 square metre (m²) is the area enclosed by a square of side length 1 m.

1 square kilometre (km²) is the area enclosed by a square of side length 1 km.

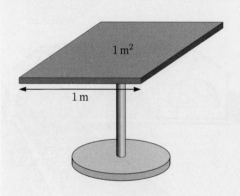

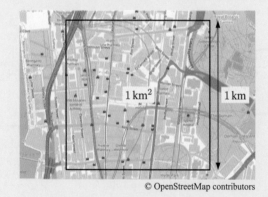

© OpenStreetMap contributors

EXERCISE 10A

1 Match each description with the correct area:

a	a picnic rug	**A**	0.8 km²
b	a sports stadium	**B**	100 cm²
c	New Zealand	**C**	5 m²
d	a drink coaster	**D**	7.5 cm²
e	this dot ●	**E**	600 m²
f	a golf course	**F**	7 mm²
g	a suburban park	**G**	268 000 km²
h	a coin	**H**	20 000 m²

2 Each of the squares in these shapes has area 1 square centimetre. Count the squares to find the area of each shape.

a 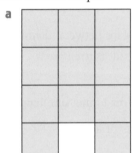   b 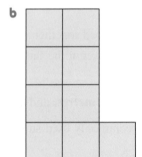   c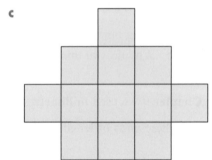

3 The diagram shows Christine's kitchen.

  a How many tiles have been used?

  b 20 tiles cover an area of one square metre. How many square metres of tiles are there in Christine's kitchen?

  c The tiles cost $44 per square metre. Find the total cost of the tiles.

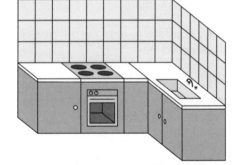

4 Look at the picture. The brick pavers in the courtyard are identical to those in the driveway.

  a How many pavers have been used for:

    i the driveway   **ii** the courtyard?

  b 50 pavers cover an area of one square metre. How many square metres of paving are there in total?

  c The pavers cost $32 per m², and the cost of laying them was $28 per m². Find the total cost of the paving.

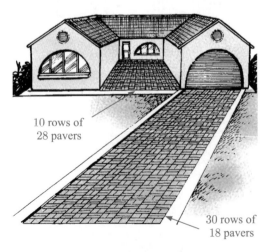

10 rows of 28 pavers

30 rows of 18 pavers

5 Each of the small squares in these shapes has area 1 square millimetre. Find the area of each shape.

a

b

c

d

DISCUSSION

When you found the areas of the shapes in question **5**, did you count each individual square?

Is there a quicker way to find the area of each shape?

B   THE AREA OF A RECTANGLE

Consider a rectangle 6 units long and 4 units wide.

The area of this rectangle is 24 units², and we can find this by multiplying $6 \times 4 = 24$.

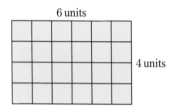

In general, the area of a rectangle is given by the rule:

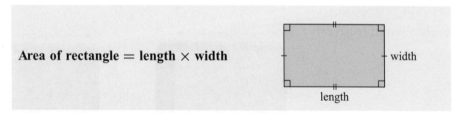

Area of rectangle = length × width

Example 1   ◀)) Self Tutor

Find the area of each rectangle:

a

5 cm

8 cm

b

16.3 m

42 m

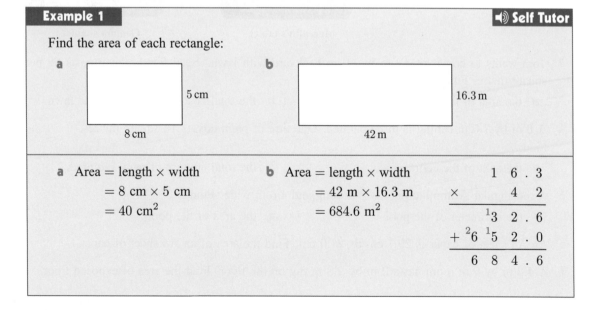

a   Area = length × width
      = 8 cm × 5 cm
      = 40 cm²

b   Area = length × width
      = 42 m × 16.3 m
      = 684.6 m²

$$
\begin{array}{r}
1\ 6\ .\ 3 \\
\times \qquad 4\ \ 2 \\
\hline
{}^{1}3\ \ 2\ .\ 6 \\
+\ {}^{2}6\ {}^{1}5\ 2\ .\ 0 \\
\hline
6\ 8\ 4\ .\ 6
\end{array}
$$

EXERCISE 10B

1 Find the area of each rectangle. Make sure you answer with the correct units.

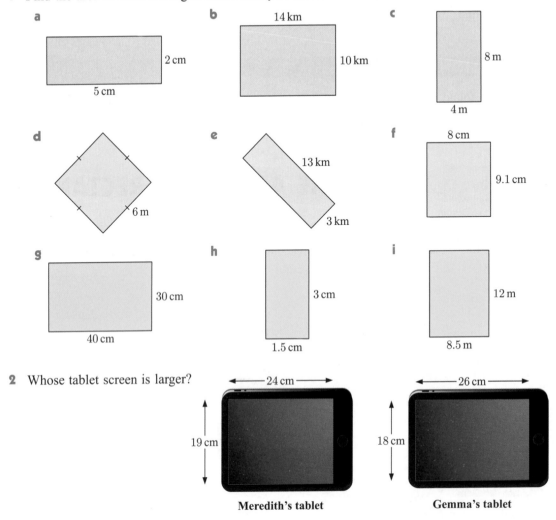

a

2 cm

5 cm

b

14 km

10 km

c

8 m

4 m

d

6 m

e

13 km

3 km

f

8 cm

9.1 cm

g

30 cm

40 cm

h

3 cm

1.5 cm

i

12 m

8.5 m

2 Whose tablet screen is larger?

24 cm

19 cm

Meredith's tablet

26 cm

18 cm

Gemma's tablet

3 Tom wants to cover his 12 m by 10 m backyard with lawn. Seed for the lawn costs $8 per square metre. Find:

   a the area of the lawn   **b** the total cost of the seed for the lawn.

4 A 6 m by 7.5 m ceiling is to be painted. One litre of paint covers 15 square metres. Find:

   a the area of the ceiling   **b** the total amount of paint required.

5 A rectangular swimming pool is 8 m long and 4.6 m wide. Find:

   a the perimeter of the pool   **b** the area of the pool.

6 An A4 sheet of paper is 29.7 cm by 21.0 cm. Find the area of an A4 sheet of paper.

7 A 4.8 m by 6 m room has a 2 m by 2.8 m rug on the floor. Find the area of exposed floor.

8

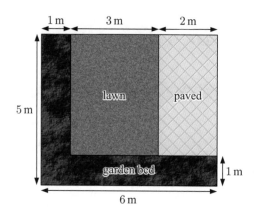

A backyard has the design shown.

Find the area of the:

  a   whole backyard

  b   paved section

  c   lawn

  d   garden bed.

9   The base of Ted's shower is 1.2 m long and 90 cm wide. It is to be covered with tiles which are 6 cm long and 5 cm wide.

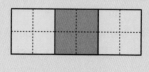

When finding areas, each measurement must be in the same units.

  a   Find the area of the shower base in square centimetres.

  b   Find the area of each tile.

  c   How many tiles are required?

PUZZLE

It is easy to put squares of *equal size* together to form a rectangle. For example, in this diagram three 2×2 squares are put together to form a 6×2 rectangle.

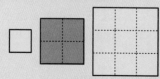

It is much harder to form a rectangle if the squares have different sizes! For example, it is impossible to form a rectangle using the 1×1 square, 2×2 square, and 3×3 square opposite.

In 1925, Polish mathematician **Zbigniew Moroń** discovered that one of each of the squares 1×1, 4×4, 7×7, 8×8, 9×9, 10×10, 14×14, 15×15, and 18×18 can be used to form a rectangle.

What to do:

1   Use grid paper to draw squares with the sizes given above, or click on the icon and print the squares.

SQUARES

2   Cut out the squares, and arrange them to form a rectangle.

    Hint: The total area of the squares can help you work out the dimensions of the rectangle.

C   THE AREA OF A TRIANGLE

INVESTIGATION 1   THE AREA OF A TRIANGLE

You will need: scissors, ruler, pencil, graph paper.

GRAPH PAPER

What to do:

1   **a**   Draw a large rectangle using the grid on the graph paper.

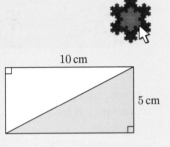

   b   Draw one diagonal, then colour one of the triangles green.

   c   Cut out the two triangles, then arrange them on top of each other so you can see they have the same shape.

   d   Copy and complete:

   The areas of the two triangles are ....

   The area of each triangle is ...... the area of the rectangle.

2   **a**   Draw another large rectangle using the graph paper.

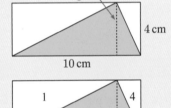

   b   Select a point where the top boundary meets a vertical grid line. Use it to draw triangles as shown.

   c   Colour in the pink triangle.

   d   Now divide the pink triangle along the grid line so you form four regions in total.

   e   Using what you found in **1**, copy and complete:

   The areas of regions 1 and 2 are ......

   The areas of regions 3 and 4 are ......

   So,   area 2 + area 3 = area 1 + area 4.

   The total area of the pink triangle is ...... the area of the rectangle.

From the **Investigation** you should have found that the area of a triangle is half the area of a rectangle which has the *same base and height* as the triangle.

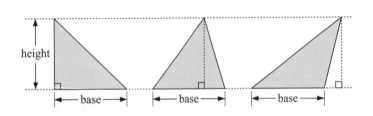

Even though they have different shapes, these triangles have the same base and height. They therefore have the same area.

DEMO

$$\text{Area of triangle} = \tfrac{1}{2} \times \text{base} \times \text{height}$$

Example 2   ◀) **Self Tutor**

Find the area of each triangle:

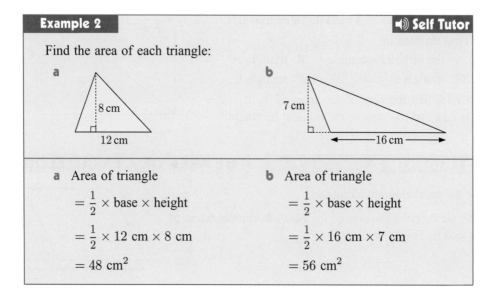

a Area of triangle

$= \frac{1}{2} \times$ base $\times$ height

$= \frac{1}{2} \times 12$ cm $\times 8$ cm

$= 48$ cm^2

b Area of triangle

$= \frac{1}{2} \times$ base $\times$ height

$= \frac{1}{2} \times 16$ cm $\times 7$ cm

$= 56$ cm^2

EXERCISE 10C

1 Find the area of each triangle:

a
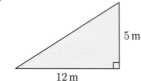

b
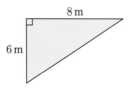

c

d
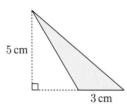

e
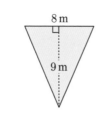

f
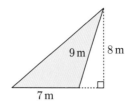

g
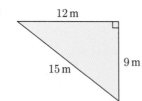

h
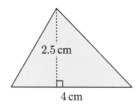

i
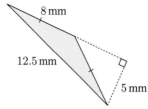

2 Alice is buying five identical shade sails with the dimensions shown. The shadecloth costs \$28 per m^2.

a Find the total area of shadecloth.

b Find the total cost of the shadecloth.

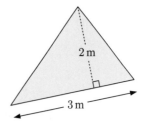

3 A rectangular tarpaulin is cut into three triangles.

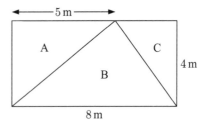

   a Find the area of:

      i the original rectangle   **ii** triangle A

      iii triangle B   **iv** triangle C.

   b Check that the sum of the areas of the triangles is equal to the area of the original rectangle.

INVESTIGATION 2   THE AREA OF A PARALLELOGRAM

Look at the parallelogram alongside.

How can we describe the area of the parallelogram in terms of its base and its height?

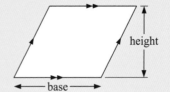

What to do:

1 **a** Using your ruler, carefully draw a large parallelogram on a piece of paper. It is important that the sides are parallel.

   b Cut out a triangle from one end of the parallelogram as shown.

      Use the two pieces to form a rectangle.

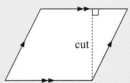

   c Hence explain why the area of the parallelogram is equal to the length of its base times its height.

2 Find the area of each parallelogram:

  a

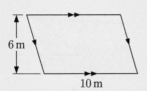

  b

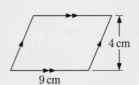

  c

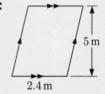

D   VOLUME

The stone occupies more space than the pebble.

We say that the stone has greater *volume* than the pebble.

stone   pebble

The **volume** of a solid is the amount of space it occupies.

As with area, the units of volume are related to the units of length.

> **1 cubic millimetre** (mm^3) is the volume of a cube with side length 1 mm.
>
> **1 cubic centimetre** (cm^3) is the volume of a cube with side length 1 cm.
>
> **1 cubic metre** (m^3) is the volume of a cube with side length 1 m.

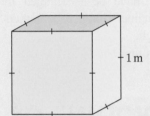

EXERCISE 10D

1 Each of the cubes in these solids has volume 1 cm^3. Count the cubes to find the volume of each solid.

  a

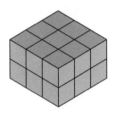

  b

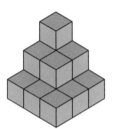

  c

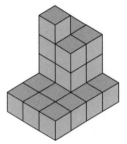

2 Each of the cubes in these solids has volume 1 cm^3. Write down the solids in order of volume, from lowest to highest.

  A

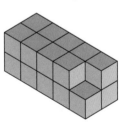

  B

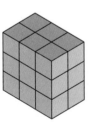

  C

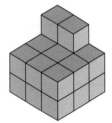

3 Using cubes with volume 1 cm^3, sketch a solid with volume:

  a 7 cm^3 **b** 12 cm^3 **c** 20 cm^3

4 The volume of a telephone box is about:

  A 2 cm^3 **B** 200 cm^3 **C** 2 m^3 **D** 20 m^3

5 The volume of a die is about:

   A 2 mm^3 **B** 2 cm^3 **C** 20 cm^3 **D** 2 m^3

6 Cubic containers of volume 1 m^3 are stored in a warehouse.

The containers have been arranged into a stack which is 4 containers long, 3 containers wide, and 2 containers high.

Find the total volume of the containers.

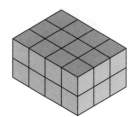

E   THE VOLUME OF A RECTANGULAR PRISM

INVESTIGATION 3   THE VOLUME OF A RECTANGULAR PRISM

In this Investigation we will discover a quick way to find the volume of a rectangular prism or box.

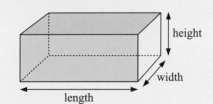

What to do:

1 Find the volume of each rectangular prism in the table below by counting the number of cubes.

Use the length, width, and height of each rectangular prism to complete the table.

Rectangular prism	Volume	Length	Width	Height	Length × Width × Height

2 Copy and complete: "The volume of a rectangular prism = ..."

From the **Investigation**, you should have discovered that:

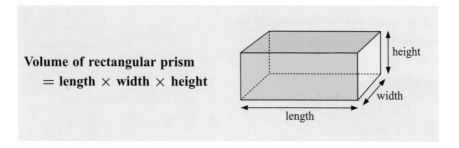

Volume of rectangular prism
= length × width × height

Example 3	◄)) **Self Tutor**

Find the volume of this rectangular prism.

Volume = length × width × height
= 10 cm × 5 cm × 4 cm
= 200 cm^3

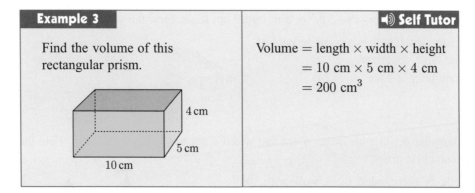

EXERCISE 10E

1 Find the volume of each rectangular prism:

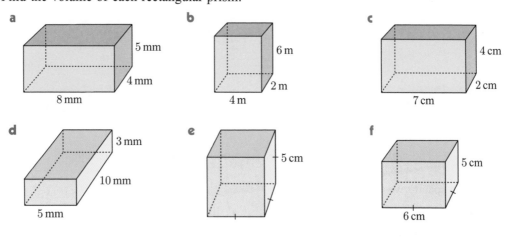

a 8 mm, 4 mm, 5 mm

b 4 m, 2 m, 6 m

c 7 cm, 2 cm, 4 cm

d 5 mm, 10 mm, 3 mm

e 5 cm

f 6 cm, 5 cm

2 Estimate the volume of this eraser.

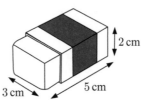

2 cm, 5 cm, 3 cm

3 A shoe box is 30 cm long, 16 cm wide, and 10 cm high. Find the volume of air inside the shoe box.

4 This rectangular prism has volume 36 cm³.
Show that there are exactly 8 different rectangular prisms with whole number sides and with volume 36 cm³.
You do not need to draw them.

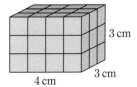

5

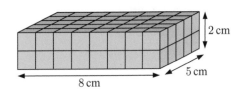

Find:

a the volume of this prism

b the sum of the areas of its six faces.

6 An industrial vat measures 2 m by 3 m by 80 cm high. Find the volume of the vat.

7 How many small pink boxes can be packed into the large container?
Illustrate your answer.

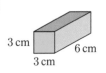

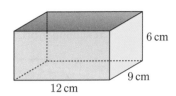

8 A rectangular prism with length 4 cm and width 5 cm has volume 120 cm³. Find the height of the rectangular prism.

9 A castle is surrounded by a wall with the dimensions shown. The wall is 1 m thick and 5 m high. The wall is broken only by a set of gates 5 m wide. Find the total volume of the wall.

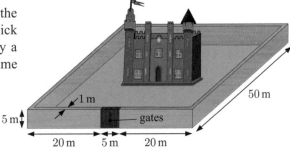

F   CAPACITY

The **capacity** of a container is the amount of fluid it can contain.

The units of capacity we use are:

- **millilitre** (mL)
  We would measure the capacity of a medicine glass in millilitres.

40 mL

- **litre** (L)
  We would measure the capacity of a milk carton in litres.

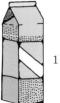

1 L

- **kilolitre** (kL)

  We would measure the capacity of an outdoor spa in kilolitres.

  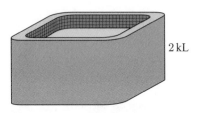

- **megalitre** (ML)

  We would measure the capacity of a lake in megalitres.

The units of capacity are related as follows:

1 L = 1000 mL
1 kL = 1000 L
1 ML = 1000 kL

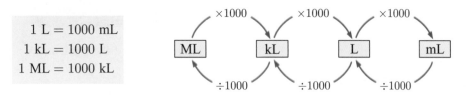

Example 4   ◀)) **Self Tutor**

Convert:

    a 8 L into mL   b 12 400 L into kL

   a   8 L   b   12 400 L

       $= 8 \times 1000$ mL $= 12\,400 \div 1000$ kL

       $= 8000$ mL $= 12.4$ kL

EXERCISE 10F

1 State the units you would use for measuring the capacity of:

    a   a perfume bottle   b   a vacuum flask

    c   an Olympic swimming pool   d   a drinking glass

    e   a water tank   f   a reservoir

    g   a baby's bottle   h   a bucket.

2 Convert:

    a   7 L into mL   b   5.6 kL into L   c   8.51 ML into kL

    d   3540 mL into L   e   760 000 L into kL   f   124 kL into ML

3 A soft drink can has capacity 375 mL. How many litres of soft drink are in a carton containing 24 cans?

4 A household used 6.3 kL of water during April. On average, how many litres of water did the household use each day?

MULTIPLE CHOICE QUIZ

REVIEW SET 10A

1 The area of a credit card is about:

A 4 cm^2 **B** 40 mm^2 **C** 4 m^3

D 4 mm^2 **E** 40 cm^2

2 A rectangular garden is 6 m long and 4.5 m wide. Find the area of the garden.

3 Find the area of each polygon:

a

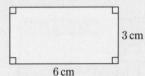

3 cm

6 cm

b

4 cm

5 cm

c

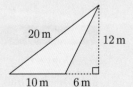

20 m   12 m

10 m   6 m

4 A postage stamp is 3 cm long and 2 cm wide.

a Find the area of the stamp.

b How many of these stamps can fit on a 20 cm by 30 cm sheet?

5 Each of the cubes in these solids has volume 1 cm^3. Count the cubes to find the volume of each solid.

a

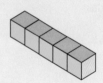

b

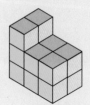

c

6 A yachting line will have 30 flags attached to it with the dimensions shown. Find the area of material required to make the flags on the line.

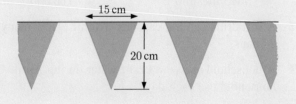

15 cm

20 cm

7 Find the volume of each rectangular prism:

a

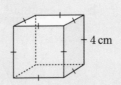

4 cm

10 cm

8 cm

b

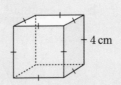

4 cm

c

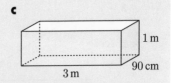

1 m

3 m

90 cm

8 How many 10 cm × 6 cm × 10 cm boxes can fit into a container with dimensions 60 cm × 60 cm × 60 cm?

9 Wendy bought three 1.25 L bottles and two 600 mL bottles of soft drink for a party. How many litres of soft drink did she buy in total?

10 An ice cream container is 10 cm long, 8 cm wide, and 9 cm high.

   a Find the area of the base of the container.

   b Find the volume of the container.

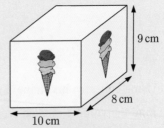

9 cm

8 cm

10 cm

11 This large rectangle has been divided into three smaller rectangles.

   a Find the area of:

   i the large rectangle

   ii the red rectangle

   iii the green rectangle

   iv the yellow rectangle.

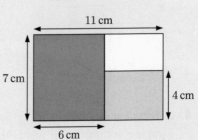

11 cm

7 cm

4 cm

6 cm

   b Check that the sum of the areas of the smaller rectangles is equal to the area of the large rectangle.

REVIEW SET 10B

1 Suggest suitable units for measuring the area of:

   a a volleyball court

   b China.

2 A billiard table has the dimensions shown.
The cloth which covers the table costs $90 per square metre.
Find the cost of covering the table.

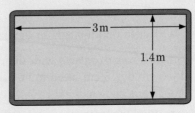

3 m

1.4 m

3 Which rectangle has the largest area?

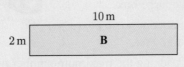

3 m

A

6 m

10 m

2 m

B

C

4 m

4 Find the area of each triangle:

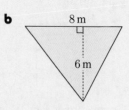 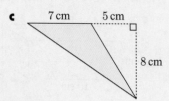

a 3 cm 5 cm

b 8 m 6 m

c 7 cm 5 cm 8 cm

5 Show that the total area of the red triangles is equal to the total area of the green triangles.

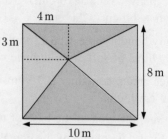

4 m
3 m
8 m
10 m

6 Using cubes with volume 1 cm³, sketch a solid with volume 15 cm³.

7 Find the volume of each rectangular prism:

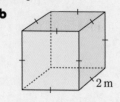 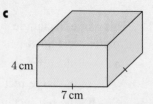

a 5 mm 8 mm 3 mm

b 2 m

c 4 cm 7 cm

8 A rectangular garden shed is 5 m long, 4 m wide, and 4.5 m high. Find the volume of air inside the shed.

9 Convert:

   a 12.4 L into mL

   b 765 kL into ML

10 A lawnmower petrol tank holds 2.5 L of fuel. Rob fills the tank, then uses 850 mL of petrol mowing his lawn. How much petrol is left in the tank?

11 This parallelogram has base 10 cm and height 6 cm.

   a Find the area of:

   i the red triangle

   ii the green triangle.

   b Hence find the area of the parallelogram.

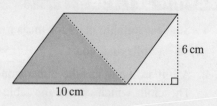

6 cm
10 cm

12 Small boxes of raisins with dimensions 5 cm by 6 cm by 15 cm, need to be packed into the larger box shown.

   a Find the volume of each raisin box.

   b Find the volume of the large box.

   c Find the maximum number of raisin boxes that will fit into the large box.

   d Illustrate a method of packing the maximum number of raisin boxes into the large box.

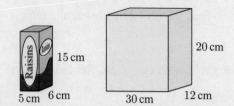

Raisins
15 cm
5 cm 6 cm

20 cm
30 cm 12 cm

Chapter 11

Time

Contents:

OPENING PROBLEM

Eight teams are competing in a junior soccer carnival.

This timetable shows the games which are to be played. Each game lasts 60 minutes.

Time	Field 1	Field 2	Field 3
8:00	1 v 2	3 v 4	5 v 6
9:15	1 v 5	2 v 7	3 v 8
10:30	3 v 5	4 v 8	6 v 7
11:45	2 v 6	1 v 7	4 v 5
13:00	3 v 6	4 v 7	1 v 8
14:15	2 v 8		

Things to think about:

a At what time does the carnival start?

b At what time does Team 4 play Team 8?

c What does the time 13:00 mean?

d What is the time difference between Team 2 starting their first game, and finishing their last game?

Time plays an important role in our everyday lives.

Understanding time allows us to answer questions such as:

- At what time does school start?
- How long will it take us to fly to Tokyo?
- When are the holidays?
- When did the Second World War start?

DISCUSSION

In small groups discuss the following topics:

1 How would the following groups be aware of time changes?

    a animals in the wild   **b** domestic animals   **c** human infants

    d farmers   **e** sailors at sea 300 years ago

2 What problems would people in the past have had in measuring time using:

    a candles   **b** sundials

    c sand-glasses   **d** pendulum clocks

    e mechanical clocks?

3 List 10 occupations where time or timing is very important, such as musicians and restaurant chefs. For each occupation, describe the consequences of wrong timing.

 A

TIME LINES

Time lines are simple graphs which tell us when important events have occurred.

In the Gregorian calendar used in most of the world, the terms *before Christ* (BC) and *anno Domini* (AD) are used with the numbers of the years.

The years BC count *down* to 1 BC. Then, instead of a year "zero", the year AD 1 immediately followed 1 BC.

The AD years count forwards. We usually write them without the AD.

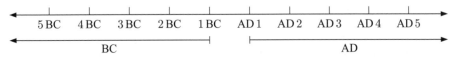

HISTORICAL NOTE

The BC and AD system was invented in 525 by the 6th century monk **Dionysius Exiguus** (470 - 544) in Scythia Minor (present day Romania).

Today, the BC and AD system is used all around the world, even in non-Christian countries. However, since *anno Domini* is short for a Latin phrase that translates to "in the year of our Lord", *Before Common Era* (BCE) and *Common Era* (CE) have been introduced as non-religious alternatives.

Example 1   ◄)) Self Tutor

This time line shows the years in which important events in Sarah's life occurred:

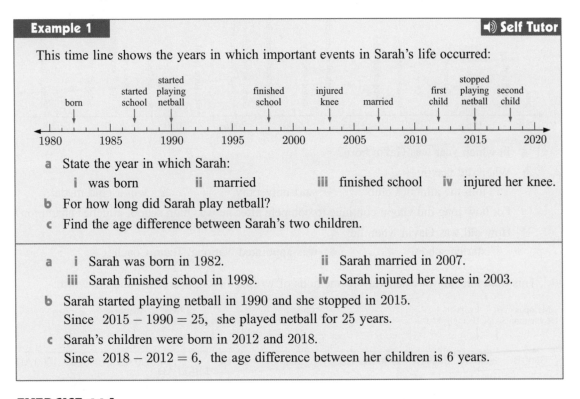

a State the year in which Sarah:
  i was born   ii married   iii finished school   iv injured her knee.
b For how long did Sarah play netball?
c Find the age difference between Sarah's two children.

a i Sarah was born in 1982.   ii Sarah married in 2007.
  iii Sarah finished school in 1998.   iv Sarah injured her knee in 2003.
b Sarah started playing netball in 1990 and she stopped in 2015.
  Since $2015 - 1990 = 25$, she played netball for 25 years.
c Sarah's children were born in 2012 and 2018.
  Since $2018 - 2012 = 6$, the age difference between her children is 6 years.

EXERCISE 11A

1 This time line shows the monarchs of England during the 20th century:

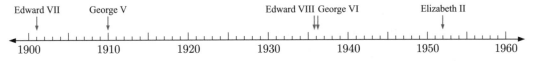

  a When did the reign of George V begin?
  b Which monarch reigned immediately after George VI?
  c How long did the reign of Edward VII last?

2 This time line shows the French Presidents since 1975:

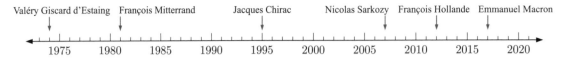

a In which year did François Hollande become President?

b Who was President in 1980?

c For how long was Nicolas Sarkozy President?

d Who was President for longer, François Mitterrand or Jacques Chirac?

e How long was there between the presidencies of Jacques Chirac and Emmanuel Macron?

3 The following time line shows the years in which important events in Gavin's life occurred:

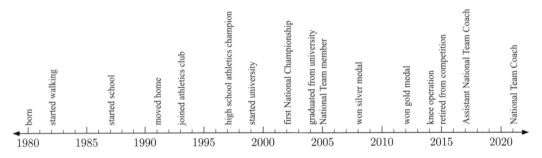

a In which year was Gavin born?

b When did Gavin:
   i join the athletics club   ii start university   iii win a gold medal?

c For how long did Gavin continue to compete after he was high school athletics champion?

d How old was Gavin when he:
   i started school   ii was appointed National Team Coach?

4 This time line shows when various methods of writing first appeared around the world:

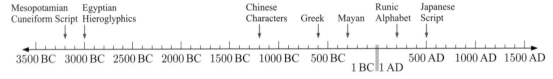

a Estimate when:
   i the Runic Alphabet first appeared   ii Greek writing was first used.

b About how long was there between the appearance of:
   i Egyptian Hieroglyphics and Chinese Characters
   ii Mayan writing and Japanese script
   iii Egyptian Hieroglyphics and the Runic Alphabet?

c i What was the earliest form of writing?
   ii About how long ago did it first appear?

5 **a** Draw a 20 cm line. Divide the line into 5 equal lengths as shown.

3000 BC   2000 BC   1000 BC   1 BC 1 AD   1000 AD   2000 AD

Using the letters of the alphabet given, place these important events on your time line:

A	1947	A polaroid camera produced pictures in under one minute.
B	1450	Gutenberg built the first printing press in Europe.
C	700 BC	Coins were used in Turkey for buying and selling goods.
D	1890	An electric counting machine was used in the American census.
E	999	The first mechanical clock was invented by a monk.
F	810	Arabic numerals were first described.
G	1636	The first accurate pendulum clock was built.
H	3000 BC	The abacus was invented by the Babylonians.
I	1569	Mercator showed a new way of drawing maps.
J	1938	The ballpoint pen was invented.
K	1642	A faster adding machine was designed by Pascal.
L	2800 BC	Egyptians devised a 12 month, 365 day calendar.
M	1614	Scottish mathematician John Napier invented logarithmic tables.
N	1946	The first electronic computer was demonstrated.
O	100	Paper was invented in China.
P	1955	The polio vaccine IPV was invented.
Q	1500	The first watches were made.

b Which of the events listed occurred most recently?

c Which of the events occurred closest to the year 1590?

d Which two of these events occurred closest together?

e How many of the events listed occurred before paper was invented?

f How many years before Pascal's adding machine was the Babylonian abacus used?

g How long after the first mechanical clock was invented, were the first watches made?

ACTIVITY 1   CREATING YOUR OWN TIME LINE

What to do:

1 Decide on a topic which particularly interests you. For example, you might choose:

- the Presidents of the USA
- the major wars of the 20th century.

The 20th century was from 1901 to 2000.

2 Research the dates of events you wish to include on your time line.

3 Choose a suitable scale for your time line and complete it with the dates you have found.

4 Write down four questions based on your time line. Ask another student to answer them.

GLOBAL CONTEXT   FAMILY TREES

Global context: Identities and relationships
Statement of inquiry: Drawing diagrams can help us to understand our
                         relationships with those around us.
Criterion: Communicating

GLOBAL
CONTEXT

B | UNITS OF TIME

> A **day** is the time it takes for the Earth to complete one rotation on its axis.

Other time units we use that are based on the day include
weeks, hours, minutes, and **seconds**.

1 week = 7 days
1 day = 24 hours
1 hour = 60 minutes
1 minute = 60 seconds

DISCUSSION

- List some activities that can be performed in approximately:
  - ▸ 1 second   ▸ 1 minute   ▸ 1 hour   ▸ 1 day   ▸ 1 week.
- Consider these statements about time:
  "It will take me 30 minutes to ride to school."
  "It will take me 2 hours to make dinner."
  "It will take me 4 days to paint the fence."
  "It will take me 10 weeks to learn to play the guitar."
  Would you expect these people to be performing the task for the *entire* time period given?
  If not, what is their statement actually describing?

To convert between units of time, we can use the following conversion diagram:

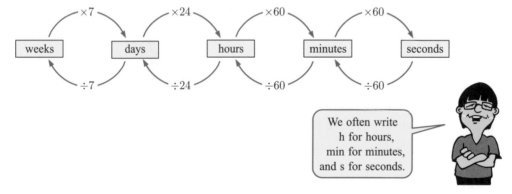

We often write
h for hours,
min for minutes,
and s for seconds.

Example 2		◀) **Self Tutor**
Convert:		
a 5 days to hours	**b** 120 minutes to hours	**c** 3 hours to minutes.

a 5 days $= 5 \times 24$ h	**b** 120 min $= 120 \div 60$ h	**c** 3 h $= 3 \times 60$ min
$= 120$ h	$= 2$ h	$= 180$ min

EXERCISE 11B

1 What units would you use when talking about the time taken to:

- **a** brush your teeth
- **b** watch a movie
- **c** run 100 metres
- **d** drive from Rome to London
- **e** play a round of golf
- **f** drink a glass of water?

2 Convert:

- **a** 7 minutes to seconds
- **b** 10 days to hours
- **c** 4 hours to minutes
- **d** 5 weeks to days
- **e** 240 seconds to minutes
- **f** 14 days to weeks
- **g** 12 minutes to seconds
- **h** 180 minutes to hours
- **i** 144 hours to days.

3 Jill has 120 cans to put in her supermarket display. It takes her 4 seconds to position each can. How long will it take Jill to complete her display?

4 Max has been told that he must practise the piano for 6 hours each week. His diary shows the times in minutes he has spent practising this week.

- **a** Write 6 hours in minutes.
- **b** Did Max practise enough this week?

Example 3	◀) **Self Tutor**
Write 9 hours and 42 minutes in minutes only.	

$$9 \text{ hours} = 9 \times 60 \text{ min}$$
$$= 540 \text{ min}$$

So, 9 hours and 42 minutes $= 540$ min $+ 42$ min
$$= 582 \text{ minutes}$$

5 Write in minutes only:

- **a** 3 hours and 24 minutes
- **b** 5 hours and 43 minutes
- **c** 6 h 7 min
- **d** 8 hours and 39 minutes

6 Write in seconds only:

    a 5 minutes and 12 seconds   **b** 35 min 27 s

    c 15 minutes and 48 seconds   **d** 49 minutes and 56 seconds

7 Jodie spent 4 hours and 40 minutes planting trees last Saturday.

    a Write this time in minutes only.

    b Jodie planted 35 trees during this time. On average, how long did Jodie spend planting each tree?

Example 4   ◀)) **Self Tutor**

Write 395 seconds in minutes and seconds.

6 minutes $= 6 \times 60$ seconds
$\qquad\qquad = 360$ seconds

So, 395 seconds $= 360$ seconds $+ 35$ seconds
$\qquad\qquad\qquad\quad = 6$ minutes 35 seconds

---

8 Write in minutes and seconds:

    a 76 seconds   **b** 95 s   **c** 110 s

    d 205 seconds   **e** 341 seconds   **f** 700 s

9 Write in hours and minutes:

    a 85 min   **b** 100 minutes   **c** 129 minutes

    d 146 minutes   **e** 258 min   **f** 499 min

10 Jason ran for 25 minutes every day for two weeks. Find the total time he spent running, in hours and minutes.

GAME   **ESTIMATING TIME**

Click on the icon to load a game for improving your time estimation skills.   **GAME**

C   **THE CALENDAR YEAR**

A **year** is the time it takes for the Earth to complete one orbit around the Sun.   **DEMO**

There are approximately $365\frac{1}{4}$ days in a year.

To avoid having to deal with fractions of days each year, we instead use **calendar years** which contain a whole number of days.

Each calendar year has either 365 days or 366 days.

Years that have 366 days are called **leap years**. A leap year occurs if the year is divisible by 4 but not by 100, except if the year is divisible by 400.

For example:
  • 1996 was a leap year.
  • 2000 was a leap year because it was divisible by 400.
  • 2100 will not be a leap year because it is divisible by 100 but not by 400.

Each year is divided into 12 **months**. The number of days in each month is shown in the table alongside.

Month	Days		Month	Days
January	31		July	31
February	28*		August	31
March	31		September	30
April	30		October	31
May	31		November	30
June	30		December	31

* February has 29 days in a leap year.

EXERCISE 11C

1   Determine whether each year is a leap year:

   a   2020   **b**   2025   **c**   2200   **d**   2400

2   Find the number of:

   a   days in 2022   **b**   months in 6 years.

3   Noah is 30 months old. Rosie is 3 years old. Which child is older?

4   In Chile, the months of spring are September, October, and November. Find the number of days of spring in Chile each year.

5   Find the number of hours in:

   a   June   **b**   March.

6   Consider a four year period which includes a leap year. Convert this period of time into:

   a   months   **b**   days   **c**   hours.

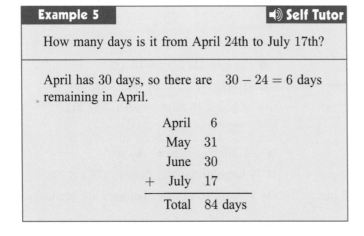

Example 5 ◀) **Self Tutor**

How many days is it from April 24th to July 17th?

April has 30 days, so there are $30 - 24 = 6$ days remaining in April.

```
      April    6
      May     31
      June    30
  +   July    17
      ─────────────
      Total   84 days
```

In questions like this we assume full days.

7 Find the number of days from:

    a March 11th to April 7th   **b** May 11th to June 23rd

    c July 12th to November 6th   **d** September 19th to January 8th

    e January 7th to March 16th in a non-leap year

    f February 6th to August 3rd in a leap year.

8 Lou Wong is saving money to buy a bicycle priced at $270. Today is the 23rd of March, and the shop will hold the bicycle until May 7th.

    a How many days does Lou have to save for the bicycle?

    b How much does Lou need to save each day, to save $270?

9 Candice must take her medication every second day, starting from April 11th. Will she take her medication on November 4th?

10 Sung Kim arrived in Australia on 17th February 2012. On what date did he celebrate being in Australia for 100 days?

D   TIME CALCULATIONS

We often need to add and subtract hours and minutes to find out when events start and finish.

Example 6   ◀⑴ **Self Tutor**

Find the time which is:

    a 2 hours 50 minutes after 3:20 pm   **b** 3 hours 40 minutes before 9:15 am.

a 3:20 pm + 2 hours = 5:20 pm	**b** 9:15 am − 3 hours = 6:15 am
5:20 pm + 40 minutes = 6 pm	6:15 am − 15 minutes = 6 am
6 pm + 10 minutes = 6:10 pm	6 am − 25 minutes = 5:35 am
The time 2 hours 50 minutes after 3:20 pm is 6:10 pm.	The time 3 hours 40 minutes before 9:15 am is 5:35 am.

EXERCISE 11D

1 Find the time which is:

    a 4 hours after 3:00 am   **b** 34 minutes after 6:15 am

    c 2 hours 13 minutes after 8:19 pm   **d** 1 hour 47 minutes after 1:30 pm

    e 3 hours 27 minutes after 12:42 pm   **f** 5 hours 48 minutes after 9:51 am.

2 Find the time which is:

    a 5 hours before 8:00 pm   **b** 21 minutes before 7:45 pm

    c 2 hours 55 minutes before 2:00 pm   **d** 1 hour 40 minutes before 5:25 am

    e 4 hours 47 minutes before 6:15 pm   **f** 3 hours 16 minutes before 2 am Monday.

3 High tide at a beach occurs at 1:45 am. The following low tide will occur 6 hours and 20 minutes later. At what time will the low tide occur?

4 David has agreed to meet some friends at their farm at 12:30 pm. It will take David 1 hour and 40 minutes to drive there. At what time should David start the journey?

5 A concert starting at 8:35 pm will last for 2 hours and 40 minutes. At what time will the concert finish?

6 Paula's air conditioner automatically shuts off 1 hour and 50 minutes after it is turned on. If the air conditioner shuts off at 12:26 am, at what time was it turned on?

Example 7   ◀) **Self Tutor**

Ken arrives at the airport at 10:45 am. His plane will depart at 3:20 pm. How long will he have to wait for his plane to depart?

10:45 am to 2:45 pm = 4 h
2:45 pm to 3:00 pm = 15 min
3:00 pm to 3:20 pm = 20 min

So, Ken will have to wait for 4 h 35 min.

---

7 Find the time difference between:
  a 7:20 am and 10:40 am
  b 11:15 am and 5:20 pm
  c 3:30 pm and 9:16 pm
  d 8:24 am and 7:11 pm.

8 A cyclist rides from 7:47 am until 11:31 am. For how long did the cyclist ride?

9 Gemma sent a text message to her friend Monique at 6:27 pm. Monique replied to Gemma at 9:09 pm. How long did Monique take to reply?

10 Shelley fell asleep at 10:26 pm. She woke up at 6:05 am the next day. For how long did she sleep?

11 Mary's watch "loses" 3 seconds every hour. If it shows the correct time at 8 am, what time will it show when the real time is 5 pm?

E   24-HOUR TIME

Consider the statement "My train leaves at 8 o'clock Tuesday".

It is unclear whether the train leaves at 8 o'clock in the morning, or 8 o'clock in the evening.

To avoid this confusion, we can use **24-hour time**.

24-hour time indicates the amount of time which has passed since midnight.

midnight	3 am	6 am	9 am	noon	3 pm	6 pm	9 pm	midnight
00:00	03:00	06:00	09:00	12:00	15:00	18:00	21:00	00:00

Although a clock might only use three digits on its display, *we* always use *four* digits to write 24-hour time. For example:

12-*hour time*	Digital display	24-*hour time*
midnight	12:00 AM	00:00
6:13 am	6:13 AM	06:13
midday (noon)	12:00 PM	12:00
9:47 pm	9:47 PM	21:47

9 hours + 12 hours = 21 hours, so 9 pm is 21:00.

Example 8   ◄) **Self Tutor**

Write in 24-hour time:

  a   8:55 am   **b**   10:25 pm

  a   8:55 am is 08:55.

  b   10 hours + 12 hours = 22 hours
       So, 10:25 pm is 22:25.

Times from 00:00 to 11:59 are **am** times. Times from 12:00 to 23:59 are **pm** times.

Example 9   ◄) **Self Tutor**

Write in 12-hour time:

  a   07:34   **b**   16:30

  a   07:34 is 7:34 am.

  b   16:30 is a pm time.
       16 hours − 12 hours = 4 hours
       So, 16:30 is 4:30 pm.

EXERCISE 11E

1   Write in 24-hour time:

  a   3:13 am   **b**   11:17 am   **c**   midnight   **d**   12:47 pm

  e   5:41 pm   **f**   9:22 am   **g**   2:09 pm   **h**   noon

  i   10:56 am   **j**   6:14 pm   **k**   8:19 pm   **l**   11:59 pm

2   Write in 12-hour time:

  a   03:40   **b**   06:35   **c**   18:26   **d**   12:00   **e**   19:39

  f   06:15   **g**   15:45   **h**   20:17   **i**   13:11   **j**   23:48

3   What, if anything, is wrong with these 24-hour times?

  a   08:62   **b**   07:13   **c**   25:41

4 Write in 24-hour time:

a  morning

b  afternoon

c evening

5 The following arrivals appear on a display at Singapore Changi Airport.

   a Which flight is due to arrive at 3:50 pm?

   b A thunderstorm delays the arrival of flight QF14 by 1 hour 35 minutes. At what time will the flight arrive? Write your answer using 24-hour time.

   c How long before flight EM16 is flight JAL130 scheduled to arrive?

ARRIVALS		
Flight	*From*	*Arrival time*
JAL130	Tokyo	14:50
BA10	London	15:50
SQ71	Rome	16:25
QF14	Perth	16:45
EM16	Dubai	17:15

F   TIMETABLES

Timetables are tables of information which give us a **schedule** of when events are to occur.

We can use timetables to find out when the next bus or train is coming, when our favourite television show will be on, and when the sun will rise tomorrow.

Example 10   ◀) Self Tutor

This timetable gives information about the phases of the moon, and the rising and setting of the planets of our solar system.

   a When is the next full moon?

   b At what time will:

      i Mercury rise tomorrow

      ii Saturn set tomorrow?

The Moon

New	First $\frac{1}{4}$	Full	Last $\frac{1}{4}$
Sep 21	Sep 29	Oct 6	Oct 12

The Sun and Planets

Tomorrow	Rise	Set
Sun	6:15 am	6:07 pm
Moon	2:29 am	1:00 pm
Mercury	5:59 am	5:20 pm
Venus	5:51 am	5:09 pm
Mars	4:43 am	3:11 pm
Jupiter	6:01 am	6:34 pm
Saturn	9:10 am	8:23 pm

   a The next full moon is on October 6th.

   b i Mercury will rise at 5:59 am tomorrow.

      ii Saturn will set at 8:23 pm tomorrow.

EXERCISE 11F

1

Spelling	9:00 - 9:45
Music	9:45 - 10:30
Recess	10:30 - 11:00
Mathematics	11:00 - 11:50
Science	11:50 - 12:40
Lunch	12:40 - 1:40
Sport	1:40 - 2:25
Language	2:25 - 3:10

This timetable shows the classes for a school day.

a At what time does the Science class start?

b At what time does the Spelling class end?

c What class is being taken at 2 pm?

d How long is the:
  i Music class
  ii Mathematics class?

e How long is the school day?

2 The timetable of activities at a school camp is shown alongside.

a At what time does the kayaking start?

b Which activity begins at 3:30 pm?

c For how long do the students sing campfire songs?

d How much free time do the students have during the day?

Breakfast	8:30 am - 9:00 am
Kayaking	9:00 am - 10:45 am
Free time	10:45 am - 12:30 pm
Lunch	12:30 pm - 1:30 pm
Nature hike	1:30 pm - 3:00 pm
Free time	3:00 pm - 3:30 pm
Volleyball	3:30 pm - 5:00 pm
Journal writing	5:00 pm - 6:00 pm
Dinner	6:00 pm - 7:00 pm
Chores	7:00 pm - 7:30 pm
Campfire songs	7:30 pm - 9:00 pm
Bedtime	9:00 pm

3 This timetable shows the tide times on a particular day.

Tide times				
Location	*High Tide*		*Low Tide*	
Port Xenon	3:00 am	1.2 m	9:56 am	0.4 m
	3:07 pm	0.7 m	7:21 pm	0.3 m
Port Dowell	3:54 am	1.5 m	10:37 am	0.2 m
	4:37 pm	1.0 m	10:09 pm	0.4 m
Coomera	2:05 am	1.9 m	8:53 am	0.6 m
	3:52 pm	1.4 m	9:02 pm	0.3 m
Joseph's Bay	3:07 am	1.6 m	8:58 am	0.5 m
	3:05 pm	1.4 m	8:52 pm	0.3 m
Paradise Point	4:35 am	2.5 m	10:27 am	0.9 m
	4:16 pm	2.2 m	10:27 pm	0.5 m
Sunny Inlet	2:44 am	1.1 m	9:27 am	0.4 m
	2:26 pm	0.7 m	8:06 pm	0.3 m

a When is the tide highest in the morning at Port Xenon?

b When is the tide lowest in the evening at Paradise Point?

c Find the time difference between:
  i the low tides at Sunny Inlet
  ii the first low tide and the next high tide at Coomera.

d A boat at Joseph's Bay must return to shore at least 70 minutes before the evening low tide. By what time must it return?

4

Channel 4

05:30	Weather Watch	14:30	Movie Matinee
06:30	Roger Robot	16:45	Cartoon Capers
07:00	Cartoon Collection	17:30	Pick a Prize
08:00	Dazzlers	18:00	News and Weather
08:30	Kids Korner	19:00	Animal Antics
09:30	Hot Hits	19:30	North Park
11:00	Growing Gardens	20:30	Saturday Special
11:30	Football Flashbacks	23:15	Sports Roundup
12:00	Spectator Sports	00:10	Cooking with Con

Use this television guide to answer the following questions:

a At what time does Kids Korner start?

b Which program starts at 7:30 pm?

c For how many minutes is the News and Weather shown?

d In total, how much time is spent showing sport?

e How much time is there from the end of Cartoon Collection to the start of Cartoon Capers?

f Leon missed the last 50 minutes of Saturday Special because he had to go to bed. At what time did he go to bed?

5 Below is the summer timetable for a tourist bus service in Christchurch, New Zealand.

Departure location	Bus A	Bus B	Bus C	Bus D	Bus E	Bus F
Central Station	09:00	09:15	09:30	09:45	10:00	10:15
Canterbury Museum	09:30	09:45	10:00	10:15	10:30	10:45
Christchurch Gondola	10:50	11:05	11:20	11:35	11:50	12:05
Lyttelton Harbour	11:20	11:35	11:50	12:05	12:20	12:35
Akaroa	13:00	13:15	13:30	13:45	14:00	14:15
Airforce World	14:30	14:45	15:00	15:15	15:30	15:45
Yaldhurst Transport Museum	15:15	15:30	15:45	16:00	16:15	16:30
International Antarctic Centre	16:30	16:45	17:00	17:15	17:30	17:45
Arrive at Central Station	17:30	17:45	18:00	18:15	18:30	18:45

a How many bus services are available?

b What is the latest departure time?

c What is the earliest arrival time back at Central Station?

d How long does it take to get from:

   i Lyttelton Harbour to Airforce World

   ii the Gondola to the International Antarctic Centre?

e How long does a complete trip last?

f If you wanted to arrive at Akaroa no later than 2 pm, which bus should you take?

g Your friend wants to meet you at Yaldhurst Transport Museum at 3:25 pm. Which bus should you catch?

6 Consider this train timetable for the Carlingford to Wynyard line.

a What does it mean by:

    i arr   **ii** dep?

b If I catch the 4:17 pm train at Rydalmere, what time will I arrive at Central?

c At what time should I catch the train from Dundas in order to arrive at Lidcombe by 6:00 pm?

d If I miss the 5:00 pm train from Clyde, what is the earliest time I can now arrive at Wynyard?

e Which train takes the longest to travel from Carlingford to Wynyard?

CARLINGFORD-WYNYARD TRAIN TIMETABLE		pm	pm	pm	pm	pm	pm	pm
Carlingford		3:32	4:11	4:45	5:23	5:55	6:26	6:52
Telopea		3:34	4:13	4:47	5:25	5:57	6:28	6:54
Dundas		3:36	4:15	4:49	5:27	5:59	6:30	6:56
Rydalmere		3:38	4:17	4:51	5:29	6:01	6:32	6:58
Camellia		3:40	4:19	4:53	5:31	6:03	6:34	7:00
Rosehill UA		3:42	4:21	4:55	5:33	6:05	6:36	7:02
Clyde	**arr**	3:45	4:24	4:58	5:36	6:08	6:39	7:05
	dep	3:51	4:26	5:00	5:48	6:18	6:48	7:06
Lidcombe	**arr**	3:55	4:29	5:04	5:52	6:22	6:52	7:10
	dep	3:57	4:31	5:06	5:54	6:24	6:54	7:12
Strathfield	**arr**	4:02	4:36	5:11	5:59	6:29	6:59	7:18
	dep	4:03	4:37	5:12	6:00	6:30	7:00	7:23
Central	**arr**	4:17	4:50	5:26	6:14	6:44	7:14	7:36
	dep	4:18	4:51	5:27	6:15	6:45	7:15	7:37
Town Hall		4:21	4:54	5:30	6:18	6:48	7:18	7:40
Wynyard		4:24	4:57	5:33	6:20	6:50	7:20	7:42

PUZZLE   CINEMA SCHEDULING

Imagine you operate a cinema complex which contains 3 cinemas. During the day, you want to show:

- 5 screenings of film A, which is 160 minutes long
- 5 screenings of film B, which is 70 minutes long
- 3 screenings of film C, which is 100 minutes long
- 3 screenings of film D, which is 120 minutes long.

In addition, these rules must be followed:

- No film must start earlier than 10 am.
- No film must start later than 9 pm.
- No film must finish later than 11 pm.
- There must be at least 30 minutes between films in the same cinema.
- There must be at least 10 minutes between the starting times of films in different cinemas.
- There must be at least 60 minutes between the starting times of the *same film* in different cinemas.

Can you create a schedule of films which satisfies all of these requirements?

ACTIVITY 2   THE JAPANESE CALENDAR

The Japanese calendar is a **cultural** calendar which is associated with the ascension of each emperor to the throne.

Click on the icon to explore this calendar.

JAPANESE
CALENDAR

MULTIPLE CHOICE QUIZ

REVIEW SET 11A

1 This time line shows some important dates in the history of The Book Company.

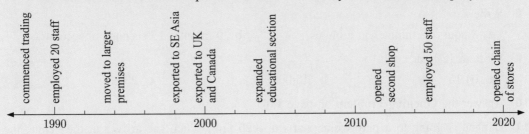

a When did The Book Company:

    i start trading   **ii** employ 20 staff

    iii export to SE Asia   **iv** expand their educational section?

b How many years was it between when The Book Company:

    i employed 20 staff and employed 50 staff

    ii opened a second shop and opened a chain of stores?

2 Convert:

    a 12 hours to minutes   **b** 4 minutes to seconds   **c** 72 hours to days.

3 Write 168 minutes in hours and minutes.

4

TIMETABLE - Melbourne to Sydney		
Melbourne	depart	7:30 am
Albury	arrive	11:10 am
	depart	11:50 am
Canberra	arrive	4:05 pm
	depart	4:45 pm
Goulburn	arrive	5:55 pm
	depart	6:25 pm
Sydney	arrive	9:30 pm

The Happy Travellers Bus Service has a regular daily run between Melbourne and Sydney.

a Find the time taken to go from:

    i Melbourne to Canberra   **ii** Canberra to Sydney   **iii** Melbourne to Sydney.

b For how long does the bus stop in:

    i Albury   **ii** Canberra   **iii** Goulburn?

c If the bus was 15 minutes late departing Goulburn, at what time did it actually depart?

5 Mitchell is spending the day at the beach. He applies sunscreen at 9:40 am. The sunscreen lasts for 2 hours and 30 minutes. At what time should Mitchell reapply sunscreen?

6 Decide whether each year is a leap year:

    a 1986   **b** 2052   **c** 2300

7 Sophia has a taekwondo black belt test on November 14th. Starting from September 22nd, Sophia will spend 20 minutes each day training for the test.

    a Find the number of days from September 22nd to November 14th.

    b How long, in hours and minutes, did Sophia spend training for the test?

8 Write:

    a 3 hours 18 minutes in minutes   **b** 9 minutes 12 seconds in seconds.

9 Write in 12-hour time:

    a 04:15   **b** 13:00   **c** 23:35

10 Answer the **Opening Problem** on page **198**.

11 Daphne is going to a play which starts at 8:20 pm. When she arrives at the venue, the clock reads 19:57.

    a Write this time in 12-hour time.

    b How long will it be before the play begins?

    c The play lasts for 135 minutes.

        i Write 135 minutes in hours and minutes.

        ii At what time will the play finish?

12 Claire's birthday is on May 9th, and Peter's birthday is on July 11th.

    a Find the number of days between Claire's birthday and Peter's birthday.

    b Hence explain why Claire and Peter's birthdays always occur on the same day of the week as each other.

    c Latisha's birthday is on August 24th. If Peter's birthday occurs on a Monday this year, on what day of the week does Latisha's birthday occur?

REVIEW SET 11B

1 The following time line shows the periods of various Chinese civilisations:

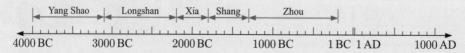

    a In which year did the Longshan period begin?

    b For how long did the Xia dynasty last?

2 Find the time:

    a 6 hours after 10 am   **b** 3 hours 21 minutes before 8 pm.

3 Find the time difference between 11:17 am and 2:56 pm.

4 Find the number of:

    a hours in September   **b** days in 2016.

5 Roger needs to cook a casserole in the oven for 75 minutes. If he put the casserole in the oven at 3:57 pm, at what time should he take it out?

6 Laura's graduation ceremony starts at 2 pm. Due to the traffic, it took her 56 minutes to get there. She arrived with only 9 minutes to spare.
At what time did she leave home?

7 Write in 24-hour time:

    a
    morning   **b**
    evening

8 Find the number of days from 7th July to 22nd October.

9 Darnell jogged from 7:26 am until 9:15 am. For how long did he jog?

10 Consider the television schedule alongside.

    a At what times does "Sport Stunts" start and finish?

    b Paul started watching television at 11:10 am, and watched for 1 hour 53 minutes. What program was showing when he turned off the TV?

Wednesday	
11:00	Festival of Films
11:30	Cartoon Mania
12:00	Car racing
12:30	Top dog
13:30	Sport Stunts
14:00	The Monsters
14:30	My Cat called Felix

11 Write in 24-hour time:

    a 12:32 am   **b** 10:15 am   **c** 5:49 pm

12 The time line below shows the cars that Gordon has owned:

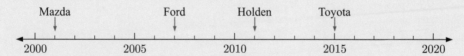

    a In which year did Gordon buy the Holden?

    b Which car did he buy most recently?

    c Which car was Gordon driving in 2005?

    d For how long did he own the Ford?

13 A City Circuit bus leaves the Town Hall every 10 minutes. The timetable shown is for the 10 am bus.

Timetable	
Town Hall	10:00 am
General Post Office	10:03 am
Garden Square	10:05 am
Bus Depot	10:08 am
Railway Station	10:10 am
Museum	10:12 am
Art Gallery	10:14 am
University	10:19 am
Shopping Mall	10:23 am
Cathedral	10:25 am
Theatre Complex	10:27 am
Town Hall	10:30 am

a How long does it take the bus to complete one circuit?

b Find how long it takes to go from:
   i the Town Hall to the Railway Station
   ii the Bus Depot to the Shopping Mall
   iii Garden Square to the Cathedral.

c Write the times that the *next* bus will depart from the:
   i Town Hall   **ii** Museum.

d How many other buses will leave the Town Hall before this bus returns?

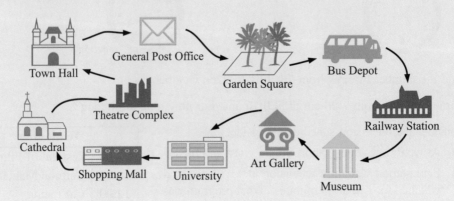

Chapter 12

Percentage

Contents:

OPENING PROBLEM

A 100 g snack bar is labelled "96% sugar free".

Things to think about:

a What does 96% *mean*?

b What percentage of the bar is sugar?

c What fraction of the bar is sugar?

d How much sugar is in the bar?

You have probably seen the symbol % many times on signs and on packaging labels.

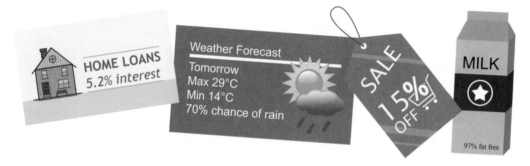

The symbol % indicates a **percentage**.

A   PERCENTAGE

A **percentage** is used to compare a portion with a whole amount.

The whole amount is represented by 100%, which has the value 1.

% reads **percent**, which means "in every hundred".

If an object is divided into one hundred equal parts, then each part is called 1 percent, written 1%.

If 1 part out of 100 is shaded, then this is 1% or $\frac{1}{100}$.

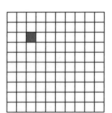

If 55 parts out of 100 are shaded, then this is 55% or $\frac{55}{100}$.

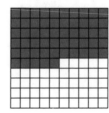

If 100 parts out of 100 are shaded, then this is 100% or $\frac{100}{100}$ or 1.

So, a percentage is like a fraction with denominator 100.

$$x\% = \frac{x}{100}$$

The word "percent" comes from the Latin *per centum*, and means "in every hundred".

Example 1   ◀) **Self Tutor**

There are 100 tiles in this pattern.

Write the portion of tiles which are coloured as a:

   a fraction   **b** percentage.

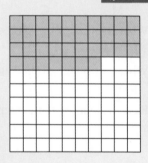

Of the 100 tiles, 37 are coloured.

a $\frac{37}{100}$ of the tiles are coloured.   **b** 37% of the tiles are coloured.

EXERCISE 12A

1 In each of the following patterns, there are 100 tiles. Write the portion of tiles which are coloured as a:

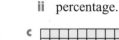

     i fraction with denominator 100   **ii** percentage.

a 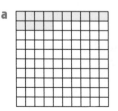 **b** 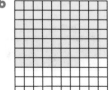 **c** 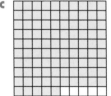 **d**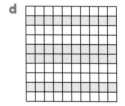

2 Estimate the percentage of each diagram which is shaded:

a

0   20   40   60   80   100

b

0   20   40   60   80   100

c

0   20   40   60   80   100

3 In a 4 player video game, the red bars show how healthy each player is.

Which player has a health level of:

a 60%   **b** 36%

c 91%   **d** 17%?

4 There are 100 symbols in the circle.

a How many of the symbols are:

   i M   **ii** C   **iii** X   **iv** V?

b What fraction of the symbols are:

   i M   **ii** C   **iii** X   **iv** V?

c What percentage of the symbols are:

   i M   **ii** C   **iii** X   **iv** V?

d Find the sum of the percentages in **c**. Explain your answer.

5 The diagram illustrates the different things we throw away.

a What percentage of waste is:

   i food and green waste

   ii rubber and leather

   iii either wood or metal?

b Does plastic or glass make up the greater percentage of waste?

c Find the sum of the percentages. Explain your answer.

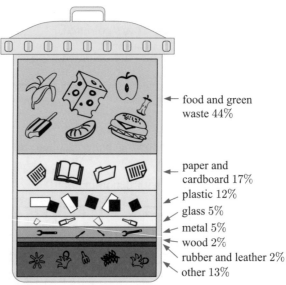

← food and green waste 44%

← paper and cardboard 17%

plastic 12%

glass 5%

← metal 5%

← wood 2%

rubber and leather 2%

other 13%

Data source: World Bank 2018

INVESTIGATION   COMMON PERCENTAGES

The printable worksheet contains squares with grids.

PRINTABLE PAGES

What to do:

1 How many little grid squares are in each big square?

2 Look at the big squares which are divided into 10 equal regions.
   a What fraction of the whole is each region?
   b Use a separate big square to shade each fraction. Hence write the fraction as a percentage.

      i $\dfrac{1}{10}$ **ii** $\dfrac{4}{10}$ **iii** $\dfrac{7}{10}$ **iv** $\dfrac{9}{10}$

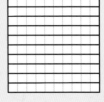

3 Look at the big squares which are divided into 4 equal regions.
   a What fraction of the whole is each region?
   b Use a separate big square to shade each fraction. Hence write the fraction as a percentage.

      i $\dfrac{1}{4}$ **ii** $\dfrac{2}{4}$ **iii** $\dfrac{3}{4}$

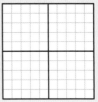

4 Look at the big squares which are divided into 5 equal regions.
   a What fraction of the whole is each region?
   b Use a separate big square to shade each fraction. Hence write the fraction as a percentage.

      i $\dfrac{1}{5}$ **ii** $\dfrac{3}{5}$ **iii** $\dfrac{4}{5}$

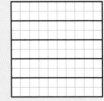

B   CONVERTING PERCENTAGES INTO FRACTIONS

To convert a percentage into a fraction, we write the percentage as a fraction with denominator 100, then write the fraction in lowest terms.

Example 2   ◀》 Self Tutor

Write as a fraction:
   a 29%   **b** 85%

   a $29\% = \dfrac{29}{100}$ **b** $85\% = \dfrac{85}{100}$

   $= \dfrac{85 \div 5}{100 \div 5}$

   $= \dfrac{17}{20}$

Remember that
$x\% = \dfrac{x}{100}$.

EXERCISE 12B

1 Write as a fraction with denominator 100:

    a 59%   **b** 13%   **c** 3%   **d** 97%

2 Write as a fraction in lowest terms:

    a 10%   **b** 50%   **c** 90%   **d** 5%

    e 22%   **f** 74%   **g** 15%   **h** 65%

    i 25%   **j** 80%   **k** 35%   **l** 75%

    m 4%   **n** 48%   **o** 56%   **p** 64%

C | CONVERTING FRACTIONS INTO PERCENTAGES

Many fractions can be converted to a percentage by first writing the fraction with denominator 100.

Example 3 | ◄)) Self Tutor

Write as a percentage:

    a $\dfrac{19}{100}$ **b** $\dfrac{2}{5}$ **c** $\dfrac{557}{1000}$

    a $\dfrac{19}{100} = 19\%$

    b $\dfrac{2}{5} = \dfrac{2 \times 20}{5 \times 20}$

            $= \dfrac{40}{100}$

            $= 40\%$

    c $\dfrac{557}{1000} = \dfrac{557 \div 10}{1000 \div 10}$

            $= \dfrac{55.7}{100}$

            $= 55.7\%$

EXERCISE 12C

1 Write as a percentage:

    a $\dfrac{21}{100}$ **b** $\dfrac{53}{100}$ **c** $\dfrac{91}{100}$ **d** $\dfrac{8}{100}$

    e $\dfrac{3}{10}$ **f** $\dfrac{7}{10}$ **g** $\dfrac{0}{10}$ **h** $\dfrac{10}{10}$

2 Write as a percentage:

    a $\dfrac{1}{2}$ **b** $\dfrac{13}{50}$ **c** $\dfrac{1}{5}$ **d** $\dfrac{41}{50}$ **e** $\dfrac{3}{20}$

    f $\dfrac{3}{5}$ **g** $\dfrac{7}{25}$ **h** $\dfrac{19}{20}$ **i** $\dfrac{12}{25}$ **j** $\dfrac{19}{25}$

3 Write as a percentage:

    a $\dfrac{29}{200}$ **b** $\dfrac{231}{1000}$ **c** $\dfrac{759}{1000}$ **d** $\dfrac{103}{500}$

4   **a** Write $\dfrac{200}{100}$ in simplest form.   **b** Write 2 as a percentage.

5 Use the illustration to complete the table below.

	Students	Number	Fraction	Percentage
a	with a bag			
b	without a book			
c	holding an open book			
d	black hair			
e	sitting down			
f	wearing something on their head			
g	wearing shoes			

PRINTABLE
TABLE

6 Copy and complete these patterns:

a $\frac{1}{5} = 20\%$

$\frac{2}{5} = \ldots\ldots$

$\frac{3}{5} = \ldots\ldots$

$\frac{4}{5} = \ldots\ldots$

$\frac{5}{5} = \ldots\ldots$

b $\frac{1}{4} = 25\%$

$\frac{2}{4} = \ldots\ldots$

$\frac{3}{4} = \ldots\ldots$

$\frac{4}{4} = \ldots\ldots$

c $\frac{1}{3} = 33\frac{1}{3}\%$

$\frac{2}{3} = \ldots\ldots$

$\frac{3}{3} = \ldots\ldots$

d $1 = 100\%$

$\frac{1}{2} = 50\%$

$\frac{1}{4} = \ldots\ldots$

$\frac{1}{8} = \ldots\ldots$

$\frac{1}{16} = \ldots\ldots$

D CONVERTING PERCENTAGES INTO DECIMALS

We have seen that $1\% = \frac{1}{100} = 0.01$ and that $100\% = \frac{100}{100} = 1.00$.

> To write a percentage as a decimal number, we **divide by 100%**.

Since $100\% = \frac{100}{100} = 1$, dividing by 100% does not change the value of the number.

Example 4 ◀)) **Self Tutor**

Write as a decimal:

a 21%   b 6.7%

a   21%   b   6.7%
    = 21. ÷ 100   = 06.7 ÷ 100
    = 0.21   = 0.067

To divide by 100, move the decimal point two places to the left.

EXERCISE 12D

1 Write as a decimal:

  a 10%   b 50%   c 25%   d 5%   e 33%   f 57%
  g 94%   h 6%   i 40%   j 11%   k 1%   l 90%

2 Write as a decimal:

  a 17.5%   b 81.6%   c 60.7%   d 9.4%
  e 3.9%   f 4.3%   g 1.7%   h 0.8%

3 Write each percentage as:

     i a decimal   ii a fraction in lowest terms.

  a 71%   b 30%   c 55%   d 6%   e 28%

E   CONVERTING DECIMALS INTO PERCENTAGES

To write a decimal number as a percentage, we **multiply by 100%**.

Example 5 ◀)) **Self Tutor**

Write as a percentage:

a 0.27   b 0.055

a   0.27   b   0.055
    = 0.27 × 100%   = 0.055 × 100%
    = 27%   = 5.5%

EXERCISE 12E

1 Write as a percentage:

  a 0.37   b 0.89   c 0.15   d 0.49
  e 0.73   f 0.11   g 0.05   h 0.02

2 Write as a percentage:

a 0.2	**b** 0.7	**c** 0.9	**d** 0.4
e 0.074	**f** 0.739	**g** 0.086	**h** 0.001

3 Copy and complete:

	Percent	Fraction	Decimal
a	20%		0.2
b	40%	$\frac{2}{5}$	
c			0.25
d			0.5
e		$\frac{3}{4}$	
f			0.85

	Percent	Fraction	Decimal
g		$\frac{2}{25}$	
h			0.35
i		$\frac{4}{5}$	
j	84%		
k	100%		
l		$\frac{3}{20}$	

F   NUMBER LINES

Placing numbers on a number line can be difficult when the numbers are given as a mixture of fractions, decimals, and percentages. However, we can make the process easier by converting all of the numbers to the same form.

Example 6   ◀ᴙ **Self Tutor**

By converting each number to a percentage, place $\frac{1}{4}$, 0.42, and 33% on a number line.

$$\frac{1}{4} = \frac{1 \times 25}{4 \times 25} = \frac{25}{100} = 25\% \qquad\qquad 0.42 = 0.42 \times 100\% = 42\%$$

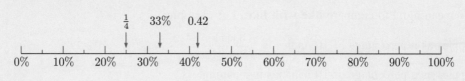

EXERCISE 12F

1 Place on a number line:

    a 30%, 70%, 50%   **b** 75%, 15%, 45%   **c** 62%, 74%, 36%

2 Write each number as a percentage, and place them on a number line:

    a $\frac{3}{5}$, 70%, 0.65   **b** 55%, $\frac{9}{20}$, 0.8   **c** 0.93, 79%, $\frac{17}{20}$

    d 0.85, $\frac{3}{4}$, 92%   **e** $\frac{27}{50}$, 67%, 0.59   **f** 47%, 0.74, $\frac{7}{10}$

3 Write each value as a percentage, as a decimal, and as a fraction with denominator 100:

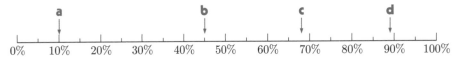

4 Write each value as a percentage:

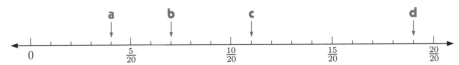

5 **a** Write each number as a percentage:

   i $\dfrac{17}{25}$ **ii** 0.43   **iii** $\dfrac{39}{50}$ **iv** 0.627

   b Hence place the numbers on a number line.

   c Write the numbers in ascending order.

GAME

Click on the icon to play a game which requires you to write fractions, decimals, and percentages in order.

GAME

G   EXPRESSING ONE QUANTITY AS A PERCENTAGE OF ANOTHER

Percentages are often used to *compare* quantities, so it is useful to express one quantity as a percentage of another.

It is only meaningful to compare **like with like**. For example:

- 3 apples as a percentage of 10 apples is $\dfrac{3 \text{ apples}}{10 \text{ apples}} = \dfrac{3}{10} = 30\%$.

- 3 apples as a percentage of 10 bananas is meaningless.

We must also make sure that the quantities are compared with the **same units**.

For example, if we are asked to express 35 cm as a percentage of 7 m, we would first convert the larger unit to the smaller one:

$$\frac{35 \text{ cm}}{7 \text{ m}} = \frac{35 \text{ cm}}{700 \text{ cm}}$$

$$= \frac{35 \div 7}{700 \div 7}$$

$$= \frac{5}{100}$$

$$= 5\%$$

To express one quantity as a percentage of another, we write them as a fraction, then convert the fraction to a percentage.

Example 7 🔊 **Self Tutor**

Express the first quantity as a percentage of the second:

a 22 marks out of 25 marks   b 60 cm out of 3 m   c 160 g out of 2 kg.

a $\dfrac{22 \text{ marks}}{25 \text{ marks}} = \dfrac{22}{25}$

$= \dfrac{22 \times 4}{25 \times 4}$

$= \dfrac{88}{100}$

$= 88\%$

b $\dfrac{60 \text{ cm}}{3 \text{ m}} = \dfrac{60 \text{ cm}}{300 \text{ cm}}$

$= \dfrac{60 \div 3}{300 \div 3}$

$= \dfrac{20}{100}$

$= 20\%$

c $\dfrac{160 \text{ g}}{2 \text{ kg}} = \dfrac{160 \text{ g}}{2000 \text{ g}}$

$= \dfrac{160 \div 20}{2000 \div 20}$

$= \dfrac{8}{100}$

$= 8\%$

EXERCISE 12G

1 Express as a percentage:
   a 76 marks out of 100   b 17 marks out of 20   c 11 marks out of 25
   d 37 marks out of 50   e 36 marks out of 40   f 138 marks out of 200.

2 Express as a percentage:
   a 72 diners in a restaurant that seats 200 diners
   b 405 books sold out of 500 printed
   c 660 square metres of lawn in a 2000 square metre garden
   d a ten pin bowler scores 186 points out of a possible 300 points.

3 28 000 spectators attend a baseball match. The stadium has 40 000 seats. What percentage of the seats are taken?

4 In a class of 25 students, 13 have blue eyes. What percentage of the class have blue eyes?

5 Maria is taking a cooking course with 20 classes. To earn her certificate, she needs to attend at least 80% of the classes. Maria was unable to attend 3 classes.
   a What percentage of the classes did Maria attend?
   b Will Maria receive her certificate?

6 Express the first quantity as a percentage of the second:
   a 20 cm, 100 cm   b 10 km, 50 km   c 3 m, 4 m

7 By writing the quantities with the same units, express the first quantity as a percentage of the second:
   a 7 mm, 2 cm   b 50 g, 1 kg   c 84 cm, 4 m
   d 48 seconds, 5 minutes   e 720 kg, 2 tonnes   f 63 cents, 9 dollars
   g 24 minutes, 10 hours   h 50 cents, $25   i 1 mL, 1 litre

8 Ray has watched 30 minutes of a 2 hour long movie.
   a What percentage of the movie has Ray watched?
   b What percentage of the movie does Ray still have to watch?

9 2 km of gas pipes need to be laid. So far, the engineers have laid 480 m of pipes. What percentage of the pipes have been laid?

10 There are 50 singers in a school choir. 9 of them are in Year 4, 17 are in Year 5, and 21 are in Year 6.

    a Find the percentage of singers who are in:

      i Year 4   **ii** Year 5   **iii** Year 6.

    b Find the sum of your percentages in **a**. What does this tell you about the choir?

11 Pauline has made 3.6 litres of fruit punch for a party. Before the party begins, she drinks 180 mL to test the recipe. What percentage of the fruit punch is left for the party?

12 The Smith family and the Jones family each put up a display of coloured lights on their house during the holiday season.

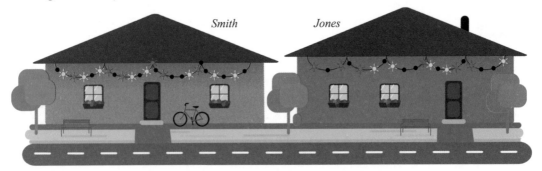

Smith   *Jones*

    a Find the percentage of lights which are working on each house.

    b Which house has the higher percentage of working lights?

    c Of all the lights that are working, what percentage are:

      i red   **ii** yellow?

13 Sven has a 3.7 kg pumpkin. He uses 600 g for dinner and 2.3 kg in soup. What percentage of the pumpkin remains?

DISCUSSION

Discuss the following examples of everyday percentage use. In each case, talk about:

- what the percentage *means*
- how the percentage may have been calculated
- why the percentage may be useful information.

1 25% of the gardens in my street have roses growing in them.

2 65% of students voted for a greater variety of food in the school canteen.

3 47% of school age children do not eat enough fresh fruit and vegetables.

4 The netball goal shooter had a 68% score rate for the season.

5 Over 52% of 5 - 14 year old children play sport outside school hours.

H | FINDING A PERCENTAGE OF A QUANTITY

A school website claims that 56% of its students are girls.

This means that for every 100 students, there are 56 girls.

Notice that $56\% = 0.56$, and that $0.56 \times 100 = 56$.

To find a percentage of a quantity, we convert the percentage to a decimal, then multiply to find the required amount.

Example 8

◀)) **Self Tutor**

Find 53% of 4000 people.

53% of 4000 people
$= 0.53 \times 4000$ people $\{0.53 \boxed{\times} 4000 \boxed{=} \}$
$= 2120$ people

"of" means multiply.

EXERCISE 12H

1   Find:

  a   28% of $100
  b   60% of 10 mushrooms
  c   85% of 1000 balloons

  d   15% of $200
  e   80% of 250 people
  f   27% of 30 kg

  g   75% of 320 litres
  h   7% of 70 cm
  i   45% of 35 seconds

2   A new company policy requires 5% of the workers in each office to have first aid training. How many workers need first aid training in:

  a   a small office containing 20 workers
  b   a large office containing 300 workers?

3   A school has 485 students. A teacher takes 20% of them on an excursion to the museum. How many students went to the museum?

4   A council collects 4500 tonnes of rubbish each year. 27% of the rubbish is recycled. How many tonnes of rubbish is this?

5   A farmer planted 2400 acres of crops.
    30% of the crop was barley, and the rest was wheat.

  a   What percentage of the crop was wheat?

  b   How many acres were planted with:

    i   barley
    ii   wheat?

6   An orchardist picks 2400 kg of apricots for drying. 85% of the weight is lost in the drying process. How many kilograms of dried apricots are produced?

Example 9

◀⬥ **Self Tutor**

Find 12% of 3 km, giving your answer in m.

> You may use your calculator if you need to.

12% of 3 km
$= 0.12 \times 3000$ m   {3 km $= 3000$ m}
$= 360$ m   {$0.12 \boxed{\times} 3000 \boxed{=}$ }

7 Find the following, giving each answer in the units indicated:

a 27% of $1 (in cents)
b 5% of 9 m (in cm)
c 35% of 2 kg (in g)
d 10% of 3 hours (in min)
e 60% of 8 kL (in L)
f 42% of 4 cm (in mm)
g 22% of 5 days (in hours)
h 7% of $14 (in cents)
i 1.5% of an hour (in seconds)

8 A soft drink is 8% sugar. How many grams of sugar are there in 1.5 kg of the drink?

9 A theatre production lasts for 2 hours and 40 minutes. 12.5% of this time is the interval between acts. How long is the interval?

10 In a series of triathlon races, prize money is awarded to the top three competitors in each race. The winner receives 50% of the prize money, second place receives 35%, and third place receives 15%.

The total prize money and results for the first two races are shown below.

	Total prize money	1st	2nd	3rd
Race 1	$3000	Daniel	Matt	Shane
Race 2	$5000	Justin	Daniel	Trent

Find the prize money won by:

a Shane
b Daniel.

I   PERCENTAGE INCREASE OR DECREASE

DISCUSSION

Here are some examples of how we observe percentage increase and decrease in our daily lives:

- A department store marks up a shirt by 50%.
- Low fat milk contains 80% less fat than whole milk.
- The cost of a laptop is €320 plus 10% goods tax.
- The price of a microwave oven is discounted by 25%.

Discuss whether each statement refers to a percentage *increase* or a percentage *decrease*.

Discuss other statements you have heard involving percentage change.

To apply a percentage increase or decrease, we:
- find the *size* of the increase or decrease, then
- *apply* the change to the original quantity by addition or subtraction.

Example 10   ◀)) **Self Tutor**

Jeremy's weekly allowance of $10 was increased by 20%.

  a Find the size of the allowance increase.   **b** Find Jeremy's new weekly allowance.

a increase $= 20\%$ of $\$10$ $\qquad\quad = 0.2 \times \$10$ $\qquad\quad = \$2$	**b** Jeremy's new weekly allowance $\qquad\quad = \$10 + \$2$ $\qquad\quad = \$12$

EXERCISE 12I

1 To purchase a laptop, Eliza must pay €320 plus 10% goods tax.

    a Find the size of the tax.

    b Find the total amount Eliza must pay.

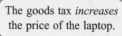

The goods tax *increases* the price of the laptop.

2 A department store buys a shirt for $12. The shirt is then marked up by 50% so the store can make a profit.

    a Find the size of the price increase.

    b For what price will the department store sell the shirt?

3 Increase: **a** 60 cm by 40%   **b** 40 L by 70%.

Example 11   ◀)) **Self Tutor**

Due to an illness, the mass of a 50 kg chimpanzee decreased by 8%.

  a Find the size of the mass decrease.   **b** Find the new mass of the chimpanzee.

a decrease $= 8\%$ of 50 kg $\qquad\qquad = 0.08 \times 50$ kg $\qquad\qquad = 4$ kg	**b** The chimpanzee's new mass $\qquad\quad = 50$ kg $- 4$ kg $\qquad\quad = 46$ kg

---

4 During a sale, a £160 microwave oven is discounted by 25%.

    a Find the size of the price decrease.

    b Find the price of the discounted microwave oven.

5 A carton of whole milk contains 8 g of fat. A low fat version of the milk contains 80% less fat than the whole milk.

    a How much less fat does the carton of low fat milk contain?

    b Find the amount of fat in the carton of low fat milk.

6 Decrease: **a** 30 minutes by 60%   **b** 200 m^2 by 35%.

GLOBAL CONTEXT   ELECTIONS

Global context:	Fairness and development
Statement of inquiry:	Mathematics can help us analyse the fairness of different voting systems.
Criterion:	Communicating

QUICK QUIZ

MULTIPLE CHOICE QUIZ

REVIEW SET 12A

1 In the pattern alongside there are 100 tiles.

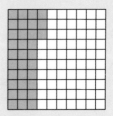

  a Write the number of coloured tiles as a fraction with denominator 100.

  b Write the number of coloured tiles as a percentage of the total number of tiles.

2 This map shows the percentage of the world's population who live on each continent.

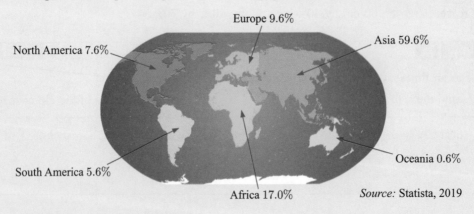

Europe 9.6%

Asia 59.6%

North America 7.6%

Oceania 0.6%

South America 5.6%

Africa 17.0%

Source: Statista, 2019

  a Find the sum of the percentages.

  b What percentage of the world's population lives in:

   i Asia   **ii** North or South America?

  c What *fraction* of the world's population lives in:

   i Africa   **ii** Europe?

3 Write as a percentage:

  a 0.9   **b** 0.47   **c** 0.306

4 Write as a fraction in lowest terms:

    a 31%   **b** 16%   **c** 94%

5 Find: **a** 45% of $60   **b** 12% of 4 m (in cm)

6 50 students attended a quiz night. 27 of them won at least one prize during the night. What percentage of the students won at least one prize?

7 Write as a percentage:

    a $\dfrac{3}{5}$ **b** $\dfrac{221}{1000}$

8 Write as a decimal:

    a 81%   **b** 2%   **c** 10.8%

9 Marcia has travelled 620 kilometres of a 2000 km journey. What percentage has she travelled?

10 Write $\dfrac{3}{4}$, 0.78, and 72% as percentages, then place them on a number line.

11 A small country town has 280 households. 15% use a wood burning fire to warm their homes, 30% use electricity, and 10% use gas.

How many households use: **a** electricity   **b** fire or gas?

12 Brenda makes her own mayonnaise. 40% of the mayonnaise is egg, 35% is oil, 20% is lemon juice, and the rest is mustard.

    a Does the mayonnaise contain more oil or lemon juice?

    b What percentage of the mayonnaise is mustard?

    c How much:

       i lemon juice is there in 300 mL of mayonnaise

       ii oil is there in 800 mL of mayonnaise?

13 The stopping distance of Lou's truck is normally 150 m. In wet weather, the stopping distance increases by 30%.

    a Find the size of the increase in the stopping distance.

    b Find the stopping distance of the truck in wet weather.

REVIEW SET 12B

1 Estimate the percentage shaded in each diagram:

    a 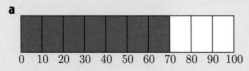   **b**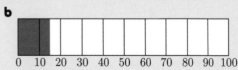

2 Write as a percentage:

    a 0.09   **b** 0.136   **c** 0.702

3 In a group of 200 children, 34 are allergic to peanuts. What percentage of the group are allergic to peanuts?

4 Write 74% as:

    a a decimal   **b** a fraction in lowest terms.

5 8% of the students at a school are left-handed. The school has 375 students. How many students at the school are left-handed?

6 Write each fraction as a percentage:

    a $\dfrac{27}{100}$ **b** $\dfrac{18}{25}$ **c** $\dfrac{13}{20}$

7 Express the first quantity as a percentage of the second:

    a 13 goals from 25 shots   **b** 58 cm of 2 m

8 Klaus spent $15 from the $50 he was given for his birthday. What percentage of his money did he spend?

9 An 800 mL bottle of cordial mixture contains 15% cordial and 85% water.
Find the amount of: **a** cordial   **b** water   in the mixture.

10 Answer the **Opening Problem** on page **218**.

11 **a** Convert each number to a percentage:

       i 0.7   **ii** $\dfrac{17}{25}$ **iii** $\dfrac{39}{50}$ **iv** 0.734

    b Hence place the numbers on a number line.

    c Write the numbers in ascending order.

12 When a painting is sold at an art gallery, the art gallery receives a fixed percentage of the selling price, and the artist receives the rest.

    a When a painting was sold for $200, the art gallery received $66. What percentage of the price was received by:

       i the art gallery   **ii** the artist?

    b A second painting is sold for $450. How much money will be received by:

       i the art gallery   **ii** the artist?

13 In an economic recession, a company was forced to reduce its 600 staff by 15%.

    a Find the size of the decrease.

    b How many staff did the company still have?

Chapter

13

Positive and negative numbers

OPENING PROBLEM

Suppose your class has 25 students. When you arrive for your lesson, you find your teacher has brought 12 cupcakes.

The first students to arrive are allowed to take a cupcake each.

Things to think about:

a How many cupcakes will be left after:

   i 3 students arrive   **ii** 8 students arrive

   iii 12 students arrive?

b How many students will miss out on getting a cupcake?

c Does it make sense to talk about *less than zero* cupcakes?

d When *does* it make sense to talk about numbers less than zero? What should we call these numbers?

You have probably seen numbers less than zero before.

Water freezes at 0°C, but this is not the end of the temperature scale.

When the temperature falls below freezing, we say it becomes *negative*.

A   THE NUMBER LINE

POSITIVE NUMBERS

> **Positive numbers** are numbers which are greater than zero.

We have seen that the **counting numbers** are the numbers 1, 2, 3, 4, 5, ...

They are positive because they are greater than zero.

We could also write them with a **positive sign** (+) before the number, for example +1. However, we normally see them without the positive sign and *assume* the number is positive.

NEGATIVE NUMBERS

> **Negative numbers** are numbers which are less than zero.
>
> They are written with a **negative sign** (−) before the number.

The negative whole numbers are −1, −2, −3, −4, −5, ...

−1 is read as "minus one" or "negative one".

THE NUMBER LINE

To show both positive and negative numbers on a number line, we extend the number line in both directions from zero.

The positive numbers are to the right of zero and the negative numbers are to the left of zero.

Zero is neither positive nor negative.

The number line continues forever in both directions.

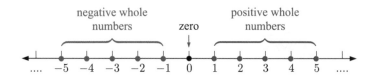

OPPOSITES

Two numbers are **opposites** if they are the same distance from zero but on opposite sides. The numbers will have *opposite signs*.

For example, $+5$ and -5 are opposites.

DISCUSSION

Does zero have an opposite?

EXERCISE 13A

1   State whether each number is positive, negative, or neither:

    a $+5$ **b** -4 **c** -1 **d** 3

    e -7 **f** 0 **g** 9 **h** -8

2   Write down the opposite of:

    a $+7$ **b** -1 **c** 2 **d** -4 **e** $+11$ **f** -13

3   Write down the values of A, B, C, and D:

    a

    b

4 Place each set of numbers on a number line:

  a 2, −5, 1, −3   **b** −2, 0, 7, −4   **c** −9, 3, −7, −6, 5

5 Write down the temperature shown on the thermometer, in degrees Celsius:

B	**ORDERING NUMBERS**

As you move along the number line from *left* to *right*, the numbers *increase*. In a set of numbers, the number furthest to the right is the *greatest* number.

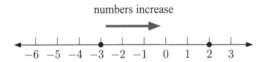

+2 is *greater than* −3 because it is further to the right on the number line.

We write 2 > −3.

As you move along the number line from *right* to *left*, the numbers *decrease*. In a set of numbers, the number furthest to the left is the *least* number.

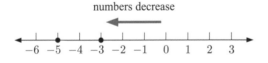

−5 is *less than* −3 because it is further to the left on the number line.

We write −5 < −3.

EXERCISE 13B

1

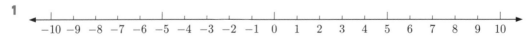

Use the number line to help you complete each statement with < or >:

  a 2 ...... −1   **b** −6 ...... −3   **c** −5 3

  d 0 ...... −8   **e** −5 ...... −9   **f** −7 0

Example 1   ◀) **Self Tutor**

Arrange the numbers −2, 3, −7, and 1 in ascending order.

Ascending means from least to greatest.

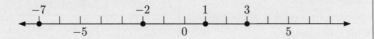

In ascending order, the numbers are −7, −2, 1, and 3.

2 Place each set of numbers on a number line, and hence write them in *ascending* order:

   a 4, −2, 0, −3   **b** −1, 5, 2, −4   **c** −1, 4, −8, 6

3 Place each set of numbers on a number line, and hence write them in *descending* order:

   a 1, −5, 3, −2   **b** −3, 6, −6, 0   **c** −4, 5, −6, −1

DISCUSSION

- When dealing with positive and negative numbers, why might we talk about *greater than* and *less than* rather than *larger* and *smaller*?
- When we write numbers in ascending or descending order, are we necessarily ordering them according to their *size*?

C   WORDS INDICATING POSITIVE AND NEGATIVE

There are many words we commonly use which are *opposites*. We can often associate them with positive and negative.

- Some words refer to our **position** on the number line. They tell us the **sign** of the quantity we are talking about.

  For example:

  ▶ A temperature *above* zero is positive.

  ▶ A temperature *below* zero is negative.

- Some words refer to the **direction** we are moving on the number line. They tell us the **operation** we are performing.

  For example:

  ▶ If a quantity is *increasing*, we are moving to the right, which is the positive direction.

  ▶ If a quantity is *decreasing*, we are moving to the left, which is the negative direction.

ACTIVITY 1

What to do:

1 The words below refer to a **position**.
Write each word with its opposite in the table according to which is positive and which is negative.

a loss	above	right of
an increase	a gain	behind
ahead	left of	below
a decrease		

Positive (+)	Negative (−)
north of	south of

2 The words below refer to a **direction**.
Write each word with its opposite in the table according to which is positive and which is negative.

winning	backwards	upwards
cooling by	decreasing	forwards
losing	warming by	downwards
increasing	right	left

Positive (+)	Negative (−)
north	south

3 Why do you think we choose:

a north to be positive and south to be negative

b east to be positive and west to be negative?

EXERCISE 13C

1 Write each temperature as a positive or negative number:

    a 7°C below zero   **b** 32°C above zero   **c** 40°C below zero

2 Write as a positive or negative number:

    a a $10 gain   **b** a $15 loss   **c** a 7 kg gain

    d a 3 kg loss   **e** 8 m in front   **f** 45 m behind

3 Assuming north is the positive direction, write each position as a positive or negative number:

    a 7 km south   **b** 12 km north   **c** 15 km south

4 Write as a positive or negative number:

    a The clock is 8 minutes fast.   **b** Suzanne is 10 minutes early.

5 The table alongside shows the elevation of various cities compared with sea level.

    a Place each value on a number line.

    b Which of these cities are *below* sea level?

    c Which of these cities has the:

        i *highest* elevation   **ii** *lowest* elevation?

Location	Elevation
Dublin, Ireland	8 m
Hachirōgata, Japan	−4 m
Tripoli, Libya	5 m
New Orleans, USA	−2 m
Jakarta, Indonesia	3 m

6 Write the opposite of:

    a a 6 point loss   **b** an $18 gain   **c** 15 km to the east

    d 20 m above   **e** 3 minutes early   **f** 7 m to the left

7 Copy and complete:

	Statement	Number	Opposite of statement	Opposite number
a	30 km to the south	−30		
b	a $25 gain			
c	4 m above the water			
d	12°C below zero			
e	an increase of 6 kg			

8 Write the opposite of:

    a travelling 6 km north   **b** gaining 4 kg   **c** 3 steps backwards

    d warming by 4°C   **e** losing $30   **f** ascending 12 stairs

9 Copy and complete:

	Statement	Operation	Opposite of statement	Opposite operation
a	cooling by 18°C	subtract 18°C		
b	gaining $26			
c	6 steps to the left			
d	winning by 7 points			
e	driving 8 km east			
f	60 m downwards			

D   ADDITION AND SUBTRACTION ON THE NUMBER LINE

So far, all of the operations we have performed have been with positive numbers.

> When we **add** a positive number, we move to the right on the number line. The quantity is increasing.

For example, in $4 + 2$, we start at 4 and move 2 units to the right.

So, $4 + 2 = 6$.

> When we **subtract** a positive number, we move to the left on the number line. The quantity is decreasing.

For example, in $4 - 2$, we start at 4 and move 2 units to the left.

So, $4 - 2 = 2$.

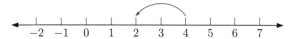

Example 2

🔊 **Self Tutor**

Use a number line to find:

a $5 - 8$ **b** $-7 + 3$

a We start at 5 and move 8 units to the left.

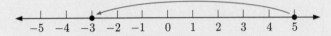

So, $5 - 8 = -3$.

b We start at -7 and move 3 units to the right.

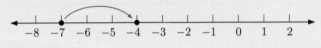

So, $-7 + 3 = -4$.

When we subtract a number greater than our starting number, the result will be negative.

EXERCISE 13D

1 Use a number line to find:

  a $5 - 3$ **b** $3 - 5$ **c** $-5 + 3$ **d** $-3 + 5$

2 Use a number line to find:

  a $4 - 4$ **b** $-4 + 4$ **c** $4 + 4$ **d** $-4 - 4$

3 Use a number line to find:

  a $2 - 7$ **b** $-1 + 4$ **c** $0 - 6$ **d** $-9 + 2$

  e $-3 - 4$ **f** $7 - 12$ **g** $-2 + 8$ **h** $1 - 9$

4 Find:

  a $-8 + 5$ **b** $-3 - 7$ **c** $6 - 9$ **d** $-1 + 7$

Example 3

🔊 **Self Tutor**

Use a number line to find $1 - 2 + 5$.

We start at 1, move 2 units to the left, and then 5 units to the right.

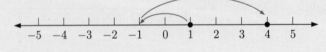

So, $1 - 2 + 5 = 4$.

5 Use a number line to find:

  a $2 + 3 - 6$ **b** $-7 + 4 - 2$ **c** $-5 + 8 + 3$ **d** $4 - 6 + 5$

  e $3 - 10 + 1$ **f** $-8 + 6 - 7$ **g** $3 - 7 + 9$ **h** $-9 - 5 - 2$

Example 4   ◀️ **Self Tutor**

A lift started 2 floors above ground level. It travelled down 5 floors then up 1 floor.

How many floors above or below ground level is the lift now?

The lift started at $+2$ or just 2.

Travelling down 5 floors means we subtract 5.

Travelling up 1 floor means we add 1.

So, the result is $2 - 5 + 1 = -2$.

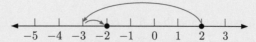

The lift is now 2 floors *below* ground level.

6   Henry entered an elevator 6 floors above ground level. He travelled down 8 floors to his car. How many floors below ground level is Henry's car?

7   A lift started 1 floor below ground level. It travelled 4 floors up then 6 floors down. How many floors above or below ground level is the lift now?

8   At midnight, the temperature in Chicago was $-3°C$. Between midnight and 9 am, the temperature dropped by $4°C$ then rose by $6°C$. What was the temperature at 9 am?

9   Wendy is 5 km east of her house. She cycles 11 km to the west to meet her friend, then 6 km to the east. Where is Wendy now?

10   An NFL gridiron team was 7 points ahead at quarter time. They lost the 2nd quarter by 15 points, won the 3rd quarter by 13 points, and lost the 4th quarter by 9 points.

    a   By how many points was the team winning or losing:

       i   at half time   **ii**   after three quarters?

    b   Did the team win or lose the game? By how much?

Example 5   ◀️ **Self Tutor**

Find the combined effect of travelling 6 km south and then 2 km north.

Suppose we start at 0.

Travelling 6 km south means we subtract 6.

Travelling 2 km north means we add 2.

So, the result is $0 - 6 + 2 = -4$.

The combined effect is travelling 4 km south.

11   Find the combined effect of travelling:

    a   3 km north and then 6 km south

    b   7 km south and then 9 km north

    c   8 km east and then 5 km west

    d   11 km west and then 3 km east.

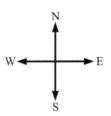

12   Boris checks the temperature in his bedroom on a regular basis. Find the combined effect if his bedroom gets:

    a   1°C warmer and then 6°C cooler

    b   4°C cooler and then 11°C warmer.

13   Find the combined effect of:

    a   earning \$5 and then spending \$15   **b**   spending €10 and then earning €30

    c   spending £40 and then earning £40.

E   ADDING AND SUBTRACTING NEGATIVE NUMBERS

DISCUSSION

We have seen that:

- to add a positive number, we move to the right
- to subtract a positive number, we move to the left.

Which direction do you think we will need to move, to:

a   add a negative number   **b**   subtract a negative number?

ADDING A NEGATIVE NUMBER

Freddy the frog is sitting at 5 on the number line.

He is getting ready to perform an addition, so he faces the *right*.

- To add a *positive* number, Freddy hops *forwards*. He moves to the right.

$$5 + 3 = 8$$

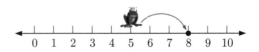

- To add a *negative* number, Freddy hops *backwards*. He moves to the left.

$$5 + -3 = 2$$

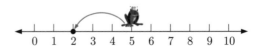

Since we know $5 - 3 = 2$, we conclude that:

Adding a **negative** number is the same as **subtracting** its **opposite**.

SUBTRACTING A NEGATIVE NUMBER

Freddy is now sitting at 7 on the number line.

He is getting ready to perform a subtraction, so he faces the *left*.

- To subtract a *positive* number, Freddy hops *forwards*. He moves to the left.

  $7 - 2 = 5$

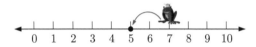

- To subtract a *negative* number, Freddy hops *backwards*. He moves to the right.

  $7 - -2 = 9$

Since we know $7 + 2 = 9$, we conclude that:

Subtracting a **negative** number is the same as **adding** its **opposite**.

Example 6 ◀)) **Self Tutor**

Find:

a $3 + -7$ **b** $3 - -7$ **c** $-3 + -7$ **d** $-3 - -7$

a $\quad 3 + -7$	**b** $\quad 3 - -7$	**c** $\quad -3 + -7$	**d** $\quad -3 - -7$
$= 3 - 7$	$= 3 + 7$	$= -3 - 7$	$= -3 + 7$
$= -4$	$= 10$	$= -10$	$= 4$

EXERCISE 13E

1 Find:

   a $6 + -2$ **b** $6 - -2$ **c** $-6 + -2$ **d** $-6 - -2$

   e $5 + -9$ **f** $5 - -9$ **g** $-5 + -9$ **h** $-5 - -9$

2 Find:

   a $10 + -4$ **b** $1 - -7$ **c** $-3 + -5$ **d** $-8 - -14$

   e $-9 - -6$ **f** $-4 + -9$ **g** $0 - -5$ **h** $-11 - -18$

   i $-4 + -5$ **j** $2 - -11$ **k** $-3 + -4$ **l** $-12 - -4$

3 Find:

   a $2 + 7 + -3$ **b** $8 - 5 + -4$ **c** $10 - -6 - 8$

   d $-3 + -8 - -5$ **e** $7 + -11 + -1$ **f** $-5 + 14 + -9$

Example 7   ◀))) **Self Tutor**

Find the difference between:

a 2 and -6 b -11 and -1

The difference between two numbers is the distance between them on the number line. It is the greater number minus the lesser number.

a 2 is to the right of -6 on the number line, so 2 is greater than -6.

The difference between 2 and $-6 = 2 - -6$
$$= 2 + 6$$
$$= 8$$

b -1 is to the right of -11 on the number line, so -1 is greater than -11.

The difference between -11 and $-1 = -1 - -11$
$$= -1 + 11$$
$$= 10$$

4 Find the difference between:

a 3 and -4 b -7 and 2   c -4 and -8

d 0 and -6 e 11 and -8 f -13 and -9

g -4 and 10   h -7 and -5 i 5 and -7

5 The seagull is flying 5 metres above sea level.
The kayaker is paddling at sea level.
The diver is swimming 2 metres below sea level.
The dolphin is 6 metres below sea level.

a Write a whole number to describe the position of each person or animal compared with sea level.

b Find the distance between the:

  i   kayaker and the diver
  ii seagull and the dolphin
  iii dolphin and the kayaker
  iv diver and the dolphin.

6 This table shows the minimum and maximum temperatures in a ski village over a one week period. Copy the table, then complete the last row with the difference between the minimum and maximum temperatures on each day.

	Mon	Tue	Wed	Thu	Fri	Sat	Sun
Minimum temperature	$-4°$C	$-6°$C	$-2°$C	$-3°$C	$-5°$C	$-12°$C	$-13°$C
Maximum temperature	$1°$C	$3°$C	$1°$C	$0°$C	$0°$C	$-3°$C	$-2°$C
Temperature difference							

7 Two teams are playing the card game canasta. The table shows the number of points scored by each team for the first three hands.

Hand	Team A	Team B
1	−50	810
2	400	140
3	900	−300

  a Find the difference between the points scored by the teams in:

    i hand 1   **ii** hand 2   **iii** hand 3.

  b Find the total number of points scored by each team so far.

  c Who is winning the game and by how many points?

8 The children at a party are trying to guess how many lollies are in a jar. The results of the game are shown below. A positive number means the child guessed too high, and a negative number means the child guessed too low.

  a How many children guessed too low?

  b How many children were within 10 of the correct answer?

  c Which child's guess was the furthest away?

  d Which child's guess was the closest?

  e Find the difference between:

    i Xavier's guess and Kevin's guess

    ii Gabrielle's guess and Luis' guess.

  f Jack's guess was 50 lollies.

    i How many lollies were in the jar?

    ii What was Molly's guess?

Child	Result
Max	+30
Xavier	−12
Lauren	−4
Molly	+21
Claire	+3
Jack	−24
Gabrielle	+9
Luis	−13
Kevin	−7

F   MULTIPLYING NEGATIVE NUMBERS

DISCUSSION

We have seen that 3×5 means "3 lots of 5" which is $5 + 5 + 5 = 15$

So, $3 \times 5 = 15$.

1 Can we use this idea to find:

  a 3×-5 **b** -3×5?

2 Do you think -3×-5 will be negative or positive?

Suppose Freddy the frog starts at 0.

- Freddy thinks of 4×3 as "4 hops of 3".
  Freddy makes four jumps of positive 3. Since each jump is positive, he faces the right.

We see that $4 \times 3 = 12$.

- Freddy thinks of 4×-3 as "4 hops of *minus* 3".
  Freddy makes 4 jumps of *minus* 3. Since each jump is negative, he faces the left.

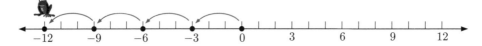

We see that $4 \times -3 = -12$.

- Freddy thinks of -4×3 as "4 *backwards* hops of 3".
  Freddy is again jumping 3 units each time, and is facing the right. However, he now jumps four times *backwards* each time.

We see that $-4 \times 3 = -12$.

- Freddy thinks of -4×-3 as "4 *backwards* hops of *minus* 3".
  Freddy is jumping three units each time, and is facing the left. He jumps four times *backwards*.

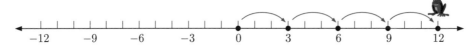

We see that $-4 \times -3 = 12$.

Our observations of Freddy lead us to the following **rules for multiplication**:

- A **positive** times a **positive** gives a **positive**.
- A **positive** times a **negative** gives a **negative**.
- A **negative** times a **positive** gives a **negative**.
- A **negative** times a **negative** gives a **positive**.

Multiplying numbers with the **same** signs gives a **positive**.

Multiplying numbers with **different** signs gives a **negative**.

Example 8			◀⟩ **Self Tutor**

Find:

  a 3×2 **b** 3×-2 **c** -3×2 **d** -3×-2

  a $3 \times 2 = 6$ **b** $3 \times -2 = -6$ **c** $-3 \times 2 = -6$ **d** $-3 \times -2 = 6$

EXERCISE 13F

1 Find:

  a 2×5 **b** 2×-5 **c** -2×5 **d** -2×-5

  e 5×-2 **f** -5×2 **g** 5×2 **h** -5×-2

2 Find:

  a 4×-2 **b** -5×3 **c** 7×-4 **d** 9×-1

  e -3×-6 **f** -8×5 **g** -1×-7 **h** -4×11

  i 5×-5 **j** -8×-8 **k** -9×7 **l** -12×10

  m -8×7 **n** -6×-11 **o** -5×9 **p** -7×-12

3 Each week, Marnie's bank account balance reduces by \$10 to pay for her television subscription. Find the change in Marnie's bank account balance after 4 weeks.

4 A multiple choice test contains 12 questions. Students gain 5 marks for each question they answer correctly, and they lose 3 marks for each question they answer incorrectly. Find:

  a the highest possible score   **b** the lowest possible score

  c the final score of a student who answers 7 questions correctly and the rest incorrectly.

5 List all the ways of writing -30 as the product of two whole numbers.

6 Find:

  a $-2 \times 3 \times -4$ **b** $5 \times -2 \times 3$ **c** $-6 \times -1 \times -7$ **d** $5 \times -8 \times -2$

7 List all the ways of writing -12 as the product of *three* whole numbers.

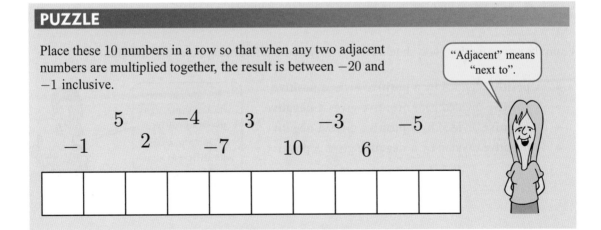

PUZZLE

Place these 10 numbers in a row so that when any two adjacent numbers are multiplied together, the result is between -20 and -1 inclusive.

"Adjacent" means "next to".

5 -4 3 -3 -5

-1 2 -7 10 6

G | DIVIDING NEGATIVE NUMBERS

In this Section we look for rules for the **division** of negative numbers.

For example, we know that $15 \div 5 = 3$, but we also need to be able to calculate:

- $15 \div -5$
- $-15 \div 5$
- $-15 \div -5$

INVESTIGATION   DIVIDING NEGATIVE NUMBERS

We have seen previously how multiplication facts can be used to help solve division problems.

For example:

- $4 \times 5 = 20$, so $20 \div 4 = 5$
- $8 \times 3 = 24$, so $24 \div 8 = 3$

What to do:

1. Copy and complete:
   a $3 \times 6 = 18$, so $18 \div 3 = \ldots\ldots$
   b $-3 \times -6 = 18$, so $18 \div -3 = \ldots\ldots$
   c $3 \times -6 = -18$, so $-18 \div 3 = \ldots\ldots$
   d $-3 \times 6 = -18$, so $-18 \div -3 = \ldots\ldots$

2. Copy and complete:
   a $9 \times 5 = \ldots\ldots$, so $\ldots\ldots \div 9 = 5$
   b $-9 \times -5 = \ldots\ldots$, so $\ldots\ldots \div -9 = -5$
   c $9 \times -5 = \ldots\ldots$, so $\ldots\ldots \div 9 = -5$
   d $-9 \times 5 = \ldots\ldots$, so $\ldots\ldots \div -9 = 5$.

3. What do you suspect is the result when:
   a a positive number is divided by a positive number
   b a positive number is divided by a negative number
   c a negative number is divided by a positive number
   d a negative number is divided by a negative number?

From the **Investigation**, you should have discovered the following **rules for division**:

- A **positive** divided by a **positive** gives a **positive**.
- A **positive** divided by a **negative** gives a **negative**.
- A **negative** divided by a **positive** gives a **negative**.
- A **negative** divided by a **negative** gives a **positive**.

Dividing numbers with the **same** signs gives a **positive**.
Dividing numbers with **different** signs gives a **negative**.

Example 9			◀) **Self Tutor**
Find:			
a $14 \div 7$	**b** $14 \div -7$	**c** $-14 \div 7$	**d** $-14 \div -7$
a $14 \div 7 = 2$	**b** $14 \div -7 = -2$	**c** $-14 \div 7 = -2$	**d** $-14 \div -7 = 2$

EXERCISE 13G

1 Find:

    a $18 \div 3$ **b** $18 \div -3$ **c** $-18 \div 3$ **d** $-18 \div -3$

    e $36 \div 9$ **f** $36 \div -9$ **g** $-36 \div 9$ **h** $-36 \div -9$

    i $5 \div 5$ **j** $5 \div -5$ **k** $-5 \div 5$ **l** $-5 \div -5$

    m $42 \div 6$ **n** $42 \div -6$ **o** $-42 \div 6$ **p** $-42 \div -6$

2 Find:

    a $-12 \div 4$ **b** $-18 \div 9$ **c** $6 \div -2$ **d** $20 \div -5$

    e $-24 \div -4$ **f** $35 \div -7$ **g** $-9 \div 3$ **h** $32 \div -8$

    i $-26 \div -2$ **j** $-54 \div 6$ **k** $-9 \div -9$ **l** $-49 \div -7$

    m $80 \div -8$ **n** $-63 \div 7$ **o** $-96 \div -12$ **p** $121 \div -11$

3 A negative number is divided by a positive number, and then the result is divided by a negative number. Is the final answer positive or negative? Explain your answer.

ACTIVITY 2   CALCULATOR USE

We can use our calculator to perform operations with negative numbers. The negative numbers are entered on the calculator using a key such as $\boxed{+/-}$ or $\boxed{(-)}$.

For example, to find $-3 - -2$, press $\boxed{+/-}\ 3\ \boxed{-}\ \boxed{+/-}\ 2\ \boxed{=}$.

What to do:

1 Use your calculator to find:

    a $-10 + 8$ **b** $23 - 48$ **c** $-57 + 39$

    d $-31 + 49 + -60$ **e** $19 - -83 + -43$ **f** $-124 + -71 - -94$

    g 13×-17 **h** -18×-22 **i** $456 \div -24$

2 Evaluate each expression using the correct order of operations. Use your calculator to check your answers.

    a $-4 \div 2 - 6$ **b** $-4 \div (2 - 6)$ **c** $4 - 6 \div 2$

    d $(4 - 6) \div 2$ **e** $-4 \times 2 - 6$ **f** $-4 \times (2 - 6)$

    g $-4 - 2 \times 6$ **h** $(-4 - 2) \times 6$ **i** $-4 \div (-2 - 6)$

    j $4 \div (-2 + 6)$ **k** $4 \times -2 + 6$ **l** $4 \times (-2 + 6)$

3 Use your calculator to solve the following problems:

   a Jerusalem has an altitude of 785 m. The Dead Sea has an altitude of -423 m. Find the difference between their altitudes.

   b The table alongside shows the daily maximum temperatures in Tokyo over one week.
Calculate the average daily maximum temperature.

Saturday	$-3°$C
Sunday	$2°$C
Monday	$3°$C
Tuesday	$-2°$C
Wednesday	$-5°$C
Thursday	$-11°$C
Friday	$-6°$C

   c At the start of the month, Harry's credit card balance was $-\$347$. This means he *owed* the bank $\$347$. During the month he bought a dishwasher for $\$549$, then made a credit card repayment of $\$250$. What is his credit card balance now?

QUICK QUIZ

MULTIPLE CHOICE QUIZ

REVIEW SET 13A

1 State whether each number is positive, negative, or neither:

   a -4 **b** 3 **c** 0 **d** -12

2 Write down the values of A, B, and C.

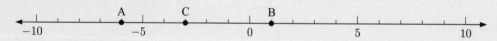

3 Complete each statement with $<$ or $>$:

   a -3 ...... 2 **b** 0 ...... -6 **c** -4 ...... -7

4 Write the opposite of:

   a travelling 10 km south   **b** getting 3 cm shorter.

5 Use a number line to find:

   a $6 - 10$ **b** $-4 + 7$ **c** $-5 - 6$

   d $5 - 10 + 3$ **e** $-8 - 3 + 7$ **f** $1 - 7 + 9$

6 Find:

   a $3 + -8$ **b** $5 - -5$ **c** $-6 - -13$

   d $9 + -9$ **e** $11 + -7 - -1$ **f** $2 + -10 - -4$

7 Find the difference between:

   a 2 and -5 **b** -4 and 0   **c** -3 and -9

8 Find:

   a 2×-7 **b** -9×-3 **c** -6×6 **d** -5×-10

9 Find:

   a $-33 \div 3$ **b** $16 \div -4$ **c** $-72 \div -9$ **d** $48 \div -8$

10 Find:

   a $3 \times -4 \times -2$ **b** $-5 \times -3 \times -2$

11 Isabella ran a lemonade stall at a school festival. She made a $10 profit in the first hour, a $25 loss in the second hour, and a $7 profit in the third hour. Find the total profit or loss made by Isabella over the three hours.

12 The top of a tree is 5 metres above ground level. A bird in the tree is 3 metres above ground level, the tree's roots are 1 metre below ground level, and a pipe is 2 metres below ground level.

   a Write a positive or negative number to describe the height of each object compared with ground level.

   b Find the difference in height between:

     i the tree top and the roots

     ii the bird and the pipe

     iii the roots and the pipe.

REVIEW SET 13B

1 Write the opposite of:

   a $+5$ **b** -8 **c** 12

2 Place each set of numbers on a number line, and hence write them in ascending order:

   a $-9, 4, 0, -2$ **b** $-6, 3, -8, 1$

3 Write as a positive or negative number:

   a 15 m below sea level   **b** 6 m to the right

4 An elevator started 3 levels below ground level. It travelled up 5 floors, then down 3 floors. How many floors above or below ground level is the elevator now?

5 Find:

   a $11 + -1$ **b** $3 - -9$ **c** $-10 - -10$ **d** $-4 + 13 + -8$

6 In a spelling quiz, students were awarded points for answering questions correctly, and they lost points for answering questions incorrectly. Nick scored 7 points, Teresa scored 12 points, and Brett scored -4 points.

Find the difference between:

   a Teresa's score and Brett's score

   b Brett's score and Nick's score.

7 Find:

   a 6×-1 **b** -3×7 **c** 10×-9 **d** -11×-12

8 List all the ways of writing -20 as the product of two whole numbers.

9 Find:

   a $14 \div -2$ **b** $-24 \div 6$ **c** $-35 \div -7$ **d** $-88 \div -11$

10 Find:

   a -12×5 **b** $-2 - -8$ **c** $-20 \div -4$

   d $-7 + -6 - 5$ **e** -11×-9 **f** $63 \div -7$

11 The temperature in Moscow at midnight was $-4°$C. In the period between midnight and midday, the temperature dropped by $3°$C, rose by $10°$C, then dropped by $2°$C.

   a Find the temperature at midday.

   b For this period, find the:

      i warmest temperature reached   **ii** coolest temperature reached.

   c Find the difference between the warmest and coolest temperatures reached.

12

Freddy the frog is on the lilypad at 0. He has spied a bug which he would like for dinner.

   a Write down a number to represent the position of the bug.

   b Freddy has forgotten his bow tie for dinner. He jumps back to his house, 2 lilypads at a time. Freddy needs 4 jumps to return home. What is the position of his house?

   c Meanwhile, the bug has moved one lilypad to the right for each of Freddy's jumps. How far away is the bug now from 0?

   d Not wanting to miss his dinner, Freddy chases after the bug. He jumps forward 3 lilypads every time, with the bug fleeing one lilypad for each of Freddy's jumps. How many jumps does Freddy need to catch the bug?

Chapter 14

Sequences

Contents:

OPENING PROBLEM

Katie-Rose has saved $72. She decides to save a further $10 from her pocket money each week from now until she has enough to buy a bicycle.

Things to think about:

a Can you write a *sequence* to show the total amount Katie-Rose will have saved at the end of each week?

b How long will it take Katie-Rose to save the $130 needed to buy her bicycle?

Look at the house numbers on this street.

The values 24, 26, 28, 30, 32 form a **sequence** of numbers.

The sequence starts at 24. Since the house numbers are consecutive even numbers, we add 2 each time to get the next house number.

$$24 \xrightarrow{+2} 26 \xrightarrow{+2} 28 \xrightarrow{+2} 30 \xrightarrow{+2} 32$$

So, we can describe the sequence using the **rule**:

start at 24 and add 2 each time.

 A   # GENERATING A SEQUENCE

We can generate a sequence if we have a **rule** telling us:

• the *starting value* of the sequence
• how to get from one number to the next.

Example 1	◀) **Self Tutor**

Find the first five numbers in the sequence:

start at 7 and increase by 4 each time.

$$7 \xrightarrow{+4} 11 \xrightarrow{+4} 15 \xrightarrow{+4} 19 \xrightarrow{+4} 23$$

The first five numbers are   7, 11, 15, 19, 23.

EXERCISE 14A

1   Copy the boxes, then use the rule to complete each sequence:

    a   start at 9 and add 5 each time

$$\boxed{9} \xrightarrow{\;+5\;} \square \longrightarrow \square \longrightarrow \square \longrightarrow \square$$

    b   start at 23 and subtract 3 each time

$$\boxed{23} \xrightarrow{\;-3\;} \square \longrightarrow \square \longrightarrow \square \longrightarrow \square$$

    c   start at 18 and increase by 7 each time

$$\square \xrightarrow{\;+7\;} \square \longrightarrow \square \longrightarrow \square \longrightarrow \square$$

    d   start at 5 and multiply by 2 each time

$$\square \xrightarrow{\;\times 2\;} \square \longrightarrow \square \longrightarrow \square \longrightarrow \square$$

    e   start at 5 and decrease by 2 each time

$$\square \xrightarrow{\;-2\;} \square \longrightarrow \square \longrightarrow \square \longrightarrow \square$$

2   Find the first six numbers in each sequence:

    a   start at 5 and add 3 each time   **b**   start at 12 and increase by 7 each time

    c   start at 19 and add 8 each time   **d**   start at 21 and subtract 2 each time

    e   start at 57 and decrease by 5 each time   **f**   start at 17 and subtract 6 each time

    g   start at -18 and increase by 7 each time.

3   **a**   Find the first eight numbers in each sequence:

          i   start at 14 and increase by 9 each time

         ii   start at 56 and decrease by 6 each time

        iii   start at 8 and add 12 each time.

    b   Which number can be found in all three sequences?

4   When asked to write the first 10 numbers of the sequence "start at 83 and subtract 7 each time", Russell wrote these numbers:

$$83, \ 76, \ 69, \ 62, \ 55, \ 46, \ 41, \ 34, \ 27, \ 20$$

    One of the numbers is incorrect. Identify the incorrect number, and correct it.

5   Find the first four numbers in each sequence:

    a   start at 4 and multiply by 2 each time   **b**   start at 10 and multiply by 3 each time

    c   start at 200 and divide by 2 each time   **d**   start at 7000 and divide by 10 each time

    e   start at 1 and multiply by -2 each time.

6   Kiri is recovering from an injury to her arm. The doctor says that she must exercise it for 3 minutes on Monday, and the exercise time must be doubled each day until Friday.

    a   List the exercise times for Kiri for the five days.

    b   Find the total exercise time for the five days.

Example 2   ◀) **Self Tutor**

Find the first six numbers of the sequence:

start at 7 and subtract $\frac{3}{8}$ each time.

$$7 \xrightarrow{-\frac{3}{8}} 6\frac{5}{8} \xrightarrow{-\frac{3}{8}} 6\frac{2}{8} \xrightarrow{-\frac{3}{8}} 5\frac{7}{8} \xrightarrow{-\frac{3}{8}} 5\frac{4}{8} \xrightarrow{-\frac{3}{8}} 5\frac{1}{8}$$

The first six numbers are $7, \ 6\frac{5}{8}, \ 6\frac{1}{4}, \ 5\frac{7}{8}, \ 5\frac{1}{2}, \ 5\frac{1}{8}.$

7 Find the first six numbers in each sequence:

  a start at 5 and increase by $\frac{1}{2}$ each time   **b** start at $\frac{1}{4}$ and add $\frac{3}{4}$ each time

  c start at 6 and decrease by $\frac{2}{5}$ each time   **d** start at 8 and subtract $\frac{5}{8}$ each time

  e start at $\frac{1}{2}$ and increase by $\frac{1}{4}$ each time   **f** start at $\frac{11}{6}$ and take away $\frac{1}{3}$ each time.

8 Martha fills her bird feeder with 5 cups of bird seed. Her birds eat $\frac{3}{4}$ cup of seed each day.

Write a sequence to show the amount of seed in the feeder at the end of each day for the first 5 days.

9 Find the first six numbers in each sequence:

  a start at 4 and add 0.6 each time

  b start at 3.6 and increase by 1.1 each time

  c start at 7.8 and take away 0.3 each time

  d start at 21 and decrease by 2.5 each time

  e start at 490 and divide by 10 each time

  f start at 0.0173 and multiply by 10 each time.

10 The cost of attending a swimming club session in 2014 was $6.40. The cost increased by $0.55 per year after that.
Find the cost of attending a swimming session each year from 2015 to 2020.

B FINDING A RULE FOR A SEQUENCE

A rule for a sequence should include both:

* the starting value of the sequence
* how to get from one number to the next.

Writing one of these without the other is not enough.

To find a rule for a sequence:

- Think about how you can get from the starting value to the second number.
- Check that the same operation will get you to the next numbers.

Example 3   ◀)) **Self Tutor**

Find a rule for the sequence   5000, 500, 50, 5, ...

To get from 5000 to 500 we can divide by 10.

So, we try dividing by 10 each time:

$$5000 \xrightarrow{\div 10} 500 \xrightarrow{\div 10} 50 \xrightarrow{\div 10} 5$$

This gives the correct results, so the rule is:

start at 5000 and divide by 10 each time.

EXERCISE 14B

1 Find a rule for each sequence:

    a 8, 13, 18, 23, 28, ...   **b** 24, 22, 20, 18, 16, ...

    c 69, 72, 75, 78, 81, ...   **d** 38, 34, 30, 26, 22, ...

    e 43, 52, 61, 70, 79, ...   **f** 83, 66, 49, 32, 15, ...

    g 2, 6, 18, 54, 162, ...   **h** 6, 60, 600, 6000, 60 000, ...

    i 112, 56, 28, 14, 7, ...   **j** 7500, 1500, 300, 60, 12, ...

2 Find a rule for each sequence and hence find its next three numbers:

    a 4, 9, 14, 19, 24, ...   **b** 38, 32, 26, 20, ...

    c 6, 15, 24, 33, 42, ...   **d** 41, 33, 25, 17, 9, ...

    e 2, 4, 8, 16, ...   **f** 4, 40, 400, 4000, ...

    g 13, 7, 1, −5, ...   **h** −1, 2, −4, 8, ...

3 Find a rule for each sequence and hence find the missing number(s):

    a 11, 14, 17, △, 23, ...   **b** 50, 43, 36, △, 22, 15, ...

    c 3, 9, △, 21, 27, □, ...   **d** 60, 51, 42, △, 24, □, 6, ...

    e 4, 20, △, 500, 2500, ...   **f** 6400, 1600, △, 100, 25, ...

4 Bruno is training for a weightlifting competition. He lifted 150 kg in the first week, 155 kg in the second week, 160 kg in the third week, and 165 kg in the fourth week.

    a Find a rule for this sequence.

    b Assuming the sequence continues, what weight will Bruno lift in the sixth week?

5 Find the rule for each sequence and hence find the next three numbers:

    a 5, 5.9, 6.8, 7.7, 8.6, ...   **b** 13.1, 12.6, 12.1, 11.6, 11.1, ...

    c 1.4, 1.34, 1.28, 1.22, 1.16, ...   **d** 5130, 513, 51.3, 5.13, ...

6 Find the missing number in each sequence:

    a 2.8, 3.1, 3.4, $\triangle$, 4, ...   **b** 6.3, 5.7, 5.1, $\triangle$, 3.9, ...

    c 9.12, 9.19, 9.26, $\triangle$, 9.4, ...   **d** 2.5, 2.38, 2.26, $\triangle$, 2.02, ...

    e 1270, 127, 12.7, $\triangle$, 0.127, ...   **f** 0.539, 5.39, $\triangle$, 539, 5390, ...

7 Molly is preparing for a long distance kayaking expedition. She paddled 5.7 km on the first day, 7.1 km on the second day, 8.5 km on the third day, and 9.9 km on the fourth day.

    a Find a rule for this sequence.

    b Assuming the pattern continues, find:

        i how far Molly will paddle on the sixth day

        ii when Molly will first paddle at least 15 km in one day.

8 Find a rule for each sequence and hence find the next three numbers:

    a $2, 2\frac{2}{3}, 3\frac{1}{3}, 4, ...$ **b** $\frac{19}{5}, \frac{16}{5}, \frac{13}{5}, 2, ...$ **c** $3\frac{1}{4}, 4, 4\frac{3}{4}, 5\frac{1}{2}, ...$

9 By writing the fractions with the same denominator, find a rule for the sequence. Hence find the next three numbers.

    a $\frac{1}{2}, \frac{2}{3}, \frac{5}{6}, 1, \frac{7}{6}, ...$ **b** $\frac{3}{2}, \frac{17}{12}, \frac{4}{3}, \frac{5}{4}, \frac{7}{6}, ...$ **c** $\frac{5}{16}, \frac{1}{2}, \frac{11}{16}, \frac{7}{8}, ...$

10 Find a rule for each sequence and hence find the missing number:

    a $6, 5\frac{1}{3}, 4\frac{2}{3}, \triangle, 3\frac{1}{3}, ...$ **b** $2, 3\frac{1}{5}, 4\frac{2}{5}, \triangle, 6\frac{4}{5}, ...$ **c** $11\frac{6}{7}, 9\frac{3}{7}, 7, \triangle, 2\frac{1}{7}, ...$

11 Find the rule for each sequence and hence find the next two numbers:

    a 0.05, 0.1, 0.2, 0.4, 0.8, ...   **b** $27, 9, 3, 1, \frac{1}{3}, ...$

12 Amber bought a book to read while she was on holidays. It has 268 pages.

Amber read 8 pages on the first day, $10\frac{1}{2}$ pages on the second day, 13 pages on the third day, and $15\frac{1}{2}$ pages on the fourth day.

    a Find a rule for this sequence.

    b Assuming the pattern continues:

        i How many pages will Amber read on the seventh day?

        ii On which day will she finish the book?

Example 4   ◀)) **Self Tutor**

Find the next three numbers in this sequence: $\frac{2}{5}, \frac{5}{9}, \frac{8}{13}, \frac{11}{17}, ...$

The numerators start at 2 and increase by 3 each time.

$$2 \xrightarrow{+3} 5 \xrightarrow{+3} 8 \xrightarrow{+3} 11$$

The denominators start at 5 and increase by 4 each time.

$$5 \xrightarrow{+4} 9 \xrightarrow{+4} 13 \xrightarrow{+4} 17$$

So, the sequence starts at $\frac{2}{5}$, and we add 3 to the numerator and 4 to the denominator each time.

$$11 \xrightarrow{+3} 14 \xrightarrow{+3} 17 \xrightarrow{+3} 20$$

$$17 \xrightarrow{+4} 21 \xrightarrow{+4} 25 \xrightarrow{+4} 29$$

The next three numbers are $\frac{14}{21}, \frac{17}{25},$ and $\frac{20}{29}.$

> In this sequence, we get from one number to the next by addition, but we are *not* adding the same fraction each time. Our rule needs to talk about the numerator and denominator separately.

13 Look at the sequence $\frac{6}{7}, \frac{11}{15}, \frac{16}{23}, \frac{21}{31}, ...$

   a Write a rule for the sequence formed by the numerators.

   b Write a rule for the sequence formed by the denominators.

   c Hence write a rule for the sequence of fractions.

14 Find the next three numbers in each sequence:

   a $\frac{3}{7}, \frac{5}{10}, \frac{7}{13}, \frac{9}{16}, ...$
      b $\frac{4}{11}, \frac{8}{14}, \frac{12}{17}, \frac{16}{20}, ...$
      c $\frac{13}{22}, \frac{20}{27}, \frac{27}{32}, \frac{34}{37}, ...$

15 Find the missing number in each sequence:

   a $\frac{1}{3}, \frac{3}{8}, \frac{5}{13}, \triangle, \frac{9}{23}, ...$
      b $\frac{2}{5}, \frac{9}{15}, \frac{16}{25}, \triangle, \frac{30}{45}, ...$
      c $\frac{4}{31}, \frac{7}{27}, \frac{10}{23}, \triangle, \frac{16}{15}, ...$

16 Find the next three numbers in each sequence:

   a $\frac{3}{4}, \frac{4}{9}, \frac{5}{16}, \frac{6}{25}, ...$
      b $\frac{32}{3}, -\frac{16}{5}, \frac{8}{7}, -\frac{4}{9}, ...$
      c $\frac{1}{7}, \frac{4}{5}, 3, 16, ...$

GAME

Click on the icon to play Codebreaker!

CODEBREAKER

INVESTIGATION   SEQUENCE USING SPREADSHEETS

A **spreadsheet** is a computer program which allows us to enter numbers and   SPREADSHEET
instructions in *cells*.

In this Investigation, we use a spreadsheet to create sequences.

What to do:

1 Suppose we want to create the sequence which starts at 6 and increases by 13 each time.

a Open the spreadsheet and enter the number 6 into cell A1.

b Move down to cell A2, and enter "= A1 + 13". This instruction or *formula* tells the computer that the value in this cell should equal the value in cell A1, plus 13.

	A	B	C
1	6		
2	= A1 + 13		
3			
4			
5			

c Activate cell A2, then "fill down" to A20. This should give you the first 20 numbers in the sequence. It does this by transferring the formula from cell A2 into the cells below it, automatically adjusting the cell it refers to in each case.

For example, if you click on cell A3, you should see the formula "= A2 + 13". In cell A4 you should see "= A3 + 13", and so on.

2 Use a spreadsheet to find the 10th term of the sequence:

a start at 11 and add 7 each time

b start at 70 and decrease by 6 each time

c start at 5.9 and increase by 2.4 each time

d start at 47.3 and subtract 3.8 each time

e start at 4 and multiply by 3 each time

f start at 1024 and divide by 2 each time.

C   PATTERNS

We can use objects such as matchsticks or dots to create **patterns**.

When we count the number of matchsticks or dots in each diagram, a number sequence is formed.

The sequence for this matchstick pattern is 3, 5, 7, ...

Example 5   ◀◉ **Self Tutor**

Consider the matchstick pattern: |__| , |__|__| , |__|__|__| , ...

a Draw the next two diagrams in the pattern.

b Copy and complete this table:

Diagram number	1	2	3	4	5
Number of matches	3	5			

c Write a rule describing the number of matches in each diagram.

a The next two diagrams are: |__|__|__|__| , |__|__|__|__|__|

b

Diagram number	1	2	3	4	5
Number of matches	3	5	7	9	11

　　　　　　　　　　　+2 +2 +2 +2

c The number of matches starts at 3, and increases by 2 each time.

EXERCISE 14C

1 Consider this matchstick pattern:  , ...

    a Draw the next two diagrams in the pattern.

    b Copy and complete this table:

Diagram number	1	2	3	4	5
Number of matches					

    c Write a rule describing the number of matches in each diagram.

2 Consider this matchstick pattern: 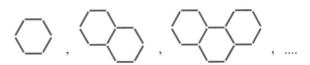 , ...

    a Draw the next two diagrams in the pattern.

    b Copy and complete this table:

Diagram number	1	2	3	4	5
Number of matches					

    c Write a rule describing the number of matches in each diagram.

3 Consider this dot pattern:

 a Draw the next two diagrams in the pattern.

 b Copy and complete this table:

Diagram number	1	2	3	4	5
Number of dots					

 c Write a rule describing the number of dots in each diagram.

4 Consider this dot pattern:

 a Draw the next two diagrams in the pattern.

 b Write a rule describing the number of dots in each diagram.

5 Create a matchstick pattern where the number of matches follows the sequence:

 a 6, 8, 10, 12, 14, ...   **b** 5, 9, 13, 17, 21, ...

6 For each sequence, write a rule describing the number of hexagons in each diagram:

 a

 b

  ,

7 In this matchstick pattern, the outside matches are red and the inside matches are green.

 a Draw the next two diagrams in the pattern.

 b Write a rule for describing:

   i the number of red matches   **ii** the number of green matches

   iii the total number of matches.

8 Find the number of matches in the 8th diagram in this pattern.

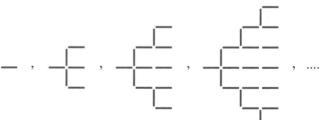

ACTIVITY

Throughout this Chapter, we have described sequences using rules which include:

- the starting value of the sequence
- how to get from one number to the next.

An alternative way to describe sequences is to use a rule which tells us directly what each number is.

For example,   1, 2, 3, 4, 5, ...   is the *sequence* of counting numbers.

What to do:

1 Write a rule to describe each sequence:

    a 1, 4, 9, 16, 25, 36, ...   **b** 2, 3, 5, 7, 11, 13, ...

    c 4, 6, 8, 9, 10, 12, ...   **d** 2, 4, 8, 16, 32, 64, ...

2 Write the first 10 counting numbers as words.
   Hence write a rule to describe the sequence   3, 3, 5, 4, 4, 3, 5, 5, 4, 3, ...

3 **a** Copy and complete this table of factors.

    b *Hence* write a rule to describe each sequence:

       i 1, 2, 2, 3, 2, 4, 2, 4, 3, 4, ...

      ii 1, 3, 4, 7, 6, 12, 8, 15, 13, 18, ...

     iii 1, 2, 3, 8, 5, 36, 7, 64, 27, 100, ...

Number	Factors
1	1
2	1, 2
3	
4	
5	
6	
7	
8	
9	
10	

GLOBAL CONTEXT   HONEYCOMBS

GLOBAL CONTEXT

Global context:	Scientific and technical innovation
Statement of inquiry:	Mathematics can be used to describe the patterns we observe in nature.
Criterion:	Investigating patterns

QUICK QUIZ

MULTIPLE CHOICE QUIZ

REVIEW SET 14A

1 Copy the boxes, then use the rule to complete each sequence:

a start at 6 and multiply by 2 each time

$$\square \xrightarrow{\times 2} \square \rightarrow \square \rightarrow \square \rightarrow \square$$

b start at 100 and decrease by 9 each time

$$\square \xrightarrow{-9} \square \rightarrow \square \rightarrow \square \rightarrow \square$$

2 Find the first six numbers in each sequence:

a start at 2 and add 7 each time   **b** start at 13 and decrease by 6 each time.

3 Helen makes jam from the fruit on her trees. She makes 2 jars of jam in the first week, and increases the amount of jam she makes by $1\frac{1}{2}$ jars each week after that.

Write down the number of jars of jam Helen makes for the first five weeks.

4 Find the first five numbers in each sequence:

a start at $\frac{1}{3}$ and add $\frac{2}{3}$ each time   **b** start at 12 and decrease by 1.1 each time.

5 Find a rule for the sequence:

a 12, 17, 22, 27, 32, ...   **b** 42, 38, 34, 30, 26, ...

6 Find the missing number in each sequence:

a 15, 30, 60, △, 240, ...   **b** 23.6, 22.1, 20.6, △, 17.6, ...

c 1.41, 1.47, 1.53, △, 1.65, ...

7 Find a rule for the sequence and hence find its next three numbers:

a 2, 2.7, 3.4, 4.1, ...   **b** 6410, 641, 64.1, 6.41, ...

8 Find the next three numbers in each sequence:

a $\frac{1}{9}, \frac{4}{14}, \frac{7}{19}, \frac{10}{24}, ...$ **b** $\frac{21}{16}, \frac{18}{13}, \frac{15}{10}, \frac{12}{7}, ...$

9 Consider this matchstick pattern:

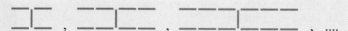

a Draw the next two diagrams in the pattern.

b Copy and complete this table:

Diagram number	1	2	3	4	5
Number of matches					

c Write a rule describing the number of matches in each diagram.

10 Consider this dot pattern:

a Draw the next two diagrams in the pattern.

b Write a rule describing the number of dots in each diagram.

11 Look at these sequences:

Sequence A: 15, 19, 23, 27, ...   Sequence B: 53, 46, 39, 32, ...

a Find a rule for sequence: **i** A   **ii** B.

b Find the next six numbers in sequence: **i** A   **ii** B.

c Which number is in both sequences?

12 Samuel is building castles out of toothpicks.

1 tower   2 towers   3 towers

a Write down the number of toothpicks needed to make a castle with:

i 1 tower   **ii** 2 towers   **iii** 3 towers.

b Draw the next two diagrams in the pattern.

c Find the number of toothpicks needed to make a castle with:

i 4 towers   **ii** 5 towers.

d Write a rule describing the number of toothpicks in each diagram.

REVIEW SET 14B

1 Find the first six numbers in each sequence:

a start at 4 and add $3\frac{1}{2}$ each time   **b** start at 2 and subtract $\frac{1}{7}$ each time.

2 Janet has a science test on Friday. She studies for 10 minutes on Monday, and doubles her study time each day after that.

List the times Janet spends studying from Monday to Thursday.

3 Determine a rule for this sequence: 3, 8, 13, 18, 23, ...

4 Find the missing number in each sequence:

a 4, 11, 18, $\triangle$, 32, ...   **b** 29, 26, 23, $\triangle$, 17, ...

5 Find the first four numbers in each sequence:

a start at 4 and multiply by 3 each time   **b** start at 500 and divide by 5 each time.

6 Create a dot pattern where the number of dots follows this sequence: 6, 10, 14, 18, ...

7 Kane drinks too much soft drink, and is trying to cut back.

He drank 12.3 litres of soft drink in January, 11.6 litres in February, 10.9 litres in March, and 10.2 litres in April.

Assuming this pattern continues, how much soft drink will Kane drink in June?

8 Consider this dot pattern:

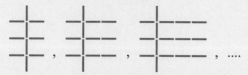

a Draw the next two diagrams in the pattern.

b Write a rule describing the number of dots in each diagram.

9 Find the missing number in each sequence:

a $6, 6\frac{2}{3}, 7\frac{1}{3}, \triangle, 8\frac{2}{3}, ...$

b $\frac{2}{3}, \frac{5}{10}, \frac{8}{17}, \triangle, \frac{14}{31}, ...$

10 Write a rule describing the number of matches in each diagram.

 , , 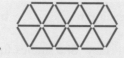 , ...

11 Brianna started selling macarons in her shop. She sold 4 macarons on the first day, 6 on the second day, 8 on the third day, and 10 on the fourth day.

a Find a rule for this sequence.

b Assuming this pattern continues:

i Write down the number of macarons Brianna will sell on the fifth and sixth days.

ii Find the total number of macarons sold in the first six days.

iii Determine when Brianna will first sell at least 20 macarons in one day.

12 In this matchstick pattern, the outside matches are red and the inside matches are green.

a Draw the next two diagrams in the pattern.

b Copy and complete this table:

Diagram number	1	2	3	4	5
Red matches	6				
Green matches	6				
Total matches	12				

c Write a rule for describing:

i the number of red matches

ii the number of green matches

iii the total number of matches.

Chapter 15

Location

Contents:

OPENING PROBLEM

Mitchell drew a map of a petrol station on grid paper.

To help him describe the location of particular sites, he could use:

- grid references   • coordinates.

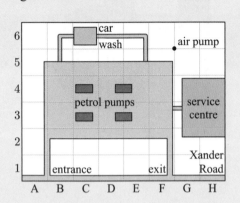   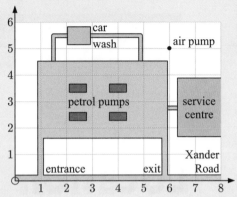

Things to think about:

a What are the similarities and differences between the maps?

b On which map is it easier to describe the location of:

  i the car wash   **ii** the air pump?

c Can you find the distance between the entrance and the air pump? If not, what extra information do you need?

d There is a shopping centre on the other side of Xander Rd. How can we extend the coordinates map to describe locations in the shopping centre?

DISCUSSION

Which maps do *you* commonly use? Do they use grid references or coordinates?

A   GRID REFERENCES

We look at a **map** to find out where a particular town or feature is located. We can also use the map to see how far away it is, and in which direction it is.

The map on the next page shows part of Adelaide, Australia.

The map is divided into squares using horizontal and vertical **grid lines**.

We use letters to identify the columns and numbers to identify the rows.

We describe the **location** of a place by the square it is in.

The **grid reference** for the square has a letter and a number.

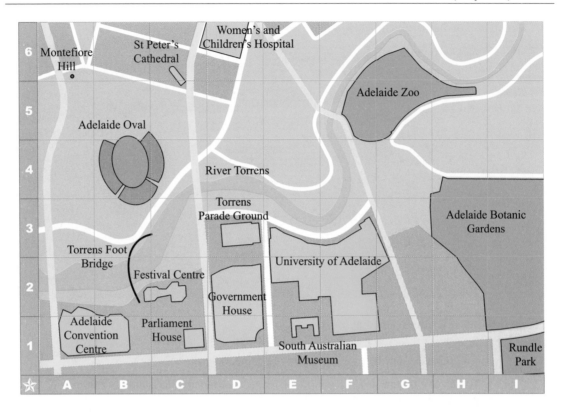

Example 1   ◀ᴑ **Self Tutor**

Look at the map of Adelaide above.
  a Name the feature located at:
      i C2   **ii** F5.
  b Write down the grid reference for:
      i Parliament House   **ii** Women's and Children's Hospital.

---

  a **i** Festival Centre   **ii** Adelaide Zoo
  b **i** C1   **ii** D6

EXERCISE 15A

1 Look at the map of Adelaide above.
  a Name the feature located at:
      i D3   **ii** A6   **iii** A1   **iv** H3.
  b Write down the grid reference for:
      i Adelaide Oval   **ii** Government House   **iii** Rundle Park
      iv St Peter's Cathedral   **v** South Australian Museum.
  c Through which grid squares does the Torrens Foot Bridge pass?
  d How many grid squares does the River Torrens pass through?

2 A map of London is given below.

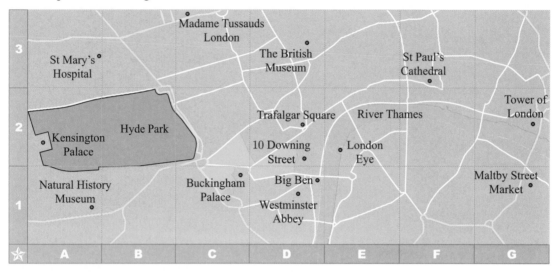

a Name the feature located at:

i D3   ii A2   iii E2   iv G1.

b Write down the grid reference for:

i Tower of London   ii Madame Tussauds London

iii Buckingham Palace   iv St Paul's Cathedral

v Natural History Museum.

c Name *two* features located at:

i D1   ii D2.

d In which squares can you find Hyde Park?

e Which other feature is closest to The British Museum?

3

Look at the school map.

a What feature is located at J6?

b Where is the canteen?

c Locate the parking area which is closest to the oval.

d i How many drinking fountains are there?

ii Locate the fountain which is closest to the gym.

4 A map of the Singapore Zoo is shown below.

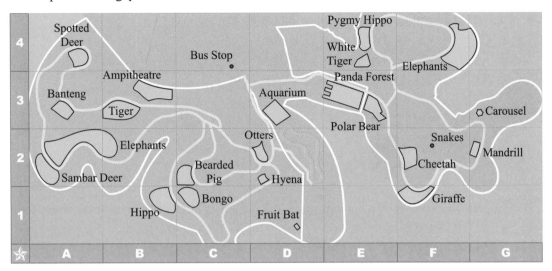

a Name the animal located at:

i C2	**ii** D1	**iii** A4
iv B3	**v** B1	**vi** F1.

b Write down the grid reference for:

i the panda forest	**ii** the mandrill	**iii** the carousel
iv the bongo	**v** the aquarium	**vi** the bus stop.

c Name the *two* animals located at:

i D2	**ii** E4	**iii** F2.

d Which squares contain elephants?

B   LOCATING POINTS

If we want to describe the position of a *point* on a map, we can place the letters and numbers *on* the grid lines, rather than between them.

Example 2	◀ Self Tutor
Mark the points B2, D5, and F4 on a grid.	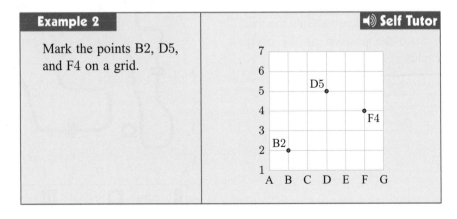

EXERCISE 15B

1 Copy this grid and locate each of these points on it:

    a C3   **b** D7   **c** E8

    d A1   **e** G1   **f** A2

    g A8   **h** H7   **i** B4

PRINTABLE GRID

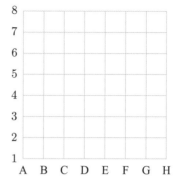

2 Plot each set of points on a separate grid. Join the points in order, then name the shape formed.

    a A4, C7, F4, C1, A4   **b** B3, C1, D4, B3

    c B2, H4, F6, C5, B2   **d** B5, F7, G5, C3, B5

    e A4, D8, H5, E1, A4

3

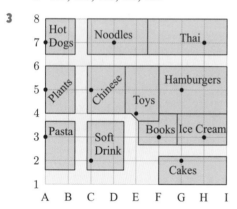

This map shows the positions of various stalls at the local markets.

    a Find the position of the:

        i cakes   **ii** toys   **iii** pasta.

    b Name the stall at:

        i A5   **ii** H7   **iii** F3.

4 This map shows the track for a car race.

    a Name the feature located at:

        i D6   **ii** H7   **iii** C2.

    b State the position of the Start/Finish line.

    c Elise is at F3.

        i Is Elise inside or outside the track?

        ii State the position of the overpass closest to Elise.

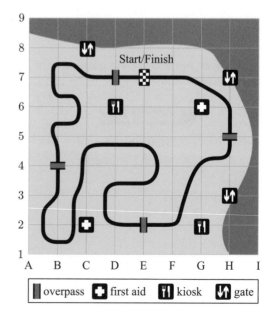

C | COORDINATES

Instead of using letters and numbers to locate positions, we can use numbers along both sides of the grid. In this case, we call the grid a **number plane**.

We draw two number lines called **axes**.

The horizontal axis is called the x-**axis**.

The vertical axis is called the y-**axis**.

The axes meet at a point called the **origin**, which we mark with O or with a small circle.

We can describe any point on the number plane using a pair of numbers called **coordinates**.

We write coordinates as an **ordered pair** of numbers, in brackets, with a comma between them.

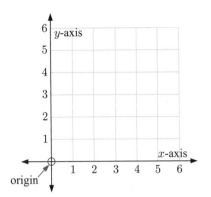

Axes is the plural of *axis*.

The coordinates of a point are written (x-coordinate, y-coordinate).

The x-coordinate gives the horizontal position along the x-axis and the y-coordinate gives the vertical position along the y-axis.

Example 3   ◀ᵢ) **Self Tutor**

Plot these points on a set of axes:
   A(3, 1), B(2, 5), C(4, 0), D(0, 1).

The x-coordinate is always given first.

DISCUSSION

What are the advantages of using numbers on both axes, instead of a letter and a number?

Are there any disadvantages to using two numbers?

EXERCISE 15C

1 a On the same set of axes, plot and label these points:

A(1, 5),   B(6, 3),   C(4, 4),   D(2, 0),   E(5, 2),   F(0, 5),
G(7, 3),   H(8, 0),   I(5, 8),   J(0, 3),   K(6, 0),   L(3, 7).

PRINTABLE
GRIDS

b Which of the points lie on the x-axis?
What do you notice about the y-coordinate of each of these points?

c Which of the points lie on the y-axis?
What do you notice about the x-coordinate of each of these points?

2

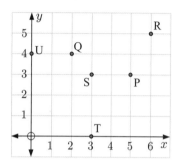

Look at the grid.

a Write down the x-coordinate of:

  i P   **ii** Q   **iii** R.

b Write down the y-coordinate of:

  i R   **ii** S   **iii** T.

c Find the coordinates of each point.

d Write down the coordinates of the origin, O.

3

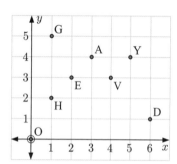

Write down the message given by these coordinates:

(1, 2), (3, 4), (4, 3), (2, 3)
(3, 4)
(1, 5), (0, 0), (0, 0), (6, 1)
(6, 1), (3, 4), (5, 4)!

4 A map of an athletics stadium is shown alongside.

a Write down the coordinates of the:

  i high jump   **ii** long jump.

b Name the sport located at:

  i (2, 2)   **ii** (1, 4).

c Which sport has the same:

  i x-coordinate as the javelin

  ii y-coordinate as the pole vault?

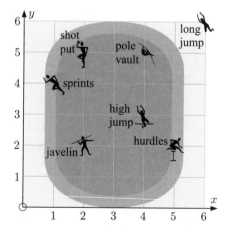

5 Explain why the points (1, 6) and (6, 1) are different. Illustrate your answer.

6 Plot these points then join them in order:

Start with: $(13, 2)$, $(16, 2)$, $(17, 1)$, $(16, 0)$, $(1, 0)$, $(0, 2)$, $(1, 4)$, $(3, 4)$, $(4, 2)$, $(6, 2)$,
$(6, 5)$, $(8, 7)$, $(13, 7)$, $(15, 5)$, $(15, 3)$, $(13, 2)$, $(9, 2)$, $(7, 4)$, $(9, 6)$, $(12, 6)$,
$(13, 5)$, $(13, 4)$, $(12, 3)$, $(10, 3)$, $(9, 4)$, $(10, 5)$, $(11, 5)$

then $(1, 4)$, $(1, 6)$, $(0, 7)$

then $(2, 4)$, $(2, 6)$, $(1, 7)$.

GAME   EGG HUNT

This is a game for two people. Each player tries to find the positions
of 6 "eggs" hidden by their opponent on a grid.

**PRINTABLE
GRIDS**

You will need: a sheet of graph paper and a pencil for each player.

What to do:

1 Draw a grid with numbers up to 8 on each axis.

2 Mark the positions of six "eggs" on your grid, but do
not show your opponent. You may place an egg at the
origin or along the axes if you wish.
An example is shown alongside.

3 The first player calls out the coordinates of a point to
try to locate one of their opponent's eggs.
If the point has an egg on it, the opponent says "yes".
If the point is *next to* an egg (either horizontally,
vertically, or diagonally), the opponent says "close".
Otherwise, the opponent says "no".

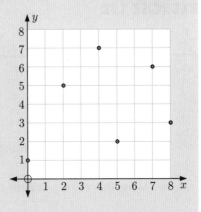

4 The players then take turns until someone locates all of their opponent's eggs. The player
who achieves this first is the winner.

D | POSITIVE AND NEGATIVE COORDINATES

In **Chapter 13** we saw how the number line was extended in
two directions to include positive and negative numbers.

In the same way, we can extend both the x-axis and the
y-axis in two directions. This allows us to consider positive
and negative coordinates.

The x-axis is positive to the right of the origin O, and negative
to the left of it.

The y-axis is positive above O, and negative below it.

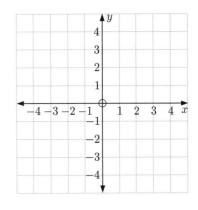

Example 4   ◆) **Self Tutor**

Plot these points on a set of axes:

A(4, 1), B(−3, 3), C(2, −4), D(−1, −3),
E(−4, 0), F(0, −1).

The x-coordinate is always given first.

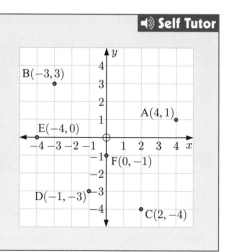

EXERCISE 15D

1 On the same set of axes, plot and label these points:

A(5, 3),   B(−1, 4),   C(2, −2),   D(0, −4),   E(3, 0),
F(−4, −5),   G(−3, 1),   H(−5, 0),   I(5, −1),   J(−4, 5).

PRINTABLE GRID

2 Look at the grid.

a Write down the x-coordinate of:
    i Z   **ii** W   **iii** S.

b Write down the y-coordinate of:
    i R   **ii** T   **iii** Q.

c Write down the coordinates of:
    i P   **ii** V   **iii** U.

d Name the point which has:
    i x-coordinate −3
    ii y-coordinate −2
    iii the same x and y-coordinates.

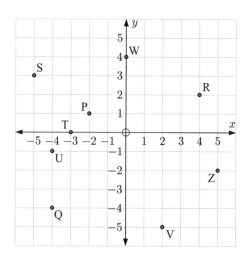

3

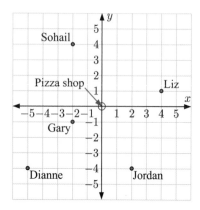

A group of friends are meeting at a pizza shop. This map shows where the friends live, using the pizza shop as the origin.

a Find the coordinates of:
    i Liz's house   **ii** Sohail's house.

b Who lives at (−5, −4)?

c Who lives closest to the pizza shop?

4 This grid shows the train stations in a city.
   The main station is at the origin.

   a Find the coordinates of:
      i station F   ii station L.
   b Name the station at:
      i $(-5, 1)$ ii $(-3, -5)$.
   c Tory lives at $(-4, -2)$. Which station is
      she closest to?

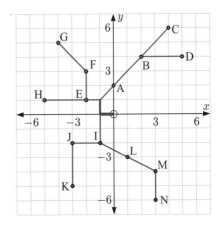

5 This map shows the attractions at a carnival.

   a Write down the coordinates of the:
      i fairy floss   ii dodgem cars
      iii pony rides.
   b Which feature is located at:
      i $(-1, 2)$ ii $(4, -2)$
      iii $(-5, -5)$?
   c Which attraction is closest to the origin?

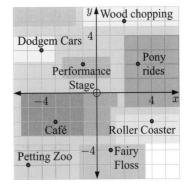

Example 5   ◀) **Self Tutor**

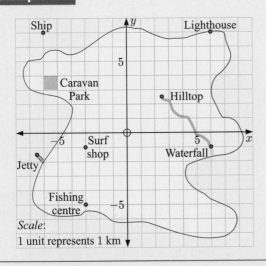

On the map alongside, 1 grid unit
represents 1 km.

a Find the actual distance between the
   surf shop and the fishing centre.

b Monique is at $(3, -1)$.
   Find the actual distance between
   Monique and the waterfall.

> The scale allows us to
> find actual distances
> represented on the map.

a The surf shop and the fishing centre are 4 grid units apart.
   So, the actual distance between the surf shop and the fishing centre is 4 km.

b $(3, -1)$ is 3 grid units away from the waterfall.
   So, the actual distance between Monique and the waterfall is 3 km.

6 On the map alongside, 1 grid unit represents 10 km.

  a Find the actual distance between Beachport and Morristown.

  b Doug is currently at $(4, -1)$. How far is Doug from Cedarville?

  c Belinda is currently at $(-2, 3)$. How far is Belinda from Stanley?

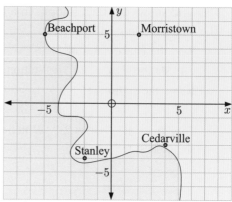

Scale: 1 unit represents 10 km

7

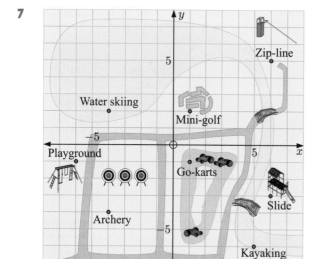

Scale: 1 unit represents 20 m

On this map of a recreational park, 1 grid unit represents 20 metres.

  a Find the coordinates of:
    i the entrance
    ii the slide.

  b Find the actual distance between:
    i the archery and the water skiing
    ii the playground and the go-karts.

  c Sam is currently at $(-1, -6)$. How far is Sam from the kayaking?

  d Lucy is currently at $(6, 2)$.
    i Is she closer to the mini-golf or the zip-line?
    ii How far is she from the nearer attraction?

8

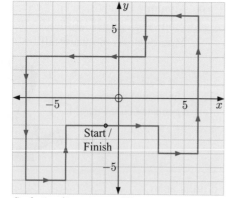

Scale: 1 unit represents 15 m

This map shows the course for a jetski competition.

  a Find the coordinates of the Start/Finish line.

  b Brad is on the course, and is currently at $(-7, -2)$.
    i How far is he from the next corner?
    ii In which direction must Brad turn at the next corner?

  c Find the total length of the course.

E   COMPASS POINTS

When describing directions, we often use the points of a compass.

The four main compass directions north (N), east (E), south (S), and west (W) are called the **cardinal points** or **cardinal directions**.

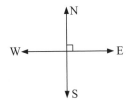

Halfway between the cardinal points are the **ordinal points** or **ordinal directions** northeast (NE), southeast (SE), southwest (SW), and northwest (NW).

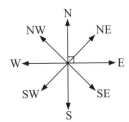

We usually draw north up the page.

Example 6   ◀)) Self Tutor

a   Plot the points   A(1, 3),   B(−2, 0),   C(1, −1),   and   D(3, 0)   on a set of axes. Draw north pointing up the page.

b   In which direction must we travel to go from:

   i   A to C   ii   D to B   iii   B to A?

a

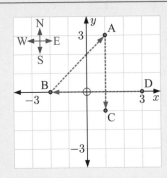

b   i   To go from A to C, we travel south.

   ii   To go from D to B, we travel west.

   iii   To go from B to A, we travel northeast.

EXERCISE 15E

1   a   Plot the points   A(3, 2),   B(−2, 4),   C(−1, 2),   and D(−2, −3)   on a set of axes. Draw north pointing up the page.

   b   In which direction must we travel to go from:

      i   D to B   ii   C to A

      iii   A to D?

PRINTABLE GRIDS

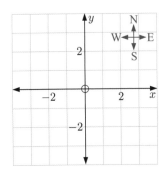

2

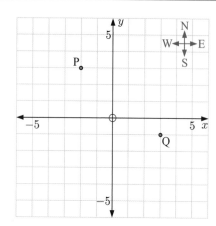

a Write down the coordinates of P and Q.

b Which of these points is south of P?

   A $(-4, 3)$ **B** $(-2, 6)$

   C $(-2, -1)$ **D** $(3, 3)$

c Which of these points is west of Q?

   A $(5, -1)$ **B** $(3, -4)$

   C $(3, 2)$ **D** $(-4, -1)$

d Which of these points is northwest of Q?

   A $(3, 2)$ **B** $(2, -2)$

   C $(0, 2)$ **D** $(5, 1)$

Example 7   ◀) Self Tutor

This map shows a walking trail.

John is at $(2, 4)$, Kyle is at $(-2, 4)$, and Emma is at $(-4, 2)$.

a Find the actual distance between John and Kyle.

b In which direction is Emma from Kyle?

c Meg is 400 m south of Emma.

   i   Find the coordinates of Meg.

   ii In what direction is John from Meg?

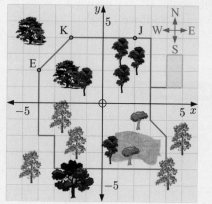

Scale: 1 unit represents 100 m

---

a On the map, John and Kyle are 4 grid units apart.
   So, the actual distance between John and Kyle is 400 m.

b Emma is southwest of Kyle.

c i   Meg is 400 m south of Emma, so Meg is 4 grid units below Emma.
       Meg is at $(-4, -2)$.

   ii John is northeast of Meg.

---

3 This map shows a playground.

a Find the actual distance between the spider net and the monkey bars.

b In which direction is the slide from the spider net?

c The swings are 5 m south of the slide.

   i   Find the coordinates of the swings.

   ii How far are the swings from the entrance?

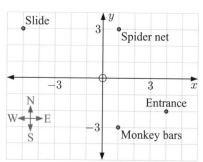

Scale: 1 unit represents 1 m

4 On this map, 1 grid unit represents 1 km.

a Find the distance between Pelican Point and Collinsville.

b In which direction is Pirate Cave from:
   i the lighthouse   **ii** Riverton Bay?

c In which direction is the nature reserve from:
   i the lake resort   **ii** the golf course?

d In which direction is:
   i Collinsville from Pirate Cave
   ii Pirate Cave from Collinsville?

e There is a windmill 3 km west of the golf course. Find the coordinates of the windmill.

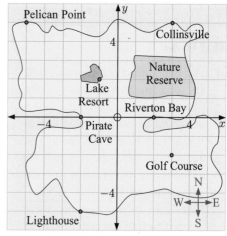

Scale: 1 unit represents 1 km

5 Each grid unit on this maze represents 2 metres.

a Find the coordinates of the:
   i entrance   **ii** exit.

b Joe is currently at $(-3, -3)$, and is very lost. Use directions and distances to guide Joe to the exit.

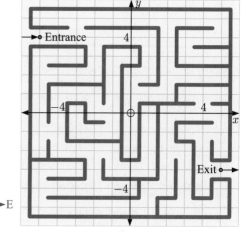

Scale: 1 unit represents 2 m

6 Erin goes on a five day hike, starting at S on the map.

Day 1: Erin hikes to T.

Day 2: Erin hikes 12 km east to U.

Day 3: Erin hikes southwest to V, which is southeast of S.

Day 4: Erin hikes 6 km west to W.

Day 5: ?

a In which direction does Erin hike on day 1?

b Copy the grid, and on it mark the points U, V, and W.

c How far, and in what direction, does Erin need to hike to return to S?

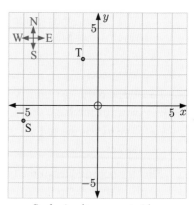

Scale: 1 unit represents 2 km

ACTIVITY   TREASURE HUNTS

What to do:

1 A wealthy farmer once owned all the land shown in the map. Fifty years later, his grandchildren Jane and Sam discovered a map and a letter he had left them. The letter told them about a fortune in gold and silver coins, hidden on the property.

Two sets of instructions were needed to find the exact location of the coins.

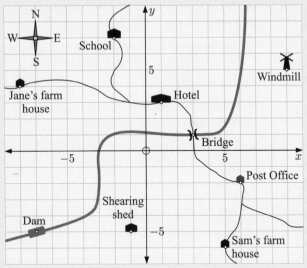

Scale: 1 unit represents 200 m

Sam's instructions: Start at your farm, travel 600 m west, then travel north until you are directly west of the windmill. The treasure is now southeast of you.

Jane's instructions: Start at your farm, travel 2 km south, then travel until you are directly south of the bridge. The treasure is now northeast of you.

Where did Sam and Jane find the coins?

2 You have found a treasure map and a set of clues for finding the treasure:

- From Pirate's Cove, head south for 100 paces, then southeast until you reach Dead Man's Creek.

- Face the lone palm tree, and walk 200 paces.

- Walk northeast until you are directly west of the large cross.

- The treasure is hidden 250 paces south of here.

Find the coordinates of the hidden treasure.

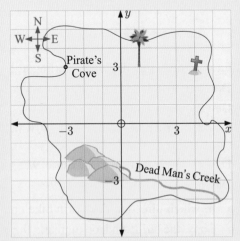

Scale: 1 unit represents 50 paces

3 Draw a treasure map of your own on grid paper. Write a set of instructions for finding the hidden treasure. Do not forget to specify a starting point.

Exchange maps with a classmate, and try to find each other's treasure.

DISCUSSION

The directions we have used in this Section are all very precise.

- How do we use directions in everyday language?
- Is B "to the south of" A?
- Why do we say that C is "*due* south" or "*directly* south" of A?

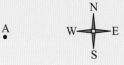

MULTIPLE CHOICE QUIZ

QUICK QUIZ

REVIEW SET 15A

1 Look at this map of a swimming centre.

   a What feature is located at A3?
   b How many grid squares does the main pool cover?
   c What is the grid reference for the:
      i diving area   ii canteen?
   d In which direction are the:
      i water slides from the kids pool
      ii change rooms from the canteen?

	N	Kids Pool		Water slides	
4	W←→E				
3	Change rooms	S			
2			Main Pool		Diving
1	Entrance	Canteen			
A	B	C	D	E	F

2 Draw a set of axes, then plot and label the following points:

   a A(1, 5)   b B(4, 6)   c C(5, 2)   d D(3, 0)

3 Copy this grid, and mark the points A4, B5, D1, and F3 on it.

PRINTABLE GRIDS

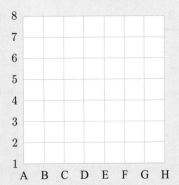

4 a Plot the points P(1, −1), Q(3, 0), R(4, −2), and S(2, −3) on a set of axes.
   b Join [PQ], [QR], [RS], and [SP]. What shape is formed?

5

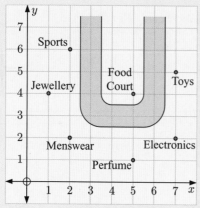

Scale: 1 unit represents 20 m

This map shows the various shops in a mall.

a Find the coordinates of:

    i the jewellery store

    ii the food court.

b Which shop is located at:

    i $(5, 1)$ **ii** $(2, 6)$?

c How far is it from the electronics store to the toys store?

6

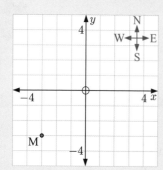

a Write down the coordinates of M.

b Which of these points is east of M?

    A $(-3, 3)$ **B** $(-1, -3)$

    C $(-5, -3)$ **D** $(-3, -5)$

7 Consider the points alongside.

a Find the coordinates of:

    i A   **ii** E.

b Name the point which has:

    i x-coordinate 3   **ii** y-coordinate 2.

c In which direction must we travel to go from:

    i C to B   **ii** E to F?

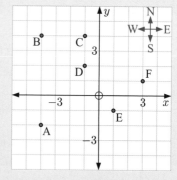

8 The map alongside shows the route for a yacht race.

a Find the coordinates of the Start/Finish point.

b Find the direction in which the yacht is travelling when it is sailing from:

    i B to C   **ii** C to D

    iii D to E.

c The race referee is 200 metres north of the Start/Finish point. Find the coordinates of the referee.

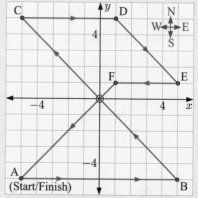

Scale: 1 unit represents 100 m

REVIEW SET 15B

1 Below is a map of Kyoto, Japan.

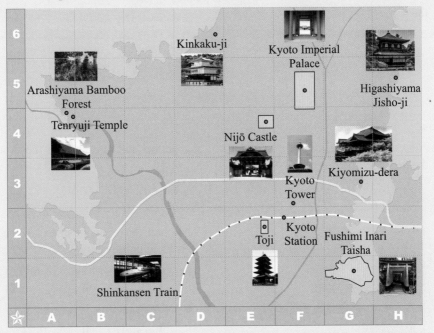

a Name the feature located at:
   i H5   **ii** D6   **iii** E2.

b Write down the grid reference for:
   i Nijō Castle   **ii** Fushimi Inari Taisha   **iii** Kyoto Tower.

c Which two features are found at A4?

d Through which grid squares does the Shinkanzen bullet train pass?

2 This map shows the positions of stalls at a Food Fair.

   a Find the location of the:
      i Italian stall   **ii** Chinese stall.

   b Which stall is at:
      i E5   **ii** H2?

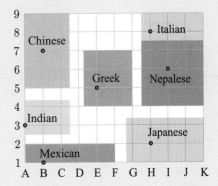

3 Draw a set of axes, then plot and label the points A(2, 3), B(−1, 5), C(3, −4), and D(−5, −3).

PRINTABLE GRIDS

4 Consider the points on the axes shown.

  a Write down the coordinates of each point.

  b For which point are the x and y-coordinates the same?

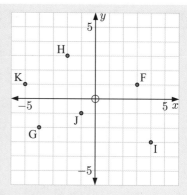

5 Construct a 10 by 10 grid, with the origin in the bottom left corner. Plot these points and join them in the given order:

  $(2, 3)$, $(8, 3)$, $(7, 2)$, $(5, 2)$, $(5, 1)$, $(4, 1)$, $(4, 2)$, $(3, 2)$, $(2, 3)$

then $(4, 3)$, $(4, 10)$, $(8, 4)$, $(2, 4)$, $(4, 10)$, $(5, 10)$, $(4, 9)$.

6

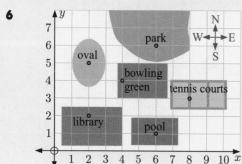

This map shows the positions of the facilities in a local community.

  a Find the coordinates of the:

   i oval   **ii** pool   **iii** library.

  b Which facility is located at:

   i $(4, 4)$ **ii** $(8, 3)$?

  c In which direction is the pool from the park?

7 **a** Plot the points A$(-1, 3)$, B$(4, -2)$, and C$(3, 3)$ on a set of axes, and connect the points to form a triangle.

  b Is triangle ABC acute angled, right angled, or obtuse angled?

8

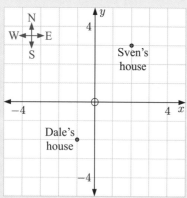

Scale: 1 unit represents 1 km

On this map, 1 grid unit represents 1 km.

  a Find the coordinates of:

   i Sven's house   **ii** Dale's house.

  b Violet lives 5 km south of Sven.

   i Find the coordinates of Violet's house.

   ii How far is Violet's house from Dale's house?

   iii In what direction is Violet's house from Dale's house?

  c There is a park located directly north of Dale's house, and directly southwest of Sven's house. Find the coordinates of the park.

Chapter **16**

Line graphs

OPENING PROBLEM

Jun is heating some water on the stove. She measures its temperature at one minute intervals from the time she turns the stove on. After a while, she realises she does not have enough water, so she adds some cold water. She plots her temperature readings on a graph.

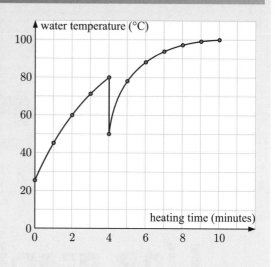

Things to think about:

a What is the temperature of the room?

b What is the temperature of the water after 2 minutes?

c When did Jun add the cold water?

d What is the maximum temperature the water reaches?

When we study the real world, we are often interested in how one quantity varies compared with another. Most commonly, we study how quantities change over *time*.

DISCUSSION

While growing up, most children measure their *height* so they can see how much they are growing over time.

What other quantities do we measure so we can observe how they change with time?

A   LINE GRAPHS

> **Line graphs** consist of straight line segments or curves.
>
> Line graphs are used to show how one quantity varies compared with another.

In general, the value of one quantity *depends* on the value of the other. When we graph data for the quantities, the quantity which depends on the other is placed on the *vertical* axis.

For example, the table below gives the temperature outside recorded at 2-hour intervals:

Time	6 am	8 am	10 am	noon	2 pm	4 pm	6 pm
Temperature (°C)	24	26	29	30	31	29	25

The temperature *depends* on the time of day, so we place *time* on the horizontal axis, and *temperature* on the vertical axis.

The data values give us *points* on the graph.

However, we know that the temperature has a value at all times. We therefore join the dots with line segments to create a **line graph**.

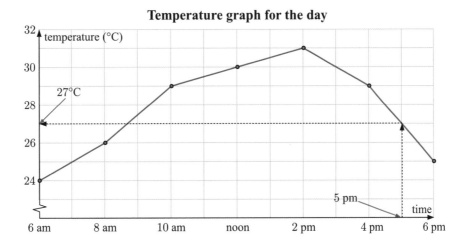

Temperature graph for the day

From the graph we can determine information such as:

- the highest recorded temperature for the day was at 2 pm
- the lowest recorded temperature was at 6 am
- the temperature at 8 am was 26°C
- the estimated temperature at 5 pm was 27°C, using the dotted lines shown.

DISCUSSION

On a line graph, why might we choose to use:

- line segments rather than curves
- curves rather than line segments?

INCREASING AND DECREASING GRAPHS

If the line or curve slopes *upwards* from left to right, we say the graph is **increasing**.

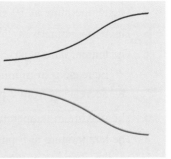

If the line or curve slopes *downwards* from left to right, we say the graph is **decreasing**.

Graphs may be increasing in some sections and decreasing in others.

For example, the temperature graph above is increasing from 6 am to 2 pm, then decreasing from 2 pm to 6 pm.

Example 1   ◀》 **Self Tutor**

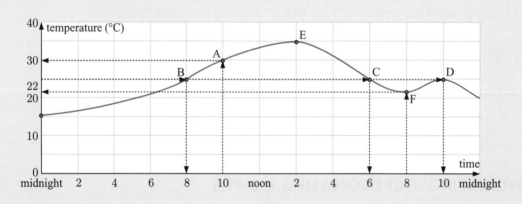

Use this line graph to find:

a the temperature at 10 am

b the times when the temperature was 25°C

c the periods when the temperature was: **i** increasing   **ii** decreasing

d the maximum temperature and when it occurred

e the decrease in temperature from 2 pm to 8 pm.

a The temperature at 10 am was 30°C.   {point A}

b The temperature was 25°C at 8 am, 6 pm, and 10 pm.   {points B, C, and D}

c The temperature was:

   i increasing from midnight to 2 pm, and from 8 pm to 10 pm

   ii decreasing from 2 pm to 8 pm, and from 10 pm to midnight.

d The maximum temperature was 35°C at 2 pm.   {point E}

e The temperature at 8 pm was about 22°C.   {point F}

   ∴   the decrease in temperature from 2 pm to 8 pm was

   $$35°C - 22°C \quad \{\text{points E and F}\}$$
   $$= 13°C$$

EXERCISE 16A

1   State whether each line graph is:

   A increasing   **B** decreasing   **C** increasing in some sections and decreasing in others.

a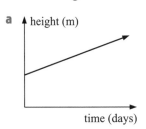

b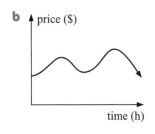

c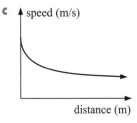

2   The temperature of water in a kettle is graphed over a 10 minute period.

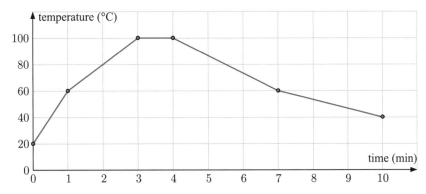

   a What was the room temperature when the kettle was switched on?

   b How long did it take for the water to boil?

   c For how long did the water boil?

   d At what times was the water temperature 60°C?

   e During what period was the temperature decreasing?

3   The manager of a café counts her customers during the day to help her decide how to roster her staff. The results are shown in this line graph.

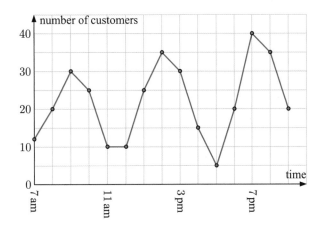

   a Find the maximum number of customers in the café, and when it occurred.

   b Find the minimum number of customers in the café, and when it occurred.

   c How many customers were in the café at 10 am?

   d Describe what happened between 6 pm and 7 pm.

   e Estimate the number of customers in the café at 4:30 pm.

   f How many fewer customers were there at closing time than at 7 pm?

4 This line graph shows the amount of water used by a sprinkler system over a 10 minute period.

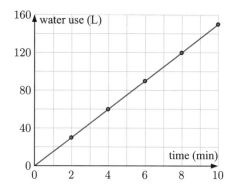

  a How much water did the sprinkler system use in 4 minutes?

  b How long did it take for the sprinkler system to use 90 litres of water?

  c How many litres of water are used by the sprinkler system each minute?

5 The graph below shows the average daily temperature for Johannesburg over a 2 year period.

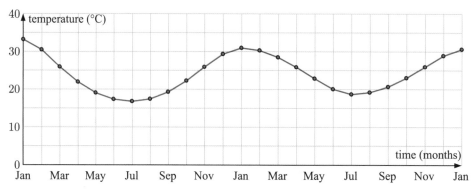

  a In which month was the average temperature: **i** highest   **ii** lowest?

  b What happens to the temperature in Johannesburg from July to January?

  c In which month (or months) was the average temperature about 26°C?

6 Caitlin flies a kite one afternoon. The line graph below shows the height of the kite above ground level.

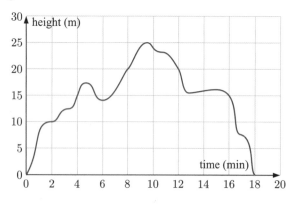

  a For how long was the kite in the air?

  b How high was the kite after 4 minutes?

  c What was the greatest height reached by the kite?

  d At what times was the kite 20 metres above the ground?

7 The graph below shows the progress of a basketball team during a match. Their points were recorded every three minutes.

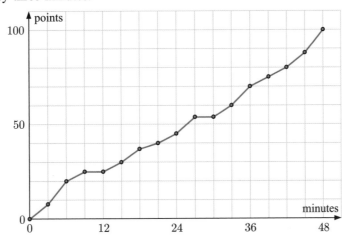

   a Find the total number of points at the end of the:

      i first quarter   **ii** second quarter   **iii** third quarter   **iv** match.

   b In which quarter did the team score the most points?

   c During which time intervals was the team unable to score?

   d During which time interval did the team's score reach 80?

8 The volume of water in a New Zealand lake over one year is shown below.

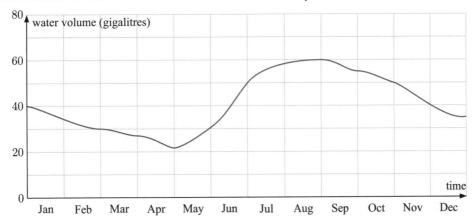

   a Estimate the volume of water in the lake at the start of July.

1 gigalitre = 1 000 000 000 litres!

   b When was the water volume least?

   c What was the maximum water volume?

   d How much water was taken from the lake between the start of January and the start of March?

   e During which months was there at least 50 gigalitres of water in the lake?

   f Over what period was the volume of water in the lake increasing?

9 This data shows the cost of covering different areas of floor with tiles.

Area (m^2)	0	5	10	15	20
Cost ($)	0	100	200	300	400

   a Draw a line graph to display the data. Place *area* on the horizontal axis.

   b Find the cost of each square metre of tiles.

10 Julie is editing her short story. This table shows the word count of the story over the course of a week.

Time (days)	0	1	2	3	4	5	6	7
Word count (thousand words)	35	32	30	29	27	26	25	23

   a Draw a line graph to display the data. Place *time* on the horizontal axis.

   b Comment on whether the graph is increasing or decreasing.

11 The data in this table gives the volume of water in a water fountain over time.

Time (days)	0	1	2	3	4	5	6	7	8	9	10
Volume (m^3)	1.6	1.5	1.4	1.3	2.2	2.1	2.0	1.9	2.1	2.0	1.9

   a Draw a line graph to display the data. Place *time* on the horizontal axis.

   b On which days do you think it rained? Explain your answer.

ACTIVITY 1   TEMPERATURE GRAPHS

When we want to compare two sets of data, it can be useful to plot both data sets on the same graph.

The graph below shows the average daily temperatures for London and Sydney over a two year period.

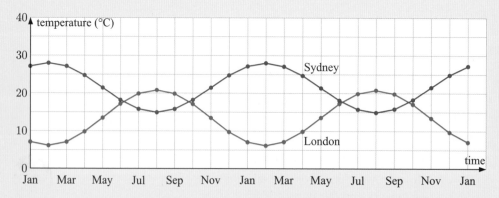

What to do:

1 Explain why the two curves are increasing and decreasing at different times.

2 In which month was the *minimum* average temperature in:

   a London   **b** Sydney?

3 In which month was the *maximum* average temperature in:

   a London   **b** Sydney?

4 In which months are London and Sydney the same temperature?

5 Overall, which city is hotter? Explain your answer.

ACTIVITY 2	COMMODITY PRICES

Items which are frequently traded around the world are called *commodities*. Gold, silver, and copper are examples of metals which are commodities.

The prices at which commodities are traded will continuously vary over time. The prices are often displayed using a line graph.

The graph below shows the price of one ounce of silver during October, 2020.

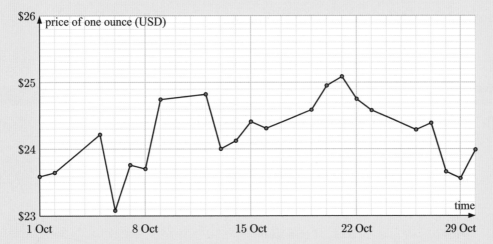

What to do:

1 Use the line graph to determine the price of one ounce of silver at:

   a the beginning of October, 2020   **b** the end of October, 2020.

2 Can you explain why the given data values are not evenly spaced?

3 On October 20, 2020, I owned 50 ounces of silver.

   a How much was my silver worth at that time?

   b How much was my silver worth at the end of October, 2020?

4 Research the prices of gold and copper during October, 2020.

   a Were they less than or greater than the price of silver?

   b Did their prices increase or decrease during the month?

B   TRAVEL GRAPHS

The **travel graph** for a journey shows the relationship between the distance travelled and the time taken to travel that distance.

The distance travelled *depends* on the time taken, so *time* is on the horizontal axis and *distance* is on the vertical axis.

If an object is travelling slowly, it will not travel as far in a given length of time.

If an object is travelling quickly, it will travel further in a given length of time.

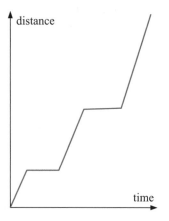

DISCUSSION

From a travel graph, how do we observe when the object is travelling:

- at a constant speed   • fast   • slow?

Example 2   ◀) Self Tutor

The graph shows the progress of Leon as he cycles to school.

a How long did Leon take to cycle to school?

b How far is it from his home to the school?

c On his way to school, Leon was stopped at a set of traffic lights.

   i How far are these lights from his home?

   ii For what length of time was he stopped?

d How far did Leon cycle:

   i in the first 5 minutes   ii between the 6th and 10th minutes

   iii between the 10th and 12th minutes?

e There is a steep hill on Leon's way to school. When did he reach the top?

---

a 12 minutes {point D}   b $4\frac{1}{2}$ km {point D}

c i The lights are 2 km from Leon's home.

   ii He was stopped for 1 minute.   {between points A and B}

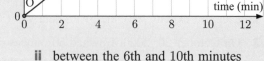

> **d i** 2 km {O to A}   **ii** $\frac{1}{2}$ km {B to C}   **iii** 2 km {C to D}
>
> **e** From B to C, the line is less steep. Leon was riding slowly, so we assume this is the hill. He reached the top after 10 minutes. {point C}

EXERCISE 16B

1 This travel graph shows the distance travelled by a family as they drove from the city to a weekend holiday destination.

   a How far did they drive?

   b How long did the journey take?

   c How far had they travelled after 3 hours?

   d How long did they take to travel the first 100 km?

   e Find the distance travelled in the:

      i first hour   **ii** second hour

      iii third hour   **iv** last 2 hours.

   f Describe what happened during the third hour.

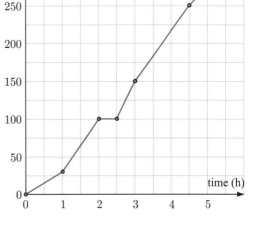

2 This graph shows the distance Peggy travelled on her morning walk.

   a For how long did Peggy walk?

   b How far did Peggy walk?

   c How far had Peggy walked after 10 minutes?

   d How far did Peggy walk each minute?

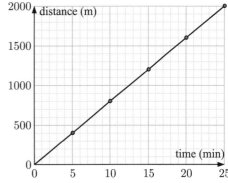

3 Two families travel 900 km by car from Boston to Cleveland. Their journeys are shown on the graph.

   a Which family arrived in Cleveland first?

   b For how long did the Williams family stop for lunch?

   c Find the distance travelled by the Murphy family in the first 5 hours.

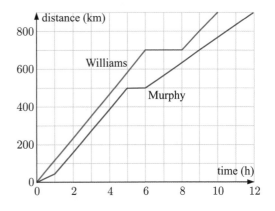

4 The graph below indicates the distance of a jogger from her home at various times.

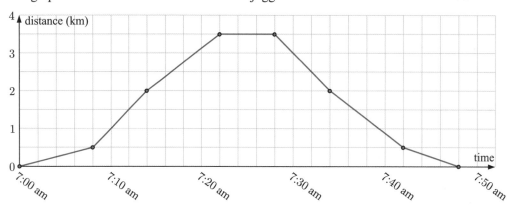

a At what time did the jogger arrive back home?

b Find the total distance travelled by the jogger.

c Find the total time the jogger was away from home.

d For how long did the jogger rest at the halfway point?

e How far was the jogger from home at:
  i 7:10 am   ii 7:30 am?

f How far did the jogger travel between:
  i 7 am and 7:14 am   ii 7:32 am and 7:42 am?

5 This table shows the progress of a cruise ship sailing between two ports:

Time (hours)	0	2	4	6	8
Distance (km)	0	60	120	180	240

a Draw a travel graph to display the data, connecting the points with straight line segments.

b Use your graph to estimate:
  i the distance travelled by the cruise ship in the first 3 hours
  ii how long the cruise ship takes to sail 150 km.

c Is the cruise ship travelling at a constant speed? Explain your answer.

6 The data below records the progress of a cyclist at various times during a time trial.

Time (min)	0	5	10	15	20	25	30	35
Distance (km)	0	3	7	11	16	19	23	28

a Draw a travel graph to display the data, connecting the points with straight line segments.

b Use your graph to estimate:
  i the distance travelled by the cyclist after 32 minutes
  ii the time taken for the cyclist to ride 15 km.

c What evidence is there that the cyclist is not travelling at a constant speed?

ACTIVITY 3   WRITING A STORY TO FIT THE GRAPH

The graph alongside shows Taylor's distance from home over a two hour period.

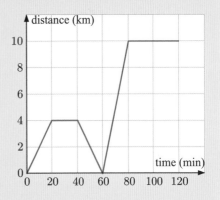

There could be many reasons for the graph taking this form.

One story describing the graph is:

"Taylor caught the train to her friend's house. She planned to go directly from her friend's house to their netball match, but Taylor realised that she had left her netball shoes at home. She returned home on the train to get her shoes, and since she was running late, her mum drove her to the netball game, arriving just in time."

What to do:

1   Draw your own travel graph, and write a short story to describe it.

2   Swap graphs with a classmate. Write a short story using your classmate's graph.

C   CONVERSION GRAPHS

Conversion graphs are special line graphs which enable us to convert from one quantity to another. We can use conversion graphs to convert between currencies or between units of measurement.

Conversion graphs are usually straight lines, but they do not always pass through the origin.

For example, the graph alongside shows the relationship between United States dollars (USD) and euros (EUR) on a particular day.

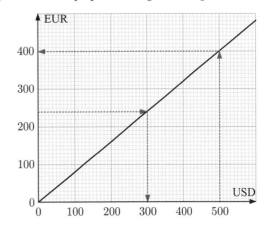

We can see that on that day:

- 500 USD was equivalent to 400 EUR
- 240 EUR was equivalent to 300 USD.

EXERCISE 16C

1   Use the currency conversion graph above to convert:

    a 200 USD to EUR   **b** 280 EUR to USD

    c 340 USD to EUR   **d** 480 EUR to USD.

2 This graph shows the relationship between British pounds (GBP) and Canadian dollars (CAD) on a particular day.

Use the graph to convert:

   a 500 GBP to CAD

   b 300 GBP to CAD

   c 450 CAD to GBP

   d 720 CAD to GBP.

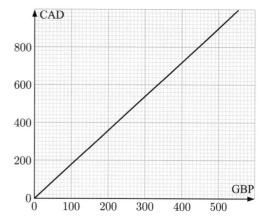

3 This graph shows the relationship between lengths in kilometres and miles.

Convert:

   a 45 km to miles

   b 28 km to miles

   c 48 miles to km

   d 30 miles to km.

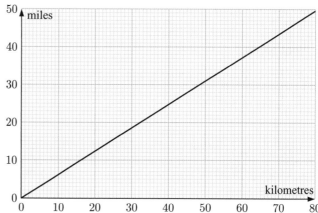

4 Fahrenheit and Celsius are two scales for measuring temperature. The graph below shows the relationship between them.

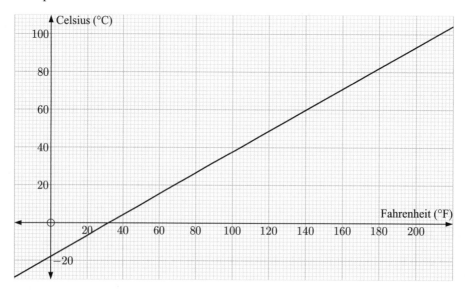

   a Convert:

      i 40°F to °C   **ii** 60°C to °F.

   b Water boils at 100°C. Find the equivalent temperature in °F.

   c Suppose the temperature today is 85°F. Write this temperature in °C.

RESEARCH

Research the Kelvin temperature scale.

1 Print or draw the conversion graph between:

   a Celsius and Kelvin   **b** Fahrenheit and Kelvin.

2 Convert each temperature to Kelvin:

   a 20°C   **b** 100°C   **c** 80°F   **d** 300°F

3 Which temperature scale do you think is most intuitive to use? Explain your answer.

4 0 Kelvin is known as "absolute zero".

   a Find what absolute zero is in:

      i °C   **ii** °F.

   b Physically, what does absolute zero *mean*?

   c Hence explain why it is not possible to have a temperature lower than absolute zero.

MULTIPLE CHOICE QUIZ

QUICK QUIZ

REVIEW SET 16A

1 The graph alongside shows the speed of a car as it accelerates away from a traffic light.

   a Is the graph increasing or decreasing?

   b Estimate the speed after 3 seconds.

   c How long does it take for the car to reach 20 km/h?

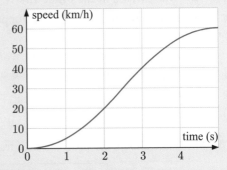

2 This data shows the measurements from a rain gauge over the course of one week.

Time (days)	1	2	3	4	5	6	7
Rainfall (mm)	3	5	6	6	13	13	18

   a Draw a line graph to display the data.

   b Comment on whether the graph is increasing or decreasing.

3 The number of diners in a restaurant was recorded throughout an evening. The results are shown in this line graph.

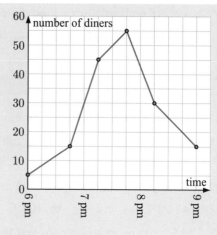

a Find the maximum number of diners in the restaurant, and when it occurred.

b Estimate when there were 25 diners in the restaurant.

c Estimate the number of diners in the restaurant at 8 pm.

4 The population of salmon in a lake over a 10 year period is displayed in the graph alongside.

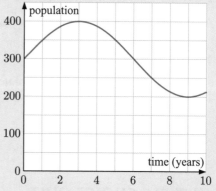

a At what time was the population greatest?

b What was the minimum population, and when did it occur?

c At what times was the population:

   i increasing   **ii** decreasing?

d Estimate the times when the population was 350.

5 Celia and Janet are housemates who also work in the same office. One day, Celia decided to ride her bicycle to work, while Janet drove her car. The travel graph shows their journeys.

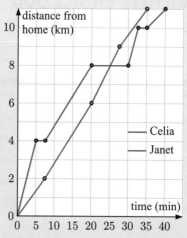

a How far is it from the house to the office?

b Who arrived at the office first?

c How many times was Janet stopped on the way to work?

d How far was Janet from work when she stopped for 10 minutes while a freight train passed?

6 This table shows the progress of a train driving between two cities.

Time (hours)	0	2	4	6	8	10
Distance (km)	0	150	300	450	600	750

a Draw a travel graph to display the data.

b Estimate the distance travelled by the train after 5 hours.

c How far does the train travel each hour?

7 The graph alongside shows the relationship between British pounds (GBP) and euros (EUR) on a particular day.

Use the graph to convert:

   a 200 GBP to EUR

   b 360 GBP to EUR

   c 500 EUR to GBP

   d 150 EUR to GBP.

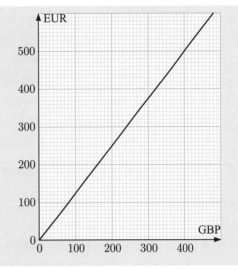

REVIEW SET 16B

1 State whether this line graph is increasing, decreasing, or increasing in some sections and decreasing in others.

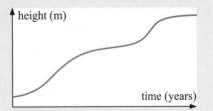

2 Joy is heating water on her stove. She is in a hurry, and decides to speed up the process by adding some boiling water straight from the kettle.

   a What was the initial temperature of the water?

   b At what time did Joy add water from her kettle?

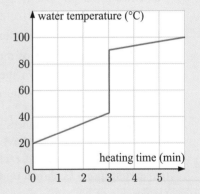

3 The graph alongside shows the relationship between distances measured in feet and metres.

Use the graph to convert:

   a 20 feet to metres

   b 5 feet to metres

   c 8 metres to feet

   d 2 metres to feet.

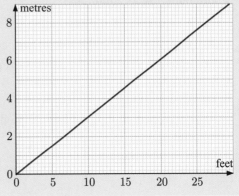

4 This table shows the battery charge level of Jessica's laptop during a day.

Time	8 am	10 am	noon	2 pm	4 pm	6 pm	8 pm	10 pm
Charge level (%)	100	80	30	30	15	0	100	70

    a Draw a line graph to display the data, connecting the points with straight line segments.

    b Estimate the charge at 9 am.

    c Estimate the times at which the charge was 25%.

5 This graph indicates how far Pradeep is from his home.

    a Find the total time Pradeep was away from home.

    b Find the total distance travelled by Pradeep.

    c How long did it take him to travel the first kilometre?

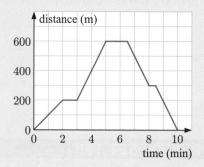

6 Some chocolate custard was placed into an ice cream churn. Its temperature was recorded at 10-minute intervals.

Time (minutes)	0	10	20	30	40	50	60
Temperature (°C)	28	18	10	6	3	−3	−5

    a Draw a line graph to display the data, connecting the points with straight line segments. Place *time* on the horizontal axis.

    b Use the graph to estimate:

        i the temperature of the custard after 8 minutes

        ii the time taken for the temperature to drop to 0°C

        iii the fall in temperature during the first 15 minutes.

7 Two long distance runners Hissam and Mohammed decided to have a race one afternoon. The distance of each runner from the starting point is shown on the graph.

Use the graph to determine:

    a the distance of the race

    b who was leading the race after 1 hour

    c the time at which Mohammed overtook Hissam

    d how far Mohammed had run before he developed cramp and had to stop and rest

    e who won the race.

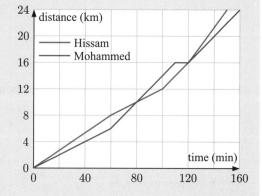

Chapter **17**

Probability

Contents:

OPENING PROBLEM

There are 25 students in Mr Donnelly's class.

On St Patrick's Day, Mr Donnelly places 25 cards in a box, one of which shows a lucky four-leaf clover. The students line up in alphabetical order ready to choose a card each.

Aaron is not happy about going first. "There are so many cards in the box," he says. "It is almost impossible for me to pick the four-leaf clover."

Zara is not happy about going last. "The four-leaf clover will almost certainly be gone by the time I get to pick!" she says.

Things to think about:

a What words did Aaron and Zara use to describe the *chance* of events occurring?

b Can you write a number to describe the chance of Aaron selecting the four-leaf clover?

c Do you think Aaron and Zara are equally likely to select the four-leaf clover?

The **probability** of an event is the likelihood or chance of it occurring.

A   DESCRIBING PROBABILITY

We often use words to describe the probability of something happening in the future.

If an event will *definitely not* happen, we say it is **impossible**.

If an event will *definitely* happen, we say it is **certain**.

Between these extremes, we can also use words or phrases such as:

- likely
- unlikely
- highly likely
- highly unlikely
- 50-50 chance
- slightly less than 50-50 chance
- slightly more than 50-50 chance

An event with a 50-50 chance is equally likely to happen or not happen.

We can place these words on a line, in order from least likely to most likely:

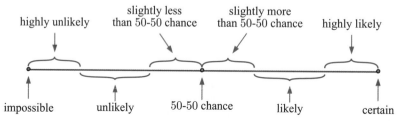

Example 1   ◄)) **Self Tutor**

Use a word or phrase to describe the probability that:

a it will snow somewhere in the world today

b a red marble will be selected from a bag containing one red marble and one blue marble.

---

a It is *highly likely* that it will snow somewhere in the world today.

b There is a *50-50 chance* that a red marble will be selected from a bag containing one red marble and one blue marble.

EXERCISE 17A

1 Use a word or phrase to describe the probability that:

a next year there will be 30 days in February

b you will eat a meal between 5 pm and 10 pm tonight

c you will roll a "6" on your next roll with a die

d the next child born at a particular hospital will be a girl.

We say "one die" or "a pair of dice".

2 Copy and complete:

a It is ...... that the spinner will stop in the white sector.

b It is ...... for the spinner to stop in a sector marked 4.

c It is ...... that the spinner will stop in a sector with a number.

d It is ...... that the spinner will stop in a sector with a number greater than 1.

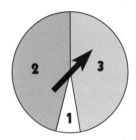

3 A bag contains 19 red marbles and 1 blue marble. A marble is randomly selected from the bag. Copy and complete:

a It is ...... that the marble will be blue.

b It is ...... that the marble will be red.

c It is ...... that the marble will be either blue or red.

d It is ...... for the marble to be green.

4 For each pair of events, determine whether event A or event B is more likely:

a A: This spinner will stop on blue.

   B: This spinner will stop on red.

b A: A randomly selected 6 year old will be taller than 120 cm.

   B: A randomly selected 10 year old will be taller than 120 cm.

c A: Your parents will buy vegetables next week.

   B: Your parents will buy a car next week.

5 You have four blue and four white cards. You have been asked to place *four* cards in a box. What cards should you place in the box so that:

    a you will be certain of drawing a blue card

    b it will be impossible to draw a blue card

    c there will be a 50-50 chance of drawing a blue card

    d you will be more likely to draw a blue card than a white card?

"Drawing a card" means taking one out without first identifying its colour.

DISCUSSION

Can you think of two *impossible* events and two *certain* events in *your* life? Remember that what may be impossible for you may be possible for someone else!

Discuss your ideas with your class.

B   USING NUMBERS TO DESCRIBE PROBABILITIES

Chermaine and Min are experienced gymnasts. Each time they perform a routine on the balance beam, it is *unlikely* that either of them will fall.

To *compare* the chance of each gymnast falling, we need a more accurate description than just words. We need a *number* that describes the probability of each gymnast falling.

An **impossible** event has probability 0 or 0%.

A **certain** event has probability 1 or 100%.

All other events have probability between 0 and 1.

The smaller the probability of an event, the less likely it is to happen.

Probabilities cannot be negative or greater than 1.

We can use fractions, decimals, or percentages to describe probabilities.

For example, we can write the probability of an event with a **50-50 chance** as $\frac{1}{2}$, 0.5, or 50%.

We can therefore place probabilities on a number line:

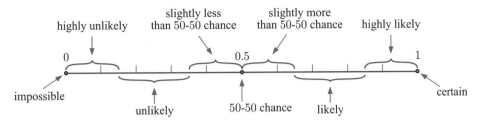

EXERCISE 17B

1 Match each probability value with the most appropriate word or phrase:

   a 0   **b** 0.3   **c** 0.92   **d** 0.5   **e** 0.56

   A highly likely   **B** 50-50 chance   **C** impossible

   D unlikely   **E** slightly more than 50-50 chance

2 Match each event with the value which best estimates its probability:

   a The next car that drives past your house will not be blue.

   b The next person you meet will be a twin.

   c In a school with two Grade 6 classes, you are placed in the same class as your best friend.

   d Your birthday will be on the same date as last year.

   e The next point in a professional tennis match is won by the player who is receiving serve.

   A 0.5   **B** 0.3   **C** 0.9   **D** 1   **E** 0.02

3 In competitions in the past year, Chermaine fell in 22% of her beam routines. We therefore estimate that the probability she will fall in her next routine is 22% or 0.22.

  In the past year, Min fell in 19% of her routines, so we estimate the probability she will fall in her next routine is 19% or 0.19.

   a Illustrate the probabilities of Chermaine and Min falling on a number line.

   b Which gymnast is more likely to fall in their next routine? Explain your answer.

4 This table shows the probability of rain for some major cities on a particular day.

   a In which city is it:

     i most likely to rain   **ii** least likely to rain?

   b Is it more likely to rain in Lima or Kuala Lumpur?

   c True or false?

     i It is likely to rain in Christchurch.

     ii It is highly likely to rain in Cairo.

City	Probability
Berlin	18%
Johannesberg	24%
Lima	27%
Cairo	2%
Kuala Lumpur	31%
Dhaka	87%
Seattle	61%
Christchurch	67%

5   Netballers Jan, Natasha, and Ellie each shoot for goal from a particular spot.

Jan has probability $\frac{4}{5}$ of shooting a goal, Natasha has probability 0.83 of shooting a goal, and Ellie has probability 58% of shooting a goal.

   a   Write each probability as a percentage.

   b   Illustrate the probabilities on a number line, clearly identifying each netballer.

   c   Write a word or phrase to describe the probability that Jan will shoot a goal.

   d   Who is most likely to shoot a goal?

   e   With her next shot, is Ellie more likely to shoot a goal or to miss? Explain your answer.

6   Each morning, Nicola has a drink with breakfast. She has milk $\frac{2}{7}$ of the time, orange juice $\frac{4}{7}$ of the time, and water $\frac{1}{7}$ of the time.

   a   On any particular morning, which drink is Nicola most likely to have?

   b   Find the probability that, on a particular morning, Nicola drinks *either* orange juice *or* water.

   c   Find the sum of all the probabilities. Explain your answer.

ACTIVITY 1   WHAT WILL HAPPEN TOMORROW?

Below is a list of things which might happen tomorrow.

What to do:

1   For each event in the table below, describe the probability of that event occurring tomorrow, using a word or phrase and a number from 0 to 1.

Event	Word or phrase	Number
You will go to school.		
You will see a horse.		
You will eat an apple.		
You will break something.		
You will receive a letter.		
You will wear a jumper.		
You will see one of your grandparents.		
You will take a photograph.		
You will use your ruler.		
You will trip over.		

PRINTABLE
TABLE

2   Compare your answers with the person next to you. Explain any similarities and differences between your answers.

OUTCOMES

When we consider the probability of a particular event occurring, it is useful to know the number of possible **outcomes**.

For example, when we toss a coin, there are 2 possible outcomes: *heads* and *tails*.

Heads   *Tails*

EXERCISE 17C

1 List the possible outcomes when:

    a this spinner is spun

    b an ordinary die is rolled.

2
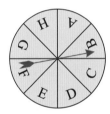
    a List the possible outcomes when this spinner is spun.

    b How many possible outcomes are there?

    c How many of the outcomes are vowels?

3 Mr Roberts is choosing a tie to wear to school today. His options are shown alongside.

    a How many possible outcomes are there?

    b How many of the outcomes include:

        i white   **ii** blue

        iii stars   **iv** stripes?

4 Look at this calendar for the month of March.

    a Terence will select a Saturday during March to hold a garage sale.

        i What are the possible outcomes?

        ii How many possible outcomes are there?

    b Janine will select a day during the week starting the 11th of March to visit her aunt.

        i What are the possible outcomes?

        ii How many possible outcomes are there?

March						
M	T	W	T	F	S	S
				1	2	3
4	5	6	7	8	9	10
11	12	13	14	15	16	17
18	19	20	21	22	23	24
25	26	27	28	29	30	31

5 Billy has a variety of pets in his house.

Billy must select one of his pets to write about for his school project.

a How many possible outcomes are there?

b How many of the outcomes:

  i are cats   **ii** are black   **iii** have legs?

6 Martine is choosing a South American country to visit for her next holiday.

a How many possible outcomes are there?

b How many of the outcomes:

  i start with P
  ii include the letter A?

7 Eliza and Patrick are playing chess. What are the possible outcomes?

D | CALCULATING PROBABILITIES

In many situations involving probability, the possible outcomes we consider are all **equally likely**.

For example, when we roll an ordinary die, the possible outcomes 1, 2, 3, 4, 5, and 6 are equally likely.

If the possible outcomes of an experiment are equally likely, the probability of a particular event is given by

$$\text{probability} = \frac{\text{number of outcomes in the event}}{\text{total number of possible outcomes}}.$$

We write P(....) to mean "the probability of ....".

Example 2

◀)) **Self Tutor**

An eight-sided die is rolled once.

Find the probability of rolling:

   a a 3   **b** an even number

   c a number larger than 5.

There are 8 possible outcomes which are equally likely:

$$1, 2, 3, 4, 5, 6, 7, \text{ and } 8.$$

a Only one of the outcomes is a 3.

   So, $P(a\ 3) = \frac{1}{8}$.

"P(a 3)" reads "the probability of rolling a 3".

b The four outcomes 2, 4, 6, and 8 are even.

   So, $P(\text{an even number}) = \frac{4}{8}$.

c The three outcomes 6, 7, and 8 are greater than 5.

   So, $P(\text{a number greater than 5}) = \frac{3}{8}$.

EXERCISE 17D

1 A coin is tossed once.

   a How many possible outcomes are there?

   b Find the probability of getting a head.

2 An ordinary die is rolled once.

   a How many possible outcomes are there?

   b Find the probability of rolling:

      i a 1   **ii** an even number.

3 A playing card is randomly selected from the group alongside.

   a How many possible outcomes are there?

   b Find the probability of selecting:

      i the 2 of ♦   **ii** a spade ♠

      iii a 4   **iv** a black card.

4 Jack says that 3 of the 5 sectors in this spinner have odd numbers, so the probability of spinning an odd number is $\frac{3}{5}$.

Explain why Jack is incorrect.

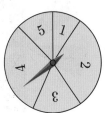

5 In a school raffle, tickets numbered from 1 to 40 are placed in a barrel. The winning ticket is drawn at random.

When we *randomly select* an object, each object is equally likely to be selected.

   a How many possible outcomes are there?

   b Find the probability that the winning ticket number is:

     i 19   **ii** 27 or 28

     iii a single digit number

     iv a prime number.

6

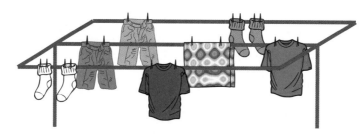

Troy hung his washing on the clothes line. Unfortunately, his dog grabbed an item at random, and pulled it off the line. Find the probability that the item was:

  a blue   **b** a sock   **c** from the middle row of the clothes line.

7 A box of chocolates contains 5 strawberry chocolates, 6 caramel chocolates, and 2 peppermint chocolates.

   a How many chocolates are in the box?

   b Prue takes a chocolate from the box at random. Find the probability that Prue selects a:

     i caramel chocolate

     ii strawberry chocolate.

8 A hockey team consists of 3 defenders, 6 midfielders, 4 attackers, and a goalkeeper.

   a How many players are in the team?

   b One player is chosen at random to be the team's captain. Find the probability that the chosen player is:

     i the goalkeeper   **ii** a defender or a midfielder.

9

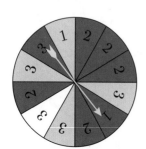

The spinner alongside is spun once.

   a Find the probability that the spinner will stop on:

     i a 3   **ii** a red sector.

   b Is the spinner more likely to stop on a 3 or a red sector?

10 A kitchen drawer contains 9 forks, 5 knives, and 6 spoons. Alexander selects an item from the drawer at random.

    a Find the probability that Alexander selects a knife. Give your answer as:

        i a fraction   **ii** a percentage   **iii** a decimal.

    b Use a word or phrase to describe the probability of Alexander selecting a knife.

11 At an event dinner, dishes are placed around a table as shown.

Scott is randomly seated at this table in front of a dish.

Find the probability that he is seated:

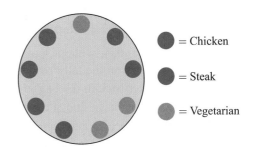

    a at a chicken dish

    b between two steak dishes

    c at a vegetarian dish, but with a steak dish next to him.

12 Ben is in Grade 6. His sister Clarissa is in Grade 4. They have both been given a list of words by their teacher, and they must learn one of the words and its meaning for homework.

Ben's words		**Clarissa's words**
exasperating	anoint	celery
pronounce	scarce	glacier
texture	junction	voyage
frugal	scent	quartet
valiant	caption	currency

Each child selects one word at random from their list.

    a Find the probability that:

        i Ben selects a word starting with "s"

        ii Clarissa selects a word which contains "a".

    b Who is more likely to select a word:

        i starting with "v"   **ii** containing at least 8 letters?

13 Shanice placed these tokens in a bag, then selected a token at random.

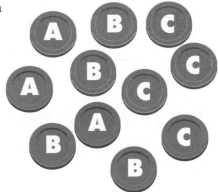

    a Find the probability that Shanice selects:

        i an A   **ii** a B   **iii** a C

        iv a blue token   **v** a red token.

    b Find:

        i P(an A) + P(a B) + P(a C)

        ii P(a blue token) + P(a red token)

    Explain your answers.

ACTIVITY 2 — EXPERIMENTAL PROBABILITY

In experiments involving chance, we can find the **experimental probability** of an event occurring by performing the experiment multiple times.

What to do:

1 Place three red, five blue, and two green counters in a bag. If you do not have these colours, use your own colours.

2 Shake the bag, then without looking, take out one counter and record its colour in the tally column of the table.
Put the counter back in the bag, then draw another counter.
Repeat until you have drawn a counter 100 times.
Copy the table below, and record in it:

   a the *number* of times you selected each colour

   b the *experimental probability* of selecting each colour, using:

   PRINTABLE TABLE

   $$\text{experimental probability} = \frac{\text{number of that colour selected}}{\text{total number of counters selected}}$$

   c the actual probability of selecting each colour.

Colour	Tally	Number of times selected	Experimental probability	Actual probability
Red				$\frac{3}{10} = 0.3$
Blue				
Green				

3 Were your experimental probabilities the same as the actual probabilities?

4 If you ran the experiment again, would you always get the same results?

5 a Run the computer simulation so you can experiment with much larger samples. Try selecting a counter 10 000 times and 100 000 times.

   DEMO

   b When you run an experiment more times, do the experimental probabilities get closer to the actual probabilities?

   c Discuss your results.

ACTIVITY 3 — PROBABILITY DEVICES

In this Chapter we have seen how coins, dice, and spinners can be used in probability experiments.

In this Activity, your task is to make devices which will generate outcomes with particular probabilities.

For example, suppose we wish to make a device offering two possible outcomes, blue and grey,

with probabilities $P(\text{blue}) = \frac{2}{3}$ and $P(\text{grey}) = \frac{1}{3}$.

We could make a **spinner** or a **die**.

- **Spinner**

$\frac{2}{3}$ of $360° = \frac{2}{3} \times 360° = 240°$

$\frac{1}{3}$ of $360° = \frac{1}{3} \times 360° = 120°$

So, the blue sector is $240°$
and the grey sector is $120°$.

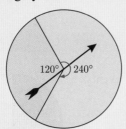

- **Die**

A die has 6 faces which are equally
likely to appear when the die is rolled.

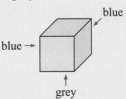

So, we colour 4 faces blue and
2 faces grey.

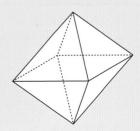

What to do:

1 The spinner above has exactly two sectors. Show, by colouring the sectors, that each of

these spinners can also be used to produce $P(\text{blue}) = \frac{2}{3}$ and $P(\text{grey}) = \frac{1}{3}$.

a

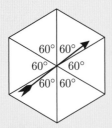

b

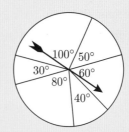

2 Look at the blue and grey die above.

Do the grey faces theoretically have to be opposite one another?

Can you think of a reason why it might be a good idea to have the grey faces opposite one another?

3 Design *two* spinners such that $P(\text{green}) = \frac{1}{6}$, $P(\text{yellow}) = \frac{1}{3}$, and $P(\text{blue}) = \frac{1}{2}$.

4 The diagram alongside shows a regular octahedron. It has
8 faces which are the same size and shape. Each face is
equally likely to appear when the octahedron is rolled.

Describe how to shade the faces of the octahedron so

that $P(\text{red}) = \frac{1}{4}$, $P(\text{blue}) = \frac{3}{8}$, $P(\text{yellow}) = \frac{1}{4}$, and

$P(\text{green}) = \frac{1}{8}$.

5   **a**   Design a spinner such that $P(\text{red}) = \frac{2}{9}$, $P(\text{purple}) = \frac{1}{6}$, $P(\text{orange}) = \frac{5}{12}$,   and the only other possible outcome is blue.

   b   Find $P(\text{blue})$,   giving your answer in lowest terms.

QUICK QUIZ

MULTIPLE CHOICE QUIZ

REVIEW SET 17A

1   Describe, using a word or phrase, the probability of these events:

   a   The spinner alongside will land on red.

   b   The next triangle you draw will have 4 sides.

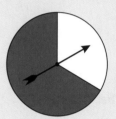

2   You have five blue cards, five white cards, and five grey cards. You must place any three of them in a hat. What cards should you place in the hat if you want:

   a   it to be impossible to draw a white or grey card

   b   to be certain of drawing a grey card

   c   there to be an equal chance of drawing a blue, white, or grey card?

3   Write a word or phrase to describe the probability value:

   a   0.14   **b**   1   **c**   0.5

4   **a**   List the possible outcomes when this spinner is spun.

   b   How many possible outcomes are there?

   c   Are the outcomes equally likely?

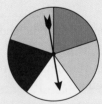

5   Jarrod placed all the letters of the alphabet in a hat, and drew one out at random.

   a   How many possible outcomes are there?

   b   Find the probability that Jarrod drew:

      i   a vowel   **ii**   an X, Y, or Z.

6   Petra has 5 petunias, 7 marigolds, and 8 roses in her garden. One of the plants was damaged by a possum. Find the probability that the damaged plant was:

   a   a petunia   **b**   a marigold *or* a rose.

7 Simon is playing Trent in a game of darts. Simon has probability 0.64 of winning, and Trent has probability 0.36 of winning.

   a Who is more likely to win the game?

   b Find the sum of the probabilities. Explain your answer.

8 A day during November is selected at random. Find the probability that the selected day is:

   a the 17th   **b** a Sunday

   c a weekday.

November						
M	T	W	T	F	S	S
		1	2	3	4	5
6	7	8	9	10	11	12
13	14	15	16	17	18	19
20	21	22	23	24	25	26
27	28	29	30			

9 Clarence the clown has a collection of balloons. He selects one at random to give to a child.

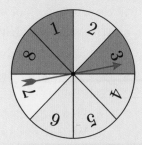

   a Find the probability that the child will receive:

      i a red balloon   **ii** a blue balloon

      iii a yellow balloon.

   b Which colour balloon is the child most likely to receive?

   c Find the sum of the probabilities in **a**. Explain your answer.

REVIEW SET 17B

1 Copy and complete:

   a It is ...... that the spinner will stop on a numbered sector.

   b It is ...... that the spinner will stop on "yellow".

   c It is ...... for the spinner to stop on "12".

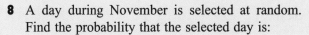

2 Peggy, Christina, Suzanne, and Chelsea go mountain biking together. The table alongside shows the probability that each girl will fall off her bike.

   a Place these probabilities on a number line.

   b Which girl is most likely to fall off her bike?

   c Write a word or phrase to describe the probability that Chelsea will fall off her bike.

	Probability
Peggy	0.15
Christina	0.3
Suzanne	0.27
Chelsea	0.1

3 A day of the week is chosen at random.

    a How many possible outcomes are there?

    b How many of the outcomes contain the letter U?

4 Justin is investigating a collection of 10 stones at the bottom of his garden. There are pill bugs under 5 of the stones, and earwigs under 3 of the stones.

Justin turns one of the stones over at random.

Find the probability that there is an earwig under the stone.

5 Bradley and Caleb have a spelling test today.

Bradley has probability $\frac{3}{5}$ of passing the test, and Caleb has probability 0.62 of passing the test.

    a Write each probability as a percentage.

    b Who is more likely to pass the test?

6 Liesl had to return 2 mathematics books, 3 science books, and 4 history books to the library. She accidentally left one of the books at home. Find the probability that she left a mathematics book at home.

7 Of the 23 passengers on a bus, 7 have a seniors card. Find the probability that a randomly selected passenger:

    a has a seniors card   **b** does *not* have a seniors card.

8 Blair selects a number from 1 to 10 at random, and Ayla selects a number from 1 to 40 at random.

    a Find the probability that:

        i Blair selects a multiple of 3   **ii** Ayla selects a multiple of 3.

    b Who is more likely to select a multiple of 3?

9 Bruce throws 4 balls up in the air, and tries to catch them all at once. The table alongside shows the probability that Bruce will catch 0, 1, 2, 3, or 4 balls.

	Probability
0 balls	0.21
1 ball	0.37
2 balls	0.31
3 balls	0.09
4 balls	0.02

    a What number of balls is Bruce most likely to catch?

    b Is Bruce more likely to catch 0 balls or 3 balls?

    c Find the sum of the probabilities in the table. Explain your result.

    d **i** Find the probability that Bruce will catch 2 balls or less.

        ii Write a word or phrase to describe the probability that Bruce will catch 2 balls or less.

Chapter 18

Statistics

Contents:

OPENING PROBLEM

A teacher asked her students "Which room at home do you usually do your homework in?"

She recorded the answers on the board, using the code B = Bedroom, K = Kitchen, F = Family room, S = Study:

  B B F S B   F K S K B   B F B S K
  B S S K B   F B S K B

Things to think about:

  a Which room was most popular for doing homework?

  b How can we *organise* and *display* this information so it is easier to analyse?

When we collect facts or information about something, we call this information **data**.

> **Statistics** is the study of collecting, organising, and analysing data.

Many groups such as schools, businesses, and government departments collect data. The information is used to help make decisions.

A   CATEGORICAL DATA

> **Categorical data** is data which can be placed in categories.

We can organise categorical data using a **tally and frequency table**.

- The **tally** is used to count the data in each category.
  We use | to represent 1, and ⊬⊬⊬ to represent 5.
- The **frequency** gives the total number in each category.

A tally and frequency table allows us to identify features of the data such as the *mode*.

> The **mode** is the most frequently occurring category.

Example 1	◀) **Self Tutor**

Rosemary recorded the types of flowers in a bouquet she received using the categories daffodil (D), lily (L), rose (R), tulip (T), and iris (I).

Her data was:

  L R T T D   L R T D T   I I L L R
  L L R R T   T T T I R   T I L T T
  L R D T D   D T T D L

a Draw a tally and frequency table for the data.

b Find the mode of the data. Explain what it means.

a	**Rosemary's flower data**			b	Tulip has the highest frequency, so it is the mode.

Rosemary's flower data

Flower	Tally	Frequency
Daffodil (D)	卌 |	6
Lily (L)	卌 ||||	9
Rose (R)	卌 ||	7
Tulip (T)	卌 卌 ||||	14
Iris (I)	||||	4
	Total	40

b Tulip has the highest frequency, so it is the mode.
The most common flower in the bouquet is the tulip.

EXERCISE 18A

1 Brody (B), Cooper (C), Hailey (H), and Maria (M) played board games on the weekend.
They recorded which person won each game:

   H C M M H   B M H C H   M H B C H

a Draw a tally and frequency table for the data.

b How many games did Cooper win?

c Who won the most games?

d Who won the least games?

2 A cinema owner recorded products sold at the candy bar using the categories popcorn (P), soft drink (S), ice cream (I), and chips (C):

   C P S P I   P S C I P   I P C S C   P C S P C   S P I P C
   I P C C P   P C S P I   C P C P S   C I I P P   C S C P I

a Draw a tally and frequency table for the data.

b How many soft drinks were sold?

c Find the mode of the data. Explain what this means.

3 A class of students went on an excursion to the aquarium. Each student was asked to name their favourite animal. Data was recorded using the categories shark (Sh), seahorse (Se), dolphin (D), and otter (O). The results were:

   D Sh Se D O   Sh D O D Sh   Se D Sh O D
   Se O D Sh D   O Sh D Se O   D Sh Sh O D

a Organise the data using a tally and frequency table.

b How many students went on the excursion?

c What was the most popular animal?

d What fraction of the students chose the seahorse as their favourite animal?

4 Guests staying in a city hotel were surveyed to find out what they thought of the hotel's service. They were asked to choose excellent (E), good (G), satisfactory (S), or unsatisfactory (U). The results were:

E G G S E   U S S G G   S G U G G   E S G U G   S S E G G

   a Draw a tally and frequency table for the data.

   b What is the mode of the data?

   c What fraction of guests responded that the service was unsatisfactory?

   d What percentage of guests responded that the service was good or excellent?

   e Why do you think the hotel would survey its guests like this?

   f Do you think the hotel manager would be pleased with the results of the survey? Explain your answer.

RESEARCH   TALLY MARKS

Humans have been using tally marks for thousands of years. In prehistoric times, people carved marks onto animal bones to record numbers.

One of the best known examples is the **Ishango bone**, believed to be over 20 000 years old!

The tally marks we use in this book are used in most of Europe, Africa, Australia, New Zealand, and North America.

Different types of tally marks are used in other countries. For example:

-   | ⌐   ⊓   □   ⧄   is used in France, Spain, and Brazil
      1   2   3   4   5

-   一   丅   干   正   正   is used in China, Japan, and Korea.
      1   2   3   4   5

What to do:

1 Which set of tally marks do you think is the most *logical*?

2 Why do you think tally marks are different in different parts of the world?

3 Why do we "bundle" tally marks in groups of 5?

4 Research what the Chinese character 正 means. Why do you think it was chosen?

5 Research the numerals in the following number systems:

   a Brahmi   **b** Roman   **c** Chinese-Japanese

   What do the first few numerals of these number systems have in common?

B | DOT PLOTS

> A **dot plot** is a graph in which each dot represents one data value.

Dot plots may be **horizontal** or **vertical**.

A horizontal dot plot for Rosemary's flower data in **Example 1** is shown below.

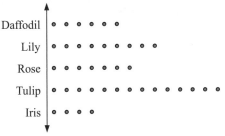

Rosemary's flower data

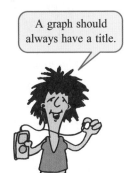

A graph should always have a title.

Check that the number of dots is equal to the frequency for each flower.

Example 2   ◀)) **Self Tutor**

The sales of drinks at the canteen were recorded one recess time. The categories recorded were orange juice (O), soy milk (S), cola (C), and iced tea (I).

  O S S C I   O C I S O   I O C S O   O O O S C   S O C O S   O O

a Draw a vertical dot plot of the data.   **b** State the mode of the data.

c What fraction of the drinks sold were soy milk?

a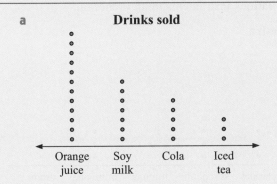

b The mode is orange juice.

c In total, 32 drinks were bought.

  The fraction that were soy milk $= \dfrac{7}{32}$.

EXERCISE 18B

1 Students at a school camp were given the choice of several afternoon activities to participate in. This vertical dot plot shows how many students chose each activity.

  a How many students chose orienteering?

  b How many students were at the camp?

  c Find the mode of the data.

Camp activities

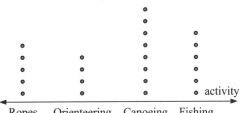

2 Lucas hosted a Halloween party. Each of the children at the party dressed up as a ghost, a pumpkin, a witch, or a mummy.

- **a** How many children were at the party?
- **b** Draw a horizontal dot plot to show how many children wore each costume.
- **c** Find the mode of the data.
- **d** One of the children is randomly chosen to win a prize. Find the probability that the child is dressed as a witch.

3 A spinner with red, blue, yellow, and green sectors is spun 30 times. The results were:

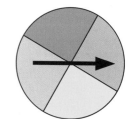

R B R Y G   Y G B B R   R G B Y Y
G R G B R   Y R R G B   G R G B R

- **a** Draw a vertical dot plot of the data.
- **b** Find the mode of the data.
- **c** What fraction of the results were yellow? Write your answer in lowest terms.

4 This dot plot shows the musicians playing various instruments in an orchestra.

Orchestra

violin	cello	double bass	flute	clarinet	saxophone	trumpet	trombone	drums
strings			woodwind			brass		percussion

- **a** Find the mode of the data.
- **b** How many musicians:
      i are in the orchestra   **ii** play the clarinet   **iii** play stringed instruments?
- **c** What fraction of musicians play a brass instrument?
- **d** What percentage of musicians play either a brass or a woodwind instrument?

C   PICTOGRAMS

> A **pictogram** is a graph made up of pictures.

Each picture in a pictogram represents a particular number of objects.

We use whole pictures and fractions of pictures to illustrate the frequency of each category.

The pictogram for Rosemary's flower data in **Example 1** is shown alongside.

The **scale** tells us that each whole picture represents 4 flowers.

Notice how fractions of pictures are used to represent 1, 2, or 3 flowers.

Rosemary's flower data

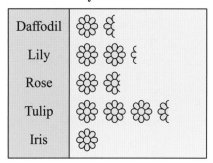

Scale: = 4 flowers

EXERCISE 18C

1   represents 4 koalas brought to an animal shelter. Show how to represent:

    a 8 koalas   **b** 3 koalas   **c** 14 koalas   **d** 21 koalas.

2   represents 8 bottles of fruit juice sold. Explain what these pictures represent:

   a    **b**   **c**   **d**

3   This pictogram shows the number of flights leaving an airport each day for a week.

Departures

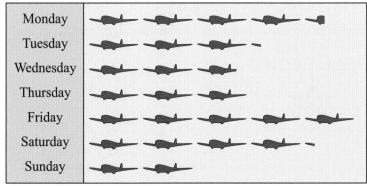

Scale:

 = 5 flights

    a How many flights left the airport on Thursday?

    b Which day had the greatest number of departures?

    c How many flights left over the weekend?

4 Ian counted the vehicles that passed as he waited for his bus.

   a How many trucks went past?

   b How many more motorbikes than bicycles went past?

   c How many vehicles went past in total?

   d What fraction of the vehicles that went past were vans?

   e Was the number of cars greater than the sum of all the other vehicles?

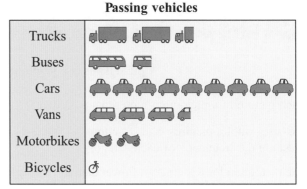

Passing vehicles

Scale: Each picture = 2 vehicles

5 Jessica recorded the activities of people using a path for one hour on Sunday morning.

Draw a pictogram to represent the results, using 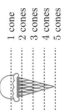 to represent 2 people.

Activity	Number of people
Walking	24
Jogging	7
Cycling	15
Rollerblading	5

6 Pete's ice cream van sells 10 flavours of ice cream, but the most popular flavours are chocolate, strawberry, boysenberry, vanilla, and rum & raisin.

Pete's sales for last Saturday are shown in the table.

Draw a pictogram to represent his sales, using this picture:

1 cone   2 cones   3 cones   4 cones   5 cones

Flavour	Number of cones sold
Chocolate	21
Strawberry	16
Boysenberry	14
Vanilla	10
Rum & raisin	15
Others	19

ACTIVITY 1   **BIRD WATCHING**

Click on the icon to run a bird watching simulation.

BIRD WATCHING

PRINTABLE TABLE

Colour	Tally	Frequency
red		
orange		
yellow		
blue		
pink		
	Total	

What to do:

1 Copy or print the tally and frequency table.

2 When you click the [Watch] button, record the colours of the birds you see using a tally.

3 Complete the frequency column in your table.

4 Draw a pictogram for your data on an A4 sheet of paper. Before you start, you will need to decide what picture will represent the birds, and how many birds each picture will represent.

5 Compare your pictogram with your classmates.
  - Did they use the same picture or scale as you?
  - Were the number of birds of each colour they saw similar to what you saw?

DISCUSSION

  - What are the advantages of using pictures to represent data values instead of dots?
  - Do the pictures in a pictogram always have to be *relevant*?

D   COLUMN GRAPHS

STATISTICS PACKAGE

Column graphs consist of rectangular columns of equal width.

The height of each column represents the frequency of the category.

The mode is the category with the highest column.

Example 3   ◀) Self Tutor

The table alongside shows the favourite subjects of students in a class.

a Draw a column graph to display the data.

b Find the mode of the data.

Subject	Frequency
Art	5
English	6
Mathematics	7
Physical Education	5
Science	4

a

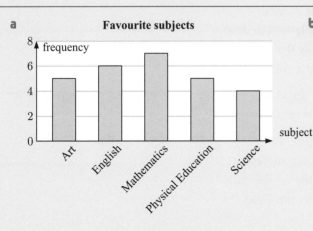

b The mode of the data is Mathematics.

The axes must be clearly labelled.

EXERCISE 18D

1 This column graph shows the items handed in to Lost Property at a gym.

   a How many T-shirts were handed in?

   b Find the mode of the data.

   c How many more towels than shoes were handed in?

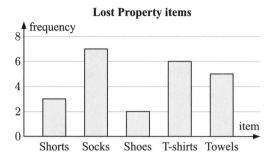

Lost Property items

2

Type of car driven

The column graph shows the types of car driven by 120 randomly selected people.

   a How many people in the sample drive a:
      i station wagon   ii sedan?

   b Which type of car is most popular?

   c What fraction of people in the sample drive a van?

3 This table describes the stalls at a market.

   a How many stalls are at the market?

   b Draw a column graph to display the data.

   c Find the mode of the data.

   d How many more clothing stalls are there than art stalls?

Stall type	Number of stalls
Food	5
Art	4
Craft	8
Clothing	6

4 The data alongside shows the ticket type of each person attending a cinema.

   The types are adult (A), concession (C), and student (S).

```
A A S S   C A C S A
C S C A A   C S S A C
C S A A S
```

   a How many people attended the cinema?

   b Draw a tally and frequency table for the data.

   c Draw a column graph to display the data.

   d What percentage of people had a concession ticket?

5 Adults completing a survey were asked whether they work full-time (F), part-time (P), are unemployed (U), or retired (R). The results were:

```
F R P P F   U P F R F   P F U P F   R F R F R   U F R P
```

   a How many adults took part in the survey?

   b Draw a tally and frequency table for the data.

   c Draw a column graph to display the data.

   d Find the mode of the data.

   e How many of the adults work either full-time or part-time?

E PIE CHARTS

A **pie chart** displays how a quantity is divided into categories.

We use a full circle to represent the whole quantity.

The circle is divided into **sectors** or wedges to show each category. The size of each sector indicates the percentage of the whole that is in that category.

This pie chart shows the languages spoken at home in the United States of America.

We see that:

- 13.4% of the population speak Spanish at home.
- $13.4\% + 1.1\% + 7.3\% = 21.1\%$ of the population speak a language other than English at home.
- The mode is English because it has the largest sector. More people living in the USA speak English at home than any other language.

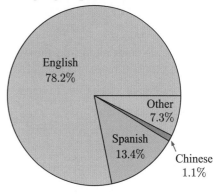

Languages spoken in the USA

Example 4   ◀) **Self Tutor**

120 Canadian Grade 6 students were asked the question "What school sport do you play in winter?"

This pie chart shows the results.

a Which is the most popular winter sport at the school?

b True or false? More than half of the students chose ice hockey or basketball.

c How many students chose volleyball?

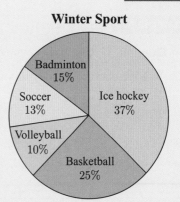

Winter Sport

---

a The most popular sport is ice hockey.

b $37\% + 25\% = 62\%$ of the students chose ice hockey or basketball. This is more than half, so the statement is true.

c 10% of the students chose volleyball.

So, the number of students who chose volleyball $= 10\%$ of 120

$$= 0.1 \times 120$$
$$= 12$$

EXERCISE 18E

1

Household water use

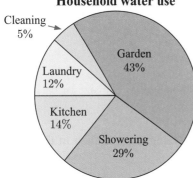

Cleaning 5%
Laundry 12%
Garden 43%
Kitchen 14%
Showering 29%

The pie chart alongside illustrates how water is used by a household.

a For what purpose is the most water used?

b True or false?

  i More water was used in the kitchen than the laundry.

  ii Less than one fifth of the water is used for laundry and cleaning.

c The household used 400 kL of water over summer. How much was used for the garden?

2 The pie chart alongside shows the clothing sizes of the Grade 6 boys in a school.

a Which size is most commonly worn?

b True or false?

  i More than half of Grade 6 boys wear size 12 or 14.

  ii Size 8 is the least commonly worn size.

c There are 180 Grade 6 boys in the school. How many boys wear:

  i size 14   ii size 10?

Clothing sizes

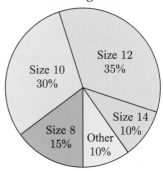

Size 10 30%
Size 12 35%
Size 8 15%
Other 10%
Size 14 10%

Example 5   ◀)) **Self Tutor**

In **Example 1**, Rosemary counted the flowers in her bouquet.

Draw a pie chart to display this information.

Flower	Frequency
Daffodil	6
Lily	9
Rose	7
Tulip	14
Iris	4
Total	40

There are 40 flowers in total.

$\frac{1}{40}$ of $360° = \frac{360°}{40} = 9°$

So each flower corresponds to an angle of 9° at the centre of the circle.

The daffodil sector has angle $6 \times 9° = 54°$.
The lily sector has angle $9 \times 9° = 81°$.
The rose sector has angle $7 \times 9° = 63°$.
The tulip sector has angle $14 \times 9° = 126°$.
The iris sector has angle $4 \times 9° = 36°$.

Rosemary's bouquet

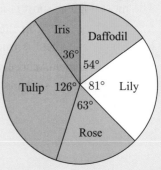

Iris 36°
Daffodil 54°
Lily 81°
Tulip 126°
Rose 63°

3 A table tennis club has 36 members. The table alongside shows their playing levels.

Playing level	Frequency
A Grade	9
B Grade	5
C Grade	10
Junior	12
Total	36

    a In a pie chart, what angle does each member represent?

    b Find the sector angle for each category.

    c Draw a pie chart for the data.

4 30 children in the school library were asked "What is your favourite type of book?" The responses are shown in this table.

Type	Frequency
Non-fiction	6
Crime	5
Adventure	5
Fantasy	10
Horror	4

    a State the mode of the data.

    b Draw a pie chart to display the data.

    c What fraction of the children prefer non-fiction? Write your answer in lowest terms.

5 A group of students in the playground were asked what they ate for lunch. Their responses are shown in this table.

Food	Frequency
Sandwich or Roll	16
Noodles	8
Baked pastry	11
Curry	4
Other	6

    a How many students were surveyed?

    b Calculate the percentage of students in each category.

    c Draw a pie chart to display the data. Include the percentage for each category with its label.

ACTIVITY 2

Use the **statistics package** or a **spreadsheet** to generate graphs for the questions in **Exercises B**, **D**, and **E**.

STATISTICS
PACKAGE

F   NUMERICAL DATA

> **Numerical data** is data which is in number form.

For example, Julio recorded the *number of people* in the cars going past an intersection. The data he collected is numerical data.

```
2  1  2  3  2    4  2  5  3  1
1  3  2  4  1    3  2  2  1  5
3  4  1  2  5    2  4  1  2  5
5  1  3  2  4    1  3  2  1  4
```

In a situation like this where there are only a small number of different data values, we can organise and display our data in the same way as for categorical data. We can use tally and frequency tables, dot plots, and column graphs.

As with categorical data, the **mode** is the most frequently occurring value. In this case, the mode is 2 people.

Number of people	Tally	Frequency
1	ℍℍℍ ℍℍℍ	10
2	ℍℍℍ ℍℍℍ ‖	12
3	ℍℍℍ ‖	7
4	ℍℍℍ │	6
5	ℍℍℍ	5
	Total	40

Number of people in each car

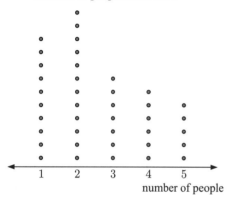

Number of people in each car

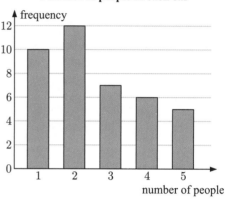

EXERCISE 18F

1   A class of students was asked how many hats they owned. Their answers are recorded in the column graph.

   a   How many students own 2 hats?

   b   How many students are in the class?

   c   Find the mode of the data. Explain what this means.

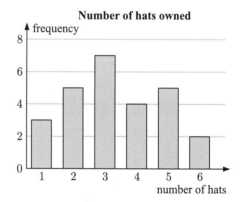

Number of hats owned

2   This dot plot shows the number of fillings that a group of children received at their last dental appointment.

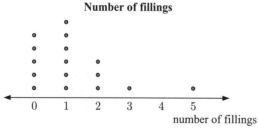

Number of fillings

   a   How many children received at least 2 fillings?

   b   Find the mode of the data.

3 A group of athletes ran laps of the athletics track at the end of their training session. The table alongside shows the number of laps they ran.

Number of laps	Frequency
2	1
3	2
4	5
5	7
6	3

   a Draw a vertical dot plot to display the data.

   b Find the mode of the data.

   c How many athletes ran less than 4 laps?

   d How many athletes were in the group?

4 The number of children in 30 families is shown below:

     0, 4, 6, 2, 1, 3, 2, 4, 0, 2, 1, 2, 4, 0, 2, 3, 1, 4, 2, 1, 2, 4, 3, 3, 0, 4, 3, 2, 2, 4

   a Copy and complete the tally and frequency table alongside.

   b Draw a column graph to display the data.

   c Find the mode of the data.

Children	Tally	Frequency
0		
1		
2		
3		
4		
5		
6		
Total		30

5 An exceptional hockey player scored these numbers of goals over 25 matches:

     4 3 6 1 5   5 4 2 2 4   6 0 5 1 0   3 1 2 6 6   8 3 6 2 8

   a Organise the data in a tally and frequency table.

   b Draw a column graph to display the data.

   c On how many occasions did the player score 5 or more goals in a match?

   d Find the mode of the data.

6 The numbers of home runs scored by a baseball team in each game of a season were:

     3 0 4 2 0   3 3 1 2 1   1 2 3 3 2   2 5 0 2 1

   a Complete a tally and frequency table for the data.

   b Draw a column graph to display the data.

   c In how many games did the team score exactly 3 home runs?

   d In what fraction of games did the team score no home runs?

   e In what percentage of games did the team score at least 4 home runs?

DISCUSSION

Do you find a dot plot or a column graph more visually appealing?

Which type of graph is more appropriate when there is a large amount of data?

G   MEASURING THE CENTRE OF A DATA SET

DISCUSSION

What do we mean by the word "average"?

For example, consider:

- the average speed of a car
- average height and weight
- the average score for a test
- the average wage or income
- the average temperature in summer.

In statistics, the **mean** or **average** of a numerical data set is a measure of its **centre**.

> The **mean** or **average** of a set of numerical data is given by:
>
> $$\text{mean} = \frac{\text{sum of data values}}{\text{the number of data values}}$$

Example 6   ◄)) **Self Tutor**

Find the mean of   7, 11, 15, 6, 11, 19, 23, 0, and 7.

There are 9 data values.

$$\text{mean} = \frac{\text{sum of data values}}{\text{number of data values}}$$

$$= \frac{7 + 11 + 15 + 6 + 11 + 19 + 23 + 0 + 7}{9}$$

$$= \frac{99}{9}$$

$$= 11$$

EXERCISE 18G

1 Find the mean of each data set:

    a 4, 5, 8, 11

    b 2, 2, 6, 7, 8

    c 6, 9, 5, 12, 9, 7

    d 13, 7, 6, 14, 11, 16, 10

    e 5, 9, 1, 2, 0, 3, 9, 3

    f 3, 4, 4, 6, 7, 8, 8, 10, 11, 12

    g 1.8, 2.5, 1.6, 2.3, 2.1, 1.7

    h 1.34, 1.45, 1.52, 1.38, 1.49, 1.41, 1.42

2 In a ski jumping competition, Lars' jumps were 110 m, 112 m, 118 m, 103 m, and 122 m.
   Calculate the average length of Lars' ski jumps.

3 People at a sweets store were asked how many chocolates they ate last week. The responses were:

2   5   0   6   1   8   0   2   5   4   1   2

The mode is always a value in the data set. The mean is usually *not* in the data set.

a Find the average number of chocolates eaten.

b Find the mode of the data.

4 The masses of a group of newborn ducklings are:

50 g, 55 g, 52 g, 61 g, 59 g, 59 g.

Find the average mass of the ducklings.

5 Olivia records how long it takes her to cycle to school each day for 15 days. The results, in minutes, are:

17   14   22   23   19   24   25   20   17   18   23   16   22   22   18

Find the average time it takes Olivia to cycle to school.

6 The data alongside shows the number of letters delivered to each house on a street in one week.

2	1	0	1	2
0	1	3	2	1
1	4	0	0	2
4	1	1	3	1

a Draw a vertical dot plot to display the data.

b How many houses received more than 2 letters?

c Find the mode of the data.

d Find the mean of the data.

7 Cameron played 16 cricket matches for his local club this season. The numbers of wickets he took in each match were:

0   3   4   2   3   5   4   4   3   0   4   2   1   5   6   2

a Draw a column graph of the data.

b Find the mode of the data.

c Find Cameron's mean number of wickets per match.

d Is it possible for Cameron to take this mean number of wickets in any particular game? Discuss your answer.

GLOBAL CONTEXT   CLOTHING SIZES

Global context: Fairness and development

Statement of inquiry: Collecting data can help businesses to make informed decisions.

Criterion: Communicating

GLOBAL CONTEXT

PROJECT   A STATISTICAL EXPERIMENT

In this Project, you will grow wheat over a 3 week period in a controlled experiment. You will use 6 grains of wheat in each of 4 plots.

You will need: 4 saucers or jar lids, cotton wool, 24 grains of wheat, an eye dropper, water, diluted liquid fertiliser.

What to do:

1 Layer the cotton wool three quarters of the way up each lid.
   Place 6 grains of wheat at equal distances apart in each lid.

2 Label the lids as plots 1, 2, 3, and 4. Saturate each plot with 15 mL of water.

3 Over a 3 week period, squeeze water and diluted fertiliser onto every grain of wheat as described in the table alongside.

Plot	Days	Water	Diluted fertiliser
1	Mon, Wed, Fri	2 drops	-
2	every weekday	2 drops	-
3	Mon, Wed, Fri	2 drops	1 drop
4	every weekday	2 drops	1 drop

4 Place all of your plots in the same safe, sheltered place with plenty of light.

5 Every Monday, Wednesday, and Friday, record the number of germinating seeds and the mean height of the germinating seeds for each plot. Avoid handling any shoots. Make a table to summarise your results.

6 Use graphs and the language of statistics to display and discuss your results.

MULTIPLE CHOICE QUIZ

QUICK QUIZ

REVIEW SET 18A

1 Yuka recorded the orders she received at her sushi restaurant on Friday.

   a How many orders did she receive?

   b Draw a column graph of Yuka's data.

   c What fraction of the orders received were ebi nigiri? Write your answer in lowest terms.

Food	Frequency
Tekkamaki	17
Hamachi	11
Kappa maki	8
Ebi nigiri	14
Maguro nigiri	6

2 a In the pictogram, what does 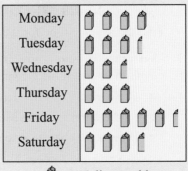 represent?

Quick Mart milk sales

b On which day were the milk sales:
  i greatest   **ii** least?

c How much milk was sold on:
  i Thursday   **ii** Friday?

 = 10 litres sold

3 This dot plot shows the shoe sizes for the Grade 6 students at a school.

Shoe sizes

a How many Grade 6 students are there at this school?

b Find the mode of the data.

c What percentage of the students wear shoe size:
  i 6 or less   **ii** 9 or more?

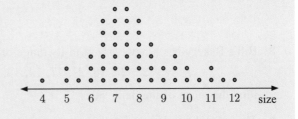

4 The column graph shows the number of points scored by a basketballer over 60 matches.

Basketball point scores

a What point score occurred most frequently?

b On how many occasions did the player score 10 or more points?

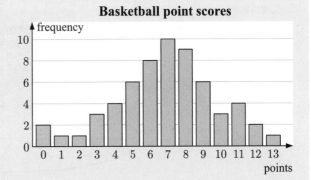

5 Tina rolled a die 35 times, and recorded these results.

a Draw a tally and frequency table for this data.

b Draw a vertical dot plot to display the data.

c How many times did Tina roll a number greater than 4?

d What fraction of Tina's rolls were less than 3?

6 The times, in minutes, for the customers at a restaurant to receive their meals were:

19   28   31   8   22   18   35   24   15   9   28   17   28   20   13

Find the average time for the customers to receive their meals.

7 Don wants to know how many flowers of each colour there are in his garden.

a Draw a tally and frequency table for the data.

b Find the mode of the data.

c Draw a pie chart to display the data.

8 Bill's Bakery has a new variety in its range of pastries. Its daily sales are:

23, 25, 18, 21, 17, 14, 15, 19, 18, 11, 15, 13, 6, 9.

Find the mean of the daily sales.

9 This pie chart shows the percentages of their budget that a council spends on various services:

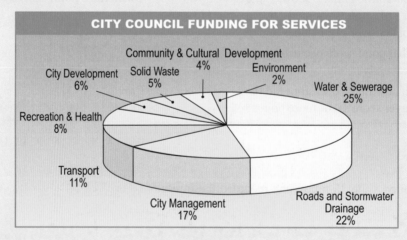

a What percentage of total funding is spent on:

  i Recreation and Health   **ii** either Transport or City Management?

b On which service is the least amount spent?

c On which service is one quarter of the funding spent?

d Find the sector angle for Solid Waste.

e The council's total budget for services was $120 million. Find the amount the council spent on City Development.

REVIEW SET 18B

1 Kirsty surveyed the bird life in her area using the categories magpie (M), sparrow (S), robin (R), wren (W), and finch (F).

During a 30 minute period she recorded these birds:

```
M  M  S  R  S  F  F  F  F  W  M  F  F  S  S  S  R
S  S  S  R  M  S  S  S  M  W  S  S  S  W  S  S
S  S  S  M  M  S  S  S  R  M  S  S  W  F  F  F
```

a Draw a tally and frequency table for the data.

b Find the mode of the data.

2 The children in a class were asked their favourite rainy day pastime.
Draw a horizontal dot plot of the data.

Rainy day pastime	Frequency
Watching TV	5
Reading	6
Computer games	9
Playing music	2
Other	4

3 Sixty people whose houses had been burgled were asked where they were at the time of the burglary.
Draw a pie chart to display the data.

Response	Frequency
At home	12
At work	20
Shopping	5
On holidays	10
Visiting friends	13
Total	60

4

House sales

= 10 houses

This pictogram shows the number of houses sold by Bill Black Real Estate in a six month period.

a How many houses were sold in
  i September   **ii** May?

b In which month were the most houses sold?

c If there were 35 sales in October, how would you represent this on the pictogram?

5 A Grade 6 class was given a mathematics test out of 10 marks.
Their results were:

8 7 6 9 10 6 7 9 8 5 9 8 7 7 7 9 4 8 7 9

Find the mean score for the class.

6 This dot plot shows the number of phone calls Susan received at work each day for 4 weeks.

   a Find the mode of the data.

   b On how many days did Susan receive less than 4 calls?

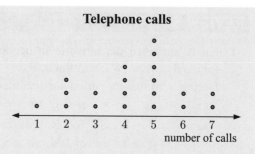

Telephone calls

number of calls

7 A group of working adults were asked what type of transportation they use to get to work. The results are shown in the column graph alongside.

   a How many adults were surveyed?

   b What percentage of the adults used the most common type of transportation to get to work?

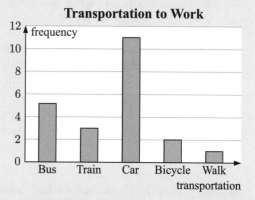

Transportation to Work

8 A teacher recorded the number of students he told off during lunch break each day for 3 weeks. His results are shown below:

   2   0   1   1   2   1   0   1   2   0   1   2   0   3   1

   a Organise the data using a tally and frequency table.

   b Draw a dot plot for the data.

   c Estimate the probability that on any given day, the teacher will tell off 2 or more students.

9 The ages of children at a party were: 8 7 8 4 7 3 7 5 6 6 7 4

   a Organise the data in a tally and frequency table.

   b How many children attended the party?

   c How many of the children were aged 7 or 8?

   d What fraction of the children were younger than 6?

   e Display the data on a column graph.

   f Find the mode of the data.

   g Find the mean of the data.

Chapter

19

Transformations

Contents:

OPENING PROBLEM

Melissa has designed this logo for the Richmond Lacrosse Club.

Things to think about:

a Which objects in the logo have the same size and shape?

b What type of *transformation* allows Melissa to start with one ball and generate the other two?

c What options does Melissa have to transform one lacrosse stick into the other?

In this Chapter we will study three types of **transformation**:

- **translation**

- **reflection**

- **rotation**

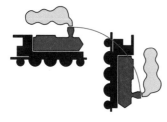

For each of these transformations, the *size* of the object is unchanged.

When we perform a transformation, the original shape is called the **object**. The shape which results from the transformation is called the **image**.

If the object is A then we can label the image A'.

 A

TRANSLATIONS

In a **translation**, every point on an object is moved the same distance in the same direction to form the image.

We can describe a translation using a horizontal step to the right or left, followed by a vertical step up or down.

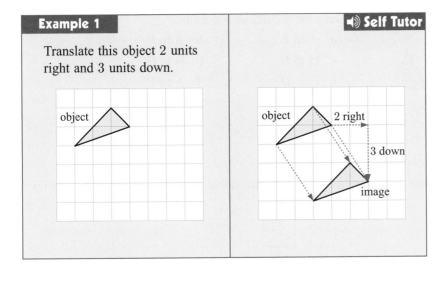

Translate each vertex of the object, then join the image vertices to complete the image.

EXERCISE 19A

1   Describe each translation using a horizontal step and a vertical step:

a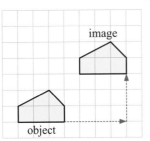

b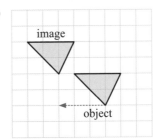

c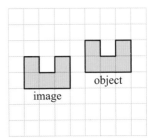

d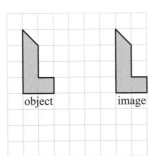

e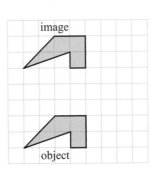

f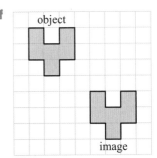

2   Describe the translation from:

   a   A to B
   b   B to A
   c   A to C
   d   C to A
   e   B to C
   f   C to B.

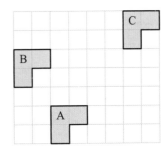

3

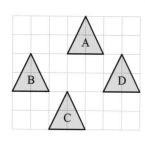

Describe the translation from:

  a A to B   **b** A to C

  c D to B   **d** B to C

  e C to D   **f** A to D.

4 Copy each figure and complete the translation given:

  a 3 units right, 2 units down   **b** 1 unit left, 4 units down   **c** 4 units right, 2 units up

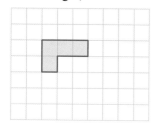 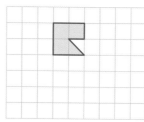 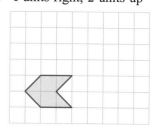

  d 2 units left, 3 units up   **e** 5 units right, 3 units down

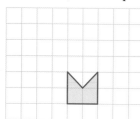 

PRINTABLE DIAGRAMS

5   **a** Translate figure A 3 units right and 1 unit down to give A′.

  b What translation is needed to move A′ back to A?

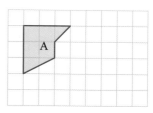

6

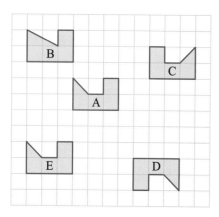

  a Which of the figures B, C, D, or E is a translation of A?

  b Describe the translation from A to this figure.

7   **a**   Translate figure A 4 units right and 3 units down to produce figure B.

    b   Translate figure A 6 units right and 5 units up to produce figure C.

    c   What translation is needed to move figure B to figure C?

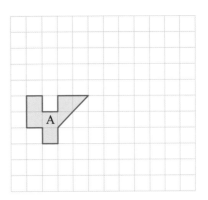

B   REFLECTIONS

When we **reflect** an object in a **mirror line**, the image is its **reflection**.

DEMO

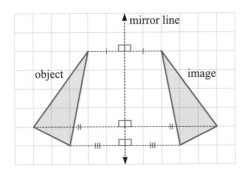

To reflect an object, we draw lines at right angles to the mirror line which pass through important points on the object.

Each image point is the same distance from the mirror line as the object point, but is on the other side of the mirror line.

EXERCISE 19B

1   Reflect each figure in the given mirror line:

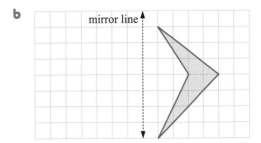

c

d

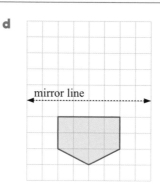

2 Reflect in the mirror line to complete the picture:

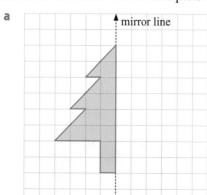

3 Is B a reflection of A? If not, copy A and the mirror line, then draw the correct reflection.

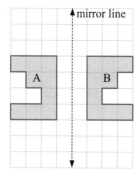

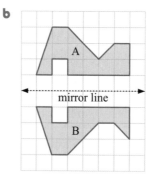

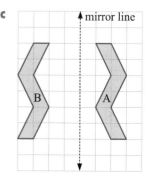

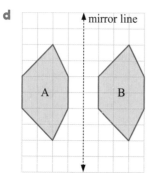

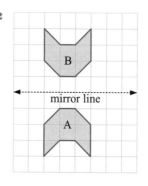

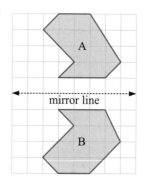

4 **a** Reflect figure R in the mirror line to give R'.

  b What happens if you reflect R' in the mirror line?

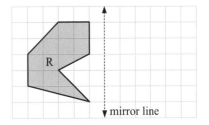

5 On a single diagram, show the images when figure A is reflected in each mirror line.

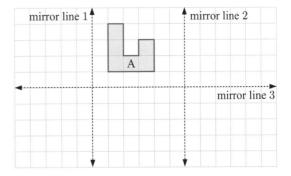

6 Julian is playing Sebastian in a game of chess. Sebastian is playing white, and Julian is playing black. Julian moves second, and his strategy on each turn is to perform the mirror image of Sebastian's previous turn.

It is now Julian's turn. Which piece will he move, and which square will he move it to?

7

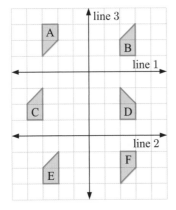

Find the two figures which are reflections of each other in one of the mirror lines. Name the mirror line in this case.

ACTIVITY 1   USING REFLECTIONS TO MAKE PICTURES

You will need: paper and scissors.

What to do:

1 Take a piece of paper and fold it neatly in half.
Cut out a shape along the fold line.
Open the sheet of paper and observe the shapes
revealed.
Record your observations.

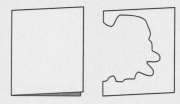

2 Repeat **1**, but this time fold the paper two or three times before cutting out your shape.
Experiment with combinations of horizontal and vertical folds.

3 **a** Make the pattern alongside by folding a piece
of paper a number of times and cutting out a
shape.

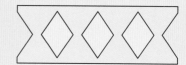

  b How many folds did you need?

  c What shape did you need to cut out?

C   ROTATIONS

Levi is riding in a Ferris wheel. As the wheel turns, he
is always the same distance from the centre of the wheel.
He therefore moves in a *circle*.

We say that Levi is *rotating* about the centre of the wheel.

> A **rotation** turns an object about a point and
> through a given angle.

The point about which the figure rotates is called the **centre of rotation,** and is often labelled O.

We will consider rotations of $90°$ (a $\frac{1}{4}$ turn) and $180°$ (a $\frac{1}{2}$ turn).

The rotations can be performed in a **clockwise** or
anticlockwise direction.

Clockwise is the
direction the hands
of a clock turn.

When we rotate objects on a grid, it is easiest to start with points or lines on the object which lie on the same horizontal or vertical grid line as O.

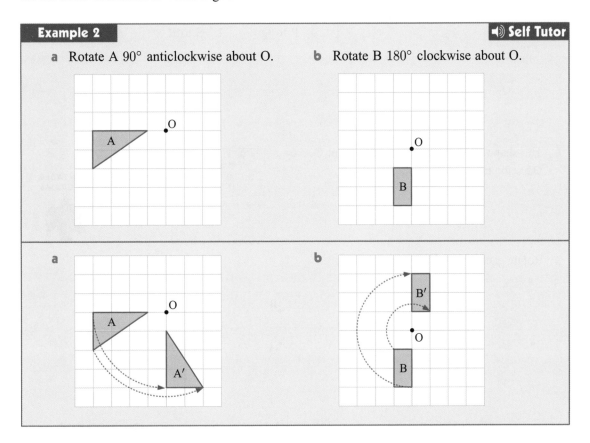

Example 2 ◀) **Self Tutor**

a Rotate A 90° anticlockwise about O.

b Rotate B 180° clockwise about O.

DISCUSSION

- When a point is rotated about O, can its distance from O ever change?
- Will a rotation 180° clockwise always give the same result as a rotation 180° anticlockwise?

EXERCISE 19C

1 Find the position of the arrow on this dial if the dial is turned:

   a 90° clockwise
      b 90° anticlockwise

   c 180° clockwise
      d 180° anticlockwise.

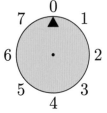

2 The hour hand of a clock is pointing at the 7. Describe the position of the hour hand if it is turned:

   a 90° clockwise
      b 180° clockwise
      c 90° anticlockwise.

3

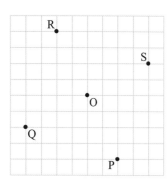

On the grid alongside, O is the centre of all rotations.

Describe the rotation from:

   a P to Q   **b** S to R   **c** Q to S.

4 The shape W is rotated about the point O. Describe the rotation from W to:

   a X   **b** Y   **c** Z.

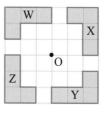

PRINTABLE DIAGRAMS

5 Rotate each point about O as directed:

a

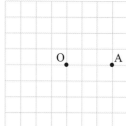

90° clockwise

b

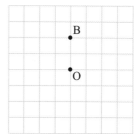

90° anticlockwise

c

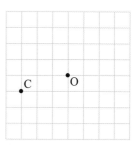

180° clockwise

d

180° anticlockwise

e

90° clockwise

f

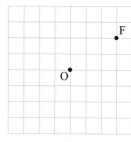

90° anticlockwise

6 Rotate each shape about O as directed:

a

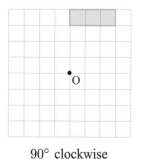

90° clockwise

b

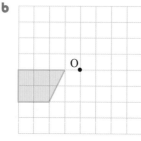

180° clockwise

c

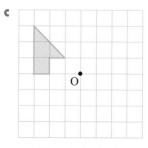

90° anticlockwise

7 Rectangle A has vertices P, Q, R, and S.

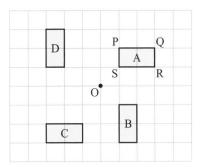

   a Which of the other rectangles is a rotation of A about O?

      Copy the grid, and mark on the image vertices P′, Q′, R′, and S′ on the image rectangle.

   b Which rectangle is a translation of A? Describe the translation.

   c Describe the transformation from D to C.

DISCUSSION

Copy and complete this table to summarise which properties of an object are changed when the object is transformed:

The *orientation* of an object refers to the direction it is facing.

Property	Translation	Reflection	Rotation
position			
size			
orientation			
shape			

D | COMBINATIONS OF TRANSFORMATIONS

In this Section we perform a combination of transformations on an object, one after another.

Example 3   ◄)) **Self Tutor**

Translate figure A 3 units right, then reflect the result in the mirror line.

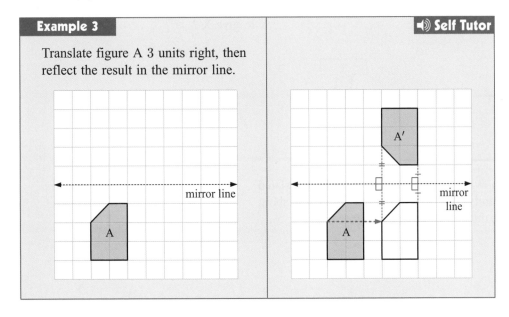

EXERCISE 19D

1 **a** Translate figure A 5 units down, then reflect the result in the mirror line.

b Reflect figure B in the mirror line, then translate the result 4 units left.

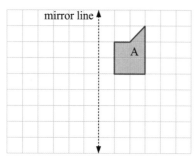

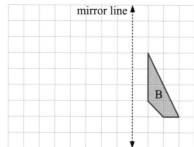

PRINTABLE DIAGRAMS

c Translate figure C 4 units up, then rotate the result 90° clockwise about O.

d Rotate figure D 180° anticlockwise about O, then reflect the result in the mirror line.

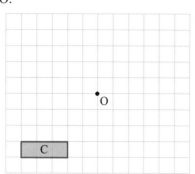

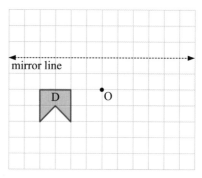

2

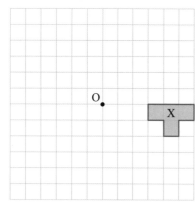

a Rotate figure X 90° anticlockwise about O, then rotate the result 180° clockwise about O to give X′.

b What single transformation could be performed on X to give X′?

3 Show the result when point P is translated 2 units right, then rotated 90° clockwise about O, then reflected in the mirror line.

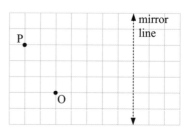

4

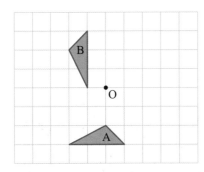

Describe how to transform A to B using a rotation about O followed by a translation.

5 Describe how to transform X to Y, using one or more reflections in the given lines, and a rotation about O.

a

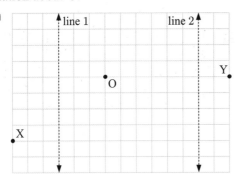

b

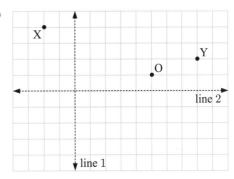

c

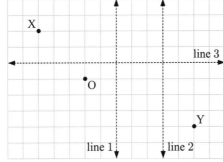

d

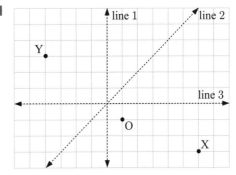

ACTIVITY 2   TESSELLATIONS

A **tessellation** is a pattern made using figures of the same shape and size which cover an area without leaving any gaps. They may be rotated or reflected to achieve this.

Martius Escher (1898 - 1972) created many clever and fascinating tessellations. One of his better known tessellations is shown above.

Here are some other examples of tessellations:

What to do:

1 Draw a tessellation using:

   a   **b**   **c**

   d   **e**

2 Form at least two different tessellation patterns using:

   a the 2×1 rectangle 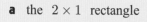   **b** the 3×1 rectangle .

3 Research how Escher designed his tesselation patterns.

MULTIPLE CHOICE QUIZ

REVIEW SET 19A

1 Describe each translation using a horizontal step and a vertical step:

a
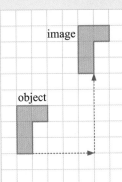

b
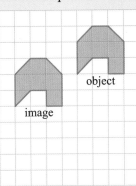

c
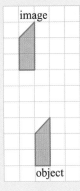

2 Is Q a reflection of P? If not, copy P and the mirror line, then draw the correct reflection.

a
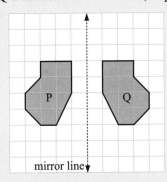

b
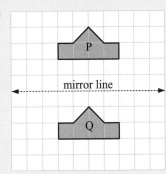

3 Copy each figure and complete the translation given:

  a 2 units right, 4 units down

  b 3 units left, 1 unit up

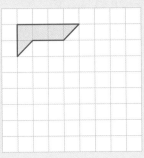

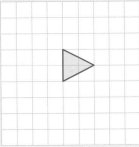

4 On the grid alongside, O is the centre of all rotations. Describe the rotation from:

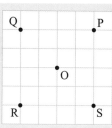

    a P to Q   **b** R to P   **c** S to R.

5 Rotate each point about O as directed:

  a

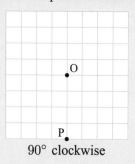

      90° clockwise

  b

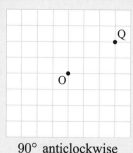

      90° anticlockwise

  c

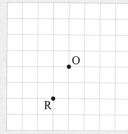

      180° clockwise

6 Translate figure A 3 units down, then reflect the result in the mirror line.

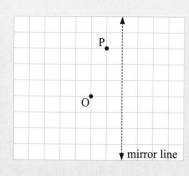

7 **a** Rotate P 180° anticlockwise about O, then reflect the result in the mirror line.

    b Repeat **a**, but perform the transformations in the opposite order.

    c Are the results from **a** and **b** the same? Comment on your answer.

8

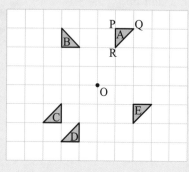

Triangle A has vertices P, Q, and R.

  a Which of the other triangles is a rotation of A about O?

    Copy the grid, and mark on the image vertices P′, Q′, and R′ on the image triangle.

  b Which triangle is a translation of A? Describe the translation.

  c Describe the transformation from B to C.

REVIEW SET 19B

1 Describe the translation from:

   a P to Q

   b Q to R.

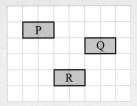

2 **a** Translate figure A 3 units left and 3 units down to give figure B.

   b Translate figure A 4 units right and 1 unit down to give figure C.

   c What translation is needed to move figure B to figure C?

PRINTABLE DIAGRAMS

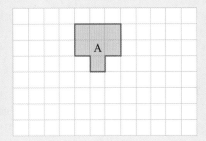

3 Reflect each figure in the given mirror line:

  a

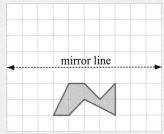

  b

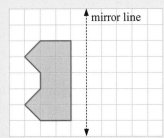

4 The figure W is rotated about the point O. Describe the rotation from W to:

   a X   **b** Y   **c** Z.

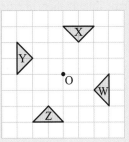

5 On a single diagram, show the images when figure A is reflected in each mirror line:

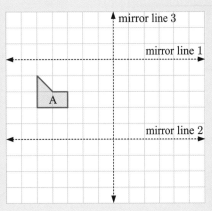

6 Rotate each shape about O as directed:

a

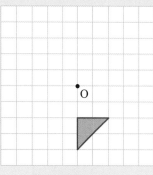

90° anticlockwise

b

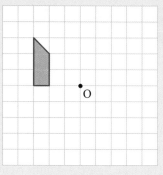

180° clockwise

7 Show the result when point P is rotated 90° clockwise about O, then translated 3 units down, then reflected in the mirror line.

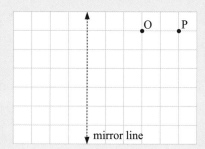

8 **a** Show the result when P is reflected in:
  i mirror line 1, then mirror line 3
  ii mirror line 3, then mirror line 1.

 b Show the result when Q is reflected in:
  i mirror line 1, then mirror line 2
  ii mirror line 2, then mirror line 1.

 c Show the result when R is reflected in:
  i mirror line 2, then mirror line 3
  ii mirror line 3, then mirror line 2.

Comment on your results.

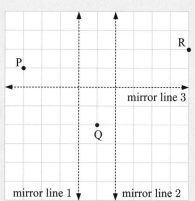

ANSWERS

EXERCISE 1A

1 a 4 tens or 40   b 4 units or 4
   c 4 hundreds or 400   d 4 hundreds or 400
   e 4 tens or 40   f 4 thousands or 4000
   g 4 units or 4   h 4 thousands or 4000

2 a 8 units or 8   b 8 hundreds or 800
   c 8 tens or 80   d 8 thousands or 8000
   e 8 hundreds or 800   f 8 ten thousands or 80 000
   g 8 thousands or 8000   h 8 hundred thousands or 800 000

3 a 2000   b 10   c 300 000   d 4   e 80 000   f 0

4 a 86   b 674   c 9638   d 50 240
   e 27 003 f 500 375 g 73 298   h 809 302

5 a 900 + 70 + 5   b 600 + 80
   c 3000 + 800 + 70 + 4   d 9000 + 80 + 3
   e 50 000 + 6000 + 700 + 40 + 2
   f 70 000 + 5000 + 7   g 600 000 + 800 + 20 + 9
   h 300 000 + 50 000 + 4000 + 700 + 10 + 8

6 a forty nine   b three hundred and fifty two
   c seven thousand, one hundred, and eighty six
   d three thousand and twenty nine
   e four hundred and one
   f six thousand, eight hundred, and fifty
   g eighteen thousand, seven hundred, and fourteen
   h two hundred and sixty three thousand, and eighty three

7 a 27   b 80   c 608   d 1016
   e 8200 f 19 538 g 75 403 h 602 818

EXERCISE 1B

1 a □ = 8   b □ = 13   c □ = 40   d □ = 100
   e □ = 40, △ = 60   f □ = 50, △ = 125
   g □ = 300, △ = 400   h □ = 2000, △ = 2500

2 a 5 < 9   b 8 > 2   c 7 < 13   d 4 < 16
   e 14 > 11 f 19 > 15

3 a

   2, 4, 7, 8, 9
   b

   13, 14, 16, 18, 19
   c

   23, 28, 30, 31, 34
   d
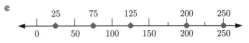
   30, 40, 60, 70, 90

   e
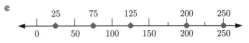
   25, 75, 125, 200, 250
   f

   500, 1500, 2500, 3000, 4000

4 a

   15, 13, 11, 8, 6
   b

   32, 28, 24, 21, 19
   c

   425, 375, 350, 300, 275

EXERCISE 1C

1 a

millions			thousands			units		
H	T	U	H	T	U	H	T	U
	2	7	4	0	6	5	9	3

   b

billions			millions			thousands			units		
H	T	U	H	T	U	H	T	U	H	T	U
		1	8	2	7	5	6	2	3	1	1	5

   c

trillions			billions			millions			thousands			units		
H	T	U	H	T	U	H	T	U	H	T	U	H	T	U
	3	2	4	0	3	9	7	6	8	1	3	2	1	4

2 a 700 000   b 7 000 000   c 700 000 000
   d 70 000 000   e 7 000 000 000   f 70 000 000

3 a twenty three million, six hundred thousand
   b seven billion, six hundred and fourteen million
   c eighteen trillion, nine hundred and forty eight billion

4 a five million, seven hundred and eighty four thousand
   b forty three million, two hundred thousand
   c one hundred and ninety eight million, thirty thousand
   d two billion, fifteen million
   e three hundred and two billion
   f seven trillion, three hundred and eighty two billion

5 a 37 000 000   b 200 000 000   c 150 000 000
   d 1 427 000 000   e 3 940 000 000   f 1 099 511 627 776

EXERCISE 1D

1 a 40   b 70   c midway   d 130   e 460
   f midway g 820   h midway   i 6740

2 a 20 and 30   b 40 and 50   c 60 and 70
   d 90 and 100   e 190 and 200   f 460 and 470
   g 780 and 790   h 1730 and 1740   i 2800 and 2810
   j 3940 and 3950

3 a 20   b 50   c 40   d 70   e 100
   f 210   g 310   h 500   i 890   j 660
   k 440   l 710   m 700   n 4080 o 3120
   p 4780 q 6560 r 7100 s 8180 t 5000

4 a 500   b 700   c midway   d 7600
e 3000   f 11 400

5 a 400 and 500   b 600 and 700   c 1800 and 1900
d 2000 and 2100   e 4900 and 5000

6 a 200   b 200   c 600   d 800   e 1100
f 2700   g 7000   h 4000   i 9000   j 13 200
k 27 700   l 18 600   m 38 500   n 55 400   o 85 100

7 a 6000 and 7000   b 14 000 and 15 000
c 86 000 and 87 000

8 a 1000   b 2000   c 1000   d 5000
e 8000   f 7000   g 10 000   h 9000
i 13 000   j 8000   k 246 000   l 500 000

9 a 20 000   b 50 000   c 50 000   d 80 000
e 90 000   f 50 000   g 90 000   h 100 000
i 100 000

10 a 200 000   b 300 000   c 700 000   d 700 000
e 100 000   f 500 000   g 300 000   h 1 000 000

11 a 38 490   b 38 500   c 38 000   d 40 000

12 a 40 musicians   b 60 singers   c $580   d €4100
e 700 kg   f $25 000   g 35 600 km   h $1400
i 40 000 km   j £460 000   k 11 900 000 people

REVIEW SET 1A

1 a $700 + 40 + 2$ b $5000 + 60 + 3$
c $20\,000 + 9000 + 100 + 80 + 8$
2 17 304
3 a $\square = 40$, $\triangle = 60$ b $\square = 100$, $\triangle = 115$
4 a

2, 5, 7, 9
b

10, 20, 30, 40, 80

5 a twenty four million, three hundred and fifty thousand
b four hundred and ten billion, seven hundred million
c eight trillion, five hundred billion, two hundred million
6 5 890 000
7 a 40   b 4000   c 460 000   d 900 000

REVIEW SET 1B

1 a 400   b 40 000   c 4 000 000
2 a 200   b 10   c 500 000   **3** 2497
4 a four hundred and twenty six
b seven thousand and eighty six
c nine hundred and thirty thousand, five hundred and forty one
5

79, 72, 67, 64

6

millions			thousands			units		
H	T	U	H	T	U	H	T	U
2	4	6	5	0	3	0	4	1

7 a 17 000 spectators   b €80   c 2300 m
d $1 000 000

EXERCISE 2A

1 a 15   b 19   c 22   d 26   e 35   f 37
g 33   h 70
2 a 16   b 29   c 20   d 91   e 138   f 85
g 257   h 144   i 90
3 a
$$\begin{array}{r} 5\ 2 \\ +\ 3\ 5 \\ \hline 8\ 7 \end{array}$$
b
$$\begin{array}{r} 7\ 4 \\ +\ 3_1\ 7 \\ \hline 1\ 1\ 1 \end{array}$$
c
$$\begin{array}{r} 6\ 2\ 8 \\ +\ \ \ 4_1\ 7 \\ \hline 6\ 7\ 5 \end{array}$$

d
$$\begin{array}{r} 4\ 9\ 2 \\ +\ {}_1 6_1\ 9 \\ \hline 5\ 6\ 1 \end{array}$$
e
$$\begin{array}{r} 7\ 5\ 3 \\ +\ 1_1 8\ 4 \\ \hline 9\ 3\ 7 \end{array}$$
f
$$\begin{array}{r} 1\ 9\ 1\ 7 \\ +\ 2\ 0\ 7_1\ 8 \\ \hline 3\ 9\ 9\ 5 \end{array}$$

g
$$\begin{array}{r} 9\ 1\ 3 \\ 2\ 4 \\ +\ 7\ 0_1\ 7 \\ \hline 1\ 6\ 4\ 4 \end{array}$$
h
$$\begin{array}{r} 2\ 1\ 7 \\ 1\ 0\ 6 \\ +\ 1\ 2\ 7_1\ 4 \\ \hline 1\ 5\ 9\ 7 \end{array}$$
i
$$\begin{array}{r} 9\ 0\ 0\ 4 \\ 2\ 1\ 6 \\ 2\ 7 \\ +\ 3_1\ 8\ 1_2\ 6 \\ \hline 1\ 3\ 0\ 6\ 3 \end{array}$$

4 a 79   b 107   c 748   d 701   e 2155
f 6565   g 3047   h 4955   i 4619
5 a
$$\begin{array}{r} 2\ 3\ 9 \\ +\ 4_1\ 7_1\ 8 \\ \hline 7\ 1\ 7 \end{array}$$
b correct   c
$$\begin{array}{r} 3\ 1\ 1 \\ 1\ 9\ 7 \\ +\ 6_1\ 4_1\ 8 \\ \hline 1\ 1\ 5\ 6 \end{array}$$
d correct

6 965 g   **7** $446   **8** 361 ice creams   **9** $432
10 3923 km

EXERCISE 2B

1 a 4   b 4   c 13   d 7
2 a 12   b 7   c 13   d 20   e 14   f 9
g 23   h 65
3 a
$$\begin{array}{r} 9\ 7 \\ -\ 1\ 5 \\ \hline 8\ 2 \end{array}$$
b
$$\begin{array}{r} {}^5\!6\ {}^{13}\!3 \\ -\ 1\ 9 \\ \hline 4\ 4 \end{array}$$
c
$$\begin{array}{r} 4\ {}^4\!5\ {}^{12}\!2 \\ -\ 1\ 3\ 8 \\ \hline 3\ 1\ 4 \end{array}$$

d
$$\begin{array}{r} {}^4\!5\ {}^{11}\!1\ 7 \\ -\ 2\ 7\ 3 \\ \hline 2\ 4\ 4 \end{array}$$
e
$$\begin{array}{r} {}^5\!6\ {}^{12}\!2\ 8 \\ -\ 3\ 3\ 3 \\ \hline 2\ 9\ 5 \end{array}$$
f
$$\begin{array}{r} 3\ {}^{17}\!4\ 7 \\ -\ 1\ 3\ 8 \\ \hline 1\ 0\ 9 \end{array}$$

g
$$\begin{array}{r} {}^5\!6\ {}^9\!{}^{10}\!0\ {}^{12}\!2 \\ -\ 1\ 4\ 9 \\ \hline 4\ 5\ 3 \end{array}$$
h
$$\begin{array}{r} {}^3\!4\ {}^9\!{}^{10}\!0\ {}^{11}\!1\ 5 \\ -\ 1\ 7\ 3\ 2 \\ \hline 2\ 2\ 8\ 3 \end{array}$$
i
$$\begin{array}{r} {}^5\!6\ {}^9\!{}^{10}\!0\ {}^9\!{}^{10}\!0\ {}^{15}\!5 \\ -\ 2\ 3\ 4\ 9 \\ \hline 3\ 6\ 5\ 6 \end{array}$$

4 a 66   b 622   c 82   d 424   e 766   f 2417
5 a 54   b 76   c 624

6 a
$$\begin{array}{r} {}^4\!5\ {}^{16}\!6\ 3 \\ -\ 2\ 8\ 1 \\ \hline 2\ 8\ 2 \end{array}$$
b
$$\begin{array}{r} 5\ {}^8\!9\ {}^9\!{}^{10}\!0\ {}^{10}\!0 \\ -\ 3\ 8\ 1\ 4 \\ \hline 2\ 0\ 8\ 6 \end{array}$$

c correct   d
$$\begin{array}{r} 3\ {}^1\!2\ {}^{10}\!{}_1\!0\ {}^{15}\!5 \\ -\ 3\ 1\ 8\ 6 \\ \hline 2\ 9 \end{array}$$

7 $16 more   **8** $60 000   **9** 82 minutes
10 173 days   **11** a 49 more fish   b 23 fewer fish

EXERCISE 2C

1 **a** 54   **b** 96   **c** 55   **d** 21   **e** 12   **f** 24

2 **a** 500   **b** 5000   **c** 50 000   **d** 6900
e 69 000   **f** 690 000   **g** 12 300   **h** 246 000
i 96 000   **j** 490 000   **k** 49 000   **l** 490 000

3 **a** 6   **b** 60   **c** 600   **d** 6000
e 35   **f** 350   **g** 3500   **h** 35 000
i 33   **j** 330   **k** 3300   **l** 330 000

4 **a** 130   **b** 1900   **c** 2100   **d** 19 000
e 2100   **f** 97 000   **g** 27 000   **h** 12 000

5 4800 pine trees

EXERCISE 2D

1 **a**
$$\begin{array}{r} 7\ 2 \\ \times\quad 3 \\ \hline 2\ 1\ 6 \end{array}$$
b
$$\begin{array}{r} 5\ 9 \\ \times\ _3\ 4 \\ \hline 2\ 3\ 6 \end{array}$$
c
$$\begin{array}{r} 1\ 2\ 5 \\ \times\ _1\ _3\ 7 \\ \hline 8\ 7\ 5 \end{array}$$
d
$$\begin{array}{r} 3\ 1\ 8 \\ \times\ _1\ _7\ 9 \\ \hline 2\ 8\ 6\ 2 \end{array}$$

2 **a** 148   **b** 496   **c** 1218   **d** 3246

3 **a**
$$\begin{array}{r} 2\ 8 \\ \times\ 1\ 2 \\ \hline ^15\ 6 \\ +\ 2_1\ 8\ 0 \\ \hline 3\ 3\ 6 \end{array}$$
b
$$\begin{array}{r} 3\ 1 \\ \times\ 2\ 6 \\ \hline 1\ 8\ 6 \\ +\ 6_1\ 2\ 0 \\ \hline 8\ 0\ 6 \end{array}$$

c
$$\begin{array}{r} 7\ 5 \\ \times\ 4\ 1 \\ \hline 7\ 5 \\ +\ 3\ ^20\ 0\ 0 \\ \hline 3\ 0\ 7\ 5 \end{array}$$
d
$$\begin{array}{r} 1\ 5\ 2 \\ \times\quad 2\ 3 \\ \hline ^14\ 5\ 6 \\ +\ ^13\ 0\ 4\ 0 \\ \hline 3\ 4\ 9\ 6 \end{array}$$

4 **a** 405   **b** 2744   **c** 3655   **d** 14 110
e 14 580   **f** 23 112

5 90 kg   **6** $1360   **7** $8246

8 **a** 300 rooms   **b** £45 000

EXERCISE 2E

1 **a** 4   **b** 4   **c** 11   **d** 12

2 **a** 200   **b** 20   **c** 2   **d** 5700
e 570   **f** 57   **g** 24 300   **h** 2430
i 243   **j** 4500   **k** 450   **l** 45
m 72 000   **n** 7200   **o** 720   **p** 600 000
q 60 000   **r** 6000

3 **a** 3   **b** 30   **c** 300   **d** 3000
e 5   **f** 50   **g** 500   **h** 5000
i 4   **j** 40   **k** 400   **l** 4000

4 **a**
$$\begin{array}{r} 1\ 4 \\ 3\overline{)4\ ^12} \end{array}$$
b
$$\begin{array}{r} 5\ 4 \\ 4\overline{)2\ 1\ ^16} \end{array}$$
c
$$\begin{array}{r} 2\ 1 \\ 8\overline{)1\ 6\ 8} \end{array}$$

d
$$\begin{array}{r} 8\ 4 \\ 6\overline{)5\ 0\ ^24} \end{array}$$
e
$$\begin{array}{r} 7\ 5 \\ 5\overline{)3\ 7\ ^25} \end{array}$$
f
$$\begin{array}{r} 2\ 9\ 1 \\ 4\overline{)1\ 1\ ^36\ 4} \end{array}$$

g
$$\begin{array}{r} 1\ 3\ 6\quad 1\ r\ 4 \\ 5\overline{)6\ ^18\ ^30\ 9} \end{array}$$
h
$$\begin{array}{r} 9\ 0\ 2\ r\ 3 \\ 7\overline{)6\ 3\ 1\ 7} \end{array}$$

5 **a** 12   **b** 25   **c** 52   **d** 48
e 29   **f** 208   **g** 41   **h** 817

6 **a** 28 with remainder 2   **b** 38 with remainder 3
c 162 with remainder 2   **d** 438 with remainder 6

7 $80   **8** 82 minutes   **9** 81 minutes

10 **a** 6000 m   **b** 7000 m   **c** 14 000 m

EXERCISE 2F

1 **a** $253   **b** $47   **2** **a** $6   **b** $54

3 54 goats   **4** $168

5 **a** $1240   **b** $1860   **6** **a** $1990   **b** failed by $10

7 426 km   **8** 600 grams   **9** 36 minutes

EXERCISE 2G

1 **a** 2^3 **b** 7^2 **c** 9^4 **d** 13^2 **e** 3^5 **f** 4^7

2 **a** 5×7^2 **b** $2^3 \times 3$ **c** $3^2 \times 5^2$
d $2^3 \times 3^2$ **e** $4^2 \times 7^4$ **f** $2^2 \times 5 \times 7$
g $2 \times 3^2 \times 5$ **h** $3 \times 5^2 \times 7^2$ **i** $3^3 \times 5 \times 7^2$

3

Numeral	Words	Exponent notation
100	one hundred	10^2
1000	one thousand	10^3
10 000	ten thousand	10^4
100 000	one hundred thousand	10^5
1 000 000	one million	10^6
10 000 000	ten million	10^7
1 000 000 000	one billion	10^9
1 000 000 000 000	one trillion	10^{12}

4 **a** 9   **b** 8   **c** 16   **d** 27   **e** 64   **f** 16
g 125   **h** 81   **i** 288   **j** 108   **k** 675   **l** 64 000

5 **a** 3^2 **b** are equal   **c** 2^5

EXERCISE 2H

1 **a** 8   **b** 10   **c** 2   **d** 4   **e** 8   **f** 5
g 18   **h** 31   **i** 3   **j** 22   **k** 16   **l** 3

2 **a** 29   **b** 6   **c** 3   **d** 25   **e** 14   **f** 18
g 3   **h** 5   **i** 95   **j** 66   **k** 4   **l** 40

3 **a** Derrick performed the addition first, but working should be done from left to right as the expression contains only + and − operations.
b 11

4 **a** 3   **b** 15   **c** 36   **d** 4   **e** 16   **f** 0
g 31   **h** 64   **i** 12

5 **a** 37   **b** 51   **c** 7   **d** 8   **e** 14   **f** 68
g 21   **h** 42   **i** 1

6 **a** 2   **b** 6   **c** 35   **d** 2   **e** 6   **f** 5
g 31   **h** 16   **i** 14   **j** 11   **k** 8   **l** 3

7 **a** 1   **b** 7   **c** 16   **d** 11   **e** 27   **f** 49
g 18   **h** 36   **i** 1   **j** 125   **k** 86   **l** 45

8 **a** $4 + 18 \div 3 = 10$ **b** $6 \times 7 - 12 = 30$
c $(17 + 3) \div 5 = 4$ **d** $(18 - 2) \div 8 = 2$
e $3^3 - 2^2 = 23$ **f** $4 + (21 \div 7) = 7$

REVIEW SET 2A

1 **a** 46   **b** 23

2 **a**
$$\begin{array}{r} 2\ 1\ 7 \\ +\ 5\ 4\ 1 \\ \hline 7\ 5\ 8 \end{array}$$
b
$$\begin{array}{r} ^5\not{6}\ ^{12}\not{2}\ 9 \\ -\ 1\ 6\ 6 \\ \hline 4\ 6\ 3 \end{array}$$
c
$$\begin{array}{r} 1\ 7\ 8 \\ 2\ 3\ 0\ 7 \\ +\ _1\ 7_1\ 6_2\ 5 \\ \hline 3\ 2\ 5\ 0 \end{array}$$

3 **a** 67   **b** 270   **c** 79   **d** 4600

4 84 points

5 **a**
```
      5 6
  ×   3 6
  ─────────
    3 3 6
```
b
```
        3 4
  4 ) 1 3 ¹6
```
c
```
          4 7
    ×     1 3
  ──────────
    1 ²4 1
  + 4₁7 0
  ──────────
    6 1 1
```

d
```
        5 6
  7 ) 3 9 ⁴2
```

6 **a** 504   **b** 43   **c** 2946   **7** €2688

8 $728   **9 a** 6^4 **b** $2^3 \times 7^5$ **10** 700

11 **a** 13   **b** 13   **c** 12   **d** 24   **e** 8   **f** 9

12 $2 \times 8 \div 4 + 2 = 6$

REVIEW SET 2B

1 **a**
```
      8 5
  −   3 2
  ─────────
      5 3
```
b
```
      3 5 7 6
  +   4 3₁8₁5
  ──────────
      7 9 6 1
```
c
```
    ¹2 ²2³ ¹⁰0̸ 6
  −      5 1 2
  ──────────
      1 7 9 4
```

2 **a** 208   **b** 1700   **c** 448   **d** 2843

3 $71   **4 a** 3400   **b** 59   **c** 28 000

5 **a**
```
        1 2 7
  ×     1 2 4
  ──────────
        5 0 8
```
b
```
        7 7
  5 ) 3 8 ³5
```
c
```
          4 3
    ×     2 8
  ──────────
        3 ²4 4
  + ₁8 6 0
  ──────────
    1 2 0 4
```

d
```
        6 1 r 4
  9 ) 5 5 ¹3
```

6 **a** 51   **b** 897   **c** 518 with remainder 6   **7** $100 000

8 15 sections   **9 a** $17   **b i** $81   **ii** $19

10 **a** $2^2 + 7^3$ **b** $11^3 − 3^4$ **11 a** 16   **b** 3   **c** 32

12 **a** addition, subtraction, multiplication, division

　　b **i** $3000 \div 20 = 150$ seats per section

　　　　ii $5 \times 3000 = 15\,000$ people

　　　　iii $15\,000 \times $30 = $450\,000$

13 **a** 12

　　b **i** $30 − 12 \div (2 \times 3) = 28$

　　　　ii $(30 − 12) \div 2 \times 3 = 27$

　　　　iii $(30 − 12 \div 2) \times 3 = 72$

EXERCISE 3A

1 **a** The line (AB) passes through A and B and continues endlessly in both directions.

b The line segment [AB] joins the two points A and B. It is only a part of the line (AB).

c The ray [AB) starts at A, passes through point B, and continues on endlessly.

d A vertex is a corner point where two line segments meet.

e A point of intersection is a point where two intersecting lines meet.

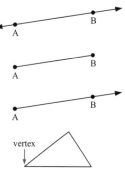

f Parallel lines are lines which are always a fixed distance apart and never meet.

2 **a** (LM) or (ML)   **b** (CD), (DC), (CE), (EC), (DE), or (ED)

3 **a** [PQ]   **b** (NM)   **c** [CD]   **d** (RS)   **e** [GF)   **f** [XY]

4 **a** B   **b** C   **5** **a** C   **b** B and C   **c** (BE) and (CD)

6 **a** B   **b** [BC]   **c** [AB]

EXERCISE 3B

1 **a**    **b**

c   **d**

e    **f**

g    **h**

2 **a** $A\widehat{B}C$ (or $C\widehat{B}A$), acute   **b** $P\widehat{Q}R$ (or $R\widehat{Q}P$), obtuse

c $K\widehat{L}M$ (or $M\widehat{L}K$), acute   **d** $C\widehat{B}D$ (or $D\widehat{B}C$), acute

e $X\widehat{Z}W$ (or $W\widehat{Z}X$), obtuse   **f** $L\widehat{J}N$ (or $N\widehat{J}L$), acute

g $X\widehat{O}Y$ (or $Y\widehat{O}X$), right

h reflex $A\widehat{D}C$ (or reflex $C\widehat{D}A$), reflex

i reflex $P\widehat{O}R$ (or reflex $R\widehat{O}P$), reflex

3 **a** acute   **b** reflex   **c** right   **d** obtuse

e acute   **f** straight   **g** reflex   **h** obtuse

4 **a** 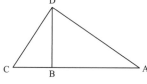   **b** $A\widehat{B}D$ and $C\widehat{B}D$

EXERCISE 3C

1 **a** 75°   **b** 60°   **c** 128°   **d** 103°   **e** 27°

f 23°   **g** 135°   **h** 155°   **i** 87°   **j** 96°

2 33°

3 **a** $A\widehat{B}C = 67°$,　$A\widehat{C}B = 30°$,　$B\widehat{A}C = 83°$

b $D\widehat{E}F = 33°$,　$E\widehat{F}D = 42°$,　$F\widehat{D}E = 105°$

4 **a**   **b**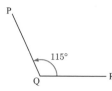

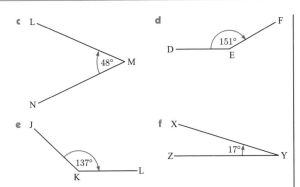

c L

48° M

N

d

D — 151° E — F

e J

137° K — L

f X

Z — 17° — Y

5 **a** **i** $\widehat{ABC} = 40°$, $\widehat{XYZ} = 38°$ **ii** $\widehat{ABC}$
   b **i** $\widehat{ABC} = 105°$, $\widehat{XYZ} = 107°$ **ii** $\widehat{XYZ}$

EXERCISE 3D

1 **a** **i** $51°$ **ii** acute   **b** **i** $100°$ **ii** obtuse
   c **i** $90°$ **ii** right   **d** **i** $20°$ **ii** acute
   e **i** $180°$ **ii** straight   **f** **i** $114°$ **ii** obtuse

2 **a** $x = 25$ **b** $x = 56$ **c** $y = 45$ **d** $m = 50$
   e $n = 107$ **f** $p = 50$ **g** $x = 60$ **h** $x = 90$
   i $x = 32$

3 **a** $a = 270$ **b** $b = 120$ **c** $c = 318$ **d** $d = 89$
   e $e = 120$ **f** $f = 81$ **g** $x = 90$ **h** $x = 148$
   i $g = 112$

4 $x = 138$, $y = 42$, $z = 138$

EXERCISE 3E

1 **a** $\widehat{DBE}$ **b** $\widehat{FBD}$ **c** $\widehat{GBE}$

2 **a** $a = 114$ **b** $b = 97$ **c** $c = 27$ **d** $d = 90$
   e $e = 100$ **f** $f = 124$ **g** $g = 41$ **h** $h = 60$
   i $i = 68$

REVIEW SET 3A

1 **a** [AB]   **b** [QP)   **c** (XY)   **2**

3 **a** $\widehat{ABC}$ (or $\widehat{CBA}$), acute   **b** $\widehat{JML}$ (or $\widehat{LMJ}$), obtuse

4 **a** obtuse   **b** right   **c** reflex   **d** acute

5 $18°$ **6** **a** $32°$, acute   **b** $91°$, obtuse

7 **a** $x = 26$ **b** $x = 111$ **c** $a = 145$

8 **a** $\widehat{DOE}$ **b** $\widehat{AOE} = 143°$

9 **a** **i** $a = 37$ **ii** $b = 122$ **b** $238°$ **c** reflex

10 **a** $\widehat{WXY} = 115°$, $\widehat{XYZ} = 60°$, $\widehat{YZW} = 75°$, $\widehat{ZWX} = 110°$
   b $\widehat{WXY}$
   c $\widehat{ZWX}$ and $\widehat{WXY}$ are obtuse, $\widehat{XYZ}$ and $\widehat{YZW}$ are acute.
   d $360°$

REVIEW SET 3B

1 **a** (AE), (EA), (EC), (CE), (AC), (CA)
   b (AB) and (DC)   **c** A and C

2 A   **3** $\widehat{XOY}$ (or $\widehat{YOX}$), acute

4 $\widehat{ABC} = 129°$, $\widehat{DEF} = 138°$. $\widehat{DEF}$ is larger.

5 **a** $\widehat{ABC} = 115°$ **b** $\widehat{ABC} = 42°$ **c** $\widehat{ABC} = 112°$
   d $\widehat{ABC} = 134°$

6 **a** $\widehat{JKL} = 82°$, $\widehat{KLJ} = 55°$, $\widehat{LJK} = 43°$ **b** $180°$

7 **a** $a = 90$ **b** $a = 100$ **c** $a = 36$

8 **a** $x = 48$ **b** $y = 70$ **c** $z = 55$

9 **a** **i** $\widehat{UOT}$ **ii** $\widehat{ROS}$
   b **i** $\widehat{SOT} = 82°$ **ii** $\widehat{POV} = 123°$

EXERCISE 4A

1 **a** 7   **b** 7   **c** 0   **d** undefined   **e** 0
   f 7   **g** 0   **h** 7   **i** 7   **j** 7

2 **a** 0   **b** 11   **c** 11   **d** 11   **e** 11   **f** 0
   g 11   **h** 11   **i** undefined   **j** 0

3 **a** 0   **b** 0   **c** 0   **d** 0   **e** 1   **f** 0
   g 1   **h** undefined

4 **a** 235   **b** 0   **c** 0   **d** 26   **e** undefined
   f 0   **g** 125   **h** 684

5 **a** 7   **b** 15   **c** 120   **d** 16   **e** 16   **f** 0
   g 18   **h** 20   **i** undefined   **j** 9   **k** 9
   l 1

EXERCISE 4B

1 **a** $5 \times 5 = \mathbf{25}$ **b** $6 \times 6 = \mathbf{36}$
    $5^2 = \mathbf{25}$ $6^2 = \mathbf{36}$

2 $1^2 = 1$, $2^2 = 4$, $3^2 = 9$, $4^2 = 16$, $5^2 = 25$, $6^2 = 36$,
   $7^2 = 49$, $8^2 = 64$, $9^2 = 81$, $10^2 = 100$

3 **a** $12^2 = 144$ **b** $15^2 = 225$ **c** $22^2 = 484$

4 **Note:** Other answers are possible.
   9 and 16, as $3^2 + 4^2 = 9 + 16 = 25 = 5^2$

5 **a** 0   **b** 0 and 1   **6** 324   **7** 196

8 Suppose • and ■ represent whole numbers.
   $\bullet^2 \times \blacksquare^2 = \bullet \times \bullet \times \blacksquare \times \blacksquare$
         $= \bullet \times \blacksquare \times \bullet \times \blacksquare$
         $= (\bullet \times \blacksquare)^2$

EXERCISE 4C

1 **a**    **b** 64

2 $1^3 = 1$, $2^3 = 8$, $3^3 = 27$, $4^3 = 64$, $5^3 = 125$,
   $6^3 = 216$, $7^3 = 343$, $8^3 = 512$, $9^3 = 729$, $10^3 = 1000$

3 180   **4** 1 and 8, as $1^3 + 2^3 = 1 + 8 = 9 = 3^2$

5 25 and 100, as $5^2 + 10^2 = 25 + 100 = 125 = 5^3$

6 **a** 0   **b** 0 and 1

EXERCISE 4D

1 **a** no   **b** yes   **c** no   **d** yes   **e** no   **f** no
   g yes   **h** no   **i** yes

2 **a** even   **b** odd   **c** odd   **d** even   **e** even   **f** odd
   g odd   **h** even

3 56   **4** Zero is even, as $0 \div 2 = 0$ with no remainder.

5 24   **6** **a** 8, 10, 12   **b** 17, 19, 21, 23, 25

7 **a** 0 and 10, 2 and 8
   b 1 and 19, 3 and 17, 5 and 15, 7 and 13

c 0, 2, 18;   0, 4, 16;   0, 6, 14;   0, 8, 12;   2, 4, 14;
2, 6, 12;   2, 8, 10;   and   4, 6, 10

8 a even   b even   c odd   d odd   e even
   f odd   g even

EXERCISE 4E

1 a yes   b yes   c no   d yes   e yes
2 a no   b yes   c no   d yes   e no
3 a yes   b yes   c no   d yes   e yes
4 a yes   b no   c yes   d no   e yes
5 a no   b yes   c no   d yes   e no
6 a yes   b no   c yes   d no   e yes
7 a □ = 0, 2, 4, 6, or 8   b □ = 2, 5, or 8
   c □ = 2 or 6   d □ = 0 or 5
8 a □ = 1, 4, or 7   b □ = 2, 5, or 8
   c □ = 1, 4, or 7   d □ = 2, 5, or 8

EXERCISE 4F

1 a yes   b no   c no   d yes
2 a 1, 5   b 1, 2, 3, 6   c 1, 7   d 1, 2, 4, 8
   e 1, 3, 9   f 1, 2, 5, 10   g 1, 11   h 1, 2, 3, 4, 6, 12
3 a yes   b no   c yes   d no   e yes
   f no   g no   h yes
4 a $22 = 2 \times 11$ b $45 = 9 \times 5$ c $30 = 3 \times 10$
   d $49 = 7 \times 7$ e $72 = 12 \times 6$ f $85 = 5 \times 17$
5 a 1, 2, 7, 14   b 1, 3, 5, 15   c 1, 2, 3, 6, 9, 18
   d 1, 23   e 1, 2, 3, 4, 6, 8, 12, 24
   f 1, 2, 3, 4, 6, 9, 12, 18, 36   g 1, 43
   h 1, 3, 5, 9, 15, 45
   i 1, 2, 3, 4, 5, 6, 10, 12, 15, 20, 30, 60
   j 1, 2, 4, 8, 16, 32, 64
   k 1, 2, 3, 4, 6, 8, 9, 12, 18, 24, 36, 72
   l 1, 2, 4, 5, 10, 20, 25, 50, 100
6 a 2 factors   b 6 factors   c 8 factors   d 8 factors
7 Every natural number greater than 1 has at least a factor of 1 and
   a factor of itself.
8 Every square number has exactly one factor pair which is made
   up of identical numbers, so this pair contributes 1 to the number
   of factors. All other factor pairs contribute 2 to the number of
   factors. So, the total number of factors must be odd.

EXERCISE 4G

1

1	neither	11	prime
2	prime	12	composite
3	prime	13	prime
4	composite	14	composite
5	prime	15	composite
6	composite	16	composite
7	prime	17	prime
8	composite	18	composite
9	composite	19	prime
10	composite	20	composite

21	composite	31	prime
22	composite	32	composite
23	prime	33	composite
24	composite	34	composite
25	composite	35	composite
26	composite	36	composite
27	composite	37	prime
28	composite	38	composite
29	prime	39	composite
30	composite	40	composite

2 one (It is 2.)   3 41, 43, 47, 53, 59, 61, 67
4 It is divisible by 5, so it is a composite number.
5 25 and 27
6 a 4 and 9 are composite numbers and their sum is $4 + 9 = 13$
      which is a prime. Other answers are possible.
   b No. Each composite number has at least 3 different factors
      and so the product of two of them has at least 3 different
      factors. So, the product cannot be a prime.
7 a 1, 2, 4, 5, 10, 20   b 2 and 5   c $20 = 2 \times 2 \times 5$
8 a 1, 3, 9, 27   b 3   c $27 = 3 \times 3 \times 3$
9 a $8 = 2 \times 2 \times 2$ b $12 = 2 \times 2 \times 3$
   c $14 = 2 \times 7$ d $15 = 3 \times 5$ e $18 = 2 \times 3 \times 3$
   f $28 = 2 \times 2 \times 7$ g $30 = 2 \times 3 \times 5$
   h $32 = 2 \times 2 \times 2 \times 2 \times 2$

EXERCISE 4H

1 a 3   b 2   c 2   d 2   e 3   f 3
   g 2   h 5   i 4   j 7   k 4   l 14
2 a 6 teams   b 7 Year 6 students, 9 Year 7 students

EXERCISE 4I

1 a 4, 8, 12, 16, 20, 24, 28, 32, 36, 40
   b 9, 18, 27, 36, 45, 54, 63, 72, 81, 90
   c 11, 22, 33, 44, 55, 66, 77, 88, 99, 110
2 12, 15, 18   3 48, 60
4 a 7, 14, 21, 28, 35, 42, 49, 56, 63, 70, 77, 84
   b i no   ii yes, $21 = 7 \times 3$ iii no   iv no
      v yes, $63 = 7 \times 9$
5 a 8, 16, 24, 32, 40, 48, 56, 64, 72, 80, 88, 96
   b 10, 20, 30, 40, 50, 60, 70, 80, 90, 100
   c 40, 80   d 40
6 a 24, 48, 72, 96   b 24   7 198   8 312

REVIEW SET 4A

1 a 13   b 0   c 0   d undefined
2 a 65   b 16, 49   3 3 cubic numbers
4 1, 3, 21;   1, 5, 19;   1, 7, 17;   1, 9, 15;   1, 11, 13;   3, 5, 17;
   3, 7, 15;   3, 9, 13;   5, 7, 13;   and   5, 9, 11
5 a no   b yes
6 a □ = 2, 5, or 8   b □ = 0, 2, 4, 6, or 8
7 a 28   b composite   c 1, 2, 4, 7, 14, 28
8 a 1, 2, 4, 8, 16   b 1, 5, 7, 35   c 1, 3, 5, 15, 25, 75
9 a composite   b composite   c prime   d composite
10 a 4   b 6   11 54, 60, 66

REVIEW SET 4B

1 a 243   b 243   c undefined   d 0

2 36   **3** 225

4 a no   b yes   c no

5 a $42 = 7 \times \mathbf{6}$ b $72 = 9 \times \mathbf{8}$ c $110 = 10 \times \mathbf{11}$

6 a 1, 3, 7, 9, 21, 63   b 1, 5, 13, 65

   c 1, 2, 4, 5, 8, 10, 16, 20, 40, 80

7 18 natural numbers   **8** a 108   b 98

9 a 1, 2, 3, 5, 6, 10, 15, 30   b 2, 3, and 5

   c $30 = 2 \times 3 \times 5$

10 8 children

11 a i 16   ii 44   iii 60   iv 76

   b When two consecutive odd numbers are added together, the result is always divisible by **4**.

12 a 6, 12, 18, 24, 30, 36, 42, 48, 54, 60, 66, 72, 78

   b 8, 16, 24, 32, 40, 48, 56, 64, 72, 80

   c 24, 48, 72   d 24

EXERCISE 5A

1 a triangle   b quadrilateral   c hexagon   d pentagon

   e heptagon   f octagon   g nonagon   h decagon

2 a not closed   b sides are not all straight

   c it crosses itself   d sides are not straight

3 a Irregular, as angles are not all equal.

   b Regular, as sides are equal *and* angles are equal.

   c Irregular, as angles are not all equal.

   d Irregular, as sides are not all equal.

   e Irregular, as sides are not all equal.

   f Regular, as sides are equal *and* angles are equal.

4 **Note:** Other answers are possible.

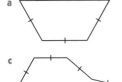

5 a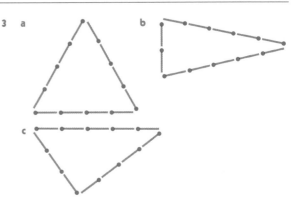

   b 90°

   c The opposite sides are parallel.

6 a Regular; all sides are equal, and all angles are equal.

   b Irregular; all sides are 4 cm long, but not all angles are equal in size.

   c Regular; all sides are equal, and all angles are equal.

   d Irregular; sides are not equal in length.

EXERCISE 5B

1 a scalene   b equilateral   c isosceles   d equilateral

   e scalene   f isosceles

2 a isosceles; with two sides 4 cm, other side 3 cm

   b scalene (3 cm, 4 cm, 6 cm)

   c equilateral; with all sides 5 cm

   d isosceles; with two sides 2 cm, other side 3 cm

3 a
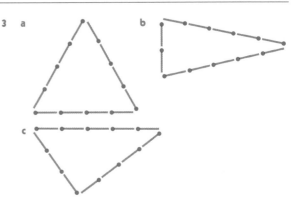

EXERCISE 5C

1
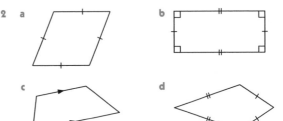

2 a
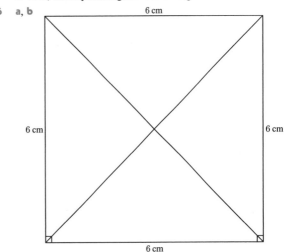
   b

   c   d

3 a rhombus   b rectangle   c kite   d trapezium

   e parallelogram   f square

4 a true   b false   c false   d true

5 a True; it is a rhombus with all angles 90°.   b false

   c True; it is a parallelogram with all sides equal in length and all angles 90°.

   d True; it is a parallelogram with all angles 90°.

6 a, b

6 cm

6 cm   6 cm

6 cm

   c They are equal in length; about 8.5 cm.

EXERCISE 5D

1 A circle does not have straight line sides.

2 **a** distance is 2 cm   **b** distance is less than 2 cm
    c distance is more than 2 cm

3

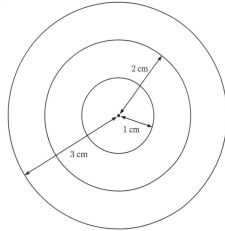

EXERCISE 5E

1 **a** cylinder   **b** cube   **c** cone   **d** sphere
   e rectangular prism   **f** square-based pyramid
   g triangular prism   **h** triangular-based pyramid

2 **a**

   b

3 **a A**   **b B**   **c A**   **d C**

4

Solid	Number of faces	Shapes of faces	Sketch
rectangular prism	6	rectangles	
pentagonal prism	7	pentagons and rectangles	
square-based pyramid	5	square and triangles	
triangular-based pyramid	4	triangles	

5 The cross-section of a cylinder is not a polygon.

EXERCISE 5F

1 **a**
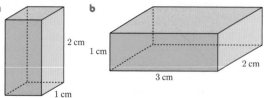

2 cm

1 cm   1 cm

b

1 cm   2 cm   3 cm

c

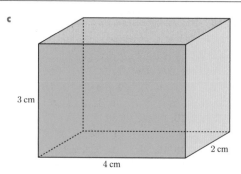

3 cm

4 cm

2 cm

2 **a**

triangular prism

b

triangular-based pyramid

c

pentagonal prism

3 **a**

b

c

4 **a**

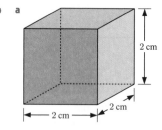

2 cm

2 cm

2 cm

b

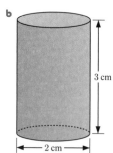

3 cm

2 cm

c

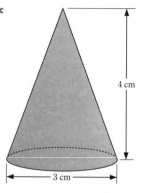

4 cm

3 cm

5

EXERCISE 5G

1 **a** **B** and **3**   **b** **A** and **4**   **c** **D** and **1**   **d** **C** and **2**

2 **a** yes   **b** no   **c** yes   **d** yes   **e** no   **f** no

3 **a**

cone

b

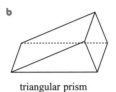

triangular prism

c

hexagonal-based pyramid

4 **a**

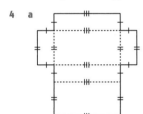

b

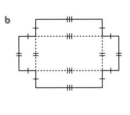

c

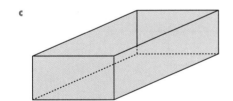

5

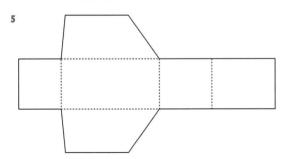

6

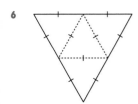

7 **a**

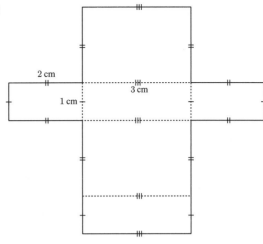

b

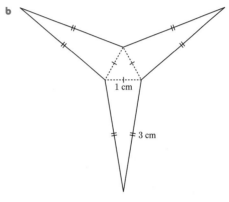

8 **a** The sides of the triangles are not long enough to meet at the apex.

b Erin's, as the sides which meet at the apex are longer than Derek's and the square base is smaller.

REVIEW SET 5A

1 **a** hexagon   **b** quadrilateral   **c** dodecagon

2 **a**   **b**   **c**

3 **a** scalene
b isosceles
c equilateral

4

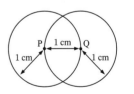

5 **a** square   **b** kite   **c** trapezium

6 **a** false   **b** true   **c** true

7 **a** Yes, an equilateral triangle has all three sides equal in length. So, it satisfies the requirements of an isosceles triangle of having two equal sides.

b Yes, a square has all four sides equal in length. So, it satisfies the requirements of a kite of having two pairs of adjacent sides which are equal in length.

8 **a** sphere   **b** cone   **c** pentagonal-based pyramid

9

3 cm

5 cm

10 a

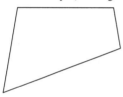

square prism   triangular prism

c

triangular-based pyramid

REVIEW SET 5B

1   a   Irregular; angles are not all equal.
    b   Irregular; sides are not all equal, and angles are not all equal.

2   scalene   3

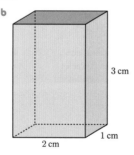

4   Yes, a rhombus is a parallelogram with all four sides equal in length.

5   a   parallelogram
    b   The obtuse angles measure 130°.
        The acute angles measure 50°.
    c   The opposite angles of a *parallelogram* are *equal in size*.

6   a Q   b T   c S   d R   e P

7   a   sphere   b   rectangular prism

8   a   b

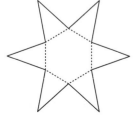

3 cm
2 cm   1 cm

9

10 a Three-dimensional means that an object has 3 dimensions: height, width, and depth.
The drawing on the page is not three-dimensional (it is two-dimensional).
    b   using small markings

    c   equilateral triangle
    d   using a net and folding along the dotted lines:

11 a, b

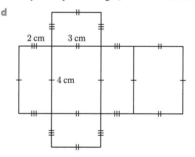

3 cm

4 cm

    c   They are equal in length, each is 5 cm long.
    d

2 cm   3 cm

4 cm

EXERCISE 6A

1   a 2   b 4   c 3   d 1

2   a 3   b 5   c 7   d 8

3   a   2 equal parts   b   4 equal parts   c   6 equal parts
    d   3 equal parts   e   10 equal parts   f   11 equal parts
    g   12 equal parts   h   100 equal parts

4   a $\frac{3}{4}$ b $\frac{1}{3}$ c $\frac{4}{5}$ d $\frac{3}{8}$ e $\frac{5}{8}$
    f $\frac{2}{7}$ g $\frac{3}{10}$ h $\frac{7}{100}$ i $\frac{6}{1000}$

5   a   two thirds   b   two quarters   c   three fifths
    d   five sevenths   e   nine tenths   f   seven eighths
    g   five twelfths   h   three hundredths
    i   eighty four hundredths   j   five thousandths

6   a $\frac{1}{2}$ b $\frac{1}{4}$ c $\frac{5}{6}$ d $\frac{3}{8}$ e $\frac{6}{16}$
    f $\frac{4}{10}$ g $\frac{15}{25}$ h $\frac{61}{100}$ i $\frac{37}{100}$

7   No, the 8 parts are not all of equal size.

8 a b c

9 a b c

d 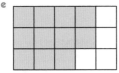 e

10 a The container is two fifths full of liquid.
   b The tank is five eighths full of fuel.
   c There are eight twelfths of a pizza left.

11 a $\frac{6}{10}$ b $\frac{6}{11}$ c $\frac{8}{15}$

12 a $\frac{2}{7}$ b $\frac{5}{7}$ c $\frac{1}{7}$ d $\frac{3}{7}$

13 a i $\frac{6}{12}$ ii $\frac{6}{12}$ b i $\frac{5}{12}$ ii $\frac{7}{12}$
   c $\frac{4}{5}$ d $\frac{5}{7}$

EXERCISE 6B

1 a $\frac{4}{5}$ b $\frac{1}{7}$ c $\frac{3}{10}$ d $\frac{8}{9}$ e $\frac{2}{11}$ f $\frac{12}{13}$

2 a $1 \div 3$ b $2 \div 5$ c $7 \div 8$ d $3 \div 4$
   e $8 \div 13$ f $11 \div 20$

3 a $20 \div 5 = 4$ b $27 \div 3 = 9$ c $55 \div 11 = 5$
   d $7 \div 7 = 1$ e $24 \div 12 = 2$ f $19 \div 19 = 1$
   g $0 \div 8 = 0$ h $108 \div 9 = 12$

EXERCISE 6C

1 a proper fraction b improper fraction c proper fraction
   d mixed number e improper fraction f proper fraction
   g mixed number h improper fraction

2 a 7 halves b $3\frac{1}{2} = \frac{7}{2}$

3 a $2\frac{3}{5}$ b 13 fifths c $2\frac{3}{5} = \frac{13}{5}$

4 a $1\frac{2}{6}$ b $3\frac{3}{4}$ c $2\frac{7}{10}$ d $4\frac{5}{8}$

5 a $1\frac{3}{4}$ L b $4\frac{1}{4}$ blocks c $2\frac{1}{2}$ cartons d $3\frac{3}{10}$ m

6 a $\frac{5}{4}$ b $\frac{5}{2}$ c $\frac{11}{3}$ d $\frac{17}{6}$ e $\frac{8}{5}$ f $\frac{16}{3}$
   g $\frac{13}{2}$ h $\frac{19}{8}$ i $\frac{25}{6}$ j $\frac{29}{10}$

7 a 4 whole sandwiches b 1 quarter c $\frac{17}{4} = 4\frac{1}{4}$

8 a $1\frac{1}{3}$ b $2\frac{1}{4}$ c $1\frac{5}{6}$ d $3\frac{1}{5}$ e $4\frac{3}{4}$ f $7\frac{1}{2}$
   g $4\frac{2}{3}$ h $2\frac{3}{7}$ i $3\frac{3}{10}$ j $4\frac{3}{8}$

9 $3\frac{4}{5}$ carrots

10 a 40 fifths

b

	Improper fraction	*Mixed number*
saucepan	$\frac{11}{5}$	$2\frac{1}{5}$
wok	$\frac{22}{5}$	$4\frac{2}{5}$
bowl	$\frac{7}{5}$	$1\frac{2}{5}$

EXERCISE 6D

1 a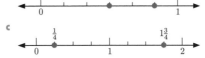
   b
   c
   d
   e
   f
   g
   h
   i

2 a $\frac{4}{5}$ b $\frac{4}{7}$ c $\frac{3}{8}, \frac{7}{8}$ d $\frac{3}{4}, 1\frac{1}{4}$
   e $\frac{5}{9}, 1\frac{7}{9}$ f $\frac{2}{3}, 1\frac{1}{3}, 2\frac{2}{3}$ g $2\frac{2}{3}, 3\frac{1}{3}$ h $3\frac{1}{4}, 4\frac{1}{4}, 4\frac{3}{4}$

3 a

b $\frac{4}{5}, \frac{6}{5}, 1\frac{2}{5}$

4 a

b $\frac{15}{6}, 2\frac{1}{6}, 1\frac{5}{6}, \frac{10}{6}$

EXERCISE 6E

1 a $\frac{18}{30}$ b $\frac{3}{5}$ **2** a $\frac{20}{60}$ b $\frac{1}{3}$

3 a $\frac{6}{8}$ b $\frac{9}{12}$ c $\frac{12}{16}$ d $\frac{15}{20}$

4 a $\frac{8}{20}$ b $\frac{12}{30}$ c $\frac{20}{50}$ d $\frac{2}{5}$

5 a $\frac{4}{24}$ b $\frac{10}{60}$ c $\frac{16}{96}$ d $\frac{1}{6}$

6 a $\frac{2}{8}$ b $\frac{4}{8}$ c $\frac{6}{8}$ d $\frac{8}{8}$ e $\frac{5}{8}$

7 a $\frac{15}{30}$ b $\frac{24}{30}$ c $\frac{25}{30}$ d $\frac{9}{30}$ e $\frac{6}{30}$ f $\frac{20}{30}$
   g $\frac{30}{30}$ h $\frac{18}{30}$ i $\frac{7}{30}$ j $\frac{39}{30}$

8 a $\frac{20}{60}$ b $\frac{24}{60}$ c $\frac{15}{60}$ d $\frac{25}{60}$ e $\frac{51}{60}$

9 a $\frac{50}{100}$ b $\frac{25}{100}$ c $\frac{80}{100}$ d $\frac{90}{100}$ e $\frac{28}{100}$ f $\frac{26}{100}$
   g $\frac{100}{100}$ h $\frac{85}{100}$ i $\frac{17}{100}$ j $\frac{122}{100}$

EXERCISE 6F

1 a $\frac{1}{2}$ b $\frac{1}{3}$ c $\frac{1}{5}$ d $\frac{1}{3}$ e $\frac{1}{6}$ f $\frac{3}{5}$
   g $\frac{2}{3}$ h $\frac{6}{7}$ i $\frac{3}{4}$ j $\frac{3}{10}$ k $\frac{9}{20}$ l $\frac{6}{5}$
   m $\frac{12}{7}$ n $\frac{10}{7}$ o $\frac{9}{2}$

2 c **3** a $\frac{1}{6}$ b $\frac{1}{18}$ c $\frac{1}{9}$ d $\frac{4}{9}$ e $\frac{2}{9}$

EXERCISE 6G

1 a $\frac{5}{12} < \frac{7}{12}$ b $\frac{4}{5} > \frac{3}{5}$ c $\frac{8}{9} < \frac{13}{9}$

d $\frac{11}{7} > 1\frac{3}{7}$ e $\frac{19}{4} < 5\frac{1}{4}$ f $\frac{28}{6} < 4\frac{5}{6}$

2 Keith

3 a $\frac{1}{2} < \frac{3}{4}$ b $\frac{1}{3} < \frac{3}{6}$ c $\frac{3}{4} < \frac{7}{8}$

d $\frac{5}{8} > \frac{1}{2}$ e $\frac{2}{3} > \frac{5}{9}$ f $\frac{4}{3} > \frac{5}{6}$

g $\frac{13}{15} < \frac{6}{5}$ h $\frac{15}{4} > 3\frac{1}{2}$ i $4\frac{1}{4} > \frac{33}{8}$

4 rent **5** a $\frac{2}{5}$ b $\frac{3}{10}$ c Trent's cage

6 a

$\frac{5}{8}, \frac{3}{4}, \frac{7}{8}$

b

$2\frac{1}{10}, \frac{12}{5}, \frac{5}{2}$

7 a $\frac{3}{12}, \frac{2}{6}, \frac{5}{12}$ b $\frac{8}{12}, \frac{5}{6}, \frac{11}{12}$ c $\frac{7}{20}, \frac{11}{20}, \frac{3}{5}$ d $1\frac{1}{4}, \frac{11}{8}, \frac{3}{2}$

8 a $\frac{4}{5}, \frac{7}{10}, \frac{3}{10}$ b $\frac{3}{4}, \frac{5}{8}, \frac{9}{16}$ c $\frac{2}{3}, \frac{3}{5}, \frac{7}{15}$ d $2\frac{2}{3}, \frac{22}{9}, \frac{7}{3}$

9 a Wednesday b Monday and Friday, Thursday and Sunday

10 Yes, improper fractions are always greater than 1, and proper fractions are always less than 1.

EXERCISE 6H.1

1 a $\frac{3}{7}$ b $\frac{1}{3}$ c $\frac{6}{5}$ d $\frac{3}{4}$ e $\frac{7}{8}$ f $\frac{9}{5}$

g $\frac{8}{7}$ h $\frac{17}{20}$ i $\frac{9}{25}$ j $\frac{29}{13}$ k $\frac{23}{14}$ l $\frac{8}{7}$

2 a $\frac{1}{2}$ b $\frac{1}{3}$ c $\frac{2}{3}$ d $\frac{5}{4}$ e $\frac{1}{2}$ f $\frac{4}{5}$

3 a $3\frac{5}{9}$ b $2\frac{7}{10}$ c $5\frac{2}{7}$ d $2\frac{1}{6}$ e $4\frac{3}{5}$ f $8\frac{5}{17}$

4 $\frac{5}{8}$ **5** $\frac{3}{10}$ **6** 1 bag of rice

7 a $4\frac{1}{3}$ b $1\frac{2}{5}$ c $3\frac{5}{7}$ d $2\frac{5}{8}$ e $7\frac{5}{9}$ f $8\frac{7}{10}$

8 a $\frac{5}{9}$ b $1\frac{3}{8}$ c $2\frac{5}{7}$ d $2\frac{7}{12}$

9 $3\frac{1}{2}$ pages **10** a $4\frac{2}{5}$ bags b $1\frac{1}{5}$ bags

EXERCISE 6H.2

1 a $\frac{3}{4}$ b $\frac{5}{6}$ c $\frac{3}{8}$ d $\frac{2}{9}$ e $\frac{5}{12}$ f $\frac{11}{10}$

g $\frac{7}{30}$ h $\frac{23}{12}$ i $\frac{56}{45}$ j $\frac{16}{49}$ k $\frac{87}{100}$ l $\frac{41}{40}$

2 a $2\frac{3}{4}$ b $4\frac{7}{9}$ c $4\frac{1}{10}$

3 a $\frac{2}{3}$ b $\frac{1}{2}$ c $\frac{5}{4}$ d $\frac{7}{5}$ e $3\frac{3}{5}$ f $2\frac{1}{6}$

4 $\frac{5}{9}$ of the cake **5** $\frac{7}{10}$ of a tub

6 a $3\frac{7}{8}$ b $1\frac{1}{6}$ c $3\frac{3}{10}$ d $1\frac{3}{4}$ e $3\frac{16}{21}$ f $3\frac{8}{15}$

7 $5\frac{3}{4}$ hours **8** $6\frac{5}{6}$ hours **9** $5\frac{5}{6}$ tonnes

10 a $1\frac{5}{12}$ cans b $\frac{7}{12}$ of a can

EXERCISE 6I

1 a $\frac{2}{3}$ b $\frac{8}{9}$ c $\frac{18}{25}$ d $\frac{6}{11}$

2 a 1 b 4 c 6 d 10

3 a $\frac{10}{3}$ b $\frac{28}{9}$ c $\frac{21}{4}$ d $\frac{20}{7}$

4 a $\frac{1}{5}$ b $\frac{3}{4}$ c $\frac{2}{3}$ d $\frac{15}{2}$ e $\frac{35}{6}$ f $\frac{5}{2}$

g $\frac{4}{3}$ h $\frac{8}{5}$

EXERCISE 6J

1 a 5 b 4 c 5 d 5 e 6 f 7

g 9 h 24

2 a 6 b 18 c 18 d 21 e 12 f 45

g 84 h 64

3 a 10 people b 14 drinks c 28 g

d 19 lollies e 45 minutes f $25

4 5 games **5** $180

6 a 12 plants b $\frac{7}{8}$ c 84 plants

7 22 school children **8** $6\frac{3}{4}$ hours

9 a 1875 kg b 1125 kg

REVIEW SET 6A

1 a $\frac{3}{5}$ b $\frac{5}{12}$ c $\frac{8}{9}$ **2** $2\frac{2}{7}$

3 a $\frac{6}{11}$ b $\frac{15}{19}$ **4** a $1\frac{4}{5}$ b $4\frac{1}{3}$ c $5\frac{5}{6}$

5 a $\frac{10}{12}$ b $\frac{8}{12}$ c $\frac{5}{12}$

6 a

b

c

7 a $\frac{6}{10} > \frac{3}{10}$ b $\frac{19}{7} > 2\frac{3}{7}$ c $\frac{4}{5} < \frac{22}{25}$ d $5\frac{2}{3} > \frac{31}{6}$

8 a $\frac{4}{7}$ b $\frac{17}{11}$ c $\frac{5}{8}$ d $4\frac{2}{9}$

9 a $\frac{8}{9}$ b 9 c $\frac{5}{2}$

10 a $50 b 40 g c 21 cm

11 a $\frac{7}{10}$ b 14 km c $\frac{3}{10}$ d 6 km

12 a i Charlie ii Matilda

b a i was easier. In a ii, the denominators of the fractions were different.

c i $\frac{7}{8}$ ii $\frac{1}{8}$

REVIEW SET 6B

1

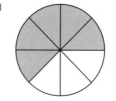

2 a $2\frac{1}{4}$ b $\frac{9}{4}$

3 a $40 \div 8 = 5$

b $72 \div 9 = 8$

c $99 \div 11 = 9$

4 5 days

5 a $\frac{23}{6}$ b $\frac{31}{7}$ c $\frac{27}{5}$

6 a $\frac{1}{8}$ b $\frac{5}{9}$ c $\frac{15}{8}$

7 a $\frac{2}{5}, \frac{7}{10}, \frac{4}{5}$ b $\frac{19}{12}, \frac{5}{3}, 1\frac{5}{6}$

8 a $4\frac{2}{5}$ b $1\frac{4}{5}$ c $\frac{47}{18}$

9 a Adam $\frac{16}{3}$, Jill $\frac{11}{3}$ b 9 sausages c $1\frac{2}{3}$ sausages

10 a $2\frac{1}{4}$ hours b $9\frac{1}{4}$ hours

11 a $\frac{12}{5}$ b 6 c $\frac{28}{5}$

12 a 20 cards b 40 cards c i 16 cards ii 24 cards

EXERCISE 7A

1 **a** 8.37 **b** 0.49 **c** 21.05 **d** 70.61
e 9.004 **f** 38.206

2 **a** zero point six **b** zero point four five
c zero point nine zero eight **d** eight point three
e eleven point seven **f** six point zero eight
g twenty point one five **h** ninety six point zero two
i five point eight six four **j** thirty four point zero zero three
k seven point five eight one **l** sixty point two six four

3 **a** 5 and 6 **b** 13 and 14 **c** 9 and 10
d 6 and 7 **e** 19 and 20 **f** 32 and 33
g 0 and 1 **h** 111 and 112 **i** 8 and 9

4 **a** 1 **b** 2 **c** 1 **d** 2 **e** 3 **f** 3
g 1 **h** 2 **i** 3

5

	thousands	hundreds	tens	units	decimal point	tenths	hundredths	thousandths	Decimal number
a				0	.	8			0.8
b				0	.	0	4		0.04
c				0	.	0	0	3	0.003
d			7	0	.	8			70.8
e				5	.	0	6		5.06
f	9	0	0	0	.	0	0	2	9000.002
g		2	0	9	.	0	4		209.04
h	8	0	0	0	.	4	0	2	8000.402
i			6	0	.	8	9		60.89

6

	Number	thousands	hundreds	tens	units	decimal point	tenths	hundredths	thousandths	Decimal number
a	$\frac{8}{10}+\frac{3}{100}$				0	.	8	3		0.83
b	$4+\frac{1}{10}+\frac{2}{100}+\frac{8}{1000}$				4	.	1	2	8	4.128
c	$9+\frac{4}{1000}$				9	.	0	0	4	9.004
d	$28+\frac{6}{10}+\frac{9}{100}+\frac{9}{1000}$			2	8	.	6	9	9	28.699
e	$\frac{5}{100}+\frac{6}{1000}$				0	.	0	5	6	0.056
f	$139+\frac{7}{100}+\frac{7}{1000}$		1	3	9	.	0	7	7	139.077

7 **a** 3 hundreds or 300 **b** 3 tenths or $\frac{3}{10}$
c 3 tens or 30 **d** 3 thousandths or $\frac{3}{1000}$
e 3 units or 3 **f** 3 hundredths or $\frac{3}{100}$
g 3 thousands or 3000 **h** 3 thousandths or $\frac{3}{1000}$

8 **a** 5 thousandths or $\frac{5}{1000}$ **b** 5 hundreds or 500
c 5 tenths or $\frac{5}{10}$ **d** 5 hundredths or $\frac{5}{100}$
e 5 thousands or 5000 **f** 5 units or 5
g 5 hundredths or $\frac{5}{100}$ **h** 5 thousandths or $\frac{5}{1000}$

9 **a** $5+\frac{4}{10}$ **b** $10+4+\frac{9}{10}$ **c** $2+\frac{3}{100}$
d $30+2+\frac{8}{10}+\frac{6}{100}$ **e** $1+\frac{3}{10}+\frac{8}{1000}$
f $3+\frac{2}{1000}$ **g** $\frac{9}{10}+\frac{5}{100}+\frac{2}{1000}$
h $4+\frac{2}{100}+\frac{4}{1000}$ **i** $20+\frac{8}{10}+\frac{1}{100}+\frac{6}{1000}$
j $9+\frac{8}{1000}$ **k** $800+8+\frac{8}{10}+\frac{8}{1000}$ **l** $\frac{6}{100}+\frac{4}{1000}$

10 **a** 0.6 **b** 0.43 **c** 0.809 **d** 0.09 **e** 0.007
f 2.503 **g** 4.037 **h** 6.52 **i** 0.568 **j** 0.0023
k 0.0308 **l** 0.006 02

11 **a** 0.3 **b** 0.15 **c** 0.23 **d** 0.65 **e** 0.79
f 0.117 **g** 0.083 **h** 0.307

12 **a** 13.5 **b** 1.91 **c** 2.137 **d** 8.034 **e** 2.7
f 3.84 **g** 4.068 **h** 51.72

13 **a** $\frac{7}{100}$ **b** $\frac{10}{100}$ **c** $\frac{28}{100}$ **d** $\frac{45}{100}$ **e** $\frac{61}{100}$

14 **a** $\frac{9}{1000}$ **b** $\frac{10}{1000}$ **c** $\frac{38}{1000}$ **d** $\frac{217}{1000}$ **e** $\frac{806}{1000}$

EXERCISE 7B

1 **a** M = 0.2, N = 0.7 **b** M = 2.6, N = 2.3
c M = 6.2, N = 7.6 **d** M = 11.7, N = 12.6
e M = 15.4, N = 17.1 **f** M = 21.5, N = 22.3

2 **a**
b

3 **a** P = 1.61, Q = 1.65, R = 1.67
b P = 2.39, Q = 2.32, R = 2.36
c P = 3.03, Q = 3.14, R = 3.08
d P = 7.64, Q = 7.77, R = 7.70
e P = 11.63, Q = 11.77, R = 11.86
f P = 13.77, Q = 13.99, R = 13.89

4 **a**
b

5 **a**
b

EXERCISE 7C

1 **a**
b 2.26, 2.3, 2.34, 2.4

2 **a**
b 4.2, 4.12, 4.1, 4.02, 4.01

3 **a** 0.7 < 0.8 **b** 0.06 > 0.05 **c** 0.2 > 0.19
d 5.01 < 5.1 **e** 0.81 > 0.803 **f** 2.5 = 2.50
g 0.304 < 0.34 **h** 0.03 < 0.2 **i** 6.05 < 60.50
j 0.29 = 0.290 **k** 5.01 < 5.016 **l** 1.15 > 1.035
m 21.021 < 21.210 **n** 8.09 = 8.090 **o** 0.904 < 0.94

4 **a** 0.4, 0.6, 0.8 **b** 0.1, 0.4, 0.9 **c** 0.06, 0.09, 0.14
d 0.46, 0.5, 0.51 **e** 1.06, 1.59, 1.61 **f** 0.206, 2.06, 2.6
g 0.0905, 0.095, 0.905 **h** 15.05, 15.5, 15.55

5   a 0.9, 0.8, 0.4, 0.3   b 0.51, 0.5, 0.49, 0.47
    c 0.61, 0.609, 0.6, 0.596   d 0.42, 0.24, 0.04, 0.02
    e 6.277, 6.271, 6.27, 6.027   f 0.311, 0.31, 0.301, 0.031
    g 8.880, 8.088, 8.080, 8.008 h 7.61, 7.061, 7.06, 7.01

6   4.01 m, 4.08 m, 4.1 m, 4.11 m, 4.4 m

7   47.103 seconds, 47.045 seconds, 47.009 seconds,
    46.982 seconds, 46.980 seconds

EXERCISE 7D

1   a 2.6   b 4.2   c midway   d 5.9
    e 18.3   f midway

2   a 2.4   b 3.6   c 4.9   d 7.8   e 0.6   f 4.3

3   a 1.5   b 7.2   c 0.1   d 6.5   e 9.0   f 13.2

4   a 4.63   b 9.11   c midway

5   a 4.24   b 2.73   c 5.63   d 10.01   e 4.38
    f 6.52   g 1.09   h 26.30

6   a 4 and 5   b 5

7   a 4   b 6   c 7   d 13   e 21   f 46

8   a 0.5   b 0.49   9   a 4   b 3.8   c 3.79

10 a 5   b 5.2   c 5.18   d 5.184

11 a 3.9   b 4   c 6.1   d 0.462   e 2.95   f 0.176

12 a 4.3 kg   b 32.7°C   c 2.94 m   d 87 seconds

EXERCISE 7E

1   a $\frac{1}{10}$ b $\frac{9}{10}$ c $\frac{19}{100}$ d $\frac{67}{100}$ e $\frac{7}{100}$
    f $\frac{191}{1000}$ g $\frac{523}{1000}$ h $\frac{49}{1000}$ i $4\frac{3}{10}$ j $6\frac{13}{100}$
    k $\frac{11}{1000}$ l $5\frac{271}{1000}$

2   a $\frac{4}{5}$ b $\frac{1}{2}$ c $\frac{13}{50}$ d $\frac{7}{20}$ e $\frac{1}{4}$ f $\frac{53}{500}$
    g $\frac{3}{200}$ h $\frac{3}{40}$ i $\frac{1}{8}$ j $7\frac{3}{5}$ k $4\frac{14}{25}$ l $3\frac{19}{20}$

EXERCISE 7F

1   a 0.8   b 0.21   c 1.4   d 0.319   e 2.83

2   a 5   b 2   c 25   d 5   e 4
    f 2   g 8   h 125   i 25   j 4

3   a 0.5   b 0.4   c 0.25   d 0.15   e 0.85
    f 0.36   g 0.84   h 0.26   i 0.276   j 0.024
    k 0.364   l 0.022   m 0.072   n 0.225   o 0.375
    p 5.75   q 7.55   r 3.168

4   a $\frac{1}{2} = 0.5$ b $\frac{1}{5} = 0.2$, $\frac{2}{5} = 0.4$, $\frac{3}{5} = 0.6$, $\frac{4}{5} = 0.8$
    c $\frac{1}{4} = 0.25$, $\frac{2}{4} = 0.5$, $\frac{3}{4} = 0.75$
    d $\frac{1}{8} = 0.125$, $\frac{2}{8} = 0.25$, $\frac{3}{8} = 0.375$, $\frac{4}{8} = 0.5$,
       $\frac{5}{8} = 0.625$, $\frac{6}{8} = 0.75$, $\frac{7}{8} = 0.875$

5   a $\frac{7}{10} = 0.7$, $\frac{13}{20} = 0.65$, $\frac{18}{25} = 0.72$
    b 0.63, $\frac{13}{20}$, $\frac{7}{10}$, $\frac{18}{25}$, 0.74

6   a 0.8 kg   b 2.5 g   c 4.75 h   d 0.35 m
    e 2.45 t   f 7.875 L

EXERCISE 7G

1   a 0.9   b 3.3   c 1.13   d 0.73   e 1.53
    f 7.82   g 18.43   h 4.7   i 0.444   j 3.209
    k 0.727   l 1.85   m 1.13   n 13.31   o 11.368

2   a 3.4   b 5.2   c 5.45   d 0.52   e 1.34
    f 13.12   g 0.8   h 1.5   i 0.4   j 1.4
    k 2.3   l 2.26   m 2.67   n 1.43   o 6.94

3   a 44.2   b 14.38   c 11.211   d 8.452

4   a 6.1   b 22.18   c 1.02   d 167.5   e 58.63
    f 2.014

5   $17.10   6 0.37 m   7 237.4 m   8 27.95 kg

9   13.079 m   10   a $91.90   b $8.10

EXERCISE 7H

1   a 25   b 63   c 2   d 0.1   e 2.38   f 606

2   a 670   b 920   c 70   d 54   e 7040   f 5.798

3   a 7400   b 16 200   c 800   d 380   e 6750   f 82.4

4

Number	× 10	× 100	× 1000
a	0.009	0.09	0.9	9
b	0.12	1.2	12	120
c	0.5	5	50	500
d	4.6	46	460	4600
e	19.07	190.7	1907	19 070

5   a $9 \times 100 = 900$ b $33 \times 10 = 330$
    c $3.4 \times 10 = 34$ d $0.02 \times 100 = 2$
    e $0.003 \times 10 = 0.03$ f $5.64 \times 1000 = 5640$

6   a $28   b $280   c $2800

7   a 1.47 kg   b 14.7 kg   c 147 kg

EXERCISE 7I

1   a 0.2   b 0.63   c 0.082   d 0.001
    e 5.402   f 60.6

2   a 0.06   b 0.092   c 0.007   d 0.53
    e 1.66   f 3.007

3   a 0.007   b 0.0062   c 0.0561   d 0.499
    e 0.070 15   f 6.8549

4

Number	÷ 10	÷ 100	÷ 1000
a	8	0.8	0.08	0.008
b	4.6	0.46	0.046	0.0046
c	50	5	0.5	0.05
d	19.07	1.907	0.1907	0.019 07
e	231.4	23.14	2.314	0.2314

5   a $6 \div 10 = 0.6$ b $33 \div 100 = 0.33$
    c $3.4 \div 10 = 0.34$ d $0.2 \div 100 = 0.002$
    e $49 \div 100 = 0.49$ f $634.1 \div 1000 = 0.6341$

6   91.4 kg   7 $275.65   8 6.284 kg

EXERCISE 7J

1   a 2.1   b 3.2   c 2.5   d 7.2
    e 0.06   f 0.49   g 0.2   h 0.048

2   a 12.6   b 6   c 19.2   d 64.8
    e 86.5   f 195   g 276.3   h 269.6

3   a 0.69   b 3.48   c 2.32   d 4.26
    e 36.45   f 22.16   g 25.48   h 57

4   a 2.6   b 5.1   c 11   d 14.4
    e 37.8   f 0.45   g 2.22   h 1.2

5   a 19.2   b 58.5   c 176.4   d 192.6   e 912.6
    f 11.62   g 96.52   h 392.7   i 599.9

6   19.6 m   7 93.6 minutes   8 $100.05   9 13.5 kg

EXERCISE 7K

1   a 3.2   b 1.5   c 0.08   d 0.42
    e 0.51   f 6.2   g 20.4   h 0.045
    i 3.02   j 22.38   k 0.903   l 1.341

2 **a** 2.65 **b** 1.22 **c** 5.85 **d** 6.205
e 0.425 **f** 1.475 **g** 2.2925 **h** 3.2625
3 2.15 kg **4** $2.29 **5** 3.35 km
6 **a** $\frac{1}{6} = 1 \div 6 = 0.166\,666....$, the 6s continue forever.
b $\frac{2}{3} = 2 \div 3 = 0.6666....$, the 6s continue forever.
c $\frac{4}{9} = 4 \div 9 = 0.4444....$, the 4s continue forever.
d $\frac{1}{7} = 1 \div 7 = 0.142\,857\,142\,857....$, the sequence of digits "142 857" repeats forever.

REVIEW SET 7A

1 **a** 0.73 **b** 0.107 **c** 5.069
2 **a** A = 2.42, B = 2.47 **b** A = 0.068, B = 0.073
3 0.069, 0.096, 0.6, 0.609, 0.69 **4** **a** 3.9 **b** 3.86
5 **a** $\frac{23}{100}$ **b** $\frac{1}{5}$ **c** $\frac{59}{1000}$ **d** $\frac{17}{25}$
6 **a** 0.71 **b** 0.8 **c** 0.95 **d** 0.162
7 **a** 0.68 **b** 2.23 **c** 20.24 **d** 5.51
8 1937.88 tonnes
9 **a** 62 **b** 215.8 **c** 0.56 **d** 0.0042
10 **a** 20.4 **b** 42.63 **c** 10.5 **d** 52.32
11 **a** 1.4 **b** 0.103 **c** 0.784 **d** 0.0375
12 **a**

b 4.85 **c** 4.9
13 $109.90 **14** **a** 26.11 kg **b** 1.09 kg **c** $78.30

REVIEW SET 7B

1 16.574 **2** 0.031 **3** 3 thousandths or $\frac{3}{1000}$
4 $2 + \frac{4}{100} + \frac{9}{1000}$
5

6 **a** 5 **b** 5.491 **c** 5.5
7 **a** 0.709 < 0.79 **b** 3.04 < 3.046 **c** 8.13 = 8.130
8 **a** 0.85 km **b** 0.12 L **c** 4.42 kg
9 **a** $203 \div 100 = 2.03$ **b** $2.03 \times 1000 = 2030$
c $0.203 \div 100 = 0.002\,03$
10 **a** 14.12 **b** 3.61 **c** 30.1 **d** 0.94
e 1.58 **f** 0.921 **g** 2.56 **h** 36.8
11 **a** $222.20 **b** $77.80 **12** 11.775 g
13 **a** $3150 **b** $6400 **c** $3250
14 **a** **i** 57.05 s **ii** 57.21 s **b** 0.16 s **c** 0.056 98 s
15 **a** $29.75 **b** $20.25 **c** $148.75

EXERCISE 8A

1 **a** 7 apples **b** 4 bags of apples
c 8 coins **d** 3 groups of coins
2 **a** **C** **b** **D** **c** **E** **d** **B** **e** **A**
3 distance in kilometres, or time in minutes
4 The weight of a bulldozer in grams is too large a number to be sensible.

EXERCISE 8B

1 **a** 2 cm **b** 6.2 cm **c** 3.6 cm **d** 0.7 cm
2 **a** 24 cm **b** 13 cm **c** 10.2 cm **d** 16.8 cm
e 25.6 cm **f** 18.5 cm

3 **a** 35°C **b** 37.4°C **c** 38.3°C **d** 35.7°C
4 **a** 120 km/h **b** 95 km/h **c** 65 km/h
5 **a** 45.2 kg **b** 71.6 kg **c** 63.65 kg
6 **a** 200 mL **b** 350 mL **c** 1.2 L **d** 0.7 L

EXERCISE 8C

1 **a** kg **b** tonnes **c** g **d** g **e** kg **f** mg
g g **h** kg **i** kg **j** g **k** g **l** tonnes
2 **a** **D** **b** **C** **c** **A** **d** **E** **e** **B** **f** **F**
3 **a** 8000 g **b** 3200 g **c** 0.38 g **d** 4.25 g
4 **a** 3400 kg **b** 150 kg **c** 13.87 kg **d** 0.786 kg
5 **a** 7000 mg **b** 3.4 g **c** 0.86 kg **d** 12 400 g
e 2516 kg **f** 4.15 t
6 2.2 kg **7** 24 kg **8** 7 t
9 Yes, as only 3.3 g of powder is needed.
10 **a** 924 kg **b** less than 1 tonne
11 40 kg **12** 102 t

REVIEW SET 8A

1 **a** **E** **b** **C** **c** **A** **d** **B** **e** **D**
2 **a** 110 km/h **b** 600 mL **c** 650 g
3 **a** g **b** t **c** kg
4 **a** 2700 kg **b** 890 kg **c** 6.23 kg
5 **a** 21 200 g **b** 0.0212 t **6** 20 t
7 **a** **i** 2500 kg **ii** 2 500 000 g **iii** 2 500 000 000 mg
b The value in **a iii** is too large a number to be sensible.
8 **a** height, mass, length, body temperature
b height and length
c The hamster weighs less than the cat. It is most sensible to write the mass of the hamster in grams, and the mass of the cat in kilograms.
d 17 times heavier

REVIEW SET 8B

1 The amount of water in a cup in kilolitres is too small a number to be sensible.
2 **a** 12.6 cm **b** 37.9°C **c** 75.3 kg
3 **a** **C** **b** **A** **c** **B**
4 **a** 3.2 kg **b** 4600 mg **c** 700 kg
5 1.7 kg **6** 80 cans
7 **a** 150 g **b** 6 kg **c** 200 boxes

EXERCISE 9A

1 **a** cm **b** mm **c** mm **d** cm **e** cm **f** m
2 **a** **B** **b** **D** **c** **C**
3 **a** 40 mm **b** 55 mm **c** 83 mm
4 **a** 60 mm **b** 97 mm **c** 800 cm **d** 1140 cm
e 208 cm **f** 4000 m **g** 700 m **h** 5260 m
i 13 145 m
5 **a** 5 cm **b** 14.3 cm **c** 3 m **d** 9.3 m
e 0.76 m **f** 10 km **g** 21.9 km **h** 4.74 km
i 0.607 km
6 **a** 1000 millimetres
b **i** 2000 mm **ii** 1240 mm **iii** 1.74 m **iv** 0.835 m
7 23.5 mm **8** 426.5 cm
9 **a** 13 cm, 7.8 cm, 9.5 cm, 8 cm
b 7.8 cm, 0.08 m, 95 mm, 0.13 m

EXERCISE 9B

1 **a** 57 cm   **b** 10.1 m   **c** 1260 mm   **d** 166.6 cm
2 **a** $(3000 + 580)$ m $= 3580$ m
   b $(1000 + 38)$ m $= 1038$ m
   c $(5000 + 674 + 0.22)$ m $= 5674.22$ m
   d $(48 + 0.91 + 0.006)$ m $= 48.916$ m
3 **a** 11 700 m   **b** 11.7 km   **4** 160 m   **5** 30 laps
6 **a** 12 m   **b** 13.2 m

EXERCISE 9C

1 **a** 14 m   **b** 100 km   **c** 28 cm   **d** 104 mm
   e 25 km   **f** 123 cm   **g** 43 m   **h** 92 mm
   i 48 m
2 **a** $(9 + 15 + 20)$ mm $= 44$ mm
   b $(80 + 70 + 100 + 200)$ cm $= 450$ cm
3 **a** 100 m   **b** 20 km   **c** 38 cm   **d** 90 mm
   e 130 m   **f** 138 cm
4 **a** 24 cm   **b** 70 cm   **c** 50 m   **d** 80 cm
   e 65 cm   **f** 144 m
5 **a** $(2 \times 8 + 2 \times 15)$ mm $= 46$ mm
   b $(2 \times 0.6 + 1.5 + 1)$ km $= 3.7$ km
   c $(3 \times 8.4 + 12.3)$ mm $= 37.5$ mm
6 **a** **A**: 11.3 cm, **B**: 9.9 cm, **C**: 11.9 cm   **b** **C**
7 **a** 760 m   **b** 55 m   **8** **a** 9.6 m   **b** $44.64
9 **a** 3.9 km   **b** 19.5 km
10 **a** 9 cm   **b** 12.3 cm   **11** 56 cm

EXERCISE 9D

1 **a** **i** 6 m   **ii** 14 m   **iii** 16.4 m   **iv** 1.6 m
   b **i** 1 m   **ii** 9 cm   **iii** 35 cm   **iv** 62 cm
2 **a** **i** 200 m   **ii** 300 m   **iii** 60 m   **iv** 35 m
   b **i** 10 cm   **ii** 6 cm   **iii** 9 cm   **iv** 19 cm
3 **a** 5.3 m   **b** 2.3 m
4 **a** 12 m   **b** 5 m   **c** 2 m by 4 m
   d 2.4 m by 1.2 m and 3.6 m by 1.2 m
5 **a** **B**   **b** **D**   **c** **C**   **d** **A**
6 **a** 5 km   **b** **i** 20 km   **ii** 9.5 km   **iii** 10.5 km
7 20 cm
8

Scale: 1 represents 2000

9

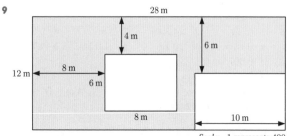

Scale: 1 represents 400

10

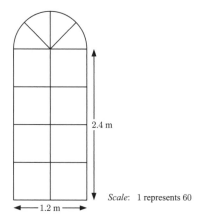

2.4 m

←— 1.2 m —→

Scale: 1 represents 60

11 **a** 1 represents 1000   **b** 1 represents 125
12 **a** 1 represents 200
   b the mandarin tree and the orange tree
   c 10 m   **d** 3 m by 2 m

REVIEW SET 9A

1 **a** cm   **b** m   **c** mm
2 **a** 3.56 m   **b** 0.45 km   **c** 7630 mm   **3** 1.84 m
4 **a** $(6000 + 207)$ m $= 6207$ m
   b $(9 + 0.38 + 0.004)$ m $= 9.384$ m
5 **a** 49 m   **b** 14.1 cm   **c** 33.4 km
6 **a** 35.2 m   **b** $704   **7** **a** 9 cm   **b** 15 cm
8 **a** 1.3 km   **b** 3.9 km   **c** $9360
9 **a** **i** 150 m   **ii** 320 m   **b** **i** 10 cm   **ii** 4 cm
10 1 represents 200
11 **a** **i** cm   **ii** m
   b The scale factor is 2000. Lengths on the scale diagram are
       2000 times longer in reality.
   c The pitch is 5 cm by 3.5 cm on the diagram. To find the
       actual dimensions, we multiply by 2000. So the dimensions
       are 100 m by 70 m.
   d Using **c**, the total distance around the boundary
       $= 2 \times 100$ m $+ 2 \times 70$ m
       $= 340$ m

REVIEW SET 9B

1 **a** 4 cm   **b** 2.8 cm
2 **a** 8100 m   **b** 59.5 cm   **c** 4.06 m
3 47.1 mm, 21 cm, 0.35 m, 423 mm   **4** 50 jumps
5 **a** 54 cm   **b** 15 m   **6** 12 cm   **7** 46 m
8 **a** 12.5 cm   **b** 16.8 cm
9 **a** 24 m   **b** 12.8 m   **c** 10.8 m
10 1 represents 20 000
11

Scale: 1 represents 100

12 **a** **i** 87.5 m   **ii** $393.75   **b** $210   **c** $630.75

EXERCISE 10A

1 a **C** b **H** c **G** d **B** e **F** f **A** g **E** h **D**

2 a 11 cm^2 b 9 cm^2 c 12 cm^2

3 a 45 tiles b 2.25 m^2 c $99

4 a i 540 pavers ii 280 pavers
   b 16.4 m^2 c $984

5 a 18 mm^2 b 16 mm^2 c 40 mm^2 d 72 mm^2

EXERCISE 10B

1 a 10 cm^2 b 140 km^2 c 32 m^2
   d 36 m^2 e 39 km^2 f 72.8 cm^2
   g 1200 cm^2 h 4.5 cm^2 i 102 m^2

2 Gemma's tablet screen is larger.

3 a 120 m^2 b $960 4 a 45 m^2 b 3 litres

5 a 25.2 m b 36.8 m^2 6 623.7 cm^2 7 23.2 m^2

8 a 30 m^2 b 8 m^2 c 12 m^2 d 10 m^2

9 a 10 800 cm^2 b 30 cm^2 c 360 tiles

EXERCISE 10C

1 a 30 m^2 b 24 m^2 c 21 cm^2 d 7.5 cm^2
   e 36 m^2 f 28 m^2 g 54 m^2 h 5 cm^2 i 20 mm^2

2 a 15 m^2 b $420

3 a i 32 m^2 ii 10 m^2 iii 16 m^2 iv 6 m^2
   b 10 m^2 + 16 m^2 + 6 m^2 = 32 m^2 ✓

EXERCISE 10D

1 a 18 cm^3 b 14 cm^3 c 21 cm^3 2 **B, A, C**

3 a  b

   c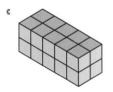

4 **C** 5 **B** 6 24 m^3

EXERCISE 10E

1 a 160 mm^3 b 48 m^3 c 56 cm^3 d 150 mm^3
   e 125 cm^3 f 180 cm^3

2 30 cm^3 3 4800 cm^3

4 **Hint:** 1 × 1 × 36, 1 × 2 × 18, 1 × 3 × 12, 1 × 4 × 9,
   1 × 6 × 6, 2 × 2 × 9, 2 × 3 × 6, 3 × 3 × 4

5 a 80 cm^3 b 132 cm^2 6 4.8 m^3

7 12 boxes

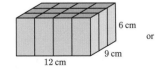 or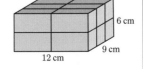

8 6 cm 9 905 m^3

EXERCISE 10F

1 a mL b L c ML d mL e kL f ML
   g mL h L

2 a 7000 mL b 5600 L c 8510 kL d 3.54 L
   e 760 kL f 0.124 ML

3 9 L 4 210 L per day

REVIEW SET 10A

1 **E** 2 27 m^2 3 a 18 cm^2 b 10 cm^2 c 60 m^2

4 a 6 cm^2 b 100 stamps

5 a 5 cm^3 b 14 cm^3 c 25 cm^3 6 4500 cm^2

7 a 320 cm^3 b 64 cm^3 c 2.7 m^3

8 360 boxes 9 4.95 L 10 a 80 cm^2 b 720 cm^3

11 a i 77 cm^2 ii 42 cm^2 iii 20 cm^2 iv 15 cm^2
    b 42 cm^2 + 20 cm^2 + 15 cm^2 = 77 cm^2 ✓

REVIEW SET 10B

1 a m^2 b km^2 2 $378 3 rectangle **B**

4 a 7.5 cm^2 b 24 m^2 c 28 cm^2

5 Total area of red triangles = 15 m^2 + 25 m^2 = 40 m^2
   Total area of green triangles = 16 m^2 + 24 m^2 = 40 m^2

6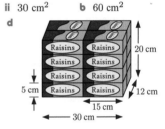

7 a 120 mm^3 b 8 m^3 c 196 cm^3 8 90 m^3

9 a 12 400 mL b 0.765 ML 10 1.65 L

11 a i 30 cm^2 ii 30 cm^2 b 60 cm^2

12 a 450 cm^3 d
    b 7200 cm^3
    c 16 boxes

EXERCISE 11A

1 a 1910 b Elizabeth II c 9 years

2 a 2012 b Valéry Giscard d'Estaing c 5 years
   d François Mitterrand, by 2 years e 10 years

3 a 1980 b i 1993 ii 1999 iii 2012
   c 18 years d i 7 years old ii 41 years old

4 a i 200 AD ii 600 BC
   b i 1800 years ii 800 years iii 3200 years
   c i Mesopotamian Cuneiform Script ii ≈ 5200 years

5 a

   H L   C   O   F E BQI M G K J N / D A P
   |-----|-----|-----|----|------|-------|--------|--------|
   3000 BC 2000 BC 1000 BC 1 BC 1 AD 1000 AD 2000 AD

   b **P** c **I** d **A** and **N** e 3 events
   f 4641 years g 501 years

EXERCISE 11B

1 a minutes b hours c seconds d days
   e hours f seconds

2 **a** 420 s **b** 240 h **c** 240 min **d** 35 days
    e 4 min **f** 2 weeks **g** 720 s **h** 3 h **i** 6 days

3 480 s or 8 minutes

4 **a** 360 min **b** No, he practised for only 310 minutes.

5 **a** 204 min **b** 343 min **c** 367 min **d** 519 min

6 **a** 312 s **b** 2127 s **c** 948 s **d** 2996 s

7 **a** 280 min **b** 8 min per tree

8 **a** 1 min 16 s **b** 1 min 35 s **c** 1 min 50 s
    d 3 min 25 s **e** 5 min 41 s **f** 11 min 40 s

9 **a** 1 h 25 min **b** 1 h 40 min **c** 2 h 9 min
    d 2 h 26 min **e** 4 h 18 min **f** 8 h 19 min

10 5 h 50 min

EXERCISE 11C

1 **a** yes **b** no **c** no **d** yes

2 **a** 365 days **b** 72 months

3 Rosie **4** 91 days **5** **a** 720 h **b** 744 h

6 **a** 48 months **b** 1461 days **c** 35 064 h

7 **a** 27 days **b** 43 days **c** 117 days **d** 111 days
    e 68 days **f** 179 days

8 **a** 45 days **b** $6 **9** no **10** 27th May 2012

EXERCISE 11D

1 **a** 7:00 am **b** 6:49 am **c** 10:32 pm **d** 3:17 pm
    e 4:09 pm **f** 3:39 pm

2 **a** 3:00 pm **b** 7:24 pm **c** 11:05 am **d** 3:45 am
    e 1:28 pm **f** 10:44 pm Sun

3 8:05 am **4** 10:50 am **5** 11:15 pm **6** 10:36 pm

7 **a** 3 h 20 min **b** 6 h 5 min **c** 5 h 46 min
    d 10 h 47 min

8 3 h 44 min **9** 2 h 42 min **10** 7 h 39 min

11 4:59:33 pm

EXERCISE 11E

1 **a** 03:13 **b** 11:17 **c** 00:00 **d** 12:47
    e 17:41 **f** 09:22 **g** 14:09 **h** 12:00
    i 10:56 **j** 18:14 **k** 20:19 **l** 23:59

2 **a** 3:40 am **b** 6:35 am **c** 6:26 pm
    d 12:00 pm (midday) **e** 7:39 pm **f** 6:15 am
    g 3:45 pm **h** 8:17 pm **i** 1:11 pm **j** 11:48 pm

3 **a** 60 minutes or more is not possible.
    b 07:13 is correct. **c** 24:00 or more is not possible.

4 **a** 09:30 **b** 12:40 **c** 19:15

5 **a** flight BA10 **b** 18:20 **c** 2 h 25 min

EXERCISE 11F

1 **a** 11:50 am **b** 9:45 am **c** Sport
    d **i** 45 min **ii** 50 min **e** 6 h 10 min

2 **a** 9:00 am **b** volleyball **c** 1 h 30 min **d** 2 h 15 min

3 **a** 3:00 am **b** 10:27 pm
    c **i** 10 h 39 min **ii** 6 h 59 min **d** 7:42 pm

4 **a** 8:30 am **b** North Park **c** 60 min
    d 3 h 55 min **e** 8 h 45 min **f** 10:25 pm

5 **a** 6 bus services **b** 10:15 am **c** 5:30 pm
    d **i** 3 h 10 min **ii** 5 h 40 min **e** 8 h 30 min
    f bus E **g** bus A

6 **a** **i** arrival time **ii** departure time **b** 4:50 pm
    c 5:27 pm **d** 6:20 pm **e** the 5:23 pm train

REVIEW SET 11A

1 **a** **i** 1988 **ii** 1990 **iii** 1998 **iv** 2004
    b **i** 25 years **ii** 8 years

2 **a** 720 min **b** 240 s **c** 3 days **3** 2 h 48 min

4 **a** **i** 8 h 35 min **ii** 4 h 45 min **iii** 14 h
    b **i** 40 min **ii** 40 min **iii** 30 min **c** 6:40 pm

5 12:10 pm **6** **a** no **b** yes **c** no

7 **a** 53 days **b** 17 h 40 min

8 **a** 198 min **b** 552 s

9 **a** 4:15 am **b** 1:00 pm **c** 11:35 pm

10 **a** 8:00 am **b** 10:30 am **c** 1:00 pm **d** 7 h 15 min

11 **a** 7:57 pm **b** 23 min **c** **i** 2 h 15 min **ii** 10:35 pm

12 **a** 63 days
    b Claire and Peter's birthdays are exactly 9 weeks apart. So, whatever day of the week Claire's birthday is on, Peter's birthday will also be on.
    c Wednesday

REVIEW SET 11B

1 **a** 3100 BC **b** 400 years **2** **a** 4 pm **b** 4:39 pm

3 3 h 39 min **4** **a** 720 h **b** 366 days

5 5:12 pm **6** 12:55 pm **7** **a** 07:15 **b** 21:25

8 107 days **9** 1 h 49 min

10 **a** 1:30 pm start, 2:00 pm finish **b** Top dog

11 **a** 00:32 **b** 10:15 **c** 17:49

12 **a** 2011 **b** Toyota **c** Mazda **d** 4 years

13 **a** 30 min **b** **i** 10 min **ii** 15 min **iii** 20 min
    c **i** 10:10 am **ii** 10:22 am **d** 2 buses

EXERCISE 12A

1 **a** **i** $\frac{14}{100}$ **ii** 14% **b** **i** $\frac{67}{100}$ **ii** 67%
    c **i** $\frac{95}{100}$ **ii** 95% **d** **i** $\frac{40}{100}$ **ii** 40%

2 **a** 50% **b** 85% **c** 25%

3 **a** Player 2 **b** Player 3 **c** Player 1 **d** Player 4

4 **a** **i** 11 **ii** 23 **iii** 39 **iv** 27
    b **i** $\frac{11}{100}$ **ii** $\frac{23}{100}$ **iii** $\frac{39}{100}$ **iv** $\frac{27}{100}$
    c **i** 11% **ii** 23% **iii** 39% **iv** 27%
    d 100%;   this represents all of the symbols in the circle.

5 **a** **i** 44% **ii** 2% **iii** 7%
    b plastic **c** 100%;   this represents all waste.

EXERCISE 12B

1 **a** $\frac{59}{100}$ **b** $\frac{13}{100}$ **c** $\frac{3}{100}$ **d** $\frac{97}{100}$

2 **a** $\frac{1}{10}$ **b** $\frac{1}{2}$ **c** $\frac{9}{10}$ **d** $\frac{1}{20}$ **e** $\frac{11}{50}$ **f** $\frac{37}{50}$
    g $\frac{3}{20}$ **h** $\frac{13}{20}$ **i** $\frac{1}{4}$ **j** $\frac{4}{5}$ **k** $\frac{7}{20}$ **l** $\frac{3}{4}$
    m $\frac{1}{25}$ **n** $\frac{12}{25}$ **o** $\frac{14}{25}$ **p** $\frac{16}{25}$

EXERCISE 12C

1 **a** 21% **b** 53% **c** 91% **d** 8% **e** 30% **f** 70%
    g 0% **h** 100%

2 **a** 50% **b** 26% **c** 20% **d** 82% **e** 15% **f** 60%
    g 28% **h** 95% **i** 48% **j** 76%

3 **a** 14.5% **b** 23.1% **c** 75.9% **d** 20.6%

4 **a** $\frac{2}{1} = 2$ **b** 200%

5

	Students	Number	Fraction	Percentage
a	with a bag	6	$\frac{6}{20}$	30%
b	without a book	10	$\frac{10}{20}$	50%
c	holding an open book	5	$\frac{5}{20}$	25%
d	black hair	5	$\frac{5}{20}$	25%
e	sitting down	2	$\frac{2}{20}$	10%
f	wearing something on their head	6	$\frac{6}{20}$	30%
g	wearing shoes	20	$\frac{20}{20}$	100%

6 **a** $\frac{1}{5} = 20\%$ **b** $\frac{1}{4} = 25\%$

$\frac{2}{5} = 40\%$ $\frac{2}{4} = 50\%$

$\frac{3}{5} = 60\%$ $\frac{3}{4} = 75\%$

$\frac{4}{5} = 80\%$ $\frac{4}{4} = 100\%$

$\frac{5}{5} = 100\%$

c $\frac{1}{3} = 33\frac{1}{3}\%$ **d** $1 = 100\%$

$\frac{2}{3} = 66\frac{2}{3}\%$ $\frac{1}{2} = 50\%$

$\frac{3}{3} = 100\%$ $\frac{1}{4} = 25\%$

$\frac{1}{8} = 12\frac{1}{2}\%$

$\frac{1}{16} = 6\frac{1}{4}\%$

EXERCISE 12D

1 **a** 0.1 **b** 0.5 **c** 0.25 **d** 0.05 **e** 0.33 **f** 0.57
g 0.94 **h** 0.06 **i** 0.4 **j** 0.11 **k** 0.01 **l** 0.9

2 **a** 0.175 **b** 0.816 **c** 0.607 **d** 0.094
e 0.039 **f** 0.043 **g** 0.017 **h** 0.008

3 **a** **i** 0.71 **ii** $\frac{71}{100}$ **b** **i** 0.3 **ii** $\frac{3}{10}$

c **i** 0.55 **ii** $\frac{11}{20}$ **d** **i** 0.06 **ii** $\frac{3}{50}$

e **i** 0.28 **ii** $\frac{7}{25}$

EXERCISE 12E

1 **a** 37% **b** 89% **c** 15% **d** 49% **e** 73%
f 11% **g** 5% **h** 2%

2 **a** 20% **b** 70% **c** 90% **d** 40% **e** 7.4%
f 73.9% **g** 8.6% **h** 0.1%

3

	Percent	Fraction	Decimal
a	20%	$\frac{1}{5}$	0.2
b	40%	$\frac{2}{5}$	0.4
c	25%	$\frac{1}{4}$	0.25
d	50%	$\frac{1}{2}$	0.5
e	75%	$\frac{3}{4}$	0.75
f	85%	$\frac{17}{20}$	0.85
g	8%	$\frac{2}{25}$	0.08
h	35%	$\frac{7}{20}$	0.35
i	80%	$\frac{4}{5}$	0.8
j	84%	$\frac{21}{25}$	0.84
k	100%	$\frac{1}{1} = 1$	1.00
l	15%	$\frac{3}{20}$	0.15

EXERCISE 12F

1 **a**
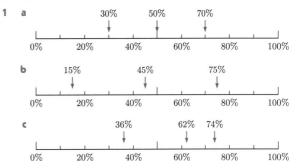

b

c

2 **a** $\frac{3}{5} = 60\%$, 70%, $0.65 = 65\%$
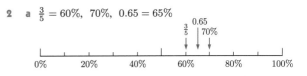

b 55%, $\frac{9}{20} = 45\%$, $0.8 = 80\%$
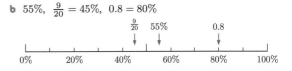

c $0.93 = 93\%$, 79%, $\frac{17}{20} = 85\%$
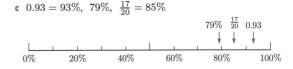

d $0.85 = 85\%$, $\frac{3}{4} = 75\%$, 92%
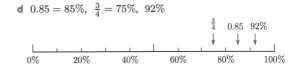

e $\frac{27}{50} = 54\%$, 67%, $0.59 = 59\%$
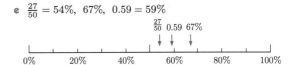

f 47%, $0.74 = 74\%$, $\frac{7}{10} = 70\%$
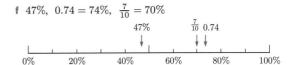

3 **a** $10\% = 0.1 = \frac{10}{100}$ **b** $45\% = 0.45 = \frac{45}{100}$
c $68\% = 0.68 = \frac{68}{100}$ **d** $89\% = 0.89 = \frac{89}{100}$

4 **a** 20% **b** 35% **c** 55% **d** 95%

5 **a** **i** 68% **ii** 43% **iii** 78% **iv** 62.7%
b
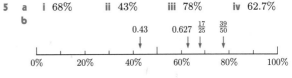

c 0.43, 0.627, $\frac{17}{25}$, $\frac{39}{50}$

EXERCISE 12G

1 a 76% b 85% c 44% d 74% e 90% f 69%

2 a 36% b 81% c 33% d 62%

3 70% **4** 52% **5** a 85% b yes

6 a 20% b 20% c 75%

7 a 35% b 5% c 21% d 16% e 36% f 7%
g 4% h 2% i 0.1%

8 a 25% b 75% **9** 24%

10 a i 18% ii 34% iii 42%
b 94%; there are singers in the choir who are *not* in Year 4, 5, or 6.

11 95%

12 a Smith's: 56%, Jones': 55% b Smith's
c i 48% ii 52%

13 $\approx 21.6\%$

EXERCISE 12H

1 a $28 b 6 mushrooms c 850 balloons
d $30 e 200 people f 8.1 kg
g 240 L h 4.9 cm i 15.75 s

2 a 1 worker b 15 workers

3 97 students **4** 1215 tonnes

5 a 70% b i 720 acres ii 1680 acres **6** 360 kg

7 a 27 cents b 45 cm c 700 g
d 18 min e 4800 L f 16.8 mm
g 26.4 hours h 98 cents i 54 s

8 120 g **9** 20 min **10** a $450 b $3250

EXERCISE 12I

1 a €32 b €352 **2** a $6 b $18

3 a 84 cm b 68 L **4** a £40 b £120

5 a 6.4 g less b 1.6 g **6** a 12 min b 130 m²

REVIEW SET 12A

1 a $\frac{33}{100}$ b 33%

2 a 100% b i 59.6% ii 13.2%
c i $\frac{17}{100}$ ii $\frac{96}{1000} = \frac{12}{125}$

3 a 90% b 47% c 30.6%

4 a $\frac{31}{100}$ b $\frac{4}{25}$ c $\frac{47}{50}$ **5** a $27 b 48 cm

6 54% **7** a 60% b 22.1%

8 a 0.81 b 0.02 c 0.108 **9** 31%

10 $\frac{3}{4} = 75\%$, $0.78 = 78\%$, 72%

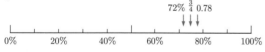

11 a 84 households b 70 households

12 a oil b 5% c i 60 mL ii 280 mL

13 a 45 m b 195 m

REVIEW SET 12B

1 a 70% b 15%

2 a 9% b 13.6% c 70.2% **3** 17%

4 a 0.74 b $\frac{37}{50}$ **5** 30 students

6 a 27% b 72% c 65%

7 a 52% b 29% **8** 30%

9 a 120 mL cordial b 680 mL water

10 a 96% means 96 in every hundred
b 4% c $\frac{4}{100} = \frac{1}{25}$ d 4 g

11 a i 70% ii 68% iii 78% iv 73.4%
b

c $\frac{17}{25}$, 0.7, 0.734, $\frac{39}{50}$

12 a i 33% ii 67% b i $148.50 ii $301.50

13 a 90 staff b 510 staff

EXERCISE 13A

1 a positive b negative c negative d positive
e negative f neither g positive h negative

2 a −7 b +1 c −2 d +4 e −11 f +13

3 a A = −3, B = 1, C = −9, D = 6
b A = 3, B = −4, C = 9, D = −7

4 a

b

c

5 a −3°C b 8°C c 0°C d −12°C

EXERCISE 13B

1 a 2 > −1 b −6 < −3 c −5 < 3 d 0 > −8
e −5 > −9 f −7 < 0

2 a

−3, −2, 0, 4

b

−4, −1, 2, 5

c

−8, −1, 4, 6

3 a

3, 1, −2, −5

b

6, 0, −3, −6

c

5, −1, −4, −6

EXERCISE 13C

1 a −7 b +32 c −40

2 a +10 b −15 c +7 d −3 e +8 f −45

3 a −7 b +12 c −15 **4** a +8 b −10

5 a

b Hachirōgata, Japan and New Orleans, USA

c i Dublin, Ireland ii Hachirōgata, Japan

6 a a 6 point win b an $18 loss c 15 km to the west
d 20 m below e 3 minutes late f 7 m to the right

7

	Statement	Number	Opposite of statement	Opposite number
a	30 km to the south	−30	30 km to the north	+30
b	a $25 gain	+25	a $25 loss	−25
c	4 m above the water	+4	4 m below the water	−4
d	12°C below zero	−12	12°C above zero	+12
e	an increase of 6 kg	+6	a decrease of 6 kg	−6

8 a travelling 6 km south b losing 4 kg
c 3 steps forwards d cooling by 4°C
e gaining $30 f descending 12 stairs

9

	Statement	Operation	Opposite of statement	Opposite operation
a	cooling by 18°C	subtract 18°C	warming by 18°C	add 18°C
b	gaining $26	add $26	losing $26	subtract $26
c	6 steps to the left	subtract 6 steps	6 steps to the right	add 6 steps
d	winning by 7 points	add 7 points	losing by 7 points	subtract 7 points
e	driving 8 km east	add 8 km	driving 8 km west	subtract 8 km
f	60 m downwards	subtract 60 m	60 m upwards	add 60 m

EXERCISE 13D

1 a 2 b −2 c −2 d 2

2 a 0 b 0 c 8 d −8

3 a −5 b 3 c −6 d −7 e −7 f −5
g 6 h −8

4 a −3 b −10 c −3 d 6

5 a −1 b −5 c 6 d 3 e −6 f −9
g 5 h −16

6 2 floors below ground level **7** 3 floors below ground level

8 −1°C **9** at her house

10 a i losing by 8 points ii winning by 5 points
b Lost the game by 4 points.

11 a 3 km south b 2 km north c 3 km east d 8 km west

12 a 5°C cooler b 7°C warmer

13 a spending $10 b earning €20 c no effect

EXERCISE 13E

1 a 4 b 8 c −8 d −4 e −4 f 14
g −14 h 4

2 a 6 b 8 c −8 d 6 e −3 f −13
g 5 h 7 i −9 j 13 k −7 l −8

3 a 6 b −1 c 8 d −6 e −5 f 0

4 a 7 b 9 c 4 d 6 e 19 f 4
g 14 h 2 i 12

5 a seagull: +5, kayaker: 0, diver: −2, dolphin: −6
b i 2 m ii 11 m iii 6 m iv 4 m

6

	Mon	Tue	Wed	Thu	Fri	Sat	Sun
Minimum temperature	−4°C	−6°C	−2°C	−3°C	−5°C	−12°C	−13°C
Maximum temperature	1°C	3°C	1°C	0°C	0°C	−3°C	−2°C
Temperature difference	5°C	9°C	3°C	3°C	5°C	9°C	11°C

7 a i 860 points ii 260 points iii 1200 points
b Team A: 1250 points, Team B: 650 points
c Team A is winning by 600 points.

8 a 5 children b 4 children c Max's guess
d Claire's guess e i 5 ii 22
f i 74 lollies ii 95 lollies

EXERCISE 13F

1 a 10 b −10 c −10 d 10 e −10 f −10
g 10 h 10

2 a −8 b −15 c −28 d −9 e 18 f −40
g 7 h −44 i −25 j 64 k −63 l −120
m −56 n 66 o −45 p 84

3 reduced by $40

4 a 60 marks b −36 marks c 20 marks

5 −1 × 30, 1 × −30, −2 × 15, 2 × −15, −3 × 10, 3 × −10,
−5 × 6, 5 × −6

6 a 24 b −30 c −42 d 80

7 −6 × −2 × −1, −6 × 2 × 1, 6 × −2 × 1, 6 × 2 × −1,
−4 × −3 × −1, −4 × 3 × 1, 4 × −3 × 1, 4 × 3 × −1,
−3 × −2 × −2, −3 × 2 × 2, 3 × −2 × 2, −12 × −1 × −1,
−12 × 1 × 1, 12 × −1 × 1

EXERCISE 13G

1 a 6 b −6 c −6 d 6 e 4 f −4
g −4 h 4 i 1 j −1 k −1 l 1
m 7 n −7 o −7 p 7

2 a −3 b −2 c −3 d −4 e 6 f −5
g −3 h −4 i 13 j −9 k 1 l 7
m −10 n −9 o 8 p −11

3 The final answer is positive.

1st step: negative ÷ positive = negative

2nd step: negative ÷ negative = positive

REVIEW SET 13A

1 a negative b positive c neither d negative

2 A = −6, B = 1, C = −3

3 a −3 < 2 b 0 > −6 c −4 > −7

4 a travelling 10 km north b getting 3 cm longer

5 a −4   b 3   c −11   d −2   e −4   f 3
6 a −5   b 10   c 7   d 0   e 5   f −4
7 a 7   b 4   c 6
8 a −14   b 27   c −36   d 50
9 a −11   b −4   c 8   d −6
10 a 24   b −30   **11** $8 loss
12 a tree top: +5,   bird: +3,   roots: −1,   pipe: −2
   b   i 6 m   ii 5 m   iii 1 m

REVIEW SET 13B

1 a −5   b +8   c −12
2 a

   −9, −2, 0, 4

   b

   −8, −6, 1, 3

3 a −15   b +6   **4** 1 floor below ground
5 a 10   b 12   c 0   d 1
6 a 16 points   b 11 points
7 a −6   b −21   c −90   d 132
8 −1 × 20, 1 × −20, −2 × 10, 2 × −10, −4 × 5, 4 × −5
9 a −7   b −4   c 5   d 8
10 a −60   b 6   c 5   d −18   e 99   f −9
11 a 1°C   b i 3°C   ii −7°C   c 10°C
12 a +6   b −8   c 10 lilypads   d 9

EXERCISE 14A

1 a 9 $\xrightarrow{+5}$ 14 $\xrightarrow{+5}$ 19 $\xrightarrow{+5}$ 24 $\xrightarrow{+5}$ 29

   b 23 $\xrightarrow{-3}$ 20 $\xrightarrow{-3}$ 17 $\xrightarrow{-3}$ 14 $\xrightarrow{-3}$ 11

   c 18 $\xrightarrow{+7}$ 25 $\xrightarrow{+7}$ 32 $\xrightarrow{+7}$ 39 $\xrightarrow{+7}$ 46

   d 5 $\xrightarrow{\times 2}$ 10 $\xrightarrow{\times 2}$ 20 $\xrightarrow{\times 2}$ 40 $\xrightarrow{\times 2}$ 80

   e 5 $\xrightarrow{-2}$ 3 $\xrightarrow{-2}$ 1 $\xrightarrow{-2}$ −1 $\xrightarrow{-2}$ −3

2 a 5, 8, 11, 14, 17, 20   b 12, 19, 26, 33, 40, 47
   c 19, 27, 35, 43, 51, 59   d 21, 19, 17, 15, 13, 11
   e 57, 52, 47, 42, 37, 32   f 17, 11, 5, −1, −7, −13
   g −18, −11, −4, 3, 10, 17
3 a i 14, 23, 32, 41, 50, 59, 68, 77
      ii 56, 50, 44, 38, 32, 26, 20, 14
      iii 8, 20, 32, 44, 56, 68, 80, 92
   b 32
4 46 is incorrect, it should be 48.
5 a 4, 8, 16, 32   b 10, 30, 90, 270   c 200, 100, 50, 25
   d 7000, 700, 70, 7   e 1, −2, 4, −8
6 a 3 min, 6 min, 12 min, 24 min, 48 min   b 93 minutes
7 a 5, $5\frac{1}{2}$, 6, $6\frac{1}{2}$, 7, $7\frac{1}{2}$ b $\frac{1}{4}$, 1, $1\frac{3}{4}$, $2\frac{1}{2}$, $3\frac{1}{4}$, 4
   c 6, $5\frac{3}{5}$, $5\frac{1}{5}$, $4\frac{4}{5}$, $4\frac{2}{5}$, 4   d 8, $7\frac{3}{8}$, $6\frac{3}{4}$, $6\frac{1}{8}$, $5\frac{1}{2}$, $4\frac{7}{8}$
   e $\frac{1}{2}$, $\frac{3}{4}$, 1, $1\frac{1}{4}$, $1\frac{1}{2}$, $1\frac{3}{4}$ f $\frac{11}{6}$, $\frac{3}{2}$, $\frac{7}{6}$, $\frac{5}{6}$, $\frac{1}{2}$, $\frac{1}{6}$
8 $4\frac{1}{4}$ cups, $3\frac{1}{2}$ cups, $2\frac{3}{4}$ cups, 2 cups, $1\frac{1}{4}$ cups

9 a 4, 4.6, 5.2, 5.8, 6.4, 7   b 3.6, 4.7, 5.8, 6.9, 8, 9.1
   c 7.8, 7.5, 7.2, 6.9, 6.6, 6.3   d 21, 18.5, 16, 13.5, 11, 8.5
   e 490, 49, 4.9, 0.49, 0.049, 0.0049
   f 0.0173, 0.173, 1.73, 17.3, 173, 1730

10

Year	2015	2016	2017	2018	2019	2020
Cost	$6.95	$7.50	$8.05	$8.60	$9.15	$9.70

EXERCISE 14B

1 a Start at 8 and add 5 each time.
   b Start at 24 and subtract 2 each time.
   c Start at 69 and add 3 each time.
   d Start at 38 and subtract 4 each time.
   e Start at 43 and add 9 each time.
   f Start at 83 and subtract 17 each time.
   g Start at 2 and multiply by 3 each time.
   h Start at 6 and multiply by 10 each time.
   i Start at 112 and divide by 2 each time.
   j Start at 7500 and divide by 5 each time.
2 a Start at 4 and add 5 each time;   29, 34, 39
   b Start at 38 and subtract 6 each time;   14, 8, 2
   c Start at 6 and add 9 each time;   51, 60, 69
   d Start at 41 and subtract 8 each time;   1, −7, −15
   e Start at 2 and multiply by 2 each time;   32, 64, 128
   f Start at 4 and multiply by 10 each time;
     40 000, 400 000, 4 000 000
   g Start at 13 and subtract 6 each time;   −11, −17, −23
   h Start at −1 and multiply by −2 each time;   −16, 32, −64
3 a Start at 11 and add 3 each time;   △ = 20
   b Start at 50 and subtract 7 each time;   △ = 29
   c Start at 3 and add 6 each time;   △ = 15, □ = 33
   d Start at 60 and subtract 9 each time;   △ = 33, □ = 15
   e Start at 4 and multiply by 5 each time;   △ = 100
   f Start at 6400 and divide by 4 each time;   △ = 400
4 a Start at 150 kg and increase by 5 kg each week.
   b 175 kg
5 a Start at 5 and increase by 0.9 each time;   9.5, 10.4, 11.3
   b Start at 13.1 and decrease by 0.5 each time;
     10.6, 10.1, 9.6
   c Start at 1.4 and decrease by 0.06 each time;   1.1, 1.04, 0.98
   d Start at 5130 and divide by 10 each time;
     0.513, 0.0513, 0.005 13
6 a △ = 3.7   b △ = 4.5   c △ = 9.33   d △ = 2.14
   e △ = 1.27   f △ = 53.9
7 a Start at 5.7 km and increases by 1.4 km each day.
   b   i 12.7 km   ii on the eighth day
8 a Start at 2 and add $\frac{2}{3}$ each time; $4\frac{2}{3}$, $5\frac{1}{3}$, 6
   b Start at $\frac{19}{5}$ and subtract $\frac{3}{5}$ each time; $\frac{7}{5}$, $\frac{4}{5}$, $\frac{1}{5}$
   c Start at $3\frac{1}{4}$ and add $\frac{3}{4}$ each time; $6\frac{1}{4}$, 7, $7\frac{3}{4}$
9 a Start at $\frac{1}{2}$ and add $\frac{1}{6}$ each time; $\frac{4}{3}$, $\frac{3}{2}$, $\frac{5}{3}$
   b Start at $\frac{3}{2}$ and subtract $\frac{1}{12}$ each time; $\frac{13}{12}$, 1, $\frac{11}{12}$
   c Start at $\frac{5}{16}$ and add $\frac{3}{16}$ each time; $1\frac{1}{16}$, $1\frac{1}{4}$, $1\frac{7}{16}$
10 a Start at 6 and subtract $\frac{2}{3}$ each time;   △ = 4
   b Start at 2 and add $1\frac{1}{5}$ each time;   △ = $5\frac{3}{5}$
   c Start at $11\frac{6}{7}$ and subtract $2\frac{3}{7}$ each time;   △ = $4\frac{4}{7}$
11 a Start at 0.05 and multiply by 2 each time;   1.6, 3.2
   b Start at 27 and divide by 3 each time; $\frac{1}{9}$, $\frac{1}{27}$

12 a Start at 8 pages and increase by $2\frac{1}{2}$ pages each day.
  b i 23 pages   **ii** on the thirteenth day
13 a Start and 6 and increase by 5 each time.
  b Start at 7 and increase by 8 each time.
  c Start at $\frac{6}{7}$, and increase the numerator by 5 each time and increase the denominator by 8 each time.
14 a $\frac{11}{19}, \frac{13}{22}, \frac{15}{25}$ **b** $\frac{20}{23}, \frac{24}{26}, \frac{28}{29}$ **c** $\frac{41}{42}, \frac{48}{47}, \frac{55}{52}$
15 a $\triangle = \frac{7}{18}$ **b** $\triangle = \frac{23}{35}$ **c** $\triangle = \frac{13}{19}$
16 a $\frac{7}{36}, \frac{8}{49}, \frac{9}{64}$ **b** $\frac{2}{11}, -\frac{1}{13}, \frac{1}{30}$ **c** $-25, -12, -9\frac{4}{5}$

EXERCISE 14C

1 a

  b

Diagram number	1	2	3	4	5
Number of matches	4	6	8	10	12

  c The number of matches starts at 4, and increases by 2 each time.

2 a
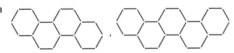
  b

Diagram number	1	2	3	4	5
Number of matches	6	11	16	21	26

  c The number of matches starts at 6, and increases by 5 each time.

3 a

  b

Diagram number	1	2	3	4	5
Number of dots	8	10	12	14	16

  c The number of dots starts at 8, and increases by 2 each time.

4 a

  b The number of dots starts at 5, and increases by 4 each time.

5 Note: Other answers are possible.
  a
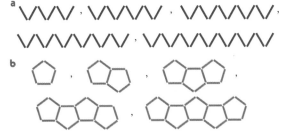
  b

6 a The number of hexagons starts at 7, and increases by 3 each time.
  b The number of hexagons is the square of the diagram number.

7 a

b i The number of red matches starts at 8, and increases by 2 each time.
  ii The number of green matches starts at 2, and increases by 5 each time.
  iii The total number of matches starts at 10, and increases by 7 each time.

8 78 matches

REVIEW SET 14A

1 a $6 \xrightarrow{\times 2} 12 \xrightarrow{\times 2} 24 \xrightarrow{\times 2} 48 \xrightarrow{\times 2} 96$
  b $100 \xrightarrow{-9} 91 \xrightarrow{-9} 82 \xrightarrow{-9} 73 \xrightarrow{-9} 64$

2 a 2, 9, 16, 23, 30, 37   **b** 13, 7, 1, -5, -11, -17
3 2 jars, $3\frac{1}{2}$ jars, 5 jars, $6\frac{1}{2}$ jars, 8 jars
4 a $\frac{1}{3}$, 1, $1\frac{2}{3}$, $2\frac{1}{3}$, 3   **b** 12, 10.9, 9.8, 8.7, 7.6
5 a Start at 12 and increase by 5 each time.
  b Start at 42 and decrease by 4 each time.
6 a $\triangle = 120$ **b** $\triangle = 19.1$ **c** $\triangle = 1.59$
7 a Start at 2 and increase by 0.7 each time;   4.8, 5.5, 6.2
  b Start at 6410 and divide by 10 each time; 0.641, 0.0641, 0.006 41
8 a $\frac{13}{29}, \frac{16}{34}, \frac{19}{39}$ **b** $\frac{9}{4}, \frac{6}{1}, \frac{3}{-2}$
9 a

  b

Diagram number	1	2	3	4	5
Number of matches	5	9	13	17	21

  c The number of matches starts at 5, and increases by 4 each time.

10 a
  b The number of dots starts at 5, and increases by 3 each time.

11 a i Start at 15 and increase by 4 each time.
    ii Start at 53 and decrease by 7 each time.
  b i 31, 35, 39, 43, 47, 51   **ii** 25, 18, 11, 4, -3, -10
  c 39

12 a i 7 toothpicks   **ii** 16 toothpicks   **iii** 25 toothpicks
  b

  c i 34 toothpicks   **ii** 43 toothpicks
  d The number of toothpicks starts at 7, and increases by 9 each time.

REVIEW SET 14B

1 a 4, $7\frac{1}{2}$, 11, $14\frac{1}{2}$, 18, $21\frac{1}{2}$ **b** 2, $1\frac{6}{7}$, $1\frac{5}{7}$, $1\frac{4}{7}$, $1\frac{3}{7}$, $1\frac{2}{7}$
2 10 minutes, 20 minutes, 40 minutes, 80 minutes
3 Start at 3 and increase by 5 each time.

4 a $\triangle = 25$ **b** $\triangle = 20$

5 a 4, 12, 36, 108   **b** 500, 100, 20, 4

6 Note: Other answers are possible.

7 8.8 litres

8 a

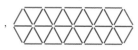

  b The number of dots starts at 5, and increases by 1 each time.

9 a $\triangle = 8$ **b** $\triangle = \frac{11}{24}$

10 The number of matches starts at 10, and increases by 3 each time.

11 a Start at 4 macarons and increase by 2 macarons each day.

  b i 12 macarons on the fifth day, 14 macarons on the sixth day

  ii 54 macarons   **iii** on the ninth day

12 a

  b

Diagram number	1	2	3	4	5
Red matches	6	8	10	12	14
Green matches	6	11	16	21	26
Total matches	12	19	26	33	40

  c i The number of red matches starts at 6, and increases by 2 each time.

  ii The number of green matches starts at 6, and increases by 5 each time.

  iii The total number of matches starts at 12, and increases by 7 each time.

EXERCISE 15A

1 a i Torrens Parade Ground   **ii** Montefiore Hill

  iii Adelaide Convention Centre

  iv Adelaide Botanic Gardens

  b i B4   **ii** D2   **iii** I1   **iv** C6   **v** E1

  c B2 and B3   **d** 17 grid squares

2 a i The British Museum   **ii** Kensington Palace

  iii London Eye   **iv** Maltby Street Market

  b i G2   **ii** C3   **iii** C1   **iv** F3   **v** A1

  c i Big Ben and Westminster Abbey

  ii Trafalgar Square and 10 Downing Street

  d A1, A2, B2, and C2   **e** Trafalgar Square

3 a staff room   **b** G6   **c** F1

  d i 3 drinking fountains   **ii** C6

4 a i bearded pig   **ii** fruit bat   **iii** spotted deer

  iv tiger   **v** hippo   **vi** giraffe

  b i E3   **ii** G2   **iii** G3   **iv** C1   **v** D3   **vi** C4

  c i otters and hyena   **ii** pygmy hippo and white tiger

  iii snakes and cheetah

  d A2, B2, F4, and G4

EXERCISE 15B

1

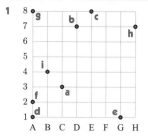

2 a

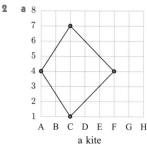
a kite

  b

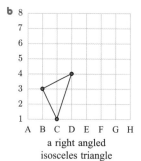
a right angled isosceles triangle

  c

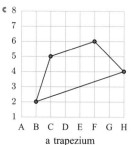
a trapezium

  d

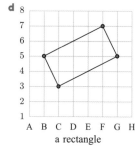
a rectangle

  e

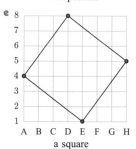
a square

3 a i G2   **ii** E4   **iii** A3

  b i plants   **ii** Thai   **iii** books

4 a i kiosk   **ii** gate   **iii** first aid   **b** E7

  c i inside   **ii** E2

EXERCISE 15C

1 a

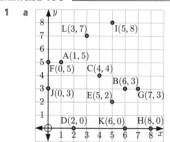

  b D, H, and K; the y-coordinate of each point is zero.

c F and J; the x-coordinate of each point is zero.

2 a i 5 ii 2 iii 6 b i 5 ii 3 iii 0
   c P(5, 3), Q(2, 4), R(6, 5), S(3, 3), T(3, 0), U(0, 4)
   d O(0, 0)

3 HAVE A GOOD DAY!

4 a i (4, 3) ii (6, 6) b i javelin ii sprints
   c i shot put ii shot put

5 The x-coordinates and y-coordinates of the points are not the same.

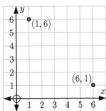

6
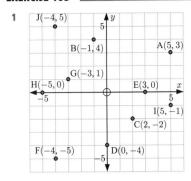

EXERCISE 15D

1
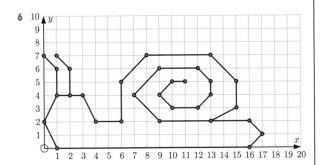

2 a i 5 ii 0 iii −5 b i 2 ii 0 iii −4
   c i P(−2, 1) ii V(2, −5) iii U(−4, −1)
   d i T ii Z iii Q

3 a i (4, 1) ii (−2, 4) b Dianne c Gary

4 a i (−2, 3) ii (1, −3)
   b i station H ii station K c station J

5 a i (1, −4) ii (−4, 3) iii (3, 2)
   b i performance stage ii roller coaster iii petting zoo
   c performance stage

6 a 70 km b 20 km c 70 km

7 a i (−6, −7) ii (6, −3) b i 120 m ii 140 m
   c 120 m d i zip-line ii 60 m

8 a (−1, −2) b i 60 m ii left c 810 m

EXERCISE 15E

1 a
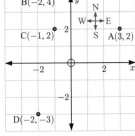
   b i north
      ii east
      iii southwest

2 a P(−2, 3), Q(3, −1) b C c D d C
3 a 6 m b west c i (−5, −2) ii 9 m
4 a 8 km b i north ii west c i east ii north
   d i northeast ii southwest e (0, −2)

5 a i (−5, 4) ii (5, −3)
   b Joe needs to travel 4 m west, then 4 m south, then 12 m east, then 2 m north, then 2 m east, then 8 m north, then 6 m east, then 2 m south, then 2 m west, then 4 m south, then 2 m east to get to the exit.

6 a northeast b
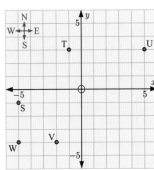
   c 6 km north

Scale: 1 unit represents 2 km

REVIEW SET 15A

1 a change rooms b 3 grid squares
   c i F2 ii C1 d i east ii northwest

2
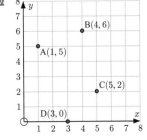

3
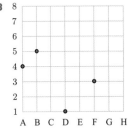

4 a
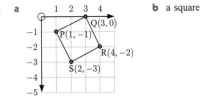
   b a square

5 a i (1, 4) ii (5, 4)
   b i the perfume shop ii the sports shop c 60 m

6 a M(−3, −3) b B

7 **a** **i** A(−4, −2)   **ii** E(1, −1)   **b** **i** F   **ii** D
c **i** west   **ii** northeast
8 **a** (−5, −5)   **b** **i** northwest   **ii** east   **iii** southeast
c (−5, −3)

REVIEW SET 15B

1 **a** **i** Higashiyama Jisho-ji   **ii** Kinkaku-ji   **iii** Toji
b **i** E4   **ii** G1   **iii** F3
c Arashiyama Bamboo Forest and Tenryuji Temple
d D1, D2, E2, F2, G2, and H2
2 **a** **i** H8   **ii** B7   **b** **i** Greek stall   **ii** Japanese stall
3
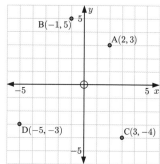

4 **a** F(3, 1),   G(−4, −2),   H(−2, 3),   I(4, −3),   J(−1, −1),
K(−5, 1)
b J
5
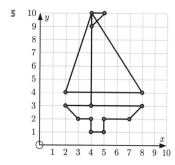

6 **a** **i** (2, 5)   **ii** (6, 1)   **iii** (2, 2)
b **i** bowling green   **ii** tennis courts   **c** south
7 **a**   **b** obtuse angled
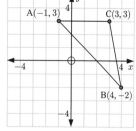

8 **a** **i** (2, 3)   **ii** (−1, −2)
b **i** (2, −2)   **ii** 3 km   **iii** east   **c** (−1, 0)

EXERCISE 16A

1 **a** A   **b** C   **c** B
2 **a** 20°C   **b** 3 min   **c** 1 min   **d** 1 min and 7 min
e from 4 min to 10 min

3 **a** 40 customers at 7 pm   **b** 5 customers at 5 pm
c 25 customers
d There was an increase in customers (from 20 to 40).
e 10 customers   **f** 20 fewer customers
4 **a** 60 L   **b** 6 minutes   **c** 15 L
5 **a** **i** January (1st year)   **ii** July (1st year)
b the temperature increases
c March and November in 1st year, and April and November
in 2nd year
6 **a** 18 min   **b** 15 m   **c** 25 m   **d** 8 min and 12 min
7 **a** **i** 25 points   **ii** 45 points   **iii** 70 points   **iv** 100 points
b fourth quarter
c from 9 min to 12 min, and from 27 min to 30 min
d from 39 min to 42 min
8 **a** 50 gigalitres   **b** the start of May   **c** 60 gigalitres
d 10 gigalitres   **e** July, August, September, October
f from the start of May to the end of August
9 **a**   **b** $20
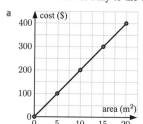
10 **a**
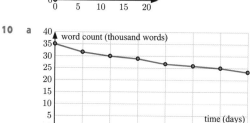
b The graph is decreasing.
11 **a**
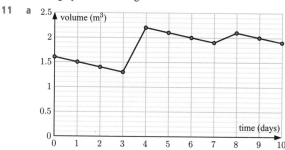
b days 4 and 8; the volume of water increases on these days

EXERCISE 16B

1 **a** 300 km   **b** 5½ hours   **c** 150 km   **d** 2 hours
e **i** ≈ 30 km   **ii** ≈ 70 km   **iii** 50 km   **iv** ≈ 120 km
f The family stopped for half an hour then continued to travel
at a faster speed.
2 **a** 25 minutes   **b** 2000 m   **c** 800 m   **d** 80 m
3 **a** the Williams family   **b** 2 hours   **c** 500 km
4 **a** 7:48 am   **b** 7 km   **c** 48 minutes   **d** 6 minutes
e **i** 1 km   **ii** 3 km   **f** **i** 2 km   **ii** 2 km

5 **a**
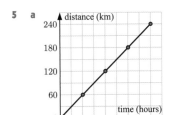

b **i** 90 km   **ii** 5 hours
c Yes, the graph is a straight line.

6 **a**
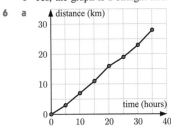

b **i** ≈ 25 km   **ii** ≈ 19 min
c The graph is not a straight line.

EXERCISE 16C

1 **a** 160 EUR   **b** 350 USD   **c** 270 EUR   **d** 600 USD
2 **a** 900 CAD   **b** 540 CAD   **c** 250 GBP   **d** 400 GBP
3 **a** ≈ 28 miles   **b** ≈ 17 miles   **c** ≈ 77 km   **d** ≈ 48 km
4 **a** **i** ≈ 4°C   **ii** 140°F   **b** 212°F   **c** ≈ 29°C

REVIEW SET 16A

1 **a** increasing   **b** 40 km/h   **c** 2 seconds
2 **a**
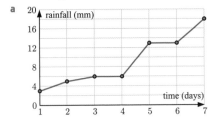

b The graph is increasing.
3 **a** 55 diners at 7:45 pm   **b** ≈ 6:55 pm and 8:30 pm
c ≈ 43 diners
4 **a** after 3 years   **b** 200 salmon, after 9 years
c **i** between 0 and 3 years and between 9 and 10 years
ii between 3 and 9 years
d after 1 year and 5 years
5 **a** 11 km   **b** Celia   **c** 3 times   **d** 3 km
6 **a**
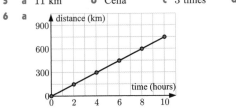

b ≈ 375 km   **c** 75 km
7 **a** 250 EUR   **b** 450 EUR   **c** 400 GBP   **d** 120 GBP

REVIEW SET 16B

1 increasing   **2** **a** 20°C   **b** after 3 minutes
3 **a** ≈ 6.1 m   **b** ≈ 1.5 m   **c** ≈ 26 feet   **d** ≈ 6.5 feet
4 **a**
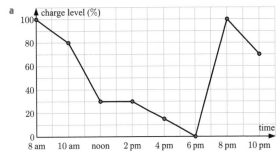

b 90%   **c** ≈ 2:40 pm and ≈ 6:30 pm
5 **a** 10 minutes   **b** 1200 m   **c** 9 minutes
6 **a**
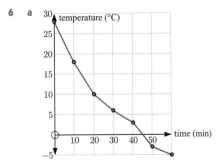

b **i** 20°C   **ii** 45 minutes   **iii** 14°C
7 **a** 24 km   **b** Hissam   **c** 80 minutes
d 16 km   **e** Hissam

EXERCISE 17A

1 **a** impossible   **b** highly likely   **c** unlikely
d 50-50 chance
2 **a** highly unlikely   **b** impossible   **c** certain
d highly likely
3 **a** highly unlikely   **b** highly likely   **c** certain
d impossible
4 **a** *A*   **b** *B*   **c** *A*
5 **a** 4 blue cards   **b** 4 white cards
c 2 blue cards and 2 white cards
d 3 blue cards and 1 white card, or 4 blue cards

EXERCISE 17B

1 **a** C   **b** D   **c** A   **d** B   **e** E
2 **a** C   **b** E   **c** A   **d** D   **e** B
3 **a**

Min   Chermaine

0   0.19 0.22   0.5   1

b Chermaine, since the probability that she will fall is higher than the probability that Min will fall (0.22 > 0.19).
4 **a** **i** Dhaka   **ii** Cairo   **b** Kuala Lumpur
c **i** true   **ii** false
5 **a** Jan: 80%,   Natasha: 83%,   Ellie: 58%

b
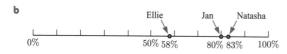
Ellie   Jan   Natasha

0%   50% 58%   80% 83%   100%

c likely   d Natasha

e Ellie is more likely to shoot a goal. The probability that she shoots a goal is greater than 0.5, so it is more likely to happen than not happen.

6 a orange juice   b $\frac{5}{7}$

c sum $= \frac{2}{7} + \frac{4}{7} + \frac{1}{7} = \frac{7}{7} = 1$. It is certain that Nicola drinks milk *or* orange juice *or* water each morning.

EXERCISE 17C

1 a yellow, green, and pink   b 1, 2, 3, 4, 5, and 6

2 a A, B, C, D, E, F, G, and H   b 8 outcomes
   c 2 outcomes

3 a 8 outcomes
   b i 5 outcomes   ii 3 outcomes   iii 2 outcomes
     iv 3 outcomes

4 a i March 2nd, 9th, 16th, 23rd, and 30th
     ii 5 outcomes
   b i March 11th, 12th, 13th, 14th, 15th, 16th, and 17th
     ii 7 outcomes

5 a 8 outcomes
   b i 2 outcomes   ii 3 outcomes   iii 4 outcomes

6 a 13 outcomes   b i 2 outcomes   ii 11 outcomes

7 Eliza wins, Patrick wins, draw, and stalemate

EXERCISE 17D

1 a 2 outcomes   b $\frac{1}{2}$

2 a 6 outcomes   b i $\frac{1}{6}$ ii $\frac{3}{6} = \frac{1}{2}$

3 a 7 outcomes   b i $\frac{1}{7}$ ii $\frac{3}{7}$ iii $\frac{2}{7}$ iv $\frac{4}{7}$

4 The sectors are not all the same size, so the outcomes are not all equally likely.

5 a 40 outcomes
   b i $\frac{1}{40}$ ii $\frac{2}{40} = \frac{1}{20}$ iii $\frac{9}{40}$ iv $\frac{12}{40} = \frac{3}{10}$

6 a $\frac{2}{9}$ b $\frac{4}{9}$ c $\frac{3}{9} = \frac{1}{3}$

7 a 13 chocolates   b i $\frac{6}{13}$ ii $\frac{5}{13}$

8 a 14 players   b i $\frac{1}{14}$ ii $\frac{9}{14}$

9 a i $\frac{5}{12}$ ii $\frac{7}{12}$ b a red sector

10 a i $\frac{5}{20} = \frac{1}{4}$ ii 25%   iii 0.25   b unlikely

11 a $\frac{3}{9} = \frac{1}{3}$ b $\frac{1}{9}$ c $\frac{2}{9}$

12 a i $\frac{2}{10} = \frac{1}{5}$ ii $\frac{3}{5}$
   b i Clarissa $(\frac{1}{5} > \frac{1}{10})$ ii Ben $(\frac{3}{10} > \frac{1}{5})$

13 a i $\frac{3}{11}$ ii $\frac{4}{11}$ iii $\frac{4}{11}$ iv $\frac{6}{11}$ v $\frac{5}{11}$
   b i P(an A) + P(a B) + P(a C) = 1, it is certain that Shanice will select either an A, a B, or a C.
     ii P(a blue token) + P(a red token) = 1, it is certain that Shanice will select either a blue token or a red token.

REVIEW SET 17A

1 a likely   b impossible

2 a 3 blue cards   b 3 grey cards   c one of each colour

3 a highly unlikely   b certain   c 50-50 chance

4 a blue, red, green, yellow, black   b 5 outcomes   c yes

5 a 26 outcomes   b i $\frac{5}{26}$ ii $\frac{3}{26}$

6 a $\frac{5}{20} = \frac{1}{4}$ b $\frac{15}{20} = \frac{3}{4}$

7 a Simon
   b Sum is 1. It is certain that either Trent or Simon will win the game.

8 a $\frac{1}{30}$ b $\frac{4}{30} = \frac{2}{15}$ c $\frac{22}{30} = \frac{11}{15}$

9 a i $\frac{3}{14}$ ii $\frac{5}{14}$ iii $\frac{6}{14} = \frac{3}{7}$ b yellow
   c Sum is 1. The child is certain to receive either a red, blue, or yellow balloon.

REVIEW SET 17B

1 a certain   b highly unlikely   c impossible

2 a
   Chelsea Peggy Suzanne Christina

   0   0.1 0.15 0.27 0.3   0.5   1

   b Christina   c highly unlikely

3 a 7 outcomes   b 4 outcomes   4 $\frac{3}{10}$

5 a Bradley: $\frac{3}{5} = 60\%$,   Caleb: $0.62 = 62\%$ b Caleb

6 $\frac{2}{9}$ 7 a $\frac{7}{23}$ b $\frac{16}{23}$

8 a i $\frac{3}{10}$ ii $\frac{13}{40}$ b Ayla $(\frac{13}{40} > \frac{3}{10})$

9 a 1 ball   b 0 balls
   c Sum is 1. Bruce is certain to catch either 0, 1, 2, 3, or 4 balls.
   d i 0.89   ii highly likely

EXERCISE 18A

1 a
Winner	Tally	Frequency
Brody (B)	‖	2
Cooper (C)	‖‖	3
Hailey (H)	╫ ‖	6
Maria (M)	‖‖‖	4
Total		15

b 3 games
c Hailey
d Brody

2 a
Product	Tally	Frequency
Popcorn (P)	╫ ╫ ╫ ‖‖	18
Soft drink (S)	╫ ‖‖	8
Ice cream (I)	╫ ‖‖‖	9
Chips (C)	╫ ╫ ╫	15
Total		50

b 8 soft drinks
c The mode is popcorn. This was the most popular product sold at the candy bar.

3 a
Animal	Tally	Frequency
Shark (Sh)	╫ ‖‖	8
Seahorse (Se)	‖‖‖‖	4
Dolphin (D)	╫ ╫ ‖	11
Otter (O)	╫ ‖	7
Total		30

b 30 students
c dolphin
d $\frac{4}{30}$

4 a

Result	Tally	Frequency
Excellent (E)	‖‖	4
Good (G)	‖‖‖ ‖‖‖ ‖	11
Satisfactory (S)	‖‖‖ ‖	7
Unsatisfactory (U)	‖‖	3
	Total	25

b good

c $\frac{3}{25}$

d 60%

e The hotel manager may want to know if guests are satisfied with the service so improvements can be made if service is seen as unsatisfactory.

f The hotel manager would be pleased with the survey results because there are very few "unsatisfactory" responses, and more than half of the guests surveyed responded with "good" or "excellent".

EXERCISE 18B

1 a 4 students **b** 23 students **c** canoeing

2 a 12 children

b

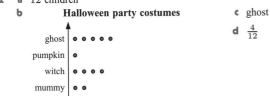

Halloween party costumes

c ghost

d $\frac{4}{12}$

3 a

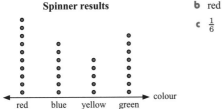

Spinner results

b red

c $\frac{1}{6}$

4 a violin

b i 28 musicians **ii** 3 musicians **iii** 12 musicians

c $\frac{5}{28}$ **d** 50%

EXERCISE 18C

1 a

2 a 24 bottles of fruit juice **b** 12 bottles of fruit juice

c 6 bottles of fruit juice **d** 18 bottles of fruit juice

3 a 15 flights **b** Friday **c** 31 flights

4 a 5 trucks **b** 3 more motorbikes **c** 38 vehicles **d** $\frac{7}{38}$

e No, as there were 18 cars and 20 other vehicles.

5

Leisure activities

Walking	👤👤👤👤👤👤👤👤👤👤👤
Jogging	👤👤👤👤
Cycling	👤👤👤👤👤👤👤👤
Rollerblading	👤👤👤

Scale: 👤 = 2 people

6

Ice cream sales

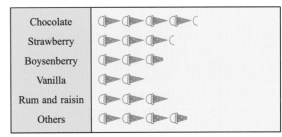

Scale: 🍦 = 5 cones

EXERCISE 18D

1 a 6 T-shirts **b** socks **c** 3 more towels

2 a i 20 people **ii** 35 people **b** Sedan **c** $\frac{25}{120}$

3 a 23 stalls

b

Stalls at market

c craft **d** 2 more clothing stalls

4 a 25 people

b

Ticket type	Tally	Frequency
Adult (A)	‖‖‖ ‖‖	9
Concession (C)	‖‖‖ ‖	7
Student (S)	‖‖‖ ‖‖	9
	Total	25

c

Cinema ticket types

d 28%

5 a 24 adults

b

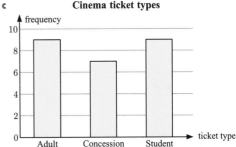

Employment type	Tally	Frequency
Full-time (F)	‖‖‖ ‖‖	9
Part-time (P)	‖‖‖ ‖	6
Unemployed (U)	‖	3
Retired (R)	‖‖‖ ‖	6
	Total	24

c

Employment type of adults

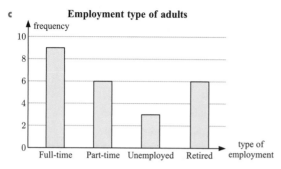

d full-time   **e** 15 adults

EXERCISE 18E

1 a garden   **b i** true   **ii** true   **c** 172 kL

2 a size 12   **b i** false   **ii** false

   c i 18 boys   **ii** 54 boys

3 a 10°   **c**

   b A Grade: 90°,
   B Grade: 50°,
   C Grade: 100°,
   Junior: 120°

Members' playing levels

4 a Fantasy   **b**

   c $\frac{1}{5}$

Favourite type of book

5 a 45 students

   b Sandwich or Roll: ≈ 35.6%, Noodles: ≈ 17.8%,
   Baked pastry: ≈ 24.4%, Curry: ≈ 8.9%, Other: ≈ 13.3%

   c   **Food for lunch**

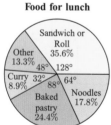

EXERCISE 18F

1 a 5 students   **b** 26 students

   c The mode is 3 hats. More students owned 3 hats than any
   other number.

2 a 5 children   **b** 1 filling

3 a   **Number of laps**

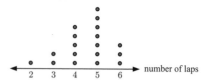

   b 5 laps   **c** 3 athletes   **d** 18 athletes

4 a

Children	Tally	Frequency
0	||||	4
1	||||	4
2	ⅢⅢ ||||	9
3	ⅢⅢ	5
4	ⅢⅢ ||	7
5		0
6	|	1
	Total	30

b   **Number of children**

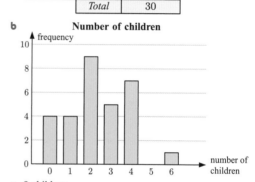

   c 2 children

5 a

Goals	Tally	Frequency
0	||	2
1	|||	3
2	||||	4
3	|||	3
4	|||	3
5	|||	3
6	ⅢⅢ	5
7		0
8	||	2
	Total	25

b   **Hockey goal data**

   c 10 occasions   **d** 6 goals

6 a

Home runs	Tally	Frequency
0					3
1						4
2								6
3							5
4			1
5			1
	Total	20

b

Home runs scored by baseball team

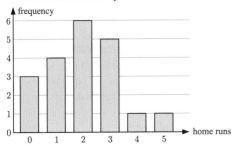

c 5 games   **d** $\frac{3}{20}$ **e** 10%

EXERCISE 18G

1 a 7   **b** 5   **c** 8   **d** 11   **e** 4   **f** 7.3
g 2   **h** 1.43

2 113 m   **3 a** 3 chocolates   **b** 2 chocolates

4 56 g   **5** 20 minutes

6 a

Number of letters delivered

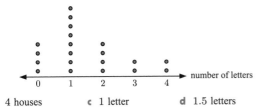

b 4 houses   **c** 1 letter   **d** 1.5 letters

7 a

Number of wickets taken

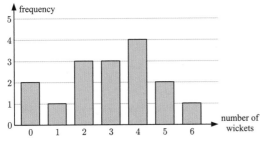

b 4 wickets   **c** 3 wickets
d Yes, Cameron took 3 wickets in 3 games. The mean value is not always one of the data values but in this case it is one of the values.

REVIEW SET 18A

1 a 56 orders

b

Sushi restaurant orders

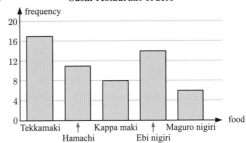

c $\frac{1}{4}$

2 a 10 litres of milk sold   **b i** Friday   **ii** Wednesday
c i 30 litres   **ii** 55 litres

3 a 50 students   **b** size 7   **c i** 14%   **ii** 24%

4 a 7 points   **b** 10 occasions

5 a

Result	Tally	Frequency
1									7
2							5
3						4
4										8
5								6
6							5
	Total	35

b

Die roll results

c 11 times

d $\frac{12}{35}$

6 21 minutes

7 a

Flower colour	Tally	Frequency
Purple	|||||		6
White	|||||	5
Pink	||||	4
Yellow	|||	3
	Total	18

b purple

c

Flower colours

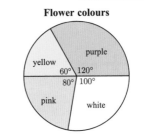

8 16 pastries

9 a i 8%   **ii** 28%   **b** Environment
c Water & Sewerage   **d** 18°   **e** $7.2 million

REVIEW SET 18B

1 a

Species	Tally	Frequency
Magpie (M)	̶H̶T̶ |||	8
Sparrow (S)	̶H̶T̶ ̶H̶T̶ ̶H̶T̶ ̶H̶T̶ ̶H̶T̶	25
Robin (R)	||||	4
Wren (W)	||||	4
Finch (F)	̶H̶T̶ ||||	9
	Total	50

b sparrow

2

Rainy day pastime

3

Location at time of burglary

4 a i 30 houses **ii** 15 houses **b** April

c 🏠 🏠 🏠 🏠

5 7.5 marks **6 a** 5 phone calls **b** 6 days

7 a 22 adults **b** 50%

8 a

Number of students	Tally	Frequency
0						4
1	̶H̶T̶		6
2						4
3			1
	Total	15

b

Students told off

(dot plot: number of students on horizontal axis 0, 1, 2, 3)

c $\frac{1}{3}$

9 a

Age	Tally	Frequency
3			1
4				2
5			1
6				2
7						4
8				2
	Total	12

b 12 children

c 6 children

d $\frac{4}{12}$

e

Ages of children at party

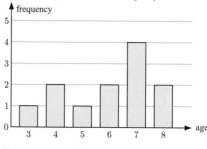

f 7 years **g** 6 years

EXERCISE 19A

1 a 4 units right and 3 units up **b** 3 units left and 2 units up
  c 4 units left and 1 unit down **d** 6 units right
  e 5 units up **f** 4 units right and 4 units down

2 a 2 units left and 3 units up
  b 2 units right and 3 units down
  c 4 units right and 5 units up
  d 4 units left and 5 units down
  e 6 units right and 2 units up
  f 6 units left and 2 units down

3 a 3 units left and 2 units down
  b 1 unit left and 4 units down **c** 5 units left
  d 2 units right and 2 units down
  e 3 units right and 2 units up
  f 2 units right and 2 units down

4 a
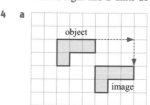
b
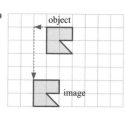

c

d
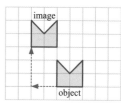

e

5 a
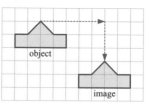
b 3 units left and 1 unit up

6 a E **b** 3 units left and 4 units down

7 **a, b**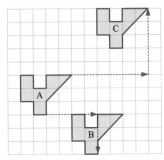

c 2 units right and 8 units up

EXERCISE 19B

1 **a**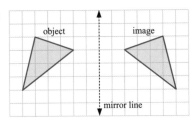

b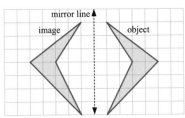

c, d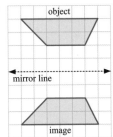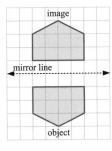

2 **a**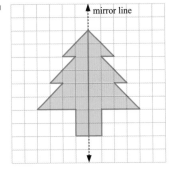

b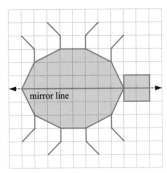

3 **a** yes
b no   **c** no

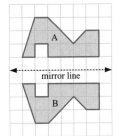 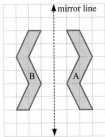

d no   **e** yes
f no

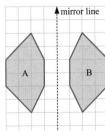 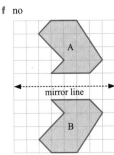

4 **a**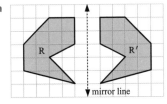

b The reflection of R′ in the mirror line is R.

5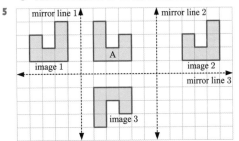

6 F1 moves to H3   **7** D and F, line 2

EXERCISE 19C

1 **a** 2   **b** 6   **c** 4   **d** 4

2 **a** pointing at the 10   **b** pointing at the 1
   c pointing at the 4

3 **a** 90° clockwise   **b** 90° anticlockwise
   c 180° clockwise or 180° anticlockwise

4 **a** 90° clockwise
   b 180° clockwise or 180° anticlockwise
   c 90° anticlockwise

5 **a**
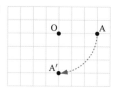
   b
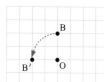

   c
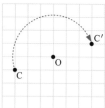
   d
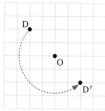

   e
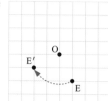
   f
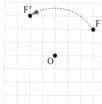

6 **a**
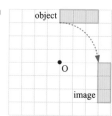
   b
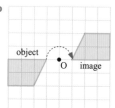

   c
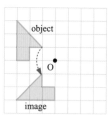

7 **a** B
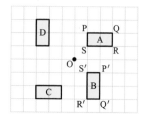

   b C, 4 units left and 4 units down.
   c A 90° anticlockwise rotation about O.

EXERCISE 19D

1 **a**
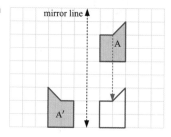

   b
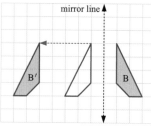

   c
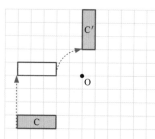

   d
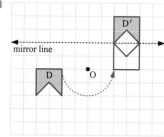

2 **a**
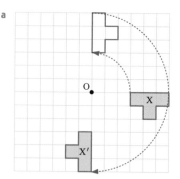

   b Rotate X 90° clockwise about O.

3

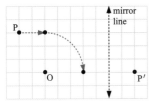

4 Rotate A 90° anticlockwise about O, then translate 4 units left and 2 units up.

5 **a** Reflect X in line 1, then rotate 90° anticlockwise about O, then reflect in line 2.

  b Reflect X in line 1, then rotate 180° (anticlockwise or clockwise) about O, then reflect in line 2.

  c Rotate X 180° (clockwise or anticlockwise) about O, then reflect in line 2 *or* rotate X 90° anticlockwise about O, then reflect in line 1.

  d Rotate X 90° anticlockwise about O, then reflect in line 2, then reflect in line 1.

REVIEW SET 19A

1 **a** 4 units right and 5 units up
   b 4 units left and 2 units down
   c 1 unit left and 6 units up

2 **a** yes   **b** no

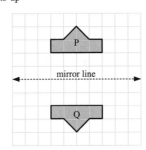

3 **a**   **b**

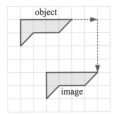   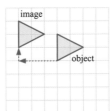

4 **a** 90° anticlockwise
   b 180° clockwise or 180° anticlockwise
   c 90° clockwise

5 **a**   **b**

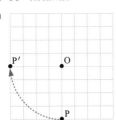   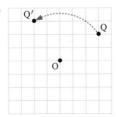

c

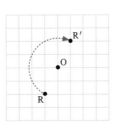

6

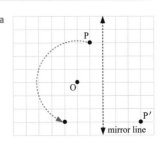

7 **a**

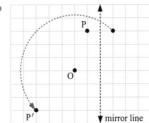

  b

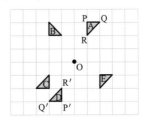

  c The results are not the same. When we perform more than one transformation, the order in which they are performed may be important.

8 **a** D

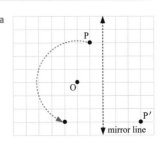

  b E, 1 unit right and 4 units down.
  c A 90° anticlockwise rotation about O.

REVIEW SET 19B

1 **a** 4 units right and 1 unit down
   b 2 units left and 2 units down

2 a, b

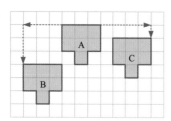

  c 7 units right and 2 units up

3 a

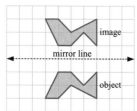

  b

4 a 90° anticlockwise
  b 180° clockwise or 180° anticlockwise
  c 90° clockwise

5

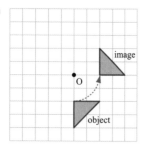

6 a

  b

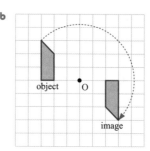

7

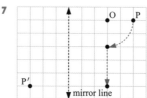

8 a

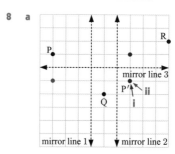

  b

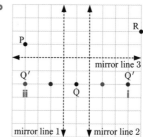

  c

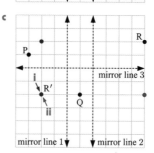

When reflections are performed in perpendicular mirror lines, the order in which they are performed is not important. When reflections are performed in parallel mirror lines, the order in which they are performed is important.

INDEX